Dictionary of Economics

*the text of this book is printed
on 100% recycled paper*

ABOUT THE AUTHORS

Harold Stephenson Sloan is a graduate of Columbia University. He has received an honorary doctorate of laws from the University of Denver and an honorary doctorate of science from Fairleigh Dickinson University. He taught economics at Montclair (N.J.) State College and at New York University and until 1958 served as Adjunct Professor of Economics in the Graduate School of Arts and Science, New York University. He was also Visiting Lecturer at Teachers College, Columbia University and at Trinity University, San Antonio, Texas. In 1959 he was appointed Professor of the Inter-American Course in Education and Economic Development held in Bogota, Colombia, S.A., and in 1963 served as consultant to the U.S. Agency for International Development Educational Project in Peru, S.A. Currently he is president of the Institute for Instructional Improvement. He is author of *Today's Economics, Farming in America,* and co-author of *Classrooms in the Factories, Classrooms in the Stores, Classrooms in the Military,* and *Classrooms on Main Street.*

Arnold John Zurcher received his Ph.D. from Princeton. His teaching career has been largely confined to New York University, where he was Professor of Political Science. He was also head of the University's Institute of Public Affairs and Regional Studies. Among various volumes of which he is author or part author are *The Experiment with Democracy in Central Europe, Propaganda and Dictatorship, The Governments of Continental Europe, Constitutions and Constitutional Trends since the Second World War, The Struggle to Unite Europe,* and *Systems of Integrating the International Community.* With Professor Edward C. Smith he is co-author of *The Dictionary of American Politics* of which Barnes and Noble, Inc. published a second and thoroughly revised edition in 1968.

Everyday Handbooks

Dictionary of Economics

Fifth Edition

Harold S. Sloan

Arnold J. Zurcher

BARNES & NOBLE BOOKS

A DIVISION OF HARPER & ROW, PUBLISHERS

New York, Hagerstown, San Francisco, London

PREFACE

In the twenty-year period which separates the first and this fifth edition of the *Dictionary of Economics* major changes have affected both the method and substance of economics. Still largely descriptive and institutional in 1949, economics in the last two decades has become a discipline increasingly analytical in temper and quantitative in its methodology. As respects its substance, there has been a growing accommodation to what is popularly known as the "new economics," a term which, however ambiguous, usually refers to the macro-economic theories and concepts provided by J. M. Keynes in his *General Theory*, published in 1936, by certain of his contemporaries, and by subsequent writers. With increasing frequency, moreover, these theories and concepts of the new economics have been used as tools by private and public bodies to formulate fiscal and monetary policies, to introduce a greater degree of social equity, to maintain equilibrium in economic life between the extremes of severe depression and intolerable inflation and, in general, to discipline and manage the economic life of individual nations.

Admittedly, an arbitrary alphabetical arrangement of terms in a dictionary is scarcely calculated to make explicit the qualitative nature, the intensity, or the range of change as fundamental as this has been. The authors are nevertheless hopeful that this change will at least be reflected in the selection of terms—both those included and those excluded—in the extent of the space accorded various entries, and in their occasional editorial comments or value judgments. As respects their policy in selecting entries, the authors are hopeful, also, that eventual users of this book will acknowledge their intention, however imperfectly executed, of providing a reference work relevant to the needs of students and practitioners of post-Keynesian economics.

The authors wish to make it clear that they have sought to make this Dictionary representative of the entire field of economics and of orthodox as well as modern thought. To that end they have culled terminology from the literature into which economics is conventionally classified. In addition to quantitative methods and concepts, especially as these relate to productivity and income, these areas include economic history and theory, international trade, finance and exchange, international commercial policy, public finance, taxation, money and credit. An examination has also been made of some of the more specialized areas of current economic study and research, such as business cycles, monopoly and competition, price and wage policies, price mechanisms, agricultural and labor economics, industrial organization and management, and social welfare problems; and appropriate words and phrases have been selected from all these areas.

Interspersed among the entries identifying "economic principles," schools of economic thought, and economic theories, that is, entries especially appropriate to economics as an academic discipline, there will be found not a few terms derived from the nomenclature of "practical" or "business" economics. Such terms embrace accounting, production costs and techniques, marketing, corporate financing and organization, securities and investments, insurance, industrial and public relations, and other activities which are of immediate interest to those engaged in commerce, industry, and finance and possibly to those in agriculture. Inclusion of such terms from the "functional" world will enhance the usefulness of this volume for the businessman and banker as well as for the student and professional economist, and may also serve to overcome, in some measure, the sometimes labored and occasionally misleading distinction between economic theory and economic practice upon which some purists insist. Where usage has established distinctions in the meaning of a term when used in formal economic discussion and when used in the marketplace, that distinction has been carefully pointed out.

The user of this book will find in appropriate alphabetical order occasional analyses of decisions of the Supreme Court that have modified economic policy or the law regulating economic practice. He will also encounter sketches of some of the more important administrative agencies of the American government, of professional or vocational associations in such fields as labor, agriculture and management, and of some of the better known international regulatory bodies. Inclusions such as these seem justified if only to mirror the growing complexity and range of the institutional framework in which contemporary economic life is being carried on. These inclusions may also serve to remind the user of the Dictionary of the discipline which private and public bodies are exerting over that increasingly mythical concept known as the "free market." Although these entries relating to public bodies, statutes, and judicial decisions have had to be compressed in the interests of editorial style and to conserve space, the authors believe that even such brief entries will be useful to anyone who has only a cursory reference interest. More detailed information may be found in appropriate encyclopedic reference works and in official sources such as the *United States Government Organization Manual, The Statistical Abstract of the United States,* the *Statutes at Large,* and the official reports of the courts.

Throughout the book, formal definitions have occasionally been supplemented by detailed explanations or illustrations to make complicated concepts more meaningful or to assist in identifying shades or nuances of meaning. Even when thus expanded the entry for a term must necessarily be brief and the investigator is referred to encyclopedias or formal treatment of the subject in books or periodical literature for more sophisticated and extensive discussion.

In Appendix A the user of the Dictionary will find a Descriptive Classification of Defined Terms. Any generic term, defined in the text, is followed by a number in parentheses. This number refers the user to an area in Appendix A in which will be found all specific terms defined in the text that have some etymological or functional relation to the generic term. This intensive effort at classification and indexing should greatly enhance the book's value as a reference tool by acquainting the user with the range of entries that may relate to the precise topic of his inquiry and placing that topic in an organized context of related ideas.

Besides the assistance provided by Appendix A, the user of the Dictionary will also find cross references in the text that suggest to him topics related to the subject of his inquiry. Thus the appearance of a word in SMALL CAPITAL LETTERS in the body of a definition means that that word is itself defined at the appropriate alphabetical point in the book. Such a word may be followed by *q.v. (quod vide)* if the authors feel that the user would find it especially helpful to inform himself of the meaning of that word. Occasionally the user will discover that an entry word or phrase is not defined but is followed by a reference to another entry in the Dictionary in which that word or phrase is printed in *italics* and its meaning is clarified by the context of the entry in which it appears.

Other useful appendices include a statement of National Income and Gross National Product, a Combined Statement of Condition of All Federal Reserve Banks, a list of the names of all national monetary units, and a list of public and some private national and international organizations and associations commonly identified by abbreviations.

Having survived five editions both publisher and authors may be forgiven if they conclude that this Dictionary has become an indispensable work of reference. Certainly it has been well received in schools and colleges in the United States and in English-speaking countries and occasionally it has been translated for use in cultures using other tongues. A brisk demand for this book has also been generated among professional persons interested in public affairs and among those concerned with the "functional" or "practical" aspects of economic life. As the Dictionary has thus found its way among these various user constituencies, there has inevitably been "feedback" of criticism, evaluation, and general comment. Usually this has taken the form of formal reviews in appropriate periodicals but, not infrequently, users of the book have sent their comments to the authors or the publisher. For such feedback the authors are especially grateful. Censure and criticism have assisted them greatly in overcoming many faults, including omissions of important terms and erroneous interpretations of words. Praise has encouraged them to continue this work, carry the book through this fifth edition and, hopefully, to improve it.

In thus expressing gratitude to reviewer and individual lay critic, the authors wish also to identify those who have directly assisted in the creation of this book and to thank them publicly for their assistance. Among individuals who provided editorial or substantive suggestions in the preparation of earlier editions of this book, the authors wish to identify and thank especially the following: Jerry Davidoff, counsellor at law; Professor Paul Clifford, of the Montclair (N.J.) State College; Mrs. Muriel P. Gaines, Assistant Secretary of the Alfred P. Sloan Foundation; the late Miss Cecile Stierli; Anne and Wallace Clark of Buttzville, New Jersey; Mrs. Carol Ann Luten; Dr. Gladys Walterhouse; and Mrs. Harold S. Sloan. In preparing the manuscript of this new edition of the Dictionary, the authors have become especially indebted to Mr. James F. Kenney, CPA, who retired recently as Vice President of the Alfred P. Sloan Foundation, and to Miss Freda Smith, secretary at the Institute for Instructional Improvement, Inc. Mr. Kenney was helpful in injecting professional usage into the authors' sometimes rather academic formulation of terms in accounting and in the broad field of financial management. Miss Smith was largely responsible for the physical preparation of the manuscript. It is probably unnecessary to add that acknowledgment of the kindness of friends and colleagues in no way saddles them with responsibility for the shortcomings of this Dictionary. Those who find the flaws—and there are many—should direct their criticisms solely to the authors.

CONTENTS

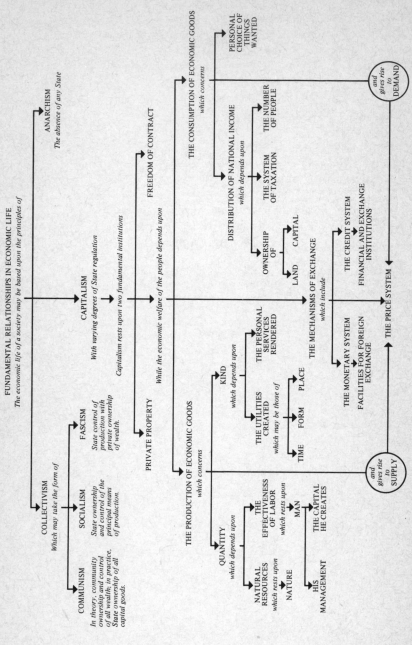

FUNDAMENTAL RELATIONSHIPS IN ECONOMIC LIFE
The economic life of a society may be based upon the principles of

COLLECTIVISM
Which may take the form of

CAPITALISM
With varying degrees of State regulation

ANARCHISM
The absence of any State

COMMUNISM
In theory, community ownership and control of all wealth; in practice, State ownership of all capital goods.

SOCIALISM
State ownership and control of the principal means of production.

FASCISM
State control of production with private ownership of wealth.

Capitalism rests upon two fundamental institutions

PRIVATE PROPERTY

FREEDOM OF CONTRACT

While the economic welfare of the people depends upon

THE PRODUCTION OF ECONOMIC GOODS
which concerns

QUANTITY
which depends upon

NATURAL RESOURCES
which rests upon

NATURE

THE EFFECTIVENESS OF LABOR
which rests upon

MAN

HIS MANAGEMENT

THE CAPITAL HE CREATES

KIND
which depends upon

THE PERSONAL SERVICES RENDERED

THE UTILITIES CREATED
which may be those of

TIME

FORM

PLACE

and gives rise to SUPPLY

THE MECHANISMS OF EXCHANGE
which include

THE MONETARY SYSTEM

FACILITIES FOR FOREIGN EXCHANGE

THE CREDIT SYSTEM

FINANCIAL AND EXCHANGE INSTITUTIONS

THE PRICE SYSTEM

THE CONSUMPTION OF ECONOMIC GOODS
which concerns

DISTRIBUTION OF NATIONAL INCOME
which depends upon

OWNERSHIP OF

LAND

CAPITAL

THE SYSTEM OF TAXATION

THE NUMBER OF PEOPLE

PERSONAL CHOICE OF THINGS WANTED

and gives rise to DEMAND

Dictionary of Economics

A

ability-to-pay principle of taxation. The principle that a tax should be levied upon individual taxpayers in accordance with their ability to pay the tax, rather than in proportion to the direct benefits received from the state or to the cost to the state of the services rendered individual taxpayers. This principle is generally applied today as, for example, in the case of PROGRESSIVE TAXATION on income. Also called *faculty principle of taxation.*

abrasion. As applied to coins, the loss in weight due to wear while in circulation.

absolute advantage. See COMPARATIVE ADVANTAGE.

abstinence theory of interest. See AGIO THEORY OF INTEREST.

accelerated depreciation. Unusually rapid DEPRECIATION caused by overloading of machinery, lack of skilled employees, inability to provide proper maintenance or to obtain repairs, or similar special conditions.

accelerating premium. Under certain incentive wage systems, a bonus which becomes progressively larger as production increases.

acceleration principle. An explanation used by Keynesian economists showing how an increase or decrease in consumer expenditures may cause changes in new CAPITAL FORMATION. For example, a sufficient increase in consumer demand for a com-

1

modity may result in added facilities for producing it and, conversely, a sufficient decrease in consumer expenditures may result in failure on the part of producers to replace worn-out equipment, or DISINVESTMENT. The acceleration factor, or *coefficient of acceleration* as it is sometimes called, is the ratio of change in investments to change in consumer expenditures. Thus, if increased consumer expenditures of $4,000,000 caused increased capital investments of $2,000,000, the acceleration factor, or coefficient of acceleration, would be ½. The equation is:

$$\frac{\Delta I}{\Delta C} = \frac{2,000,000}{4,000,000} = \frac{1}{2}.$$

See also INDUCED INVESTMENT, KEYNESIAN ECONOMICS.

acceptance. A draft or bill of exchange on the face of which the debtor against whom the draft or bill is drawn has affixed his signature indicating his intention to pay. See (17).

acceptance bill. See BILL.

acceptance supra protest. An agreement to pay a protested note, draft, or similar credit instrument by a person other than the debtor named on the document. See ACCEPTANCE.

accommodation paper. A promissory note that has been indorsed by one or more persons in order that the one who originally made that note may obtain credit at a bank, the indorser or accommodator thus assuming the maker's risk or guaranteeing his credit. If the credit is advanced by an individual, the accommodation paper may contain only the signature of the debtor without indorsements.

account. As applied to double-entry bookkeeping, a ledger record displaying charges or debits on the left-hand side of the page and credits on the right-hand side. Each account bears either a proper name or a title descriptive of the item to which the debits and credits are applied; for example, capital account, cash account, bank account, sales account. See (1).

accountant. A person versed in bookkeeping methods, in the planning, installation, and analysis of financial records, and in the preparation of statements displaying the assets and liabilities and the operating results of business and other enterprises. See also CERTIFIED PUBLIC ACCOUNTANT.

accounts payable. A term used in double-entry bookkeeping to indicate the records of the amounts credited to others for goods and services purchased, and the amounts paid for those purchases. See ACCOUNT.

accounts receivable. A term used in double-entry bookkeeping to indicate the records of the amounts charged to others for goods and services sold, and the amounts received. See ACCOUNT.

accrual basis. A method of accounting in which financial transactions are recorded prior to the actual receipt or expenditure of the funds involved in such transactions; for example, charging purchases before bills covering those purchases are paid and crediting sales before the money income represented by those sales is received.

accrued interest. Interest that has accumulated but which has not been paid or collected. In the case of bond purchases, it is customary for the buyer to pay the seller accrued interest up to but not including the date of delivery, in addition to the purchase price. See INTEREST.

accumulated dividend. A dividend which has not been paid when due and which has become a liability of the corporation, to be paid, presumably, at some future time. See DIVIDEND.

accumulated profits tax. A tax designed to penalize corporations for failure to declare dividends on accumulated earnings "beyond the reasonable needs of business" when the purpose is to enable the stockholders to avoid an income tax for which they would otherwise be liable. Only closely held corporations would be in a position to pursue such a policy. See TAX.

accumulation. 1. An increase in the calculated value of a bond, bought at a DISCOUNT, as it approaches maturity. Annual accumulation is the amount of the discount divided by the number of years to maturity. **2.** The purchase of stock or other securities at a time when the prices are considered low, for sale on an anticipated advancing market. **3.** The transfer of undistributed profits or income to capital.

accumulative dividend. See CUMULATIVE DIVIDEND.

acid-test ratio. In a BALANCE SHEET, the proportion of the sum of cash, ACCOUNTS RECEIVABLE, and the market value of securities, if any, to CURRENT LIABILITIES. If, for example, the balance sheet shows $5,000 cash, $1,000 in accounts receivable, and securities valued at $3,000, and the current liabilities amount to $3,000, the acid-test ratio is 3 to 1. The acid-test ratio is frequently used as one test to determine CREDIT RATING. Sometimes called *quick ratio.* See RATIO.

acknowledgment. A personal declaration before a notary, judge, or other official that a certain act is one's own. The act of signing certain documents is often required to be so acknowledged in order to make certain the identity of the person signing the document.

across-the-board. A popular term frequently applied to a wage policy which provides for a uniform rate of increase of wages for all employees of an establishment.

active stock. See CAPITAL STOCK.

active trade balance. See FAVORABLE BALANCE OF TRADE.

actuary. In the United States, a person who calculates insurance risks and premiums. In Europe the term is sometimes applied to a clerk, especially one employed by a corporation.

Adair v. United States. An early case, 208 U.S. 161 (1908), in which the Supreme Court declared unconstitutional an act of Congress outlawing yellow-dog employment contracts in interstate commerce. Such contracts called for a promise by a prospective employee not to join a labor union. The Court based its decision on the theory that legislative interdiction of such contracts violated contractual liberty protected by the due process clause of the 5th Amendment. The case is similar to COPPAGE V. KANSAS *(q.v.).*

Adamson Act. An act of Congress, 1916, establishing the 8-hour day as the basis of pay for railroad employees in interstate commerce.

added value tax. A tax levied at all levels of manufacture, processing, and distribution, but based only on the amount a particular level adds to the price. Also known as the *value-added tax.* The tax has been used frequently in France and is being adopted by other countries, principally by those countries associated with France in the EUROPEAN ECONOMIC COMMUNITY. See TAX.

add-on-loan. See INSTALLMENT INTEREST.

Addyston Pipe and Steel Co. case. A case, *United States* v. *Addyston Pipe and Steel Co.,* 175 U.S. 211 (1899), in which the

Supreme Court liberalized somewhat its earlier ruling in the KNIGHT CASE *(q.v.)* involving the application of the SHERMAN ANTI-TRUST ACT. In the instant case, the Court applied the act to a combination among certain steel companies to fix prices of their product in the United States, declaring that the commerce power of Congress extended to the regulation of contracts among individuals or companies if such contracts directly and substantially affected interstate and foreign commerce.

adjusted gross income. Gross personal or corporate income—a figure used for income tax purposes after certain legally allowable deductions have been subtracted. See INCOME.

adjuster. A person who examines the damage and estimates the loss created by a fire, or other disasters covered by insurance, and attempts to arrive at an agreement with the insured in settlement of the claim against the insurance company.

adjustment bond. See BOND.

Adkins v. *Children's Hospital.* See MINIMUM-WAGE CASES.

Adler v. *Board of Education.* A case, 342 U.S. 485 (1952), in which the Supreme Court upheld New York's so-called Feinberg Law (1949). This provided for the removal of teachers and other employees in the state's public schools who advocate overthrow of the government by unlawful means. The Court also held that the due-process clause of the 14th Amendment does not protect a school employee in his tenure if he knowingly joined an organization which educational authorities, after appropriate hearings, had held to be subversive in its aim.

administered price. A predetermined price arrived at from a calculation of costs and desired profits, from a fairly accurate knowledge of the total quantity of goods likely to be offered on the market, and from an estimate of the probable sales volume at the predetermined price. The process of establishing an administered price cannot be described either as COMPETITION or MONOPOLY, but is one which combines elements derived from both of these concepts. It suggests the existence of an OLIGOPOLY or a DUOPOLY. See PRICE.

administrator. A person authorized to settle an estate when the deceased has left no will or has named no executor. In common speech the term may refer to a person who manages business affairs of any kind or the activities of some public agency.

administrative budget. A form of budget used by the United States government until 1967 which embraced only expenditures from general funds and excluded expenditures and receipts from trust funds. See BUDGET.

admission temporaire. The free admission of dutiable goods which are destined for export after undergoing some sort of processing.

ad valorem duty. A customs duty based on the value of the goods. Such a duty is a fixed percentage of the foreign or domestic valuation of imported goods. It is used in contradistinction to SPECIFIC DUTY. See CUSTOMS DUTY.

advance. 1. A loan. **2.** A payment before it is due.

advance bill. See BILL.

advertising. The business of making known to the public, in one way or another, goods and services offered for sale, and of employing various methods of persuasion to induce the public to buy those goods and services.

advertising agency. A business organization that prepares and places advertising for others.

advice. Information concerning a shipment of goods or some other matter pertaining to a business transaction.

affidavit. A written statement to which the maker takes oath or makes affirmation before a NOTARY PUBLIC or other appropriate officer.

afforestation. The creation of a forest where none existed before; for example, planting trees on submarginal soil or on abandoned farm or grazing land. The term should not be confused with REFORESTATION.

Agency for International Development. A unit within the U.S. Department of State responsible for all foreign nonmilitary assistance programs under the Foreign Assistance Act of 1961 and subsequent statutes and appropriations. It makes loans and grants to promote economic development; finances surveys of investment opportunities for private enterprise in underdeveloped countries and insures private investments; and furthers technical and financial cooperation among the American Republics under the ALLIANCE FOR PROGRESS program.

agency shop. An establishment in which a nonunion employee is required to pay the local bargaining union a fee equivalent to union dues but is not required to join the union. See SHOP.

agent. Generally, any person who acts for another with the latter's consent. The term is sometimes used also to indicate a broker, as in the case of an insurance agent, or a representative of a labor union or welfare organization.

agents of production. See FACTORS OF PRODUCTION.

aggregate corporation. A corporation consisting of more than one natural person. See CORPORATION.

aggregative index number. An INDEX NUMBER *(q.v.)* computed by finding the sum of the figures applicable to each period of time under consideration, assigning the index number 100 to the period designated as the base period, and finding for each of the other periods a figure which bears the same relation to 100 that the sum of the figures for that period bears to the sum of the figures of the base period.

Example:

Item	Period	
	A	B
A	9.00	10.00
B	5.00	4.00
C	7.00	9.00
Totals	21.00	23.00
Index No.	100	*x*

$x : 100 : : 23.00 : 21.00.$
$x = 109.52$, index number for B.

This method provides no logical means for assigning relative importance to the various items constituting the lists of figures. The resulting index numbers, therefore, even though mathematically valid, may fail to disclose the full significance of changes that may have occurred from one period to another. For example, in calculating variations in the cost of living, changes in consumer buying habits will alter the relative quantities of various commodities purchased and may affect the cost of living quite as much as do price changes. For this reason, a WEIGHTED AVERAGE is often incorporated in this method of constructing an index number. In the case of a cost of living index, the weights might logically be the quantities purchased. For tests to determine the mathematical validity of an index number, see FACTOR REVERSAL TEST, TIME REVERSAL TEST.

agio. A premium paid for the exchange of one kind of money for another. The premium may be for the exchange of the money of one nation for the money of another, or it may be in the form of an allowance for coins, short in weight due to wear, exchanged for coins of full weight. Occasionally the term is used to indicate a premium paid for a foreign BILL OF EXCHANGE.

agio theory of interest. The theory that explains interest as a premium paid for the immediate possession of goods which otherwise could be had only at some future time. This premium is paid, according to the theory, because most people expect to be more bountifully supplied with goods in the future than they are at the moment, because present satisfactions are more vivid than future possibilities, or because present goods may offer the possibility of immediately increasing the profits of production. Also called *abstinence theory of interest.*

Agricultural Adjustment Act (first). An act of Congress, 1933, designed to control the prices of farm products by regulating the production of those products. Farmers were asked to cooperate by reducing acreage planted in certain products, and received cash payments from the government to compensate them for such reduction in acreage. The funds for these payments were to be raised by a PROCESSING TAX *(q.v.).* This tax was declared unconstitutional by the Supreme Court in 1936. See also HOOSAC MILLS CASE.

Agricultural Adjustment Act (second). An act of Congress, 1938, which redefined and extended the agricultural policies of the first act of that name, held unconstitutional by the courts in 1936. As supplemented by more recent statutes and a variety of executive orders, this new act continued the provision of earlier legislation for MARKETING AGREEMENTS and AGRICULTURAL PARITY payments for certain agricultural staples. It also continued the policy of SOIL CONSERVATION, inaugurated by the Soil Conservation and Domestic Allotment Act of 1936, authorizing payments out of the federal treasury to farmers and others who carry out approved soil conservation policies. In addition, the new act provided producers of certain staples with a system of insurance against growing hazards and, through loans to farmers on surpluses, developed the nucleus of the idea of the *ever-normal granary.*

Agricultural Adjustment Act case (second). A case, *Mulford* v. *Smith,* 307 U.S. 38 (1939), in which the Supreme Court sustained the constitutionality of the second AGRICULTURAL ADJUSTMENT ACT (1938). The precise issue in the case was the act's provision for tobacco-marketing quotas and the imposition of penalties on those who exceeded such quotas. The Court argued that Congress' real motive in passing this act, which was the general stabilization of agriculture, was irrelevant to the act's validity, it being clear that the attempt to regulate the flow of an agricultural commodity to the market affected interstate commerce, that such regulation was an attempt to "foster, protect and conserve that commerce" or to "prevent the flow of commerce from working harm to the people of the nation," and hence was within the competence of Congress.

Agricultural Credit Act. An act of Congress, 1923. It provided for the establishment of 12 FEDERAL INTERMEDIATE CREDIT BANKS *(q.v.).*

agricultural economics. That part of the study of economics which treats particularly of the production and distribution of agricultural products together with the economic agencies serving agriculture such as credit institutions, marketing associations, and the like. See ECONOMICS.

agricultural ladder. A figurative expression of the idea that farmers start as farm laborers, then successively become sharecroppers, tenant farmers, and owner-operators.

agricultural parity. The ratio between the price INDEX NUMBERS *(q.v.)* for what the farmer buys and what the farmer sells, both being calculated from some base period when farm income standards were considered to be approximately equivalent to the income standards of other sectors of the economy. For example, in May, 1967, the index figure for prices received by farmers was 252 (all items), and for prices paid by farmers, the index figure was 342 (all commodities, services, interest, taxes, and wage rates). Parity, therefore, was $\frac{252}{342} = .74$, the base period being 1910-1914 $= 100$. See PARITY.

agricultural price support. Any measure intended to maintain or increase prices which farmers and ranchers receive for their products, and which thus helps to keep their income levels more nearly in balance with the income levels of producers in other sectors of the nation's economy. It may take such forms as a marketing agreement, a direct payment to producers by government, a low cost school lunch program, or governmental subsidization of purchasers of agricultural products. See MARKETING AGREEMENTS, AGRICULTURAL PARITY, FOOD STAMP PLAN, NONRECOURSE LOANS, FARM SUBSIDIES.

Agricultural Research Service. A major division of the U.S. Department of Agriculture engaged in experimental, demonstration, and research activities relating to the production, utilization, and marketing of farm products. It is also responsible for the regulatory programs involving the enforcement of plant and animal quarantines, the eradication of animal and plant diseases, meat inspection, and related work. Projects are carried on at the Agricultural Research Center, Beltsville, Md., as well as in other localities in the United States and in foreign countries. Much of the research is in cooperation with state agricultural experiment stations and land-grant universities.

agricultural revolution. 1. In England, the transition from medieval to modern conditions in rural areas during the 18th century. Lands formerly held in common were enclosed for the benefit of great landowners. As a result of these *enclosures* yeoman farmers were thrown out of work, causing great distress and unrest. **2.** The application of modern science and technology to the cultivation and exploitation of land, a development especially apparent after 1870, although its beginnings may be noted earlier in the 19th century.

Agricultural Stabilization and Conservation Service. A major unit of the U.S. Department of Agriculture which, since 1961, has had direct responsibility for the administration of the nation's agricultural support program, including *(a)* acreage allotments and marketing quotas; *(b)* various policies to encourage conservation practices and more effective land-use management by farmers and ranchers, including the payment of relevant subsidies; *(c)* the price support programs including loans, purchases, and incentive payments for various staples, programs carried on in conjunction with the Commodity Credit Corporation and the management and disposal of the Corporation's inventory of surplus commodities; and *(d)* certain agricultural emergency relief programs.

Air Quality Act. An act of Congress, 1967, which authorizes the establishment of federally funded interstate agencies to provide standards for measuring air pollution and to enforce such standards, enforcement authority being vested in the Department of Health, Education, and Welfare if the states fail to act. The legislation also makes funds available for research into the sources of air pollution.

Aldrich-Vreeland Act. An act of Congress, 1908, which authorized associations of national banks to issue bank notes secured by commercial paper and state and municipal bonds. The act was regarded as a temporary one pending a reorganization of the banking system. Hence, the act provided for appointment of a *National Monetary Commission* to make a thorough investigation of the then existing banking facilities of the country. The establishment of the FEDERAL RESERVE SYSTEM was the ultimate outcome of this investigation.

Alliance for Progress. A program to hasten the economic development of Latin American states, formulated and adopted at a twenty-state Inter-American Economic and Social Conference at Punta del Este, Uruguay, August 17, 1961. The United States agreed to provide "soft" loans and grants of as much as $20 billion over a ten-year period in return for pledges from recipient states that they would direct a greater flow of resources to their own social and economic improvement. Administration of the program in the United States is confided to the Agency for International Development.

allonge. A piece of paper attached to a document to provide space for indorsements when no space is left for this purpose on the document itself.

allowed time. The time allowed employees for machine upkeep, fatigue, and personal needs in calculating the base pay in piecework or other incentive pay systems.

11

amalgamation. The formation of a new business enterprise to take over the assets and liabilities of existing enterprises, the latter then being dissolved; or the fusion of the assets and liabilities of two or more business establishments as in a CONSOLIDATION or MERGER *(qq.v.).* See COMBINATION.

American Arbitration Association. A private organization with offices in New York and Washington which, since 1926, has promoted the use of arbitration procedures in labor and commercial disputes and which seeks to extend arbitration, conciliation, mediation, and other similar procedures to the adjustment of various kinds of economic controversies.

American Column and Lumber Co. v. United States. See LUMBER INDUSTRY CASE.

American Communications Association v. *Douds.* A case, 339 U.S. 382 (1950), in which the Supreme Court upheld the validity of the provisions of the Taft-Hartley Act of 1947 which withdraw collective bargaining and other privileges guaranteed to labor unions by the National Labor Relations Act (1935) when officers of such labor unions refuse to swear or affirm that they are not members of the Communist party or of any organization which advocates the overthrow of the government by force and violence. See also LABOR-MANAGEMENT RELATIONS (TAFT-HARTLEY) ACT, NATIONAL LABOR RELATIONS (WAGNER-CONNERY) ACT.

American depository receipt. A document attesting to the ownership by an American person, corporate or individual, of a specific number of shares in a European corporation, the shares being deposited with a European bank acting as the agent of an American bank which sponsors the issuance of the receipt. The receipt entitles the holder to all privileges accorded a shareholder. The arrangement eliminates the necessity of shipping actual stock certificates and facilitates the owner's right to transfer his ownership and secure his dividends. When a similar arrangement is made by a European bank for the purchase and custody of stock in non-European countries, the receipt is known as a *European depository receipt.* See RECEIPT.

American Economic Association. A professional organization of economists founded in 1885 to stimulate thought and discussion relating to economic problems and to encourage research in that field. The association has approximately 7,700 members and publishes the *American Economic Review,* the *Journal of Economic Abstracts,* and occasional monographs.

American Farm Bureau Federation. An organization of farm and ranch families with voluntary membership in 49 states and Puerto Rico. (Alaska is the only state without a Farm Bureau organization.) Founded in 1920, the Federation is nongovernmental, nonpartisan, and nonsectarian in character and serves the needs of its member families through informational, legislative, and cooperative activities. In the depression thirties it supported emergency farm legislation calling for production controls of certain basic commodities. It has generally sought to reduce federal intervention in the pricing and production of farm products. An audited membership report of the Federation as of November 30, 1965, showed a total of 1,677,820 families in the organization. Generally known as *Farm Bureau.*

American Federation of Labor. A loose, decentralized organization established in 1886, consisting of autonomous trade union members in the United States and Canada. In 1955 it merged with the CONGRESS OF INDUSTRIAL ORGANIZATIONS to form the AMERICAN FEDERATION OF LABOR AND CONGRESS OF INDUSTRIAL ORGANIZATIONS *(q.v.).*

American Federation of Labor and Congress of Industrial Organizations. A national organization of labor unions formed in 1955 by the merger of the previously separate AFL and CIO. The organization comprises over 125 national and international unions with a total membership of approximately 13 million. In addition, there are some 350 directly affiliated local unions with about 100,000 members whose occupations do not fall within the jurisdiction of established national unions. The AFL-CIO is financed by per capita dues paid by its affiliates. The federation exercises no authority over member unions except to require them to abide by its constitution and ethical-practice codes, under penalty of suspension or expulsion.

American Management Association. A private organization, founded in 1923, with headquarters in New York, which, through appropriate publications, study groups, academic courses, and professional meetings, seeks to advance the art of management in industry, government, and nonprofit organiza-

13

tions including such special phases of management as labor relations, marketing, finance, data processing, and production and quality control.

American selling price. A provision in law which requires United States customs officials to determine the foreign valuation of certain imports, especially chemicals and chemical by-products, by adjusting that valuation to the level of the price of a competitive American product. A.S.P. has been a major stumbling block in the GATT negotiations that led to the KEN-NEDY ROUND, *(q.v.).* See PRICE.

American Statistical Association. A society consisting of statisticians, applied mathematicians, and others, founded in 1839, with headquarters in Washington, which is concerned with the professional development of statistical methods and the application of the statistical discipline to other professional disciplines and to the management of human affairs. It publishes the quarterly *Journal of the American Statistical Association.*

American Stock Exchange. One of the two principal stock exchanges in New York City. It was organized before the Civil War, and for many years conducted its trading in the open street. For that reason it was known as the CURB EXCHANGE. Since 1921 it has been located at 86 Trinity Place.

American system. The policy of encouraging American industry through protective tariffs, and of promoting extensive internal improvements. The term thus used was common during the early part of the 19th century and was usually attributed to Henry Clay.

American Tobacco Co. v. United States. A case, 328 U.S. 781 (1946), in which the Supreme Court appears to have taken the position that PRICE LEADERSHIP *(q.v.)* and the resulting phenomenon of parallel pricing in an oligopolistic market were illegal, whether or not such pricing was predicated upon an agreement between the individual firms.

amortization. 1. A provision made in advance for the gradual liquidation of a future obligation by periodic charges against the capital account or by the creation of a money fund sufficient to meet the obligation when due. **2.** As applied to finance, a reduction in the cost of a bond bought at a PREMIUM to reduce the cost to par at maturity. Annual amortization is the amount of the premium divided by the number of years to maturity.

analog computer. An electronic device which uses electrical circuits for simulating physical phenomena. It expresses results in approximate figures proportional to the magnitude of the phenomenon under study. An analog computer is thus a continuous-reading device in which numbers are represented by physical magnitudes such as flow, temperature, or pressure. Although commonly mechanical rather than electrical, a simple clock mechanism or automobile speedometer functions in a manner similar to that of an analog computer. A clock computes divisions of the day by means of a minute hand which revolves 24 times as fast as the earth. A speedometer computes speed by means of a dial or a pointer, the movement of which is in proportion to the revolutions per unit of time of the automobile wheels. See COMPUTER.

anarchism. A theory of society which advocates the abolition of all forms of coercive government. Such a theory anticipates that harmony among the members of society as well as the production of necessary and desired goods can be attained by voluntary cooperation. Private property would be abolished and collective ownership by cooperating groups substituted. See also ECONOMIC SYSTEM.

annual wage. A provision in law or labor-management contracts which guarantees a wage earner stable employment at established rates of pay for a period of at least one year. Usually called *guaranteed annual wage.* See WAGE.

annuity. The payment to or receipt by a beneficiary of an amount of money at uniform intervals of time. Usually an annuity is paid out of a fund created at one time or accumulated over a period of years, and payments may liquidate such a fund on the basis of generally accepted statistics indicating the life expectancy of the annuitant. Provisions for an annuity are sometimes incorporated in life-insurance policies and may be paid either to the insured or to beneficiaries. See (21).

annuity bond. See BOND.

antagonistic cooperation. A term used to describe the thesis that it is not mutual good will that engenders human cooperation but practical necessity. Antagonisms are suppressed because it is mutually advantageous to do so.

antibank movement. Legislative enactments and constitutional provisions promulgated during the 1840's and early 1850's that discouraged normal banking operations and even prohibited banking in the states of Arkansas, California, Florida, Illinois, Iowa, Minnesota, Oregon, and Texas, and in the District of Columbia. The movement was an extreme reaction against the WILDCAT BANKING ERA and the result of a disposition to hold the banks responsible for the DEPRESSION of 1837-42.

anticipation rate. An extra discount sometimes permitted on an invoice in addition to the cash discount stated in the terms for payment. If the stated terms are, for example, 2 per cent for cash in 10 days or 90 days net, the customer may pay the bill within 10 days, deducting not only the 2 per cent but an additional anticipation rate calculated on the basis of, say, 6 per cent per annum for 90 days or 1½ per cent. On an invoice of $1,000 the calculation would be as follows:

Invoice	$1,000.00
2 per cent cash discount	20.00
	980.00
Anticipation rate, 1½ per cent	14.70
	$965.30

See RATE.

Anti-Corn-Law League. An organization founded in Manchester, England, in 1839 under the leadership of Richard Cobden to seek repeal of the CORN LAWS.

antidumping duty. A customs duty which attempts to discourage or prevent dumping; that is, the importation of goods to be sold at a price less than that for which they are sold in the country of origin. Such a duty may achieve its purpose if it equals the difference between the selling price of the goods in the country of origin and the selling price in the country where the goods have been dumped. See CUSTOMS DUTY.

Anti-injunction *(Norris-LaGuardia)* **Act.** An act of Congress, 1932, which protects labor by regulating the issuance of INJUNCTIONS, outlawing YELLOW-DOG CONTRACTS, protecting union officials from the consequences of certain unauthorized acts committed by union members, and requiring trial by jury in certain contempt-of-court cases.

Antiracketeering Act. An act of Congress, 1934, which, with subsequent amendments, identifies as federal offenses acts constituting crimes of robbery or extortion when these have the effect of interrupting the free flow of interstate commerce.

Antistrikebreaking *(Byrnes)* **Act.** An act of Congress, 1936, which, as amended in 1938, prohibits the transportation between the states of any person employed for the purpose of interfering by force or threats with peaceful picketing during any labor dispute or with the self-organization or collective bargaining of employees. The act does not apply to common carriers.

antitrust. A term descriptive of any policy or action which has for its object the curtailment of monopolistic power.

antitrust acts. See CLAYTON ACT, SHERMAN ANTITRUST ACT.

Antitrust Division. A unit of the Department of Justice charged with the enforcement of antitrust and related legislation. It receives complaints and conducts investigations in cooperation with the Federal Bureau of Investigation and the Federal Trade Commission. Criminal prosecutions and suits in equity are instituted when necessary to curb monopolies and restraints of interstate and foreign trade. The division also studies and advises other government agencies on the competitive impact upon the economy of policies they may be pursuing or be contemplating and of their control of government resources and rights.

Apex Hosiery case. A case, *Apex Hosiery Co.* v. *Leader,* 310 U.S. 469 (1940), in which the Supreme Court ruled that the loss of production and trade entailed by a sit-down strike to coerce an employer into signing a closed-shop agreement was not substantial enough to constitute the kind of restraint of interstate commerce which the Sherman Antitrust Act was intended to curb and that, therefore, the provisions of the Sherman Act were not applicable to the strike.

Appalachia. The region embracing parts of nine states from Pennsylvania to Alabama along the Appalachian highlands, and characterized by economic blight.

applied economics. The application of economic theory to the solution of economic problems. See ECONOMICS.

apportioned tax. A tax, the proceeds of which are distributed among other political units after having been collected by one of them. Thus, in some of the states of the United States, property taxes may be collected by the county and subsequently shared by the state government, the counties, and other subdivisions. The extension of this concept to federal-state fiscal relations has been advocated, especially as respects the income tax. See TAX.

appraisal. A formal valuation of property, especially for levying property taxes or customs duties, made by a competent authority.

appreciation. A more or less permanent increase in value because of an upward change in the market price or because of inherent qualities that enhance the desirability of, and hence the demand for, a product over a period of time.

apprentice. A person who learns an art, trade, or calling by association with, and under the supervision of, skilled workers. Apprenticeship is of ancient origin. It is identified particularly with a medieval GUILD in which apprentices served under master craftsmen in return for the opportunity to learn a trade. During recent years, in the United States, employers and labor unions in certain industries, notably the printing and building trades, have developed systematic plans for apprenticeship and on-the-job training. The Bureau of Apprenticeship and Training of the U.S. Department of Labor formulates standards for the welfare of apprentices and for their instruction.

appropriation. The action of setting money aside and formally authorizing its expenditure, especially such action when taken by a legislature or similar public body. See (21).

appropriation, law of. See MARXIAN LAW OF CAPITALIST ACCUMULATION.

arbitrage. The process of buying a thing in one market and selling it at the same time in another market in order to take advantage of price differences.

arbitration. An arrangement whereby two parties to a dispute agree to the appointment of an impartial chairman or group of competent persons to decide the issue, the disputants agreeing to abide by the decision rendered. Arbitration is often used in labor and industrial disputes.

arbitration of exchange. The payment by a person in one country of a debt payable in another country by means of a BILL OF EXCHANGE purchased in a third country. The price of bills of exchange payable in the currencies of foreign countries differs in the various financial centers of the world. It may be more profitable, therefore, at any particular moment for a person in the United States, for example, wishing to settle a debt in London, to purchase a bill of exchange in France payable in English currency rather than to purchase a bill in New York payable in English currency. Such an operation may be more profitable even if it is necessary first to purchase a bill in New York payable in French currency.

area agreement. As applied to labor relations, an agreement signed by a labor union or unions and individual employers engaged in a particular industry within a geographic area. The latter is usually more extensive than that enclosed by the boundaries of a municipality.

area sample. A limited number of observations selected from an entire aggregate of phenomena on the basis of geographical subdivisions. For example, suppose that a sample of SPENDING UNITS within a state is desired, and there exists no comprehensive list from which such a sample might be obtained. The state, in such a case, might be divided into geographical units, say counties, and a certain number of counties selected for the sample. Each county included in the sample might then be divided into municipalities and a certain number of municipalities selected for the sample. Each municipality included in the sample might then be divided into streets and a certain number of streets selected for the sample. Finally, from each street included in the sample, a certain number of spending units might be identified. See SAMPLE.

arithmetic chart. See RATIO CHART.

arithmetic mean. A calculated average computed by finding the sum of the numbers to be averaged and dividing the result by the total quantity of numbers. The mathematical formula is:

$$M = \frac{\Sigma m}{N}$$

when

M = arithmetic mean,
m = numbers to be averaged,
N = total quantity of numbers.

The arithmetic mean is the average most commonly used. It emphasizes extremes, however, and is hence unsuitable for certain types of economic computation. For example, out of 25 contributions, one $10 contribution, when all the rest are less than $1, makes the average contribution seem unduly large if computed according to the arithmetic mean. See AVERAGE.

arithmetic progression. See PROGRESSION.

arm's length. The absence of nepotism, influence, or collusion, and the observance of prevailing business practices and established ethical standards in business dealings between a parent and subsidiary company, or between an eleemosynary foundation and a profit-making enterprise, both of which are under the control of the same person or company.

articles of incorporation. A document setting forth the purpose, duration, principal place of business, and other details of a proposed corporation. It is submitted to an appropriate government official for approval, and, if approved, copies of the document must usually be filed in one or more government offices in order that the existence of the corporation be made a matter of public record. Also called *certificate of incorporation.*

artificial capital. See CAPITAL GOOD.

artisan. A person skilled in some trade or craft; for example, a carpenter, mechanic, or mason.

Asian Development Bank. An investment bank with headquarters in Manila, Philippines, whose creation grew out of a recommendation of the Economic Commission for Asia and the Far East in 1963. (See REGIONAL ECONOMIC COMMISSIONS OF THE UNITED NATIONS.) Its membership consists of a minority of Western states, including the United States, and a majority of Asian states such as Japan, India, Pakistan, and others, particularly those of Southeast Asia. Japan and the United States have each contributed one-fifth of the total capital of $1 billion, half of which is working capital, the other half serving as a guarantee fund for the bank's bonds. The bank intends to make strategic investments in developing member countries and to serve as a multinational agency for extending financial aid to such countries. See BANK.

assaying. The testing of an ore or other commodity by chemical means or otherwise to determine its degree of purity. The United States government maintains *assay offices* for the testing of bullion used in coins and a customs laboratory to test imported ores for the determination of a DUTY.

assay office. See ASSAYING.

assembly-line technique. A system of production in which, by a rather extreme application of the principle of DIVISION OF LABOR, a number of individual INTERCHANGEABLE PARTS, or subassemblies, are brought together into a completely assembled or finished unit. A conveyor belt is frequently used to carry the work under construction between lines of employees, each of whom performs a given operation on the partially constructed unit as it reaches a designated point in the line, the last employee in the line performing his operation to complete the unit.

assented bond or stock. See BOND, CAPITAL STOCK.

assessable stock. See CAPITAL STOCK.

assessment. 1. A valuation placed upon property for the purpose of taxation; usually called a *tax assessment*. See also EQUALIZATION OF ASSESSMENTS, SPECIAL ASSESSMENT. **2.** The amount exacted as a tax. **3.** A demand for payment, the liability for which has already been incurred. Thus, the owners of certain classes of CAPITAL STOCK may be assessed for additional payments; or the holders of shares of stock, not fully paid for, may be assessed the unpaid balance, or a part of it.

assessor. 1. A person with specialized knowledge who assists a judge in cases requiring such knowledge. **2.** A government official, usually appointed or elected locally, who appraises property for purposes of taxation.

asset. As used in accounting, something of value that is owned.

21

It may be something tangible or something intangible such as a claim on another person. See (1).

asset and liability statement. Usually a balance sheet. The term is sometimes used by accountants, however, to indicate a statement of what is owned and what is owed, prepared from single-entry books or sources other than double-entry books. See FINANCIAL STATEMENT.

asset enter mains. A term used in the transactions of executors or trustees, indicating an asset available to meet immediate obligations. See ASSET.

assignat. A form of paper currency issued by the Revolutionary government in France between 1790 and 1795. It was secured by expropriated lands of the church and the *émigré* nobility. The assignats were redeemed in 1796 by another form of paper currency, and both were subsequently repudiated.

assignee. One to whom a title, interest, or right of some kind has been transferred. The person from whom the transfer is received is the assignor.

assignment. The formal transfer of any property or right from one person to another.

assimilation. As applied to finance, the purchase by the general public of a new issue of securities, and the establishment of its price in the stock markets.

association agreement. As applied to labor relations, an agreement signed by an association of employers and a labor union or a board representing several unions.

assumed bond. See BOND.

assumption of risk. A common-law doctrine that an employee assumes the risk of personal injury when engaged in an unusually dangerous or hazardous occupation. Such a doctrine has now been largely replaced in most of the states of the United States by WORKMEN'S COMPENSATION LAWS.

assurance. A term used by some insurance companies instead of the term "insurance."

astronomical theory of the business cycle. A theory that attempts to correlate the constantly recurring economic crises with the periodic appearance of sunspots. The varying intensity of the sun's rays is said to cause good and bad harvests, and these, in turn, influence economic life. The theory was suggested to

Stanley Jevons, an English economist, by the apparent regularity of the 10-year intervals between economic crises during the 19th century. Also called *sunspot theory of the business cycle.* See BUSINESS CYCLE.

Atomic Energy Act. An act of Congress, 1946. The act stated that "subject at all times to the paramount objective of assuring the common defense and security, the development and utilization of atomic energy shall, so far as practicable, be directed towards improving the public welfare, increasing the standard of living, strengthening free competition in private enterprise and promoting world peace." The act provided for public assistance to private research, the dissemination of technical knowledge (consistent with national security), federal research and development, and control over the production, ownership, and the use of fissionable materials. The administration of the act was committed to a newly formed ATOMIC ENERGY COMMISSION *(q.v.).*

Atomic Energy Commission. A five-man commission of the United States government charged by law with the development of policies which will promote public and private research in nuclear fission, the dissemination and exchange of scientific information on such research, governmental ownership and exploitation of fissionable materials in the interests of national security, and the application of atomic energy to industrial pursuits after proper international safeguards have been provided.

atomistic society. An economy in which there is a distinct preponderance of small, independent, producing units. The term is used to indicate the condition that existed previous to the establishment of huge aggregates of capital in industry and trade, originally organized as such or created through an AMALGAMATION, HOLDING COMPANY, MERGER, or TRUST.

at the market. An order to a stockbroker to buy or sell immediately at the current market price.

auction sale. A sale in which goods are offered to the highest bidder. Such a sale usually involves a series of oral bids which begin at a low price and proceed to the highest one offered, at which point the sale is consummated. See also DUTCH AUCTION.

audit. A verification of an accounting record.

auditor. A person qualified to audit records either of private businesses (public auditor) or of governmental agencies (state auditor).

austerity program. A national economic policy which deliberately reduces the level of living of the people in order to accomplish desired ends such as a balanced budget, increased capital equipment, the payment of the external national debt, or the balancing of international payments.

Austrian school. See PSYCHOLOGICAL SCHOOL.

autarchy. **1.** Economic self-sufficiency. **2.** Unlimited sovereign power.

automatic balance. As applied to economic life, the idea that automatic forces always restore equilibrium when excesses occur. Thus, when interest rates are too low, savings are curtailed, and the demand for capital will force an advance in interest rates. In international trade an excess of exports will be checked by the importation of gold and the resulting advance in the general price level. Prices, when too high, will meet resistance through lack of purchasing power, and when too low will be advanced through increased consumer demand.

automatic checkoff. See CHECKOFF.

automatic data processing system. A DIGITAL COMPUTER with peripheral interacting equipment such as is used for data collection, conversion, and input and output operations. See COMPUTER.

automatic stabilizer. A BUILT-IN *(q.v.)* measure which tends to offset some economic trend inimical to the welfare of the economy. For example, unemployment insurance offsets, to some extent, shrinking payrolls in a time of increasing unemployment.

automatic wage adjustment. A system of wage payments which provides for advancing or lowering employees' wages according to some factor other than the purely economic demand for labor. This factor may be an advance or decline in the cost-of-living index, or of prices or profits. The term may also refer to wage adjustments made in accordance with some established formula relating to years of employment or to a record of service.

automation. The performance of tasks, formerly requiring human labor and some thought, by self-acting and self-regulating machines. The term was first applied to the mere automatic transfer of materials from one machine tool to another, each machine tool performing some operation contributing to the completion of the final product. Only human labor was thus replaced. With the advance of technology, communication was added, and a variety of precision controls were perfected. Communication occurs when the machine tools, or other fabricating or processing devices, follow a sequence of instructions such as might be programed in an AUTOMATIC DATA PROCESSING SYSTEM. Control is effected when any deviation from a predetermined program actuates a mechanism that causes the necessary correction to be made. These two latter functions replace human thought, at least on a low level.

autonomous investment. New CAPITAL FORMATION motivated by reasons independent of the rate of interest or the level of NATIONAL INCOME. Public investments are usually of this nature. Investments deemed necessary for the national defense, those designed for PUMP PRIMING purposes, or for the general peacetime welfare of the community, such as public parks, baths, playgrounds, etc., are cases in point. Even PUBLIC WORKS of a SELF-LIQUIDATING nature may be undertaken with little regard for the rate of interest or the level of national income. Private investments are not generally autonomous. Only when made on the basis of long-term plans divorced from considerations of immediate profits and losses can they be so regarded. The term is used in contradistinction to INDUCED INVESTMENT. See INVESTMENT.

autonomous tariff system. A system of tariff duties in which the rates are established by legislative action exclusively, and not wholly or partly by commercial treaties. The term is used in contradistinction to CONVENTIONAL TARIFF SYSTEM. See TARIFF.

autonomous variable. In statistics, a variable that depends, in part, upon factors other than those which are strictly economic; for example, changes due to political, social, or psychological influences.

avail. In general, an amount remaining after the deduction of expenses or a discount; for example, the PROCEEDS of a promissory note, the amount of an estate after the debts have been paid, or the income from an auction sale after the deduction of selling expenses.

average. A medial number calculated from a set of numbers, also called a *mean,* or placed in a medial position with reference to them. See (10).

B

backlog. An accumulation. For example, a backlog of orders indicates orders as yet unfilled.

back spread. The condition which exists when the difference in price of the same commodity or security in two markets is less than normal. The term is used in contradistinction to SPREAD which indicates a price differential greater than normal. The terms are used in ARBITRAGE transactions.

backtracking. As applied to labor relations, the policy of retaining employees with the longest record of service in preference to those with shorter records when the labor force of an establishment is being reduced. Sometimes called *bumping.*

bad faith. Resort to deceit or fraud to avoid a legal obligation, or willful refusal to honor an obligation.

Bailey v. ***Drexel Furniture Co.*** See CHILD-LABOR CASES.

bailment. Generally, the transfer under a contract by one person to another of goods, money, or other valuable personal property for some specified purpose, the property to be returned when the contractual conditions have been fulfilled.

balance of payments. In the case of any particular country, the difference between the total payments made to foreign countries and the total receipts from foreign countries during a given period. Payments and receipts include gold, the value of all merchandise and services, such as freight and insurance charges, expenditures by travelers, capital movements occasioned by loans and investments, the payment of interest and dividends, and the repayment of the principal of loans. The balance is said to be favorable if the receipts exceed remittances, unfavorable if the reverse is the case. Computation of a particular country's balance of payments may be limited to its relations with another country or group of countries, or it may embrace its relations with the rest of the world. In calculating the balance of payments, reference is sometimes made to INVISIBLE ITEMS OF TRADE and to VISIBLE ITEMS OF TRADE *(qq.v.).*

balance of trade. The difference between the money value of a country's merchandise imports and the money value of its merchandise exports. The balance of trade is an important item in calculating BALANCE OF PAYMENTS. See FAVORABLE BALANCE OF TRADE, UNFAVORABLE BALANCE OF TRADE.

balance sheet. A condensed list of assets and liabilities displaying net worth or a deficit as of a given date. See FINANCIAL STATEMENT.

balloon note. A promissory note which requires only token payments during the early period of the loan, more substantial payments being deferred until near the date of maturity. See NOTE.

bank. A general and somewhat vague term applied to many different kinds of financial institutions carrying on one or more of the functions of deposit, discount, investment, and issue, and offering other financial services of various kinds. There are also many financial institutions not designated as banks which carry on one or more of the functions above mentioned. See (18), (19).

bankable bill. See BILL.

bank acceptance. A draft or bill of exchange accepted for payment by a bank. See ACCEPTANCE.

bank call. A demand by an appropriate government official made upon banks for balance sheets showing their financial condition as of a specified date. In the United States such demands may be made by a state superintendent of banks and, in the case of national banks, by the comptroller of the currency.

bank clearings. See CLEARINGS.

bank credit. Credit created by a bank. It is usually created by adding the proceeds of a loan to a depositor's account by discounting a depositor's promissory note, in which case the face value of the note becomes an ASSET of the bank and the amount of the discount becomes UNEARNED INCOME, in the form of unearned interest. Such credit may also be created by the purchase, by the bank, of United States government bonds, in which case the purchase price of the bonds may be placed to the government's credit to be drawn when needed, and the bonds become an asset of the bank. See CREDIT.

bank credit proxy. A statistical measure of current bank credit conditions in the United States consisting of a daily estimated average total of all time, demand, and federal government deposits in federal reserve member banks (excluding any currency in circulation). It is used by various agencies, including the Board of Governors of the Federal Reserve System, in determining monetary and credit policy.

bank debits. The value of checks and commercial paper charged to depositors' accounts by banks within a certain territory during a designated length of time. The statistics on bank debits, which are compiled by the FEDERAL RESERVE BANKS, are based on reports from member banks and serve as a general index of the volume of business being transacted.

bank deposit. The right to receive a stated sum of money from a bank, this right having been created by previously paying an equivalent amount of money or other currency to the bank, or by a credit to the depositor's account of the proceeds of a loan made by the bank. Evidence of a bank deposit is the bank's books of account and the depositor's passbook, duplicate deposit slip or other form of receipt. See (20).

banker's bill. See BILL.

bank examiner. A public official who periodically audits the accounts of banks under his jurisdiction to determine whether their practice conforms with the law and whether they are in sound financial condition. The examination of national banks is under the jurisdiction of the U.S. Comptroller of the Currency, who appoints the examiners. Each bank is examined at least twice a year and more often if deemed necessary. State banks are examined by bank examiners appointed under the laws of the individual states of the United States.

bank for cooperatives. One of a system of 13 credit institutions, one operating nationally and 12 regionally, which were created by act of Congress in 1933 to provide both short- and long-term credit to farm cooperatives. These banks are a part of the FARM CREDIT ADMINISTRATION. See BANK.

Bank for International Settlements. A bank organized in 1930, under a Swiss charter, by representatives of the central banks of certain Western European states and by representatives of banking interests of the United States, to administer reparations payments under the YOUNG PLAN and engage in a limited general banking business. Since its creation it has become a highly influential and useful institution. Among its special services are those as agent for the EUROPEAN MONETARY AGREEMENT *(q.v.)*, as depository for loans of the EUROPEAN COMMUNITY FOR COAL AND STEEL *(q.v.)*, and as an international institutional framework through which central banks cooperate to maintain equilibrium in the world's monetary system. See BANK.

Bankhead-Jones Farm Tenant Act. An act of Congress, 1937, which authorized the Farmers Home Administration to finance 40-year mortgage loans to enable tenant farmers, and others in a similar position, to purchase small farms.

bank holiday. Any holiday or other period during which banks are legally permitted to remain closed. The term is applied particularly to the period from March 4 to 14, 1933, when a presidential proclamation closed all banks in the United States pending examination into their operations and the restoration of public confidence.

Banking (Glass-Steagall) Act. An act of Congress, 1933, which denied commercial banks and trust companies the right to engage in INVESTMENT BANKING, established the FEDERAL DEPOSIT INSURANCE CORPORATION, and canceled the DOUBLE LIABILITY feature of national bank stock.

banking system. A term indicating the general characteristics of the structure and operation of a nation's banks. See (20).

bank note. A form of paper currency carrying a bank's promise to pay a specific amount of money to the bearer on demand. Bank notes, secured by certain United States bonds, were issued by NATIONAL BANKS in the United States from 1865 to

1935, when the bonds were retired. No national bank notes have been issued since that date. See NOTE.

bank of issue. A bank that issues bank notes. See BANK.

Bank of North Dakota. A bank owned and operated by the state of North Dakota, officially designated as the "State of North Dakota doing business as the Bank of North Dakota." The bank opened for business in 1919. Its capital was obtained through the sale of bonds—since retired. It conducts a commercial banking business, accepting time and checking accounts from individuals and corporations. Loans are made only to departments and political subdivisions of the state, and to individuals solely under the rules of the Federal Home Administration, veterans' legislation, or Farmers Home Administration. It is the only bank of its kind in the United States. See BANK.

Bank of the United States. A quasi-public bank, operating under a congressional charter, which through a central office and various branches did a general banking business throughout the United States, issued bank notes, and served as a depositary for federal funds and as a fiduciary agent for the United States government. Technically there were two such banks. The first, created at the instance of Hamilton and the Federalists in 1791, ceased operations with the expiration of its 20-year charter in 1811. The second bank was chartered in 1816, also for 20 years. President Jackson became its unrelenting foe. In 1833 he ordered the federal government's deposits removed and, by his use of the veto and other tactics, succeeded in defeating legislation to recharter the bank. It accordingly ceased operating as the Bank of the United States in 1836. See BANK.

bank post remittance. A foreign bill of exchange converted into a money order or cash by the bank to which it is directed, the money order or cash then being forwarded by mail to the payee.

bank rate. The rate of interest or discount for business loans which is prevalent among commercial banks. See RATE. See also PRIME RATE.

bank reserves. The amount of money or its equivalent kept available by a bank to meet the demands of depositors. Since the demands of depositors for money normally represent only a small proportion of a bank's deposits, it is never necessary for a bank to have on hand an amount of money equal to the total deposits entrusted to it. In the United States the amount of money that a bank must keep available for such a purpose is specified by law in the form of a percentage of its deposits, called the RESERVE RATIO. The *legal reserve* requirement of a bank which is a member of the FEDERAL RESERVE SYSTEM depends upon the location of the bank and is determined by the Board of Governors of the Federal Reserve System for all member banks similarly located. Except for cash in its vaults, a member bank's reserves must be kept on deposit with the district federal reserve bank. The legal reserves of state banks in the United States are specified in the laws of the several states. Contraction or expansion of legal reserves, through changes in the reserve ratio, directly affects the volume of a bank's lending capacity. See RESERVES. See also DEPOSIT CURRENCY.

bankruptcy. The condition of a debtor who has been adjudged insolvent by a court of competent jurisdiction and whose existing property is administered under the court's order for the benefit of his creditors. This condition may be brought about by a petition filed with the court by the insolvent debtor himself, in which case it is known as *voluntary bankruptcy;* or it may be brought about by a petition filed with the court by the requisite number of creditors, in which case it is known as *involuntary bankruptcy.*

bankruptcy acts. Various acts passed by Congress under its constitutional power to make uniform laws on the subject of bankruptcy. Such national laws supersede existing state legislation on the same subject. Among the more recent federal acts are those of 1898 and 1933. The latter act, amended somewhat in 1934, was passed during the depths of an economic depression and was designed to ease the lot of certain creditors. Railroads and other corporations, unable to meet maturing fixed obligations, were permitted to reorganize under their existing management or under the control of a trustee, and to scale down or otherwise modify their liabilities. Certain classes of individual debtors were also given the opportunity by law to make compositions with their creditors or to secure an extension of time for the payment of indebtedness. In 1938 Congress passed the

Chandler Act to consolidate existing bankruptcy legislation. See BANKRUPTCY.

bankruptcy case. See *STURGES* v. *CROWNINSHIELD.*

bank term loan. A bank loan terminating in a year or more, sometimes used instead of a long-term bond issue especially during periods of high interest rates. See LOAN.

bantam store. A small neighborhood grocery store which is open late in the evening and provides quick service and easy parking. By enabling housewives to piece out supplies or fill in forgotten items, it provides an effective supplement to a supermarket. Also called *convenience store.*

bargaining unit. Employees of a company, or of an industry in a particular area, whose representatives bargain collectively with management—often so designated by the National Labor Relations Board.

barometer stock. See CAPITAL STOCK.

barter. The direct exchange of one commodity or service for another without the use of money.

base pay. Wages exclusive of overtime, bonuses, or premiums of any kind.

base period. See INDEX NUMBER.

base rate. As applied to the payment of wages for labor, the pay for a specified amount of production. When bonuses are paid for production beyond a certain minimum, the base rate determines the point from which any increased production and pay are calculated. See RATE.

basic crops. A term used to designate certain staple commodities subject to price supports. In farm-price support programs enacted by Congress, basic crops include wheat, corn, cotton, rice, peanuts, tobacco, oats, barley, grain sorghums, flaxseed, soybeans, wool, and milk, among others.

basic yield. The annual return, expressed as a percentage, on a hypothetical investment presenting no risk. In the United States, the nearest approach to a basic yield is the return on long-term federal bonds. See YIELD.

basing-point system. The selection by a seller of a certain place called the "basing point," from which freight charges, paid by the buyer, are calculated, regardless of the actual place from which the goods are shipped. If, for example, the seller has a plant in San Francisco and another in Chicago, and the basing point is San Francisco, a buyer nearer to Chicago than to San Francisco will have to pay the equivalent of freight charges on his order from San Francisco even though his goods are produced and shipped from the Chicago plant. Recent court decisions in the United States will have the effect of outlawing this practice.

bazaar. A marketplace, especially in Eastern countries, particularly one where fancy goods are sold.

bear. As applied to trading on the security exchanges, an expression indicating a person who believes that the value of corporate stocks will decline. Used in contradistinction to BULL.

bearer. An individual who holds a negotiable instrument, such as a note or check made payable to the bearer on demand, and which is transferable without indorsement.

Bedford Cut Stone Co. v. Journeymen Stone Cutters' Assn. A case, 274 U.S. 37 (1927), in which the Supreme Court, following its decision in the DANBURY HATTERS' CASE *(q.v.)*, held that the federal antitrust laws prohibited a national labor organization from instructing its members not to work on an unprocessed commodity, in this instance quarried stone, which their employer had purchased from a nonunion enterprise.

Beech-Nut Packing case. A resale price-maintenance case, *Beech-Nut Packing Co.* v. *Federal Trade Commission*, 257 U.S. 441 (1922), in which the Supreme Court upheld an order of the Federal Trade Commission requiring a company to desist from certain practices involving maintenance of resale prices by local dealers. The Court held that the Sherman Act is violated when producers or distributors of goods or services exact a promise from dealers to maintain fixed resale prices or solicit dealer cooperation to that end. The decision has been modified as a result of legislation permitting resale price agreements, which the courts have sustained. See OLD DEARBORN DISTRIBUTING CO. V. SEAGRAM DISTILLERS CORP.

beneficiary. One who receives something as a gift. The term is commonly applied to the person named in a life-insurance policy who receives the proceeds upon the death of the insured.

benefit society. See BUILDING AND LOAN ASSOCIATION.

benefits-received principle of taxation. The principle that taxes should be levied upon individual taxpayers in proportion to the benefits they receive from the state. To a certain extent this principle is used in the case of special assessments for improvements, but its general application is subject to the same difficulties as is the COST-OF-SERVICE PRINCIPLE OF TAXATION *(q.v.)*. Sometimes called *compensatory principle of taxation.*

Benelux. A term used to identify the CUSTOMS UNION and certain limited aspects of an economic union which have come into being among the Low Countries.

bequest. Usually a gift of personal property provided for in a will. Also called *legacy.*

betterment tax. A SPECIAL ASSESSMENT *(q.v.)*. See TAX.

Beveridge plan. A plan elaborated by Sir William Beveridge in 1942 for revising the British social-insurance system. The plan provided for eight primary causes of need: (1) unemployment; (2) disability; (3) loss of means of support when not regularly employed; (4) retirement; (5) marriage needs of women; (6) expenses of childhood; (7) funeral expenses; and (8) sickness or incapacity.

bid. An offer to sell a commodity or service at a stipulated price or an offer to purchase at a price, as at an auction.

bidding. As applied to labor relations, the procedure of notifying employees of other jobs in a plant or industry in order that any who wish to do so may apply.

big board. See NEW YORK STOCK EXCHANGE.

big business. Collectively the largest corporations, sometimes identified as the 100 largest or the 500 largest in such areas as manufacturing, mining, construction, distribution, and finance, which hold a disproportionately large share of the total assets devoted to enterprise and are responsible for a disproportionately large percentage of total sales, total profits, and total employment.

big steel. A popular term for the United States Steel Corporation. See also LITTLE STEEL.

bilateral agreement. An agreement between two parties.

bilateral monopoly. The condition which would exist if there were only one buyer for a commodity or service, the entire supply of which was controlled by one seller. See MONOPOLY.

bill. 1. As used in commerce and finance, a generic term identifying a variety of documents having to do with currency, the shipment of goods, and the collection of debts. The term is used as an abbreviation of BILL OF EXCHANGE or as synonymous with DRAFT, often in association with any one of a number of qualifying or descriptive adjectives. Thus, *acceptance bill* is a bill of exchange accepted for eventual payment; *advance bill,* one drawn in advance of a shipment; *bankable bill,* one easily discounted; *banker's bill,* one drawn on a bank; *blank bill,* one with the name of the creditor omitted; *clean bill,* one with no documents attached; *continental bill,* one payable on the continent of Europe; *credit bill,* one drawn against credit already established by the debtor; *demand bill,* one payable at sight; *documentary bill,* one having documents attached; *domestic bill,* one drawn and payable in the same country (in the United States one drawn and payable in the same state); *finance bill,* one drawn by a bank in one country on a bank in another country usually against securities held by the latter bank, and good for a relatively long period of time; *foreign bill,* one drawn in one country and payable in another (in the United States a bill drawn in one state and payable in another); *inland bill,* one drawn in one country and payable in the same country; *investment bill,* one purchased at a discount for the interest it will yield at maturity; *payment bill,* one presented for payment rather than for acceptance; *prime bill,* one which is an excellent credit risk; *sight bill,* same as demand bill; *time bill,* one payable at a future date; *treasury bill,* a promissory note issued to a lender by the United States government as evidence of a short-term loan. A *bill of sale* formally transfers ownership of property from one person to another. **2.** An itemized list of charges for goods or services issued to a buyer by a seller. **3.** Popularly, a piece of paper currency. See (14).

bill of credit. In the United States, an unsecured promissory note issued by a government and intended to circulate as money. Art. I, Sec. 10, of the Constitution enjoins the states against emitting bills of credit, but no such injunction applies to the federal government, since it issued such notes as GREEN-BACKS, and its authority to do so was upheld by the courts. See LEGAL-TENDER CASES.

bill of exchange. A sight or time draft arising from payments to or from a foreign country. Occasionally the term is applied to domestic drafts. See BILL.

bill of lading. A contract between a shipper and a transportation company in which the latter agrees to transport goods under specified conditions which limit its liability. See (6).

bill of sale. See BILL.

bills payable. A term used in double-entry bookkeeping to indicate the records of the value of promissory notes and commercial paper given to others, and the amounts paid on such obligations. Also called *notes payable.* See also ACCOUNT.

bills receivable. A term used in double-entry bookkeeping to indicate the records of the value of promissory notes and commercial paper received from others, and the amounts paid on such obligations. Also called *notes receivable.* See also ACCOUNT.

bimetallism. A monetary system in which the monetary unit is defined by law in terms of two metals, presumably gold and silver, in a specific ratio of weight one to the other, each metal being accepted in unlimited quantities for coinage, and each kind of coin being made legal tender. Also called *double standard.* See MONETARY SYSTEM.

binary notation. A numbering system which uses the base two instead of the base ten as in the conventional decimal system. Only two digits (called bits) are used, 0 and 1. When 1 is moved one place to the left, and its previous position is replaced with zero, the resulting binary number is two times the original number instead of 10 times the original number as in the decimal system. Thus, in the binary system, two is 10 or two times the original number which was one. Four is 100 or two times the original number which was two. Eight is 1000 or two times the original number which was four, etc. Intervening binary numbers can be found by combinations. Thus, three is binary 10 plus 1 or 11. Five is binary 100 plus 1 or 101. Six is binary 10 plus binary 100 or 110. Seven is binary 100 plus binary 10 plus 1 or 111. Nine is binary 1000 plus 1 or 1001. Various adaptations of binary notation are used in DIGITAL COMPUTERS.

binder. As applied to insurance, a temporary document informing the person insured that the risk is covered. An insurance policy usually replaces the binder within a period of 15 days.

birth rate. The number of births per 1,000 persons in any given area during the period of a year—for example, 18.5 for the United States in 1966. This is called the *crude birth rate.* If corrections are made to allow for differences in the composition of the population, the crude birth rate becomes a *refined birth rate.* Thus, the birth rate established for 1,000 women of child-bearing age would be a refined birth rate. See RATE.

bituminous coal cases. Two cases which came before the Supreme Court to test the validity of two separate acts of Congress purporting to establish fair-practice codes for the soft-coal industry. In 1935 Congress passed the first of these acts, popularly known as the first Guffey Coal Act. In the case of *CARTER v. CARTER COAL CO.,* 298 U.S. 238 (1936), the Court held the act invalid because of its attempt to fix wages and control working conditions in the mines. The majority of the Court considered this to be an attempted regulation of production and not of commerce and hence an effort to exercise a power which belongs to the states and not to Congress. The second GUFFEY COAL ACT, passed in 1937, re-enacted price-fixing provisions of the first act, and this regulation was sustained in *SUNSHINE ANTHRACITE COAL CO. v. ADKINS,* 310 U.S. 381 (1940).

black Friday. A term designating any one of a number of historic dates occurring on Fridays when disastrous financial events took place. Two of the most important instances are: Friday, May 11, 1866, when Overend and Gurney, an important banking concern in London, failed, with resultant widespread financial distress; Friday, September 24, 1869, when the United States government purchased with gold 4 million dollars' worth of its BONDS in the open MARKET, thus breaking the CORNER in gold then being manipulated by Jay Gould and James Fiske.

black list. As applied to industrial disputes, a list of the names of certain workers believed to have incited discontent in some plant, circulated among other employers as a warning against employing the workers whose names appear on the list.

black market. A general term indicating all transactions in violation of price and rationing laws. See MARKET.

Bland-Allison Act. An act of Congress, 1878, which authorized the Secretary of the Treasury to purchase not less than $2 million and not more than $4 million worth of silver monthly and coin it into silver dollars of 412½ grains. Provision was also made for SILVER CERTIFICATES to be issued against an equivalent deposit of silver dollars in the Treasury.

blank bill. See BILL.

blanket bond. See BOND.

blank indorsement. An indorsement that specifies no particular person to whose order a check, note, or similar paper is made payable or to whom it is assigned, and which is therefore payable to bearer. The term is used in contradistinction to SPECIAL INDORSEMENT. See INDORSEMENT.

blighted area. A neighborhood in which real estate values have declined and which has deteriorated in appearance, because land use is inharmonious with the surroundings and property owners are unable or unwilling to invest in new structures or to renovate or maintain existing structures. Blight ensues when, because of zoning changes or failure to zone, business and industrial establishments encroach on residential areas, and when residents of relatively higher economic status move out of a neighborhood and are succeeded by residents lower in the economic scale.

block diagram. Any graphic representation using parallelograms. As applied to DIGITAL COMPUTERS, see PROGRAM.

blocked currency. Limitations imposed upon holders of a national currency preventing them from using it (except under certain conditions) to discharge obligations abroad. See CURRENCY.

blocked exchange. The condition which exists when importers and others, desiring to make payments abroad, are prohibited from doing so by their government; that is, they are prevented from purchasing bills of exchange payable in foreign currencies. Under such conditions, deposits in local currency are sometimes made to cover the prospective remittances, but foreign creditors must wait until the block is removed or find some way of using the local currency credited to them. See EXCHANGE.

Block* v. *Hirsh. See RENT-CONTROL CASE.

blue chip. A vague term indicating a well-seasoned common stock of a leading American corporation with a sustained dividend record, superior management, and favorable future prospects.

blue eagle. An emblem used by the National Recovery Administration in 1933. It appeared on citations issued to employers who agreed to a general code of fair competition formulated by the administration.

blue-sky laws. Laws which protect the inexperienced investor against fraud and misrepresentation in the purchase of corporate securities.

board of directors. See DIRECTOR.

Board of Governors of the Federal Reserve System. A seven-member body appointed by the President and Senate for 14-year terms, one of whom is designated chairman. Among other activities it *(a)* determines from time to time the ratio of reserves against deposits to be observed by member banks of the Reserve System; *(b)* participates with the FEDERAL OPEN MARKET COMMITTEE *(q.v.)* in regulating reserve bank purchases and sales of federal obligations and other securities for reserve purposes, and transactions in foreign currency; *(c)* reviews the rediscount rate as set by individual reserve banks; *(d)* supervises the issuance and retirement by reserve banks of federal reserve notes, the bulk of the nation's currency; *(e)* controls admission to the System of member banks, examines them, and under certain circumstances requires them to observe legal standards or established policy; *(f)* exercises powers relating to the establishment of domestic branches of member banks and authorizes them to invest in foreign banks and to establish branches in foreign countries and in United States possessions; *(g)* determines the rate of interest to be paid by member banks on time and demand deposits; *(h)* prescribes regulations under which the reserve banks may serve as government fiscal agents; and *(i)* generally supervises the Reserve System and, in conjunction with the Treasury and the reserve banks, especially the Federal Reserve Bank of New York, exercises a major influence in determining national credit and monetary policies. See FEDERAL RESERVE SYSTEM.

board of trade. **1.** In the United States, usually a voluntary community organization of business and professional men having as its object the promotion of civic, industrial, and general social welfare. Frequently called *chamber of commerce.* **2.** In the case of the CHICAGO BOARD OF TRADE the term refers to a COMMODITY EXCHANGE.

boiler room. The headquarters of promoters who seek to sell highly speculative securities to the general public, chiefly by telephone. Their operations are usually illegal.

Bolling v. Sharpe. See BROWN V. BOARD OF EDUCATION OF TOPEKA.

bonanza. A highly profitable enterprise, especially a mine or similar high-risk venture.

bond. 1. An agreement in which one of the parties establishes himself as surety for others or guarantees to protect others against loss, e.g., a *bail bond* guaranteeing the appearance of a defendant in a trial, or a bond posted by the administrator of an estate to protect prospective beneficiaries of the estate against loss through possible misfeasance or malfeasance by the administrator. See also FIDELITY BOND, SURETY BOND. 2. A certificate of indebtedness. As generally regarded in the security markets, a bond is evidence of a debt issued by a government, an agency of a government, or by a private corporation.

A *public bond* is one issued by a foreign government or its subdivisions, or by the federal government of the United States, an agency of the federal government, a territory, a colonial possession, one of the various states of the United States, or a local subdivision of a state, such as a county, township, borough, parish, or school district, as well as any one of a great variety of special assessment districts, such as a district engaged in levee construction, drainage of farm lands, building of irrigation works, construction of roads, and other similar projects. A bond which is a direct obligation of the United States government is designated by the words "United States of America" as a part of the title.

Savings Bonds are special United States bonds, issued in two series, E and H. Series E bonds are sold at a discount and mature in 7 to 10 years, depending upon the date of purchase, but may be retained 10 years beyond the date of maturity or exchanged for H bonds. The approximate investment yield for the entire period from issuance to maturity is 4.15 per cent. The interest of H bonds is paid semiannually. They mature in 10 years. The approximate investment yield on the face value from each interest date to maturity is 4.15 per cent.

Some federal agencies have authority to issue obligations guaranteed by, or on the credit of, the United States govern-

ment. The principal agencies having such authority are COM-
MODITY CREDIT CORPORATION, DEPARTMENT OF HOUSING AND
URBAN DEVELOPMENT, FEDERAL DEPOSIT INSURANCE CORPO-
RATION, FEDERAL HOUSING ADMINISTRATION, Housing Assis-
tance Administration, and TENNESSEE VALLEY AUTHORITY.

The principal federal agencies issuing obligations not guar-
anteed by the United States government are: BANKS FOR COOP-
ERATIVES, EXPORT IMPORT BANK, FEDERAL HOME LOAN BANK
SYSTEM, FEDERAL INTERMEDIATE CREDIT BANK, FEDERAL LAND
BANK, FEDERAL NATIONAL MORTGAGE ASSOCIATION, and the
FEDERAL SAVINGS AND LOAN INSURANCE CORPORATION.

A bond issued by a colonial possession is called a *colonial
bond* or *insular bond;* one issued by a city, county, district,
town, or village, a *municipal bond.* In a few cities of the United
States certain *municipal bonds* are called CORPORATE STOCK. A
bond issued by a state is called a *state bond,* and one issued by
a territory, a *territorial bond.* A business corporation bond is
customarily spoken of as an *industrial, public utility,* or *railroad
bond,* according to the nature of the business carried on by the
issuing corporation.

Bonds carry an almost infinite variety of titles which, in
addition to the name of the issuing agency, the interest rate,
and date of maturity, may indicate in a general way the purpose of the issue, the form of the issue, the nature of the security, if any, pledged in support of the bond, and the terms of
payment of interest and principal.

The purpose for which a bond is issued is frequently indicated by such terms as *bridge, construction, development, dock
and wharf, equipment, ferry, highway improvement, public works,
purchase money, reclamation, school,* or some other such descriptive term appearing as a part of the name of a bond. An *adjustment bond* is issued to aid in the recapitalization of a business.
Consol or *consolidated bonds* are issued to retire two or more
outstanding issues and thus bring the indebtedness together
under one issue. An *industrial revenue bond* is a municipal bond
issued to finance construction for commercial purposes. The
new facilities are leased and the bonds are retired from rental
income. An *interest bond* is a bond issued to pay the interest on
other bonds when the necessary cash is not available. A *refund-*

ing bond is issued to retire other indebtedness. A *reorganization bond* is the same as an adjustment bond, defined above. A *tax-anticipation bond* is issued by a governmental unit in order to raise immediate cash and is frequently accepted in payment of taxes when the taxes are due. A *terminal bond* is usually one sold to finance the construction of a railroad terminal. A *unified bond* is the same as a consolidated bond, defined above.

The name of a bond may give some indication of the form in which it is issued. A *coupon bond* has coupons attached—one for each interest date—which can be torn off and deposited as checks. Transfer is effected by delivery. An *interchangeable bond* can be exchanged for one issued in another form—a coupon bond for a registered bond, for example. An *interim bond* is a temporary certificate to be exchanged for a definitive bond in due course of time. A *registered bond* is recorded in the name of the owner. Interest is paid by check, and transfer of ownership requires formal notice. A *registered coupon bond* is registered in the name of the owner, but it has coupons attached, payable to the bearer.

Bonds may be unsecured or secured. The term *debenture bond* usually indicates an unsecured bond backed only by the general credit standing of the issuing agency. Direct obligations of governments are generally unsecured, being backed only by the taxing power of the government. However, a *revenue bond* is a government bond backed by revenue received from a specific project, such as the Golden Gate Bridge of San Francisco and the Triboro Bridge of New York, and a *special-assessment bond* is backed by the power of the government to assess particular individuals for benefits presumably received in the form of public improvements financed by the bond issues.

Other bonds are secured in varying degrees often indicated in a general way by the name of the bond. An *assumed bond* is guaranteed in the matter of principal, interest, or both by a corporation other than the one issuing the bond. The term *blanket bond* indicates, as a rule, a general mortgage pledged as security, but it may be subject to an indefinite number of prior claims on the mortgaged property. A *bottomry bond* is secured by a mortgage on a ship. A *collateral trust bond* is secured by deposits of other securities with a trustee. A *divisional bond* has the backing of a mortgage on some part or division of a railroad. An *equipment trust bond* is usually secured by tangible property, the title of which rests with a trustee while the property is leased to the user, usually a railroad or an airline company. An *extension bond* is one secured by a mortgage on property coming into possession of a railroad or other agency by virtue of an extension of its services. The term *first-lien bond* indicates a first claim on whatever property, tangible or intangible, is pledged to secure the loan. A *guaranteed bond* is the same as an assumed bond, defined above. An *indorsed bond* is also the same as an assumed bond. A *joint and several bond* is one for which the payment of the entire principal and interest is guaranteed by two or more parties. A *junior-lien bond* is one that ranks inferior to some other issue in the matter of its claim on the property pledged as security. A *land-grant bond* is usually issued by a railroad and secured by a lien on land granted to the railroad by the government. The term *mortgage bond* indicates a pledge of real estate or other property. Mortgage bonds are usually classified as first, second, or third, indicating priority of claims against the security. An *overlying bond* is subject to the prior claims of some other bonds. A *plain bond* is the same as a debenture bond, defined above. The term is also used to indicate a bond on which certain terms and conditions pertaining to the bond have not been stamped thereon. A *prior-lien bond* enjoys a prior lien over some other issue on the property pledged for security, but itself may be subject to prior claims of other issues. A *sinking-fund bond* is one paid from a SINKING FUND (*q.v.*). The sinking fund may be invested until the bonds are due, or, if the bonds are subject to "call from sinking fund," numbers identifying the bonds may be drawn by lot and the corresponding bonds redeemed, or the sinking fund may be used to buy the bonds in the open market. A *stamped bond* is one on which special terms and conditions have been stamped. The term *underlying bond* means that such a bond has a priority claim against the property securing its payment.

The name of the bond may indicate the terms of payment of the interest, principal, or both. An *annuity bond* bears no maturity date, the interest continuing indefinitely. A *callable bond* is redeemable upon due notice to the bondholder. A *continued bond* need not be presented for payment at maturity, but may be held for an indefinite period at the same rate of interest or possibly some different rate. A *convertible bond* grants the holder the right to exchange it for some other type of security, usually common or preferred stock. A *currency bond* may be paid in any kind of legal tender. The term *deferred bond* indicates that the payment of interest is postponed for a specified length of time. An *extended bond* is one the maturity date of which has been postponed with the sanction of the bondholders. A *gold bond* specifies that payment shall be made in gold coins of a certain weight and fineness. Such a clause has no real significance in the United States since the possession of gold coins is illegal. An *income bond* is one the payment of interest on which is contingent upon current earnings. *Installment bonds* are paid off in installments over a period of years. An *irredeemable bond* is the same as an annuity bond, defined above. A *legal-tender bond* is the same as a currency bond. A *noninterest-bearing discount bond* provides that the interest shall be paid, together with the principal, upon maturity. An *optional bond* may be redeemed prior to the maturity date if the issuing agency so elects. A *participating* or *profit-sharing bond* is one that shares in the profits of the issuing agency in addition to a guaranteed interest rate. A *passive bond* bears no interest. Presumably it holds some other advantage for the owner. The term is rarely used. A *perpetual bond* is the same as an annuity bond, defined above. A *redeemable bond* is the same as a callable bond, defined above. *Serial bonds* represent an issue of bonds the maturity dates of which are arranged through a series of years. The terms of serial bonds are usually the same, regardless of maturity date, although sometimes the terms may differ according to the dates on which the bonds are due. *Series bonds* are bonds which are issued at regular intervals over a period of years. All the bonds have the same backing, but the terms may differ according to the year a series is issued.

An *assented bond* is a bond the owner of which has agreed to some voluntary organizational change in the corporation issuing the bond and has deposited it pending the issue of a definitive bond. A bond the owner of which has not consented to the change is called a *nonassented bond.* See (15).

For bonds of historic interest see FIVE-TWENTY BOND, TEN-FORTY BOND, LIBERTY BOND.

bondage. A form of involuntary servitude such as slavery or peonage.

bonded goods. Imported goods subject to duty or domestic goods subject to excise tax which are stored in a BONDED WAREHOUSE (*q.v.*) and upon which the duty or tax must be paid if and when the goods are removed for sale.

bonded warehouse. A warehouse under government supervision, in which goods subject to excise taxes or customs duties are temporarily stored without the taxes or duties being paid. Security is given for the payment of all taxes and duties that may eventually become due, and the establishment is supervised by public revenue officers.

Bonneville Power Administration. A division of the U.S. Department of the Interior which administers the distribution of power generated at the Bonneville Dam on the Columbia River in the state of Washington. It is authorized to build power transmission systems and to market power.

bonus. A payment, usually in money, in addition to payments normally due for services rendered.

bonus stock. See CAPITAL STOCK.

book credit. See STORE CREDIT.

bookkeeping. The systematiç recording of business transactions so as to show the state of a business at any time. See also DOUBLE ENTRY, SINGLE ENTRY.

book value. 1. As applied to stocks, the proportionate amount of money that would accrue to each share of outstanding capital stock of a corporation if all the corporation's assets were converted into cash at the values appearing on the books, and all of its creditors and other prior claimants, if any, were paid in full. **2.** The value of an asset as recorded on the account books of an enterprise. See VALUE.

boom. Rapid growth in market values and expansion of business facilities and activity.

boondoggling. Wasteful or UNECONOMIC labor. The term was commonly used in the United States during the depression years after 1929 when government efforts to create employment sometimes resulted in useless or frivolous activity.

boot. As applied to trading, something given in addition to the thing exchanged to equalize the exchange.

bootlegging. Traffic in goods or services which is prohibited by law or which avoids payment of taxes on the goods or services.

borrowing. Obtaining funds through loans, the evidence of indebtedness taking the form of promissory notes, bonds, or other credit instruments.

borrowing power. Authority given a corporate officer or public official to pledge credit in order to obtain a loan.

bottomry bond. See BOND.

bounty. An additional payment or subsidy sometimes supplied by a government to encourage a particular industry or the export of specified commodities. See also EXPORT BOUNTY.

bourgeoisie. The middle class. In feudal society this term identified merchants, independent artisans, and similar groups, and distinguished them from the nobility and gentry on the one hand and the manual workers and peasantry on the other.

bourse. A French word meaning a stock or some/similar exchange. It is commonly used on the continent of Europe.

boycott. Concerted action by a group involving refusal to have business or other relations with another person or group with a view to punishing the latter or securing redress of some grievance. A boycott is often used in labor disputes, a union resorting to it in order to compel an employer to meet its terms. When those instituting a boycott bring pressure directly upon the person or group against whom they have a grievance, the boycott is called a *primary boycott* and it remains such even if those instituting the boycott use noncoercive tactics such as publicity or peaceful picketing to influence others to join with them. A boycott becomes a *secondary boycott* if those instituting action attempt to increase pressure against the object of their grievance by coercing third parties into assisting them. Thus, efforts of a union to force an employer against whom its members have no grievance, by strike or other coercive tactics, to cease doing business with an employer against whom its members do have a grievance would be a secondary boycott. The same would be true where employees of a factory not on strike were ordered by a union not to process the goods of an employer whose employees were on strike, the purpose of such an order being to aid the striking employees. Secondary boycotts are considered illegal.

bracero. See MIGRANT WORKER.

branch banking. A banking system in which there are relatively few parent institutions each of which has branches operating over a wide area. Some 17 states of the United States permit a bank to establish a state-wide system of branches and, subject to restrictions as respects location, capitalization, and other matters, a national bank may establish branches in states that permit branch banking. Various agencies, chief of which are the Office of Comptroller of the Currency and the Board of Governors of the Federal Reserve System, exercise federal jurisdiction over the establishment of bank branches in the United States and abroad. See BANKING SYSTEM.

brand. A symbol used to identify a product in commerce, thus distinguishing it from a similar product of a competitor.

Brannan plan. A plan which was never embodied in legislation, proposed by Secretary of Agriculture Charles F. Brannan in 1949, which, in lieu of the then existing system of agricultural parity payments, would have allowed agricultural prices to seek their own level on a free market. Producers would have been compensated by a subsidy equaling the difference between the market price and the higher price level established for agricultural produce during the ten-year period 1939–49. See also AGRICULTURAL PARITY.

brassage. A charge made by a government for converting bullion into coins. This charge is just sufficient to cover the costs of the coinage.

brazen law of wages. See IRON LAW OF WAGES.

break-even chart. A graphic device in which one curve shows the total FIXED COSTS and VARIABLE COSTS of an enterprise and another curve shows the total INCOME, both at various production levels. The intersection of the two curves represents the break-even point. The appended diagram shows a break-even chart when the following conditions prevail:

$10,000.00 = fixed costs.

0.70 = LABOR and material COST per unit of product.

1.50 = selling PRICE per unit of product.

x = quantity sales necessary to break even.

$10,000.00 + 0.70x$ = total fixed and variable costs.

$10,000.00 + 0.70x = $1.50x$.

x = 12,500 = break-even point shown on chart.

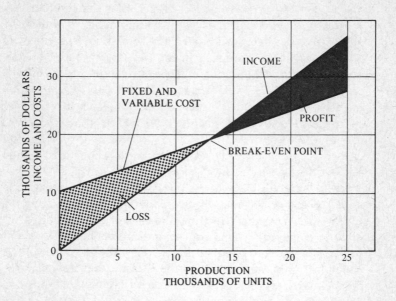

breakthrough. A vague popular term indicating some basic new discovery. Progress in some given area of knowledge may seem to remain static for a relatively long period of time. When an important advance is made in such an area, there is said to be a breakthrough. The word is especially applicable to technological advances and scientific discoveries such as the first fission of uranium isotope U 235 (nuclear chain reaction) at the University of Chicago in 1942. It is occasionally applied, however, to some relatively unimportant happening in order to give the impression of a significant accomplishment.

broad market. As applied to security exchanges, a period during which a large variety of stocks and bonds are bought and sold. See MARKET.

broker. A person who acts as an intermediary between two or more persons engaged in a business transaction of some kind. His services may consist of effecting a sale or of facilitating the arrangements preparatory or subsequent to a sale or to some similar transaction. There are numerous kinds of brokers designated, as a rule, by some descriptive term such as bond broker, insurance broker, real-estate broker, or stockbroker.

brokerage. The fee received by a broker. It is sometimes a percentage of the amount involved in a transaction, as in the case of security sales by a stockbroker, and sometimes a specific sum per carload or other unit, as in the case of a produce broker.

Brown v. Board of Education of Topeka. One of a series of five cases, 347 U. S. 483 (1954), known as the *school desegregation cases* brought before the Supreme Court, in which that tribunal overturned the so-called separate but equal doctrine of the case of *Plessy* v. *Ferguson,* 163 U. S. 537 (1896), which originally gave judicial sanction to segregated white and Negro public schools. In delivering the opinion of the Court, Chief Justice Warren declared that segregation of children in the public schools solely on the basis of race, countenanced historically by the separate but equal doctrine, did in fact deprive such children of equal educational opportunities and hence was contrary to the concept of equal protection of the laws guaranteed under the 14th Amendment to the Constitution. In *Bolling* v. *Sharpe,* 347 U.S. 497 (1954), the Court took the same position with respect to public-school segregation in the District of Columbia, declaring such segregation forbidden by the guarantee of due process in the 5th Amendment to the Constitution.

Brown v. Maryland. See ORIGINAL-PACKAGE CASES.

bubble. As applied to SPECULATION, any unsound business venture where the price of participation advances to a point having no relation to the value of the assets or to the possibilities for profit from the operation of the venture. In this sense, the term was first used during the early part of the 18th century when joint-stock undertakings came into popular favor but when the uses of CREDIT were little understood. The most famous bubbles of the time were the MISSISSIPPI BUBBLE in France and the SOUTH SEA BUBBLE in England, both of which reached their climax in 1720.

bucket shop. A place where bets are made on the prices of securities or commodities bought and sold on the stock and commodity exchanges. The bettors do not themselves trade in the securities or commodities. Such operations are considered to be wagers, and the maintenance of a bucket shop is generally held to be illegal.

budget. A formal estimate of future income and expenses, covering a definite period of time. Budgets are commonly used wherever necessary and desirable expenses must be carefully weighed against anticipated income. Thus, they are applicable as much to personal affairs and private enterprise as they are to public finance. The United States government provided for an annual budget in the *Budget and Accounting Act* of 1921 and vested its preparation and administration in the director of the federal Bureau of the Budget. Practically all of the states of the United States have also established an executive or legislative budget agency, and equivalent agencies are common in most American municipalities. See (1).

Budget and Accounting Act. See BUDGET.

budgetary control. Financial discipline exerted over the operation of an enterprise by adherence to a budget previously adopted. See BUDGET.

buffer stock plan. A term used by a few economists to describe a plan to overcome possible disastrous effects of cyclical fluctuations upon certain industries, particularly raw-material industries. Because of the technical nature of their operations some industries, notably those engaged in certain mining operations, cannot reduce their output rapidly when demand lessens and prices fall. If resulting losses compel the closing of plants, productive capacity is often lost when the products are again in active demand. The buffer stock plan proposes an intergovernmental agency which, under proper safeguards, would offer to buy at a minimum price any quantity of a given commodity and to sell any quantity of that commodity at a maximum price. Thus, it is argued, in times of depression the price could not fall below the minimum, and in times of prosperity, as long as the agency possessed stocks, the price could not rise above the maximum. The price would thus be stabilized within limits presumably narrower than those occasioned by cyclical fluctuations.

building and loan association. A general term indicating an organization, usually incorporated under the law of one of the states of the United States, that provides a presumably safe investment for the savings of its members and serves as a source of loans to its members for home-building purposes. Organizations of this nature are known as *homestead-aid benefit associations* in Louisiana, and *benefit societies, building societies,* or *mutual loan associations* in various other places. Many of these state-chartered building and loan and similar associations have been converted into SAVINGS AND LOAN ASSOCIATIONS.

building society. See BUILDING AND LOAN ASSOCIATION.

built-in. A descriptive prefix indicating laws, regulations, contractual obligations, or entrenched customs which speed or retard current economic trends. For example, intermittent wage increases required by escalator clauses in wage contracts to meet advancing prices are a form of built-in inflation since the higher wages, in turn, cause higher costs and still higher prices. Unemployment insurance is a form of built-in purchasing power tending to sustain a certain amount of consumer spending during periods of recession.

bulk-line costs. Costs at which 80 to 90 per cent of the total supply of a product is said to be produced. The term was used during World War I when the United States government investigated the costs of various products in the course of determining and fixing fair prices for such products. See COST.

bull. As applied to trading on the security exchanges, an expression indicating a person who believes that the value of corporate stocks will advance. Used in contradistinction to BEAR.

bullion. Gold or silver considered as a metal without regard to its form or any value that may be stamped upon it. Bullion usually is in the form of bars or ingots but may be in the form of old coins or foreign coins.

bumping. See BACKTRACKING.

Bunting v. Oregon. A case, 243 U.S. 426 (1917), in which the Supreme Court upheld an Oregon statute limiting the working day in certain industries to 10 hours and prescribing pay at the rate of time and one-half for employment beyond 10 hours. In effect, the Court's decision in this case removed the judicial obstacle to state regulation of the maximum working day, which had been interposed by earlier decisions such as that of LOCHNER V. NEW YORK (*q.v.*), and gave judicial blessing to such legislation as a proper exertion of the state's police power and a necessary limitation on the contractual freedom of employer and employee.

Bureau of Employees' Compensation. A unit of the U.S. Department of Labor which administers WORKMEN'S COMPENSATION LAWS as they may affect the federal government's civilian employees and certain private employees, particularly those engaged in maritime pursuits.

Bureau of Engraving and Printing. The agency of the U.S. Department of the Treasury which physically produces U.S. paper currency, bonds, notes, certificates, savings stamps, and the blank forms of certain public documents such as commissions, etc.

Bureau of Family Services. A unit of the Social Security Administration of the U.S. Department of Health, Education, and Welfare, and successor to the Bureau of Public Assistance, which reviews, appraises, and assists (with federal grants) state public-assistance programs, that is, the programs of state and local welfare departments which aid the needy with funds for general purposes and with allowances for medical and other unusual expenses. The local programs include special provisions to extend medical aid to the totally disabled, the needy aged, the blind, and dependent minors.

Bureau of Federal Credit Unions. An agency of the U.S. Department of Health, Education, and Welfare which supervises credit cooperatives chartered under the Federal Credit Union Act of 1934.

Bureau of International Commerce. An agency within the U.S. Department of Commerce which seeks to stimulate American exports by providing information services and other forms of assistance to businessmen and by setting up commercial exhibitions, trade centers, and other similar marketing services abroad. It enforces compliance with restrictions on exports of strategic materials to countries deemed to be unfriendly to the United States.

Bureau of Labor Standards. A unit of the U.S. Department of Labor which, through appropriate research activities and the collection of necessary statistical data, develops educational, health, safety, and other standards to improve working conditions in industry. It is also concerned with drafting model labor legislation and establishing standards for the effective administration of such legislation. The administration of the child-labor provisions of the FAIR LABOR STANDARDS ACT is entrusted to this bureau.

Bureau of Labor Statistics. A unit of the U.S. Department of Labor which compiles and distributes information on subjects concerning labor.

Bureau of Land Management. An administrative unit of the U.S. Department of the Interior which enforces federal laws relating to the use and disposition of federal public lands and their resources.

Bureau of Mines. A unit of the U.S. Department of the Interior concerned with establishing and enforcing safety regulations in mines, and with providing statistical and research data on the global mineral output, the needs of domestic consumers of minerals, and the development, conservation, and more efficient utilization of mineral resources.

Bureau of Public Roads. A unit of the U.S. Department of Transportation which administers federal grants-in-aid to the states for the construction and maintenance of major highways, and cooperates with the Departments of Agriculture and the Interior in the construction of roads in national forests, national parks, and elsewhere.

Bureau of Reclamation. A principal bureau of the U.S. Department of the Interior. It is engaged in irrigation projects supplying water to arid sections of 17 western states, and in related activities, such as construction of dams and reservoirs, power plants, transmission lines, canals, tunnels, and aqueducts. Major projects of the bureau include the Colorado-Big Thompson, the Missouri Basin, the Central Valley, and the Columbia River projects.

Bureau of the Budget. A division of the executive office of the President which prepares and administers the annual federal budget and assists in the formulation of governmental fiscal programs.

Bureau of the Census. An administrative unit of the Department of Commerce which is the chief statistical agency of the United States government. It is responsible for the decennial census embracing population and other important statistics and publishes numerous reports, tabulations, and current bulletins on almost every phase of national life, including the *Statistical Abstract of the United States.*

Bureau of the Customs. A service of the U.S. Department of the Treasury which assesses and collects import duties, combats smuggling, and enforces various regulations affecting vessels used in foreign trade.

Bureau of the Mint. A branch of the U.S. Department of the Treasury having general supervision of the United States mints, assay offices, and depositaries.

Bureau of the Public Debt. A part of the fiscal service branch of the U.S. Department of the Treasury which administers the national debt. It prepares the papers incident to the offering of a new debt issue, allocates the new issue among potential subscribers, handles the subscriptions, and makes regulations governing transactions in national debt issues already in existence.

business. 1. Any activity concerned with the production or exchange of goods or the rendering of financial or other services to the public for profit. **2.** An economic enterprise organized for profit.

business affected with a public interest. Any business, especially a public utility, which, because of the virtual absence of any competitive conditions in the area in which it operates, and because of the important contribution it makes to the public welfare and convenience, may be subject to governmental regulation in respect to rates and services.

business agent. As applied to labor unions, a full-time employee of such organizations who negotiates labor agreements with employers, observes the manner in which such agreements are carried out, and attempts to secure faithful performance of the terms of the agreements.

business barometer. A statistical device that estimates the extent of business activity by means of composite index numbers. See INDEX NUMBER.

business cycle. A recurring sequence of changes in business activity. Beginning with a period of prosperity, business activity declines until a low point, called a DEPRESSION, is reached. A period of recovery then follows when business conditions become more and more active until prosperity is again restored and a cycle is thus completed. There are many explanations of the business cycle. For some of the more important see ASTRONOMICAL THEORY OF THE BUSINESS CYCLE, CREDIT THEORY OF THE BUSINESS CYCLE, OVERSAVING THEORY OF THE BUSINESS CYCLE, PSYCHOLOGICAL THEORY OF THE BUSINESS CYCLE.

business interruption insurance. See USE-AND-OCCUPANCY INSURANCE.

buyers' market. The market condition which exists when, under competitive conditions, the schedules of supply and demand are such that market prices are at a relatively low level, giving the buyers an advantage. In other words, the sellers are disposed to accept a low price rather than fail to dispose of their goods and services, and the buyers are disposed to retain their money rather than to acquire the goods and services at anything but a low price. The term is used in contradistinction to SELLERS' MARKET. See MARKET.

buyer's monopoly. The condition which exists when there are numerous sellers but only one buyer. For example, during World War II the British government controlled the refrigeration space on ships serving South America. The South American meat packers, therefore, had virtually but one customer—the British government. Also called *monopsony.* See MONOPOLY.

buyers' strike. A concerted movement by consumers to refrain from buying until prices are reduced.

buyer's surplus. The hypothetical difference between what a buyer actually pays for a product and what he would have been willing to pay if necessary. See SURPLUS.

buying on margin. The practice of purchasing securities paid for in part out of funds borrowed by using the purchased securities as collateral. Buying on margin is done in anticipation of an advance in price. If an advance occurs, it may enable the trader to pay the loan and make a profit. If the market price declines, however, the value of the collateral deposited to secure the loan may depreciate to such an extent that it has to be sold to liquidate the loan. In that event the trader loses all that he has advanced. It is to prevent such a loss that a STOP-LOSS ORDER is given. Also referred to as *marginal trading*.

by-product. A product resulting as an incident of the manufacture of some other product. In the production of lignite coal, for example, coal-tar dyes, ammonium salts, and other valuable derivative products are produced.

Byrnes Act. See ANTISTRIKEBREAKING ACT.

C

cable transfer. Usually a foreign bill of exchange by cable, resorted to in order that a transfer of funds may be effected without delay.

cadastre. An official inventory of the real property in any district and the appraised values of such property. The inventory is used for apportioning taxes.

call. 1. As applied to security trading, an option purchased for a fee, which permits an investor to buy a specified security at an agreed price within a stipulated period of time. Thus, by buying a call at the prevailing market price, instead of buying a stock at that price, the investor is able to exercise his option and then sell the security at a profit if the market advances; but if the market declines, he is protected against the loss he would have sustained had he originally bought the stock. **2.** In a more generalized sense, any demand for payment. See also CALLABLE BOND.

callable bond. See BOND.

callable preferred stock. See CAPITAL STOCK.

call-back pay. The extra amount paid to employees when, after having left for the day, they are recalled to their places of work because of an emergency.

call compensation. Pay guaranteed an employee who reports for work in an establishment and has no work assigned him.

call loan. A loan payable on demand. The term is used in contradistinction to TIME LOAN. See LOAN.

cambist. **1.** A person who buys and sells bills of exchange. **2.** A specialist in matters pertaining to foreign exchange. **3.** A volume supplying data about the currencies of various countries, the rates of exchange, and related matters.

Cambridge school. See NEOCLASSICAL SCHOOL.

Cameralism. A variety of mercantilism that appeared in Germany and Austria during the middle part of the 18th century. Its economic theory was closely interwoven with considerations of financial policy, governmental administration, and technology. Hence, Cameralism was concerned not only with the best ways in which a state might acquire wealth but also with the best uses to which that wealth, once acquired, might be put. The term is sometimes used today to indicate an economic theory which places particular and perhaps undue emphasis upon public revenue as a factor in national prosperity. Sometimes spelled *Kameralism.* See SCHOOLS OF ECONOMIC THOUGHT.

canons of taxation. Stipulations as to a sound tax policy. Those set forth in Adam Smith's *Wealth of Nations* are as follows: *(a)* A tax should be apportioned among the taxpayers in proportion to the revenue they receive under the protection of the state; *(b)* a tax should be certain and not arbitrary; *(c)* a tax should be levied at the time when it is most convenient for the taxpayers to pay it; and *(d)* a tax should cost as little as possible to collect.

capillarity, law of. As applied to population growth, the generalization that as civilization advances, individuals avoid parenthood in order that they may devote their time and means to advancing their social status. The ambition to rise in the social scale is thus likened to the phenomenon of liquids rising by capillary attraction. The term is attributed to Arsène Dumont (1849-1902), a French sociologist, who, together with others, rejected the MALTHUSIAN THEORY OF POPULATION in favor of the idea that BIRTH RATES decline as STANDARDS OF LIVING increase. Although the theory seems applicable in some cases, the science of demography has not as yet offered a thoroughly satisfactory, comprehensive explanation of changes in the rate of population growth.

capital. In classical economic theory, one of the major factors of production, the others being land and labor. It consists of property or wealth from which income is derived, expressed in terms of money, and which can be used to produce additional property or wealth. A distinction is sometimes made between *money capital,* or that part of the capital held in the form of money and bank deposits, and *property capital,* or that part of the capital held in the form of evidences of ownership such as stocks, bonds, and mortgages. Then again, such instruments, together with money, are sometimes referred to as *lucrative capital* in contradistinction to capital goods. A few economists include acquired knowledge within the meaning of capital on the ground that it, too, is a source of income. In business practice the term may refer merely to the net worth of an enterprise, or it may refer to all of the more permanent investments made by the owners or borrowed by them on a long-term basis. In a still more general sense, the term may refer to the total assets of an enterprise. See (12).

capital asset. Property which produces income as distinguished from property which is consumed or which is used for the direct satisfaction of human wants. As applied to income-tax computations in the United States, the term refers only to items not bought and sold in the ordinary course of the taxpayer's business. Thus, a washing machine would be a capital asset when used in a commercial laundry, but it would be an ORDINARY ASSET to the dealer in such machines. Generally, in commercial speech the term is synonymous with FIXED ASSET. See ASSET.

capital budget. A budget listing expenditures planned for construction and the acquisition of capital goods and identifying the source of the funds required to meet such expenditures. See BUDGET.

capital consumption allowance. A deduction made in the amount of the GROSS NATIONAL PRODUCT when reconciling the total gross national product with the total NATIONAL INCOME. Capital consumption allowance consists of: *(a)* DEPRECIATION charges; *(b)* accidental damage to fixed capital such as that caused by transportation wrecks, fire, hurricanes, etc.; and *(c)* capital outlays charged to current expense, such as the purchase of new CAPITAL GOODS which are used up during the current period.

capital formation. The creation of CAPITAL GOODS made possible through savings. Savings may be spent directly for labor, materials, and other expenses involved in the creation of capital goods or, through the purchase of a security, they may be loaned to others for such a purpose. If deposited in a bank, they may become the basis of a bank loan used to create capital goods.

capital gain (loss). The increase (or decrease) in value of a capital asset such as a security—more specifically, the amount by which the sale price of a capital asset exceeds its cost.

capital-gains tax. In the United States, a federal tax levied upon the profits from the purchase and sale of capital assets. Such profits are reported as income although the rates and regulations may vary from those imposed on other income. Losses sustained in a like manner are deductible from income under specified conditions. See TAX.

capital good. A material economic good other than land which is used for the production of wealth. Most authorities exclude land from the meaning of this term on the ground that capital goods are created by man and are, for all practical purposes, unlimited in quantity whereas land is an original gift of nature and is limited in quantity. Other authorities regard land as a particular kind of capital good, terming it *natural capital,* thereby distinguishing it from other capital goods which they designate as *artificial capital.* Still other authorities make the term capital goods synonymous with WEALTH. They prefer to use such terms as *instrumental capital* or *producers' capital* to indicate wealth used to produce additional wealth, and the term *comsumers' capital* to indicate what others would call CONSUMER GOODS. However defined, the term capital goods normally excludes such items as stocks, bonds, mortgages, and money, which are sometimes called REPRESENTATIVE GOODS. Capital goods are occasionally classified according to their durability as FIXED CAPITAL GOODS and CIRCULATING CAPITAL GOODS, and again, according to their degree of specialization as FREE CAPITAL GOODS and SPECIALIZED CAPITAL GOODS. Capital goods are sometimes called *intermediate goods* because of their function of serving consumers only indirectly in the satisfaction of their WANTS. When so designated however, consumer goods, while still in the possession of producers or MIDDLEMEN, must be considered capital goods serving consumers indirectly. See GOOD.

capitalism. An economic system based upon the private ownership of all kinds of property and the freedom of the individual to contract with others and to engage in economic activities of his choice for his own profit and well-being. Such governmental restrictions as are placed on private property and freedom of contract are designed for the protection of the public. Zoning restrictions regulating building operations or land use and the exclusion of agreements involving an illegal act are cases in point. In a capitalistic economy the government plays a relatively minor role in economic life, its functions being mainly those of maintaining order, preventing abuses, and carrying on such activities as private enterprise cannot pursue with reasonable assurance of profit. Also called *free enterprise.* See (11).

capitalist. 1. An investor in a business enterprise. **2.** The individual who provides the capital needed to initiate or reorganize a business enterprise. **3.** In Marxist terminology, one who owns or shares in the ownership of the means of production and employs the labor of others.

capitalistic production. See INDIRECT PRODUCTION.

capitalization of land taxes. Capitalization at a prevailing rate of interest of the sum paid as taxes on a piece of land, the result of such calculation being the amount by which the capital value of the land in question might be reduced in case it were offered for sale. For example, if the annual taxes on a piece of land are, let us say, $100 and the prevailing rate of interest is 4 per cent, a capital sum of $2,500 will be needed to yield an amount equal to the taxes. This sum of $2,500 may be taken into consideration by a prospective purchaser and deducted from the price that he would otherwise be willing to pay. See CAPITALIZED VALUE.

capitalized value. The value arrived at by dividing annual earnings by a stipulated rate of interest, usually the prevailing rate.

Thus, if the net earnings of a productive enterprise are, let us say, $2,550 per year, and the prevailing rate of interest is 3 per cent, then the capitalized value is $85,000. See VALUE.

capitalized-value standard. In determining the value of an enterprise, the amount obtained by dividing the annual earnings by a stipulated interest rate. Virtually identical with EARNING CAPACITY STANDARD. See VALUATION.

capital levy. A nonrecurring tax on capital. The term may refer to a special nonrecurring tax placed only on new capital values acquired during some particular period such as during a war. Thus conceived, a capital levy is similar to a CAPITAL-GAINS TAX except that it is levied on an appraised instead of a realized gain. Or the term may refer to a levy on the entire existing capital in a nation. As such, a capital levy is similar to a general PROPERTY TAX levied only at one particular time.

capital liability. A fixed liability which is incurred primarily to acquire fixed assets or for refunding purposes, for example, a corporate bond. Capital stock may be considered a capital liability, although technically it represents ownership and hence not the claim of a creditor. See LIABILITY.

capital market. Collectively, securities exchanges, underwriters, and investment banks, especially when concentrated at some major financial center such as New York or London. See MARKET.

capital movement. The liquidation of capital investments of one kind and the reinvestment of the realized capital funds in investments of another kind; or the liquidation of investments in one place and reinvestment of proceeds elsewhere. The term is used particularly in describing the capital movements, as thus defined, from one nation to another.

capital rent. A price paid for the use of improvements permanently attached to the land. The concept is a hypothetical one inasmuch as the improvements cannot be used apart from the land on which they rest. The term is used when it is desired to separate ordinary rent into two parts: GROUND RENT and capital rent. See RENT.

capital stock. The permanently invested capital of a corporation contributed by the owners either at or subsequent to the time the corporation is organized. Capital stock is divided into *shares,* each share representing a proportionate ownership in the corporation. Shares are issued in the form of a *stock certificate* which is usually transferable only by indorsement. Shares of the capital stock may be assigned a PAR VALUE, in which case they are called *par-value stock*; or the shares may be issued without par value, in which case they are called *no-par-value stock.*

Capital stock is frequently divided into classes with different rights and privileges accorded each class. *Common, equity,* or *ordinary stock* enjoys exclusive claim to the net assets and to the profits of the corporation if no other class of stock is issued. *Preferred stock,* if issued, takes precedence over the common stock according to whatever terms are determined upon. Usually it is accorded a prior claim on the net assets and a specified amount of the profits. Such stock is also known by the terms *prior* or *preference stock.*

Sometimes a certain class of stock is itself divided. Thus, the preferred stock may be divided into first, prior, or class A preferred stock and second or class B preferred stock, the rights and privileges of each being still more closely defined. These subclasses are called *classified stock.* The term *debenture stock* is very seldom used in the United States. When used it has indicated a class of stock enjoying some right or privilege over some other class of stock.

Special rights and privileges accorded or denied a stock, and special liabilities attached to it or from which it is free, are frequently indicated in the name of the stock or in the terms used to describe it. An *assessable stock* is a stock subject to an assessment if the financial affairs of the corporation make such an assessment necessary. The term *callable preferred stock* indicates that the corporation issuing the stock reserves the right to buy it back from the owners at its option. It is frequently stipulated that when such stock is repurchased a premium shall be paid for it. *Convertible stock* is stock which grants the owner the privilege of exchanging it for some other issue either at any time or prior to some fixed date and in accordance with specified terms. The term *cumulative stock* indicates that if the dividends are not paid in any one year, they become a liability of the corporation and, if conditions permit, will be paid during some subsequent year. *Full-paid stock* is stock the full amount of the par value of which has been paid to the corporation issuing it. The term *guaranteed stock* indicates that dividends on the stock are guaranteed by some corporation other than the one responsible for the issue of the stock. *Nonassessable stock* is stock free from all liability of assessments. The term *noncumulative stock* indicates that dividends not paid one year do not become a liability of the company and hence will not be paid during any subsequent year. *Paid-up stock* is the same as full-paid stock, defined above. *Participating preferred stock* is a preferred stock which, in addition to the privileges accorded it as such, participates, together with other stock, in profits usually above a specified sum. *Part-paid stock* is stock only a part of the par value of which has been paid the corporation. *Redeemable preferred stock* is the same as callable preferred stock, defined above.

Other terms applicable to stocks indicate more general characteristics, some of which have little to do with the actual worth of the stock to an investor. An *active stock* is one that is bought and sold continuously on the market in fairly large volume. A *barometer stock* is a stock the market price of which is said to indicate the general condition of the market. The term *bonus stock* refers to the particular stock certificates which are given free to an investor in consideration of the purchase of some other issue. Bonus stock also refers to the particular stock certificates which are issued in return for services rendered such as, for example, those services performed by a promoter. *Clearinghouse stock* is stock which is handled by the clearinghouse of the New York Stock Exchange. *Curb stock* is stock which is listed on the American Stock Exchange. *Donated stock* is stock which is given the corporation by the owners, usually to allow the corporation to resell it in order to raise cash capital. The terms *full stock* and *half stock* indicate that the par value of a stock is $100 and $50 respectively. An *inactive stock* is one which is bought and sold relatively infrequently. *International stock* is a term used to indicate that the stock of a corporation located in one country is bought and sold on the security exchanges of another country. A *listed stock* is one accepted for trading on any recognized stock exchange. *Management stock* is stock with special voting rights. It is issued for the purpose of giving management, or some other small group, complete control over the affairs of the corporation. The term is also used to indicate simply the stock held by the management of a corporation. A *nonclearinghouse stock* is one not handled by the clearinghouse of the New York Stock Exchange. *Original-issue stock* refers to the particular certificates which are issued to the initial subscribers to the capital stock of a corporation. *Potential stock* is the unissued portion of the authorized capital stock of a corporation. *Premium stock* is stock which commands a premium in the form of an extra fee if it is borrowed for trading purposes. *Quarter stock* is stock the par value of which is $25. A stock issued for some particular purpose such as the payment of a stock dividend is occasionally called *special stock*. It is sometimes accorded some right or privilege over other classes of stock. *Treasury stock* is stock which has been issued and subsequently reacquired from the owner by the corporation originally issuing the stock. *Unissued stock* is the same as potential stock, defined above. *Unlisted stock* is a stock not traded on any recognized stock exchange. *Watered stock* is stock the book value of which is materially in excess of the amount of money that could be paid to the owners at any time if the corporation were liquidated.

An *assented stock* is a stock the owner of which has agreed to some voluntary organizational change in the corporation issuing the stock and has deposited it pending the issue of a definitive stock certificate. A stock the owner of which has not consented to the change is called a *nonassented stock*. See (16).

capital-stock tax. A tax imposed as a percentage of either the market or par value of the capital stock of a corporation. A capital-stock tax, levied by the United States government in 1916, was repealed in 1926. Many of the states of the United States, however, impose such a tax. See TAX.

capital surplus. The excess of assets over liabilities plus the value ascribed to issued capital stock, less any amounts in PAID-IN or EARNED SURPLUS. See SURPLUS.

capitation tax. See POLL TAX.

Capper-Volstead Act. See COOPERATIVE MARKETING.

capsule cargo. See CONTAINERIZED FREIGHT.

captive mine. A coal mine owned by a company that itself uses the entire, or almost the entire, output of the mine.

car loadings. The number of freight cars loaded during a specified period. The figure is frequently used as an index of general business activity.

carry-back. The privilege, sometimes extended under tax laws, to "average out" gains and losses over more than one year, thus offsetting gains in one year with losses in an earlier year and reducing the tax for the period in which gains were recorded.

carryover funds. Funds authorized in a particular budgetary period which an administrative agency may encumber and then spend in a succeeding budgetary period. See FUND.

cartel. A contractual association of independent business organizations, located in one or more countries, formed for the purpose of regulating the purchasing, production, or marketing of goods by the members. Because such activities have a tendency to restrict markets and fix prices, cartels in the United States are sometimes considered to violate antitrust statutes. See COMBINATION.

Carter* v. *Carter Coal Co. See BITUMINOUS COAL CASES.

cash. See CURRENCY.

cash flow. A statement showing all actual cash receipts and disbursements for a specifically delimited period of time, or showing estimates of such receipts and disbursements for some future period. See FINANCIAL STATEMENT.

cashier's check. A check issued by a bank and usually signed by its cashier. See CHECK.

caste system. The separation of different groups in society by rigid social and other barriers, usually originating in political or religious differences. The term should be distinguished from the term *class* which suggests greater social mobility and differences of economic origin.

casualty insurance. A generic term customarily applied to various kinds of insurance other than life, fire, and marine. For example, liability, title, credit, and explosion insurance all fall within the category of casualty insurance. See INSURANCE.

casual workers. Temporary workers who acquire no seniority rights with a company and no permanent affiliation with a labor union. In a CLOSED SHOP, casual workers are issued permit cards by the union.

caveat emptor. Let the buyer beware.

caveat venditor. Let the seller beware.

ceiling prices. See PRICE CONTROL.

cement case. A case, *Cement Mfrs'. Protective Assn.* v. *United States,* 268 U. S. 588 (1925), in which the Supreme Court greatly weakened earlier decisions such as the one in the LINSEED OIL INDUSTRY CASE *(q.v.)* that had invalidated the exchange of price and other related trade information among enterprises in an industry on the ground such exchange violated the antitrust statutes. In this case, the Court held that agreements by members of a trade association to exchange pertinent trade information might facilitate more efficient commercial operations and that there was no necessary tendency for such information to lessen competition.

Cement Mfrs'. Protective Assn.* v. *United States. See CEMENT CASE.

central bank. A bank which exists primarily for public fiscal purposes, which is controlled in whole or in part by the government, and which turns over a large proportion of its profit to the government either directly or in the form of a tax. A central bank is usually charged with the responsibility of maintaining an adequate liquid reserve against the nation's bank credit, controlling the importation and exportation of money or precious metals, and providing a sound note issue. It also acts as fiduciary agent for the government and as a banker's bank. The Bank of England and the United States FEDERAL RESERVE BANKS may be considered central banks, although in discharging central bank functions, the reserve banks are supplemented by the Board of Governors and other parts of the Federal Reserve System. See BANK.

Central Certificate Service. A centralized clearing system for handling stock certificates, devised by the New York Stock Exchange. When in full operation, it will materially reduce certificate volume and physical deliveries of stock certificates among brokerage firms, lending banks, and transfer agents.

central reserve cities. Three cities, New York, Chicago, and St. Louis, where, prior to the establishment of the Federal Reserve System, NATIONAL BANKS were required to maintain all of their legal BANK RESERVES in the form of cash in their own vaults. At that time it was customary for COMMERCIAL BANKS in smaller cities and in rural regions to maintain balances with commercial banks in large cities and these balances counted as the reserves of the banks in the smaller communities.

central reserve city banks. National banks in New York, Chicago, and St. Louis which, under the terms of the NATIONAL BANK ACT *(q.v.),* were required to maintain minimum legal reserves of 25 per cent in their own vaults and served as depositaries for reserves from RESERVE CITY BANKS and COUNTRY BANKS *(qq.v.).* See BANK.

certificate. An instrument giving formal assurance of the existence of some fact or set of facts. Such an instrument is used as evidence of some right or obligation. Many kinds of certificates are in common use. See (17).

certificate of beneficial interest. A document which identifies an owner's interest in the assets and earnings of a business enterprise. Such certificates may be issued to stockholders when the stock of a corporation is surrendered to a trustee or trustees. They also serve as evidence of interest in a MASSACHUSETTS, or *common-law,* TRUST. See CERTIFICATE.

certificate of deposit. Usually a bank receipt for a cash deposit not subject to withdrawal for a stipulated length of time. The certificate may draw interest and is negotiable. See CERTIFICATE.

certificate of incorporation. See ARTICLES OF INCORPORATION.

certificate of indebtedness. Documentary evidence of a short-term debt. Such certificates are sometimes issued by a government to raise funds to meet current expenses. See CERTIFICATE.

certificate of origin. A document which identifies the place of origin of imported goods. Such a document is usually required by customs officials. See CERTIFICATE.

certificate of public convenience and necessity. A license to operate issued by a state public-utility commission to a private business affected with a public interest. See CERTIFICATE.

certified check. A check bearing the indorsement of a bank guaranteeing its payment. See CHECK.

certified public accountant. A degree or title conferred upon an accountant under the laws of a state of the United States. It indicates that the holder has met the state's legal requirements for the practice of the profession of accountancy and testifies to his competence in installing accounting systems and in making audits and related reports. See also ACCOUNTANT.

chain banking. Direction of the policies and operations of a group of banks by some one bank or other organization which has acquired its control or influence by a system of interlocking directorates, majority stock ownership, or some other means, the various banks in the group being nominally autonomous and independent of one another. Also called *group banking.* See BANKING SYSTEM.

chain store. One of a number of retail stores, all owned and managed by one company.

chain-store tax. A progressive tax levied by many states of the United States on chain stores when the number of such stores under one management exceeds a certain maximum. The tax is usually levied in the form of a fee exacted to obtain a LICENSE. See TAX.

chamber of commerce. See BOARD OF TRADE. See also UNITED STATES CHAMBER OF COMMERCE.

chapel. As applied to labor organizations in the printers' trade, a division of a local labor union composed of those members who are employees of one particular printing establishment.

charter. 1. As applied to corporations, a document, issued by authority of a government, evidencing the creation of the corporation. Such a charter may consist of a special document, usually issued only when the corporation is authorized by special act of the legislature, or it may consist, for all practical purposes, of the approved and recorded ARTICLES OF INCORPORATION together with the general corporation laws of the government involved. 2. The fundamental statute of some public body, for example, the charter of the UNITED NATIONS.

Chartism. An English reform movement (1840–48) which sought to achieve its objectives by legislation. A parliamentary petition drafted by the leaders of the movement took the form of a charter identifying the principal desired reforms. These included universal adult male suffrage, vote by ballot, equal electoral districts, annual meetings of Parliament, payment of salaries to members of the House of Commons, and abolition of the property qualification for membership in that body. The movement disintegrated after 1848, but many of its objectives were later incorporated in the programs of the developing cooperative and trade-union organizations.

chattel. Almost any kind of personal property; this may include an interest in real estate which is less than a freehold, as a lease.

chattel mortgage. An instrument in which personal property earmarked as security for a debt or other obligation and pledged in such a way that if the debtor fails to meet the terms of the contract, the creditor can take possession of the property. See MORTGAGE.

cheap money. 1. A term used to describe a condition when the general price level is high. At such a time a relatively small quantity of goods or services exchanges for a relatively high quantity of money; hence, money is cheap, or its value low, compared with the value of goods and services. **2.** Money lent at relatively low interest rates. **3.** An inflated currency as, for example, the German mark after World War I. See MONEY.

check. A written order of limited negotiability usually issued by a depositor of a bank authorizing that bank to pay on demand a specified sum of money to some person named in the order or to the depositor, the payment to be charged to the depositor's account. See (17).

check credit. A service offered by some banks whereby a client or customer is granted a certain amount of credit, draws checks against this credit from time to time, and repays the bank periodically. See CREDIT.

check currency. See DEPOSIT CURRENCY.

checkoff. As applied to labor relations, the deduction by the employer of labor-union dues and assessments from the pay of the workers and the payment of such deductions directly to the union by the employer. The arrangement may be a *voluntary checkoff,* in which case the deductions are made only from the pay of those workers who authorize such deductions, or the arrangement may be a *compulsory checkoff*—sometimes called *automatic checkoff*—in which case the workers have no choice in the matter. See also LABOR-MANAGEMENT RELATIONS (TAFT-HARTLEY) ACT.

checkweighman. A worker in a coal mine who weighs the coal produced by each miner, a practice required when miners are paid according to the number of tons of coal they individually produce.

chemurgy. The application of chemistry to the industrial utilization of organic raw materials, particularly farm products.

Chicago Board of Trade. A produce exchange organized in 1848, and the leading grain market in the United States. The board is organized as an incorporated association of grain dealers. It supplies the physical facilities, and drafts and enforces the rules under which the trading takes place.

Chicago, Milwaukee and St. Paul Railroad Co. v. Minnesota. See STONE V. FARMERS' LOAN AND TRUST CO.

child labor. As determined by the FAIR LABOR STANDARDS ACT *(q.v.)*, generally the gainful employment of children under 16 years of age. The act declares such employment unlawful in establishments producing goods for interstate commerce. In the case of six particularly hazardous occupations this law raises the age barrier to employment to 18. Certain exceptions are made in nonmining and nonmanufacturing industries. Child labor is variously defined in the statutes of nearly all of the states of the United States, the minimum age beyond which the employment prohibitions of such laws are inapplicable varying usually between 14 and 18. These state statutes may provide protection for situations not covered by federal law. See also CHILD-LABOR CASES, LABOR.

child-labor cases. 1. *Hammer* v. *Dagenhart.* A case, 247 U. S. 251 (1918), involving the first serious attempt by Congress to prohibit child labor in the United States. The legislation under review denied transportation in interstate commerce to the products of establishments which employed children under certain ages. In its decision the Supreme Court declared that the legislation violated the Constitution because it was not a bona fide attempt to regulate transportation among the states but an attempt to control the conditions of employment and manufacture within the states. Authority to control the latter, said the Court, did not belong to Congress but was within the police power of the states. **2.** *Bailey* v. *Drexel Furniture Co.* A case, 259 U. S. 20 (1922), involving a second attempt by Congress to prohibit child labor in the United States. Under review in that case was a federal tax of 10 per cent of the net profits of any establishment which had employed children under certain ages. In a decision holding the measure invalid, the Supreme Court refused to regard the authorized tax as a bona fide one. The Court decided it to be a regulatory and prohibitory measure which, if allowed, might open the way for congressional invasion, ostensibly under the taxing power, of all the powers reserved to the states under the 10th Amendment of the federal Constitution. The decisions in both this and the first child-labor case have been impliedly if not explicitly overruled in later cases where the Supreme Court has supported federal legislative regulation of the employment of minors. See especially UNITED STATES V. DARBY LUMBER CO.

chrematistic. Having to do with the acquirement of WEALTH. Originally, as used by the Greek writers, *chrematistike* meant the science of SUPPLY in contrast to *oeconomia,* from which the word "economy" is derived, which meant the science of household management. A distinction was thus drawn between those activities devoted to the pursuit of PROFIT and those devoted to the acquisition of the necessities of life, the distinction being set forth in Aristotle's *Politics,* Book I, Chaps. VIII-XI. See also POLITICAL ECONOMY.

Christian Socialism. As used in the United States and England, a term applying to a movement started in England about 1850 which protested against the hardships suffered by the working classes at that time and devoted itself chiefly to their welfare. Charles Kingsley and Frederick Maurice were prominent Christian Socialists. At one time the movement fostered small self-governing workshops which were not successful; later it applied itself to the cooperative movement. Christian Socialism, unlike UTOPIAN SOCIALISM, based its program upon definite religious convictions. See SOCIALISM.

circular letter of credit. See LETTER OF CREDIT.

circulating capital good. A capital good which, in the course of production, is destroyed by a single use. Coal used to generate power in a factory is an example. The term is used in contradistinction to FIXED CAPITAL GOOD. See GOOD.

circulating medium. Any medium of exchange which has general acceptance and passes from person to person without indorsement. Ordinarily, the recognized medium of exchange is MONEY.

Civil Aeronautics Board. An independent federal five-member administrative agency, created in 1938, which authorizes domestic and foreign carriers to engage in interstate air transportation and in air transportation between the United States and foreign countries, regulates rates and fares and accounting practices of carriers operating in the United States, and reviews, and passes upon, mergers among air carriers, interlocking or cooperative relationships among them, and allegations of unfair practices.

civil corporation. A corporation created for business purposes. See CORPORATION.

Civil Service anti-strike law. See TAYLOR LAW.

class. See CASTE SYSTEM.

Classical school. A school of economic thought that originated in England with Adam Smith's *Inquiry into the Nature and Causes of the Wealth of Nations* (1776) and which included the writings of such English economists as David Ricardo, Thomas R. Malthus, and John Stuart Mill, as well as the French economist Jean Baptiste Say. In the writings of the Classical economists, man's self-interest is assumed, and man's economic behavior is generalized in the form of principles or laws which are believed to be universally applicable. For example, the general principle that both individuals as such and society as a whole prosper most without government intervention in economic life is indicated in one form of another in the writings of the Classical school. A belief in economic freedom and private property, therefore, is one of its fundamental conceptions. Classical doctrines were used by a group known as the *Manchester school* to support certain reforms, notably the repeal of the CORN LAWS. During recent years the doctrines have been either materially modified or abandoned. Also called *economic liberalism, Individualist school, Liberal school, Orthodox school.* See also SCHOOLS OF ECONOMIC THOUGHT.

classified stock. See CAPITAL STOCK.

classified tax. A tax system in which property is classified according to its nature and purpose, different tax rates being applied against each class, and some classes being exempted altogether from taxation. See TAX.

class price. A relatively high price charged to a buyer because he is willing and able to pay it and is ignorant of the fact that the same article can be bought at a lower price elsewhere. See PRICE.

class struggle. A doctrine of Marxian socialism which asserts that modern industrial society is characterized by an inevitable and constant struggle between the capitalistic or ownership class, on the one hand, and the proletariat or propertyless class, on the other, until such a time as the capitalistic class is overthrown.

Clayton Act. An *antitrust act* of Congress, 1914, which aims to prevent monopolies by prohibiting combinations of corporations that control so large a proportion of an industry as to lessen competition. The act specifically prohibits: *(a)* price discrimination; *(b)* tying clauses in contracts; *(c)* interlocking directorates under conditions that lessen competition; and *(d)* the holding of the stock of one corporation by another when by so doing competition is lessened. The act states that because human labor is not a commodity, labor organizations are not to be considered conspiracies in restraint of trade and are therefore exempt from the operation of antitrust laws.

clean bill. See BILL.

Clean Waters Act. An act of Congress, 1966, which authorizes substantial sums to assist municipalities and communities in constructing sewage treatment plants and provides for payment of bonuses, in addition to federal grants-in-aid, to those states which improve their standards as to quality of water.

clearing agreement. 1. An agreement between two or more nations to buy and sell goods and services among themselves according to specified rates of exchange. Payments are made by buyers in the buyers' home currency, balances being settled, at stipulated periods, among the central banks of the nations which are parties to the agreement. See also EXCHANGE CONTROL. **2.** Any local, national, or international plan for the periodic mutual exchange by banks of charges against them by others in the plan and the settlement of adverse balances.

clearinghouse. A central agency through which banks in a given area clear claims, that is, offset one another's claims arising from the issuance of checks and various forms of commercial paper and settle any resulting adverse balances.

clearinghouse agent. A bank which is a member of a clearinghouse and which accepts the checks of another bank, not a member, for settlement through the clearinghouse. Sometimes called *redemption agent.* See also CLEARINGHOUSE.

clearinghouse stock. See CAPITAL STOCK.

clearings. Checks, promissory notes, and other such instruments presented by a bank to the clearinghouse for collection. Also called *bank clearings.* See CLEARINGHOUSE.

close (closed) corporation. A corporation the stock of which is held by relatively few persons and which usually is not bought and sold in the open market. See CORPORATION.

closed-end investment company. An INVESTMENT COMPANY that sells a definitive quantity of CAPITAL STOCK and normally acquires ownership of this stock again only through retirement. The stock may be bought and sold through the regular market channels.

closed mortgage. A mortgage used as collateral security for a loan of a fixed amount and which, therefore, cannot be used as security for additional loans of any kind. See MORTGAGE.

closed shop. A shop in which only union workers are employed and in which only union members are accepted for employment. See also SHOP.

closed union. A labor union that either accepts no new members or else imposes regulations which make it very difficult for new members to qualify for admission. See LABOR UNION.

coalition bargaining. COLLECTIVE BARGAINING *(q.v.)* in which the leadership of different national or international unions presents a united front and a single composite schedule of demands to the management for all plants of a particular corporation and for all corporations within an industry such as steel, motor cars, electrical goods, etc. The aim is to promote industry-wide bargaining.

coaxial cable. Insulated copper wire inside a metallic tube, used for high-frequency transmission of telephone, telegraph, or television signals. Frequently abbreviated as coax or co-ax.

cobweb chart. A graphic representation of the conditions that may exist in a competitive market when the sale of a perishable

GOOD, requiring a period of time to produce, is confined to a short seasonal DEMAND, but enjoys a fairly constant demand from year to year during that season. The seasonal sales period is too short and the time required for production too long to permit changes in the SUPPLY by any producer after sales have begun. Each year, therefore, the supply depends upon the MARKET PRICE of the previous year. This tends to cause price oscillations from year to year, a relatively high price and short supply alternating with a relatively low price and plentiful supply. The appended diagram shows a cobweb chart. P-0 and S-0 represent a theoretical price and supply, respectively, around which actual prices and supply fluctuate. S-1 shows a relatively plentiful supply, the price during the previous season presumably having been profitable. But with the supply at S-1, the price at P-1 is relatively low. The following year, therefore, the supply drops to S-2, but the price advances to P-2. Theoretically, the price oscillations tend to widen as time goes on.

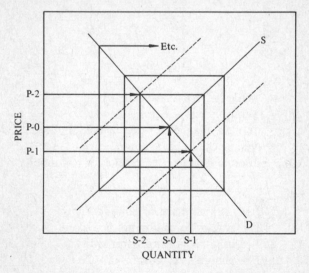

codes of fair competition. Regulations applying to specific industries, compiled by trade associations under authority of the NATIONAL INDUSTRIAL RECOVERY ACT of 1933, and having to do with maximum hours of employment, minimum wages, and, in many cases, the control of prices. When approved by the President, these codes had the authority of law governing the industries to which they applied. The codes became inoperative after the National Industrial Recovery Act was declared unconstitutional on May 28, 1935. See also SCHECHTER CASE.

codetermination. As used in the German Federal Republic *(Mitbestimmung)*, the association of representatives of labor with management on corporate boards to determine corporate policy. The institution's origins date back to the Weimar Republic, but received legislative endorsement in 1951, particularly as respects the Ruhr.

coefficient of acceleration. See ACCELERATION PRINCIPLE.

coefficient of correlation. See SCATTER CHART.

coefficient of cross-elasticity. The relationship, expressed arithmetically, between a percentage change in the price of a particular commodity or service and the resultant percentage change in the sales of a substitute or competitive commodity or service. The generalized equation is:

$$CC = \frac{\dfrac{P_a}{\Delta P_a}}{\dfrac{Q_b}{\Delta Q_b}} = \frac{P_a \times \Delta Q_b}{\Delta P_a \times Q_b}$$

when

CC = coefficient of cross-elasticity,
P_a = average price of commodity *a,*
ΔP_a = absolute change in price of commodity *a,*
Q_b = average quantity of commodity *b,*
ΔQ_b = absolute change in the sales of commodity *b.*

Example:

10 = original price of commodity *a.*
16 = new price of commodity *a.*
100 = original sales of commodity *b.*
110 = new sales of commodity *b.*

$P_a = 13.$ $Q_b = 105.$
$\Delta P_a = 6.$ $\Delta Q_b = 10.$

$$\frac{13 \times 10}{6 \times 105} = \frac{130}{630} = 0.206.$$

coefficient of elasticity. In the case of DEMAND, the arithmetical relationship between the percentage change in the quantity of a COMMODITY or service bought and the percentage change in the PRICE; in the case of SUPPLY, the relationship between the percentage change in the quantity offered and the percentage change in the price.

The generalized equation is:

$$C = \frac{\dfrac{\Delta q}{Q}}{\dfrac{\Delta p}{P}} = \frac{P \times \Delta q}{Q \times \Delta p}$$

when

C = coefficient of elasticity,
P = average price,
Q = average quantity,
Δp = absolute price change,
Δq = absolute quantity change.

Example:

10,000 units demanded at price 50.
20,000 units demanded at price 30.

$P = 40.$ $\Delta p = 20.$
$Q = 15,000.$ $\Delta q = 10,000.$

$$C = \frac{40 \times 10,000}{15,000 \times 20} = \frac{400,000}{300,000} - 1.33.$$

If the coefficient of elasticity is more than unity, the demand (or supply) is said to be *elastic;* if less than unity, it is said to be *inelastic;* if just unity, it is said to be *unitary.* If the demand (or supply) curve is vertical, the coefficient of elasticity is zero; if horizontal, it is infinity. See also ELASTIC DEMAND, ELASTIC SUPPLY.

coefficient of variation. A statistical measure of the relative dispersion, variability, or scatter in a FREQUENCY DISTRIBUTION *(q.v.)* obtained by dividing the STANDARD DEVIATION *(q.v.)* by the ARITHMETIC MEAN *(q.v.)* and multiplying the result by 100.

coin. A piece of metal or alloy identified by certain designs or marks and issued by the government to be used as money. See (33).

coinage. 1. The manufacture of coins for use as money, and coins so manufactured. 2. A country's entire system of metallic money. See (33).

Coinage Act of 1965. See SUBSIDIARY COIN.

coinsurance. A term referring to a clause frequently inserted in a fire-insurance policy, and sometimes made mandatory, to the effect that, in the event of loss to the insured, the liability of the company issuing the policy is limited to a certain per cent of the total loss occasioned by the fire. See INSURANCE.

collateral. Property, or evidence thereof, deposited with a creditor to guarantee the payment of a loan.

collateral trust bond. See BOND.

collective bargaining. As applied to employer-employee relations, the meeting in good faith of employers with representatives of their employees for the purpose of discussing and ultimately agreeing upon wages, hours of employment, working conditions, and the like. "Good faith," according to the NATIONAL LABOR RELATIONS BOARD, consists of "a forthright candid effort to reach a settlement." See COALITION BARGAINING.

collective ownership. The ownership of goods by the public as a whole, or by a group of persons, no specific proportion of ownership being assigned to individuals. For example, public parks, roads, and buildings are owned collectively by the people generally as members of a political community.

collectivism. A politico-economic system that places considerable economic power in the hands of the central government. Such power may be exercised through outright government ownership as in the case of SOCIALISM or COMMUNISM, or it may take the form of such a large degree of ECONOMIC PLANNING that FREEDOM OF CONTRACT is sacrificed even though PRIVATE PROPERTY is maintained in full or in part.

collector of the customs. An official of the U. S. Treasury Department who is responsible for the collection of import duties at a port of entry. See also DUTY, PORT OF ENTRY.

***Collector* v. *Day*.** A case, 11 Wallace 113 (1870), in which the Supreme Court upheld the exemption of the salary of a state judicial officer from federal taxation and, impliedly, the exemption of any other state instrumentality from such taxation. The ruling complemented that in MCCULLOCH V. MARYLAND *(q.v.)* in which federal instrumentalities were exempted from state taxation. Both decisions have been at least partially overruled. See FEDERAL TAX IMMUNITY CASE *(Helvering* v. *Gerhardt)* and STATE TAX IMMUNITY CASE *(Graves* v. *New York* ex rel. *O'Keefe).*

Colombo Plan. A British Commonwealth plan for the industrial and general economic development of the countries of Southeastern Asia, so called because it was first broached at a Commonwealth conference held in Colombo, Ceylon (January, 1950). The plan was formally put into effect on June 30, 1951, for a 6-year period, but in 1955 was extended for 4 years and in 1959 extended again. Membership in the plan, limited originally to Britain, Australia, Canada, Ceylon, India, New Zealand, and Pakistan, was subsequently extended to include some 15 Southeast Asia nations.

colonial bond. See BOND.

colonial system. Regulations and practices, largely exclusive and discriminatory in nature and common during the 17th and 18th centuries, by means of which a state possessing colonies managed them in such a way as to enhance its power and wealth.

column diagram. See FREQUENCY DISTRIBUTION.

combination. Any temporary or permanent association of business or other proprietary establishments which is formed to lessen competition, reduce costs, centralize management, control and allocate markets, or provide large amounts of capital for a common venture. See (4).

combination in restraint of trade. Any agreement between two or more persons which attempts to restrict competition. The agreement may take the form of a CARTEL, POOL, HOLDING COMPANY, or some other organizational device. It may attempt price fixing, the creation of a MONOPOLY, or resort to some other device to reduce competition.

combination rate. As applied to railway traffic, a rate charged for carrying freight between two points not on the same railroad which is the sum of all the local rates between the point of origin, the junction points of the two or more railroads, and the point of destination. A combination rate is used when no JOINT RATE exists. See RATE.

Comecon. See COUNCIL FOR MUTUAL ECONOMIC ASSISTANCE.

commerce. The buying and selling of commodities or services, particularly on a large scale, nationally or internationally, including necessarily related activities, such as storage and preservation of goods, transportation and movement of goods and persons, financial transactions, etc. As interpreted by the Supreme Court, the word "commerce" embraces production of commodities. See also INTERSTATE COMMERCE, INTRASTATE COMMERCE.

commercial bank. A bank, the principal function of which is to receive deposits subject to check, and to make loans to its customers. Besides these primary banking functions a commercial bank performs a variety of incidental functions. It keeps the community supplied with various kinds of legal currency, acts as a collection agent for promissory notes, drafts, and similar COMMERCIAL PAPER, and transmits funds to distant points upon request. It may offer its vaults for the safekeeping of valuables, offer interest for TIME DEPOSITS, and perform the functions of a TRUST COMPANY. Commercial banks may be NATIONAL BANKS, or STATE BANKS. All national banks are commercial banks. See BANK.

commercial credit. Short-term loans furnished a business undertaking for temporary needs. See CREDIT.

commercial credit company. A company engaged in certain specialized forms of financing, particularly the purchasing of accounts receivable, the extension of credit to retail dealers, and the discounting of installment accounts. In the automobile business, for example, dealer purchases from manufacturers are frequently settled in cash by a commercial credit company in return for a trust receipt signed by the dealer. As the cars are sold, the dealer settles with the credit company. Promissory notes of consumers who purchase on the installment plan are discounted by such companies. Also called *discount house* and *sales finance company.* See COMPANY. See also FACTOR.

commercial paper. One of various types of short-term negotiable instruments, particularly a promissory note, which calls for the payment of a specific amount of money at a given time.

commercial policy. Governmental policies relating to the industrial and commercial welfare of the nation. The term applies particularly to public policies to control or encourage foreign trade, investment and shipping, and the maintenance of facilities in foreign countries to aid business interests.

commercial revolution. The expansion of European commerce from the Mediterranean to the Atlantic and throughout the globe following the age of discovery, the geographical explorations of the 15th and 16th centuries, and the establishment of new trade routes.

commercial treaty. An agreement between two or more countries setting forth the conditions under which the nationals of one country, party to the agreement, may do business in the other contracting country or countries. For example, a commercial treaty may set forth tariff privileges, terms on which property may be owned, or the manner in which claims may be settled.

commission. 1. As applied to commercial transactions, compensation to a broker or agent for conducting some business project for another person. The term infers that the payment is a percentage of some amount involved in a transaction. 2. A public regulatory body. 3. Documentary authorization to an appointed official to discharge the duties of his office.

Commissioner of Customs. The officer in charge of the Bureau of Customs of the U. S. Department of the Treasury. He is responsible for the enforcement of customs regulations and regulations applicable to maritime commerce.

commissioner of deeds. 1. A local officer in the United States who administers oaths and takes acknowledgments to be used in the state from which he received his appointment. Unlike a NOTARY PUBLIC, he has no authority to PROTEST negotiable instruments. 2. An appointive officer having similar duties in New York City.

Commissioner of Internal Revenue. The head of the Internal Revenue Service of the U. S. Department of the Treasury. He has general supervision over the determination, assessment, and collection of all federal internal revenue taxes.

Committee for Economic Development. An organization of American businessmen created in 1942 to plan for maximum employment and production in the period following World

War II. The committee has published various statements relating to national economic policy and many research reports relating to such subjects as taxes, employment, wartime controls, agriculture, and world trade.

commodity. Any article of commerce or trade. The term is often used instead of the singular for "goods," because "good" has other common meanings, and a specialized meaning in economics such as ECONOMIC GOOD.

commodity agreement. An agreement, usually made between nations, covering the production and distribution of commodities, existing quantities of which exceed normal world demands. Such an agreement may include provisions for the control of production, exports, and prices, the creation of reserve stocks, and means of expanding existing markets. Usually called *international commodity agreement*.

Commodity Credit Corporation. A public corporation of the United States government, with an authorized and paid-in capital of $100,000,000, attached to the Department of Agriculture. It provides the necessary financial services for carrying forward public price-support activities with respect to certain agricultural commodities, including governmental lending, purchase, sale, storage, transport, and subsidization of such commodities.

commodity dollar. See COMMODITY THEORY OF MONEY.

commodity exchange. An association of traders providing an organized market for the buying and selling of certain commodities. The commodities dealt in are not brought to the marketplace; their existence is attested by documents which identify the amounts and quality. Much of the trading on the commodity exchanges is for HEDGING purposes, involving purchases and sales for future delivery. Commodity exchanges exist for wheat, cotton, sugar, corn, coffee, and other products that can be accurately classified as to standards of quality.

Commodity Exchange Authority. An administrative unit of the U. S. Department of Agriculture created in 1947 to carry out the provisions of the Commodity Exchange Act of 1922 aimed at maintaining fair trading practices and competitive pricing on certain COMMODITY EXCHANGES.

commodity paper. Drafts, promissory notes, or similar commercial paper representing a loan and secured by order bills of lading or warehouse receipts as collateral. In case the loan, represented by the commodity paper, is not paid at maturity, the creditor, usually a bank, may secure the goods, sell them, and apply the proceeds to the amount of the loan. See also ORDER BILL OF LADING.

commodity standard. A monetary system in which some commodity, other than a precious metal, is accepted as standard money. The difficulty of convertibility and portability, and the absence of stability of value and homogeneity of the commodity itself make a commodity standard impracticable in a modern economy. See MONETARY SYSTEM.

commodity theory of money. The assertion that the value of money is determined by the value of the commodity of which it is composed or which it represents. For example, when the MONETARY UNIT is defined in terms of gold, the value of money is determined by the supply of gold and the demand for gold arising by virtue of its use in manufacture and the arts, and there exists at all times a definite exchange ratio between gold and other commodities whether the gold is in the form of BULLION, COINS, or REPRESENTATIVE MONEY. Hence, when, in 1934, the gold content of the United States dollar was reduced from 25⁸⁄₁₀ or 15⁵⁄₂₁ grains ⁹⁄₁₀ fine, prices should have advanced proportionally. They did not, and it is generally conceded today that the value of money is not determined by so simple a formula. Also known as the *commodity dollar.*

common carrier. An individual or company, normally regulated by public authority and operating under a franchise, which engages in the transportation of goods or persons in return for a fee, such service being available at the same rates for all. Railroads, truck and bus lines, commercial aircraft, ferries and certain other water-borne craft, and pipelines are considered to be such carriers, but telephone and telegraph companies, which convey intelligence, are technically not so considered, although they may be subject to the same rules governing common carriers.

common-law trust. See MASSACHUSETTS TRUST.

Common Market. See EUROPEAN ECONOMIC COMMUNITY.

common stock. See CAPITAL STOCK.

common stock index. A compilation showing the average current market value of common stocks compared with their average market value at some previous base period. An index may include all the common stocks traded on an exchange or only specialized stocks, such as financial, industrial, transportation, or utility issues. Each index discloses a general market trend against which the record of specific issues may be measured. Such indexes are compiled by the New York and the American Stock Exchanges although in somewhat different form.

common trust. Two or more relatively small trust funds combined for economy in administration. See also TRUST, TRUST FUND.

Commonwealth (Mass.) v. Hunt. See COMMONWEALTH (PA.) V. CORDWAINERS.

Commonwealth (Pa.) v. Cordwainers. The first recorded labor case in the United States, tried before the Mayor's Court in Philadelphia, Pa., March, 1806. Eight bootmaker defendants, who had previously participated in a STRIKE, were charged with the offense of combining and conspiring to raise wages. It was the law, rather than the facts, upon which the court was called to decide, the decision hinging on whether or not the English doctrine of common-law conspiracy was applicable in the state of Pennsylvania. The court accepted the English doctrine, and the defendants were convicted, fined, and committed to jail pending the payment of the fines. Subsequent cases, for example *Commonwealth v. Hunt* [Mass. (1842)], modified the decision that concerted action through labor organizations violated common-law doctrines of conspiracy, and paved the way for the acceptance of LABOR UNIONS as a legitimate instrument of economic action by workmen.

communism. Government or community ownership of all wealth. Communism abolishes the concept of private property. Production by individuals is ideally in accordance with capacity, and consumption is in accordance with need. The term is sometimes used to describe the contemporary economic system of Soviet Russia, mainland China, and other states where private property in all capital goods has been abolished but has been retained in various types of consumer goods, and where standards of income vary considerably. Soviet and comparable theoreticians, however, usually refer to this system as SOCIALISM and suggest that actual communism is a condition to be achieved in the vague and indefinite future. The term is also used to suggest social revolution by force. See ECONOMIC SYSTEM.

community-property principle. The principle, derived from Spanish law and accepted in several states of the United States, that husband and wife create a community estate in the property accumulated by them, and that they have an equal interest in such estate as long as the marital relationship endures. In the states where this principle governs, it is therefore permissible for husband and wife to divide equally the total of their joint income for tax purposes, each being regarded as having an equal share in such income. Revision of federal revenue laws in 1948 authorized the application of the community-property principle to joint income-tax returns of husband and wife throughout the United States.

company. An association of persons organized for the purpose of carrying on some commercial or industrial activity. A company may be a CORPORATION or a PARTNERSHIP, or it may assume some other FORM OF BUSINESS ORGANIZATION. Companies are frequently designated by some descriptive title indicating the nature of their business or their relation to some other company, such as insurance company, operating company, parent company, and the like. See (4), (19).

company store. A retail store owned and operated by an enterprise for the use of its employees and conducted as an adjunct to its regular business.

company town. A community located on property owned in whole or in major part by an industrial or similar concern and inhabited chiefly by that concern's employees. A company town is controlled in many of its corporate activities by whatever policies the concern may pursue.

company union. A labor union, the membership of which is made up of workers employed by one company only and which is usually not affiliated with any other labor union or group of unions. See LABOR UNION.

comparative advantage. The condition which exists when one nation or region can produce each of two products at less cost than some other nation or region, and the relative saving in the case of one of these products is greater than in the case of the second. The nation or region thus favored is said to enjoy an *absolute advantage* in the case of both products over the nation or region not so favored and to enjoy a comparative advantage in the case of the product where the relative saving is greater. For example, nation A can produce both sugar and automobiles at less cost than can nation B. Nation A thus has an absolute advantage over nation B in the case of both of these products. But the relative saving of nation A over nation B in the production of automobiles is greater than the saving which nation A enjoys over nation B in the case of sugar. Hence nation A has a comparative as well as an absolute advantage over nation B in the production of automobiles.

The term "comparative advantage" may also be employed to mark the fact that in the less favored of two nations or regions, the cost of production of one commodity is less than that of another. In the above example, nation B is at an absolute disadvantage vis-à-vis nation A in the production of both sugar and automobiles. But it is also true that within nation A, the production of sugar is relatively cheaper than the production of automobiles, and in this somewhat negative sense, nation B is said to have a comparative advantage in the production of sugar. The distinction is significant because, in view of these internal circumstances, nation A might find it profitable to concentrate its productive resources on automobiles and import sugar from nation B despite the fact that sugar as well as automobiles can be produced cheaper in nation A than in nation B. Sometimes referred to as *comparative costs*.

comparative costs. See COMPARATIVE ADVANTAGE.

compensated dollar. A proposal once advocated by certain American economists to create a commodity dollar by constantly varying the gold content of the STANDARD MONEY dollar according to fluctuations in the general PRICE LEVEL. In the event of a marked advance in the general price level, the gold content of the standard money dollar would be increased, thus making it possible to offer more gold for commodities, but with fewer dollars since each dollar would contain more gold. Conversely, in the event of a marked decline in the general price level, the gold content of the standard money dollar would be decreased, thus making it possible to offer less gold for commodities, but with more dollars since each dollar would contain less gold. According to the proposal, this procedure would keep prices, or the number of dollars exchangeable for commodities, more or less constant, although the dollars would contain a larger or smaller quantity of gold at one time compared with some other time. See also COMMODITY THEORY OF MONEY.

compensatory duty. **1.** A customs duty sometimes levied on imported manufactured articles in order to offset the increased costs of a domestic manufacturer of similar articles when such costs are attributable to a tariff on the raw materials used by such domestic manufacturer. The plan has been used intermittently, for example, in the application of United States' duties on wool and woolen cloth. In 1861 the duty on wool was 3 cents a pound. On the assumption that it takes about 4 lb. of wool to produce 1 lb. of cloth, a compensatory duty of 12 cents a pound was placed on woolen cloth. At that point the domestic producer of wool cloth could compete with imported cloth on equal terms. Such additional duty as was imposed on wool cloth at that time was for the benefit of merchants dealing in this commodity. **2.** A duty on an imported commodity designed to offset an excise tax placed on the same commodity when produced in the importing country. Also called *countervailing excise duty.* See CUSTOMS DUTY.

compensatory fiscal policy. Procedures for the collection of PUBLIC REVENUE, regulation of government expenditures, and management of the NATIONAL DEBT designed to influence directly or indirectly the general level of economic activity and particularly inflationary or deflationary tendencies in the economy. The attempt to check INFLATION by heavy taxation and concomitant retirement of band-held government bonds is a case in point. Also called *functional finance.* See also MONETARY POLICY.

compensatory principle of money. As applied to bimetallism, the assertion that the ratio between the mint and market values of two metals in a bimetallic monetary system will be maintained through the normal operation of the forces of supply and demand. Thus, a high market demand and an augmented market value for one metal will be offset through fewer deliveries to the mint and more to the market. Conversely, a low market demand and a declining market value for one metal will be overcome through fewer deliveries to the market and more to the mint. See also BIMETALLISM.

compensatory principle of taxation. See BENEFITS-RECEIVED PRINCIPLE OF TAXATION.

compensatory spending. See DEFICIT FINANCING.

competition. The condition that exists in a market when there are an indeterminate number of traders all dealing in the same product and when no one trader can demand or offer a quantity sufficiently large materially to affect the market price. This condition is frequently referred to as *free competition, perfect competition,* or *pure competition.* See (6).

compliance director. An employee of a securities firm who seeks to uncover fraud or unauthorized or unethical behavior in the buying and selling of securities.

composite commodity standard. A proposed monetary system in which the value of the monetary unit would be defined in terms of a selected number of commodities called a "composite commodity unit" instead of in terms of one or more precious metals. See MONETARY SYSTEM.

composite demand. The total demand for a product or service originating in an indefinite number and variety of wants, all of which can be satisfied by that particular product or service. The demand for day laborers, for example, may originate in agricultural production, construction work, or a large number of other activities. Also called *rival demand.* See DEMAND.

composites. Synthetic substances having industrial value, generally made from familiar ingredients but which display new properties when combined.

composite supply. An indefinite number and variety of goods each of which is capable of satisfying a specific want. Transportation requirements, for example, can often be satisfied by buses, railroads, streetcars, or some other means of conveyance. Also called *rival supply.* See SUPPLY.

composition. An agreement between a debtor and a creditor in which, for proper consideration, the creditor agrees to accept part of the amount due him in satisfaction of the whole.

compound duty. A customs duty consisting of a specific duty to which is added an ad valorem duty. See CUSTOMS DUTY.

compound interest. Interest added to a principal sum at uniform intervals over a period of time, the accumulated interest and the principal sum at any given interval providing the basis for calculating succeeding interest payments. For example, a principal sum of $1,000 at 6 per cent interest, compounded annually over a three-year period, amounts to $1191.02.

$1,000.00	original principal sum
60.00	interest earned during first year
$1,060.00	principal sum beginning of second year
63.60	interest earned during second year
$1,123.60	principal sum at beginning of third year
67.42	interest earned during third year
$1,191.02	principal sum at end of third year

The generalized equation is:

$$x = a (1 + i)^n$$

x = principal at the end of the final interval
a = original principal sum
i = interest rate
n = number of intervals

In the above example

$$1,191.02 = 1,000 (1 + .06)^3$$

See INTEREST.

Compromise Tariff. The United States Tariff Act of 1833. It provided for a gradual reduction of all duties exceeding 20 per cent ad valorem. So called because the purpose of the act was to conciliate Southern opposition, particularly that of South Carolina where the tariff law of 1828 (TARIFF OF ABOMINATIONS) had been declared null and void because it was considered discriminatory toward Southern producers.

comptroller. Usually the executive head of the accounting staff of a large corporation or governmental agency who may analyze and interpret its financial position. Usually spelled *controller*.

compulsory arbitration. A legal or contractual requirement that a labor dispute be settled by ARBITRATION *(q.v.)*. See also *WOLFF PACKING CO.* v. *INDUSTRIAL COURT OF KANSAS*.

compulsory checkoff. See CHECKOFF.

computer. An electronic device capable of processing data in accordance with a prearranged PROGRAM and supplying the results of the processing in some prescribed form. See ANALOG COMPUTER, DIGITAL COMPUTER.

computer-assisted instruction. A method of self-instruction directed by a COMPUTER which actuates a typewriter-like console to print subject matter automatically and, at intervals, to print questions or problems to test the student's comprehension. The student replies, using the same console. Depending upon the correctness of his reply, the computer may proceed to the next unit of the course of study, or, if the student falters, the computer may cause supplementary explanations to be typed followed by new questions, drills, or additional study matter.

Comsat. See INTELSAT.

concentration. The creation or encouragement of oligopolistic conditions when a relatively large percentage of the production and marketing of specific products and services is handled by one or a few producers.

concession. A grant of land or other property for some specific use, or the right to the use of, or access to, all or a portion of some land or other property made either by a government or a private agency. Thus, a government may grant land to a private company for the construction of a canal or the building of a railroad, or the management of a county fair may grant an individual the right to operate a lunch counter on the fairground.

conciliation. As applied to labor relations, the appointment of a third party, in the event of a labor-management dispute, who attempts to settle the dispute by suggesting various ways in which the differences might be resolved but who has no authority to compel a settlement.

condemnation. 1. The determination by a public authority that a certain property is unfit for use. Thus, a ship or a tenement house may be condemned as unsafe. **2.** The acquisition of private property by public authority under the power of EMINENT DOMAIN *(q.v.)*. See also EXCESS CONDEMNATION. **3.** An official declaration that certain property is forfeited to the state because of a violation of law.

conditional indorsement. An indorsement which contains some condition affecting the indorser's liability. See INDORSEMENT.

conditional sale. A sale made with the understanding that title to the property sold will not pass to the buyer until payment of the sale price is made, or, conceivably, until some other condition has been met.

condominium. A form of ownership which gives the purchaser of an apartment in a multi-family dwelling a recordable deed for that apartment and for a proportionate share of the building site and of the common areas, such as halls and lobby, the maintenance cost of these areas being apportioned among all the owners. Such ownership differs from the cooperative apartment organizational structure which provides that ownership of the entire premises be vested in a corporation, the capital stock of which is held by the tenant owners who are liable for the corporation's tax assessments, interest on mortgage loans, if any, and upkeep on all areas not covered by proprietary leases.

confirmed letter of credit. See LETTER OF CREDIT.

confiscation. Seizure of private property by the government, without compensation to the owner.

conflict of interest. The condition that exists when a person finds that certain of his interests can be benefited only at the expense of another of his interests, or when a holder of a public office finds that certain of his interests might benefit because of the office he holds.

conglomerate. A single legal entity, the product of MERGER of several business enterprises producing different goods and services, in order to protect itself against the dangers of product specialization and to make possible the advantages of superior management and economies of scale. See COMBINATION.

Congress of Industrial Organizations. A federation of industrial labor unions in the United States from 1935 to 1955. At first it was affiliated with the American Federation of Labor as the Committee for Industrial Organizations. In 1937 it became an independent organization. On December 5, 1955 it merged with the AFL to form the AMERICAN FEDERATION OF LABOR AND CONGRESS OF INDUSTRIAL ORGANIZATIONS *(q.v.)*.

consent decree. A means of settling certain cases in equity by agreement of the parties in court. This means of settlement has been extensively used by the antitrust division of the U. S. Department of Justice. A party against whom an antitrust suit is pending offers to introduce reforms satisfactory to the Department of Justice which, instead of proceeding with the contemplated suit, accepts the offer. The agreement takes the form of a judicial decree.

conservation. As applied to natural resources, care and preservation in such a way as to prolong their use or make for their most effective use.

conservator. 1. In the United States, an official appointed to administer the affairs of a national bank which is in unsound condition or which is being liquidated. **2.** An official charged with the protection of a legally incompetent person, or one who enforces certain statutes in the public interest.

consignment. 1. Goods shipped by one person to another. **2.** Goods shipped on condition that they will be paid for when sold.

consol bond. See BOND.

consolidated bond. See BOND.

consolidation. A fusion of the assets and liabilities, in whole or in part, of two or more business establishments to form an entirely new establishment. See COMBINATION, MERGER.

conspicuous consumption. The use of consumer goods in such a way as to create a display for the purpose of impressing others rather than for the satisfaction of a normal consumer demand. See CONSUMPTION.

constant costs. Costs which, under a given set of conditions, remain the same, per unit of product, despite an increase in the total production. Handicraft articles made by individual craftsmen complete from beginning to end are subject to constant costs. See COST.

constant dollar. A statistical term indicating that prices, displayed in a time series, have been corrected to reflect a price level that existed at a certain date called the base period. See INDEX NUMBER.

consul. A government official stationed in a foreign country who cares for the commercial interests of the citizens of his own government and protects the interests of its seamen and its traveling nationals. In the United States Foreign Service consular officials rank as follows: *consul general, consul, vice-consul,* and *consular agent.*

consular agent. See CONSUL.

consular invoice. An INVOICE which has been stamped by a consul of the nation for which the goods represented on the invoice are destined. Such an invoice is frequently required for customs or statistical purposes.

consul general. See CONSUL.

Consumer and Marketing Service. A part of the U. S. Department of Agriculture which, in order to protect the consumer, is charged with *(a)* supervision of the inspecting, grading, and labeling of many commodities in foreign and interstate commerce; *(b)* the promotion of orderly marketing of agricultural commodities by directing surpluses to new markets or providing new uses; and *(c)* administration of the food stamp plan and several other special programs to improve nutrition and stimulate consumption of farm and dairy products by the young and the needy.

consumer cooperative. See COOPERATIVE.

consumer credit. Credit extended to consumers for the purchase of consumer goods and services. Consumer credit may be extended by means of charge accounts, an installment purchase plan, or through money loans. See CREDIT.

consumer economics. In the broadest sense of the term, a study of economics considered from the standpoint of the consumer. Much the same range of subject matter is involved as in the case of the more formal study of economics, but some problems, for example those involving credit terms and consumer purchasing, are stressed, and other problems are given more cursory treatment. See ECONOMICS.

consumer good. An economic good which is used directly in the satisfaction of human desires. The term is used in contradistinction to CAPITAL GOOD. The distinction is one of use. An automobile used by an individual for pleasure is a consumer good. The same automobile used in a business for delivery purposes is a capital good. When used for pleasure it is satisfying a human desire directly. When used for delivery service it is being used intermediately for the creation of additional wealth for its owner. It should be noted, furthermore, that the distinction between consumer goods and capital goods is not one of durability. Coal used by the manufacturer is a capital good, although it is spent with one use. The automobile mentioned above, when used for pleasure, is a consumer good even though it may yield satisfaction over a long period of time. On the other hand, a capital good in the form of a steam locomotive is relatively lasting, while a consumer good in the form of bread on the dining-room table is destined to be short-lived. Consumer goods are frequently classified according to their durability as: *(a)* durable, *(b)* nondurable, and *(c)* semidurable. See GOOD.

consumer price index. An index of prices obtaining in various parts of the United States for services and commodities deemed essential to maintain a standard of living for a working class family unit and compiled at intervals by the Bureau of Labor Statistics of the Department of Labor. The index uses a BASE PERIOD and shows the increase in cost attributable to inflation. The index is sometimes used to compute pay increases in wage contracts.

Consumers Advisory Council. Representatives of federal agencies and private citizens appointed by the President to advise on programs to protect consumer interests and interpret the impact on the consumer of national economic policies and trends. A consumer advisory program is also a part of the Department of Labor.

consumers' capital. See CAPITAL GOOD.

consumer sovereignty. The conception that consumers control economic life. If prices are higher than consumers will pay, demand will slacken and prices will fall; if prices are low, consumers will buy and thereby provide an incentive to producers to satisfy consumer wants at a profit. If a product is no longer wanted, producers will cease making it, and if a demand arises for a new product the prospect for profits will cause it to be produced. In such ways, according to this conception, the consumer is the ultimate ruler of economic life through his control of the market.

consumption. The utilization of services or material goods for the gratification of human desires. As thus defined, consumption means the destruction of UTILITY and is one of the main topics customarily included in the study of ECONOMICS. In popular parlance consumption may also mean the use of goods and services for productive purposes as, for example, when it is said that raw materials are consumed in the finished product. See (12).

consumption tax. See CUSTOMS DUTY, EXCISE TAX.

containerized freight. Freight shipped in a large metal box similar to a truck trailer. The box is often equipped with detachable wheels and, because it can be handled as a unit, provides flexibility as to form of transport in handling the commodities. This form of shipping is often used for relatively small commodities. Also called *capsule cargo*.

continental bill. See BILL.

contingent asset. An asset which may become actual or unqualified if, at some future time, conditions currently unfulfilled are fulfilled. See ASSET.

contingent duty. See COUNTERVAILING DUTY.

contingent fund. Money or its equivalent set aside for use only in the event of an unforeseen expense or loss. See FUND.

contingent liability. Liability which may become definitive and unqualified if, at some future time, certain specific events transpire or certain circumstances develop. See also LIABILITY.

continued bond. See BOND.

continuous market. A market in which active trading is constantly reaffirming or modifying an existing price, thus enabling purchases and sales to be consummated at any time—for example, a stock exchange. See MARKET.

contract. A legally binding agreement between two or more parties in which, for a consideration, one or more of the parties agree to do or not to do a certain thing. See (30).

contract clause. A clause in the Constitution of the United States (Art. I, Sect. 10) which specifies that no state may pass any law impairing the obligation of a contract. Although corporate franchises are considered contracts and protected by it, this clause cannot serve as a bar to the regulatory and police power of the state.

contract labor. Immigrants brought into a country under an agreement to work for a particular person who advances their transportation expenses. Contract labor has been forbidden in the United States since 1885. See LABOR.

contract rent. Payment for the use of land arrived at through the process of bargaining. The term is used to establish the fact that the actual rent paid, or contract rent, may differ from ECONOMIC RENT although the former always tends to approximate the latter. See RENT.

contract research. An agreement to conduct, for a fee, some investigation of a scientific or technical nature, often involving experimentation in some area of knowledge, the object being to discover new facts or procedures or to revise old ones. Most United States military research is carried on by contract with private firms. Universities and nonprofit institutes often conduct research of various kinds for business establishments and government agencies.

contract system. As applied to penal institutions, a contractual arrangement between a government and a private employer for the latter's use of convict labor. Work is done in the prison with materials furnished by the employer; supervision is provided by the prison authorities. Because of opposition by LABOR UNIONS and by employers competing with prison-made products, as well as agitation for more humanitarian and scientific correction methods, the contract system has been practically abolished in the United States. See also CONVICT LEASE SYSTEM, PUBLIC WORKS AND WAYS SYSTEM, STATE USE SYSTEM.

contributory negligence. A common-law doctrine that carelessness on the part of an employee absolved the employer from responsibility in the event of an accident resulting in an injury to the employee. This has been modified in most states of the United States by WORKMEN'S COMPENSATION LAWS. However, contributory negligence may be valid grounds for defense in other cases, such as traffic accidents.

contributory pension. A PENSION for the benefit of employees, contributions to the cost of which are made by both the employer and the employees.

control. 1. Public regulation of some phase of economic life. There are many kinds of controls. See (23). **2.** The measurement of performance in an enterprise against plans or fiscal estimates, as budgetary control, or the observance of certain standards in the production of goods or services, as quality control.

controlled economy. An economy which is extensively regulated by government. Such an economy does not necessarily involve government ownership of the means of production, but it may embrace a certain amount of economic planning by government and a variety of public controls over such matters as credit, production, foreign trade, and the disposition of the labor force. Also called *directed economy.* See ECONOMIC SYSTEMS.

controller. See COMPTROLLER.

controlling account. An account appearing in a general ledger summarizing detailed accounts carried in some other ledger. Thus, the general ledger may carry an accounts-receivable page showing the total of the balances in the customers' or accounts-receivable ledger. See ACCOUNT.

controlling company. See HOLDING COMPANY.

convenience store. See BANTAM STORE.

conventional tariff system. A system of tariff duties in which rates are largely or wholly determined by bilateral or multilateral commercial agreements with other countries and are subject to change as the relevant international agreements are altered or because of the operation of a MOST-FAVORED-NATION CLAUSE *(q.v.)* in existing agreements. The term is used in contradistinction to AUTONOMOUS TARIFF SYSTEM. See TARIFF.

conversion. 1. The exchange of one form of property for another, as a bond for a stock or real property for personal property. 2. The manufacture of a finished or semifinished product from raw materials.

conversion price. The price applicable to the stock of a corporation for which the holder of a convertible bond of the same corporation may exchange such bond. The conversion price is usually indicated at the time the bond is issued and may differ from the market price of the stock at the time the right of conversion is exercised. See PRICE.

convertible bond. See BOND.

convertible money. Money which is redeemable in standard money. See MONEY.

convertible stock. See CAPITAL STOCK.

convict labor. See STATE USE SYSTEM.

convict lease system. A contractual arrangement between a government and a private employer for the latter's use of convict labor at so much per head, the private employer supplying materials, tools, food, housing, and supervision, as well as guards to preserve order and to prevent escape. The government is thus relieved of all financial responsibility for the penal population so engaged. Serious abuses developed under the system, and it has now been abolished in all states of the United States. See also CONTRACT SYSTEM, PUBLIC WORKS AND WAYS SYSTEM, STATE USE SYSTEM.

Cooley v. Board of Wardens. A case, 12 Howard 299 (1851), in which the Supreme Court established the principle that states of the United States may make local regulations, such as pilotage regulations, affecting interstate and foreign commerce which are valid until such time as Congress chooses to supersede them by exercising its commerce powers.

cooling-off period. A specified interval of time which must elapse before any overt action is taken by either party to a labor dispute. It may be provided for in a labor agreement or may be a requirement of law, and its purpose is to provide time for amicable adjustment of differences before the parties resort to economic pressure such as a strike.

cooperative. Generally, a form of business organization operating for the mutual benefit of members who own the company, are responsible for its management, and share any surplus of income over expenses frequently in proportion to the business each contributes to the joint enterprise. Cooperatives operate for such purposes as the purchasing, production, processing, marketing, and retailing of goods *(consumer cooperatives),* the supplying of housing, and various services including banking and the extension of credit. See FORMS OF BUSINESS ORGANIZATION. See also COOPERATIVE COMMONWEALTH, ROCHDALE PRINCIPLES.

cooperative commonwealth. An economy in which production, processing, and distribution of goods and the supplying of various services would be carried on by COOPERATIVES *(q.v.).* Retail cooperatives would create and become members of processing or wholesale cooperatives which would supply their needs.

Similarly, processing or wholesale cooperatives would, in turn, create and become members of producing cooperatives. Thus the entire economy, or most of it, would be organized on a cooperative basis. Some cooperative theorists hold the view that such an economy would eventually establish a decentralized cooperative democracy, replacing present governmental structures. See ECONOMIC SYSTEMS.

Cooperative Marketing (*Capper-Volstead*) Act. An act of Congress, 1922, which exempted bona fide cooperative associations from the operation of the federal antitrust statutes. The act encouraged farmers, ranchers, and growers to combine in such associations for the purpose of obtaining more efficient distribution of their products.

***Coppage* v. *Kansas*.** A case, 236 U. S. 1 (1915), in which the Supreme Court held invalid, as a deprivation of contractual liberty protected by the due process clause of the 14th Amendment, a Kansas statute which attempted to outlaw the so-called yellow-dog employment contract. In such a contract a person agrees that, if employed, he will not join a labor union and that he may be dismissed if he subsequently joins a union or is found to belong to a union. The decision in this case is almost identical with that of the earlier case of ADAIR V. UNITED STATES *(q.v.)*, and the reasoning is similar. Legislation outlawing yellow-dog contracts has since been sustained by the courts.

copyright. An exclusive right conferred by a government upon a person or organization, for a term of years, to reproduce a literary or artistic creation, including a book, map, article, drawing, chart, photograph, or musical composition. The right thus granted may be enforced in the courts. In the United States a copyright is issued through the Copyright Office of the Library of Congress. The term of a copyright is 28 years with the right of renewal for the same length of time.

corner. As applied to stock-market trading, the possession of all or the major part of the available supply of a security. The object of a corner is to profit by advancing the price. The term has a similar meaning in the commodity markets.

corn laws. A term usually applying to the British regulations covering trade in grains, in force from 1436 to 1846. Heavy import duties were levied on grain imports for home consumption as long as the domestic price remained below a stipulated figure. Agitation against such regulations became particularly intense after 1837, and led to repeal of the laws. See ANTI-CORN-LAW LEAGUE.

Coronado case (first). A case, *United Mine Workers* v. *Coronado Coal Co.,* 259 U. S. 344 (1922), in which the Supreme Court ruled that where damages may be assessed against a labor union because of the operation of the Sherman Antitrust Act, a suit for recovery will be directly against the labor union. This decision thus changed the old common-law rule that a union was a partnership, that liability attached only to each individual member, and that when suit was brought it had to be brought against each member as an individual.

corporate stock. 1. The shares of the capital stock of a corporation. See CAPITAL STOCK. **2.** The term is sometimes applied to the debt, or part of the debt, of New York and a few other cities in the United States which is held in the form of long-term municipal bonds secured by a SINKING FUND.

corporation. A legal entity, created either for a limited period or in perpetuity, which, within the scope of its charter issued by the state, is treated in many respects as a natural person. Thus a corporation normally has the broad contractual discretion of a natural person and may own property, incur debts, and sue and be sued in a court of law. There are many types or classes of corporations, each type or class being governed by laws which normally apply only to that type or class. The corporation's control and direction are vested in its membership or board of directors or trustees. Occasionally referred to as *incorporation*. See (4).

corporation income tax. A tax levied upon the earnings of corporations. See TAX.

correspondent bank. A bank that carries on continuing mutually advantageous business and financial relations with a bank in some other locality. Although the advent of the FEDERAL RESERVE SYSTEM has reduced the role of correspondent banks in the United States, particularly in the matter of clearing checks, they still perform some collection services for one another, exchange information regarding local conditions, and, on occasion, lend and borrow surplus funds. See BANK.

cost. **1.** As used in theoretical economics, the total payments made by an enterprise to the FACTORS OF PRODUCTION, and for RAW MATERIALS, and other materials and services incidental to the enterprise. **2.** Generally, the amount paid for a commodity or service. See (1).

cost accounting. A system of ascertaining the total cost of a finished product. Individual items making up the total cost include raw material, labor applied directly to the raw material, and a proportionate amount of FIXED COSTS allotted to a finished unit of the product.

cost-of-living adjustment. A term designating an arrangement, included in some important labor contracts since 1948, whereby wages are increased or decreased in the same proportion as increases or decreases in an appropriate index of prices reflecting the living costs of the workers affected.

cost-of-production theory of value. The theory that assumes the value of a product depends upon the amount of labor and the amount of time necessary to produce it. The theory is more comprehensive than the LABOR THEORY OF VALUE in that it includes in the value of the finished product the productive efficiency contributed by capital as well as the contribution of labor. The theory was set forth by David Ricardo in the early part of the 19th century. See also VALUE.

cost-of-service principle of taxation. The principle that taxes should be levied upon individual taxpayers on the basis of the cost to the government of the services rendered those individual taxpayers. The principle is quite impossible of application except in the case of charges for postal or electric power and light services, which are in the nature of prices rather than taxes. The cost of police or fire protection supplied one individual taxpayer may be much greater or less than the same services supplied some other taxpayer, but to determine just how much greater or less and to calculate the taxes accordingly is generally considered to be impracticable.

cost plus contract. A contract which, instead of setting a fixed selling price, permits the seller to charge whatever his costs may be plus a fixed percentage of that cost.

Council for Mutual Economic Assistance. An intergovernmental organization consisting of the U.S.S.R. and seven Communist satellite states—Czechoslovakia, Poland, Hungary, Romania,

Bulgaria, East Germany, and Mongolia—established in 1949 partly in response to the organization of Western Europe's Recovery Plan (Marshall Plan), to integrate their respective economies. After 1964, the growing nationalist spirit in such states as Romania and Czechoslovakia heralded the gradual disintegration of the Council and it has lost much of its earlier importance.

Council of Economic Advisers. A three-man division of the executive office of the President of the United States, established under the EMPLOYMENT ACT of 1946 to assist in the preparation of the President's annual economic report to Congress and to recommend to the President measures and policies to promote the economic well-being of the nation.

counter check. A form of receipt for cash supplied by a bank to despositors who, having executed and signed it, use it to withdraw funds from their accounts in the bank supplying the receipt. A counter check is not negotiable. See CHECK.

counterfeit money. Money made to resemble legal money and passed as such with the intent to defraud. Such actions are universally considered criminal. See MONEY.

counterpart fund. A sum, in local currency, which European and other countries benefiting by American aid are required to set aside to offset the amount of the aid. A principal purpose of the fund is to dampen inflation. Such local offsets may be used subsequently to finance internal improvements. See FUND.

countervailing duty. A customs duty levied by an importing country as a protective surtax to offset an EXPORT BOUNTY paid by the exporting country. The term is also applied to a tariff duty levied on imported goods when the country of origin levies duties on similar goods imported by it. Such a duty is sometimes called a *contingent duty*. See CUSTOMS DUTY.

countervailing excise duty. See COMPENSATORY DUTY.

country banks. 1. Small national banks in the United States which, under the National Bank Act, were required to maintain reserves at 15 per cent of deposits but could deposit 60 per cent of these in RESERVE CITY and CENTRAL RESERVE CITY BANKS *(qq.v.)*. 2. Similar small banks which are required to maintain the smallest minimum reserve against deposits of any federal reserve member bank as a deposit in a federal reserve bank. See BANK.

county agricultural agent. See EXTENSION SERVICE.

coupon bond. See BOND.

covenant. An agreement between two or more persons or states, or one of the stipulations in such an agreement.

craft guild. A medieval association of artisans that enjoyed a virtual monopoly in the production of articles identified with its craft. The guild maintained certain standards of quality in the output of its members and sought to guarantee standards of workmanship and to preserve its monopoly by appropriate regulations concerning apprenticeship and admission to its ranks. See GUILD.

craft union. A LABOR UNION composed of workers in one skilled trade or in two or more closely allied skilled trades. Also called *horizontal labor union.*

credit. 1. A promise of future payment in kind or in money given in exchange for present money, goods, or services. See (21). 2. An entry on the right or credit side of an account in a DOUBLE-ENTRY system of BOOKKEEPING. See ACCOUNT. 3. The reputation as a risk which a borrower enjoys with an actual or potential lender.

credit bill. See BILL.

credit card. A document, usually of the dimensions of a calling card, indicating that the person to whom it is issued is entitled to credit. Credit cards are frequently issued by companies to their customers gratuitously. Similar cards are issued for a fee by finance companies to whom bills are sent for purchases of goods or services from any of a large number of suppliers, one consolidated monthly charge being made to the person to whom the card is issued.

credit control. Any policy designed to expand or contract credit, such a policy being applied by government, banks, a central banking organization such as the FEDERAL RESERVE SYSTEM, or other appropriate agencies according to the economic conditions that obtain at any particular time. Credit may be expanded or contracted to a certain extent by changing the REDISCOUNT RATE, or by lowering or increasing the requirements for BANK RESERVES. An advance in the rediscount rate of the federal reserve banks in the United States, for example, may discourage loans because of the higher interest charges, and this contracts credit. Conversely, a reduction in the rediscount rate may encourage loans and thus expand credit. Likewise, higher bank reserves may discourage loans and contract credit, whereas lower bank reserves may encourage loans and expand credit. Such credit policies affect the volume of DEPOSIT CURRENCY; and the volume of deposit currency, in turn, affects the PRICE LEVEL, this being governed in part by the volume of currency in circulation. Hence, credit control may be regarded as one means of controlling prices. See CONTROL.

credit life insurance. Insurance which, upon the death of a trader, meets, within limits, a debt incurred by him through BUYING ON MARGIN *(q.v.)* See LIFE INSURANCE.)

Crédit Mobilier. In the United States, a JOINT-STOCK COMPANY organized in 1863 in Pennsylvania, originally for the purpose of conducting a general credit and contract business. It was reorganized in 1867 under this name for the specific purpose of building the Union Pacific Railroad. Charges of corruption among its officers and of alleged bribes offered to members of Congress by representatives of the company brought about a congressional investigation and its collapse.

credit money. See FIDUCIARY MONEY.

creditor. One to whom a debt is owed.

creditor nation. A nation whose international trade and finance is such that the total amount owed to its government, private business, and banking interests from foreign sources exceeds the sum owed to foreign creditors: in other words, a nation which enjoys a creditor position in its BALANCE OF PAYMENTS.

credit rating. A rating given a business establishment by a mercantile agency indicating that establishment's record of performance in meeting its financial obligations and its ability to meet such obligations in the future.

credit theory of the business cycle. The theory that the volume of economic activity is primarily dependent upon the ebb and flow of bank credit. According to this theory, expansion of bank credit inflates prices, enhances business activity, and expands employment. When, on the other hand, prudence and the canons of safe banking policy dictate retrenchment, the economy enters upon a deflationary phase to the accompaniment of falling prices, declining business activity, and decreased employment. See BANK CREDIT, BUSINESS CYCLE.

credit union. A cooperative organization which makes small loans to its members for personal needs. Shares in the organization are usually sold for about $5, and members may buy as many shares as they wish. Applications for loans are considered by a designated committee. Most credit unions are chartered under state laws; others are chartered by the federal government under the provisions of the Credit Union Act of 1934.

Crime of 1873. A derogatory term applied to the action of the United States government, taken in 1873, to discontinue the free coinage of silver dollars. The term did not come into use until some time after the event. At the time the silver dollar was discontinued as standard money, silver was undervalued at the mint, and none of that metal was being delivered for coinage. After 1873, however, during a period of depression and falling prices, a strong agitation developed for legislation which would increase the money in circulation. It was then and thereafter that the action of the government in demonetizing silver some years earlier was termed the "Crime of 1873."

critical material. See STRATEGIC MATERIALS.

crop insurance. Insurance against loss of certain crops owing to unavoidable hazards. In the United States such insurance is provided by the FEDERAL CROP INSURANCE CORPORATION and insures about 24 individual crops as well as crops under a combined crop-protection plan. Approximately one-half of the nation's agricultural counties participate in the crop-insurance program. See INSURANCE.

cross-elasticity. The effect of a change in price of one commodity or service on the sales of a substitute commodity or service. For example, an increase in the price of fuel oil might engender an increase in the sales of coal. For examples of commodities that have such a competitive effect, see COMPOSITE SUPPLY. See also COEFFICIENT OF CROSS-ELASTICITY.

cross of gold. A phrase used by William Jennings Bryan (1860-1925) at the Democratic National Convention held at Chicago in 1896. The GOLD STANDARD versus BIMETALLISM or the FREE COINAGE of silver at fixed ratios with gold was the political issue at the time. A faction in the Democratic party, under the leadership of David B. Hill of New York, was opposed to FREE SILVER but was voted down after Bryan had delivered the oration in which he said in part, "You shall not press down upon the brow of labor this crown of thorns. You shall not crucify mankind upon a cross of gold."

cross picketing. Picketing by two or more rival unions, each claiming to represent the employees of the establishment being picketed. See PICKETING.

cross purchase. A practice which makes it possible for a broker, without recourse to the market, to fulfill an order to buy and an order to sell the same security. The practice is forbidden by the rules of the New York Stock Exchange.

cross-rate. The rate of exchange between two currencies calculated by reference to the rates of exchange between each and a third currency. For example, in April, 1952, cable transfers for pound sterling were quoted at $2.8079 in New York. Simultaneously, transfers of Mexican pesos were quoted at 0.11569 per dollar in New York. The cross-rate between pound sterling and the Mexican peso, calculated by their relation to the dollar, was, therefore, 1 pound sterling for 24.271 Mexican pesos. This was slightly above the par rate of exchange established by the INTERNATIONAL MONETARY FUND, which was 24.220 pesos per pound sterling. See RATE.

crude birth rate. See BIRTH RATE.

crude death rate. See DEATH RATE.

culture lag. The condition which exists when changes in ideas and practices pertaining to political, social, and economic life fail to keep pace with physical changes in the environment caused by mechanical invention, technological innovation, depletion of essential natural resources, or similar circumstances.

cum rights. A term describing the privilege extended to stockholders to purchase shares of a new issue of stock in a company in proportion to existing holdings. Such STOCK RIGHTS *(q.v.)* are offered to stockholders of record as of a certain date. A person buying existing stock of the corporation on the market before this date will therefore receive these stock rights, and stock sold at such a time is said to be sold "cum rights." The term is used in contradistinction to EX RIGHTS.

cumulative dividend. A dividend which, if not paid, becomes a liability of a corporation and must be paid in subsequent years before any dividends are paid on the common stock. Sometimes called *accumulative dividend.* See DIVIDEND.

cumulative stock. See CAPITAL STOCK.

cumulative voting. As applied to corporate elections, a method of voting which permits each stockholder as many votes as the number of shares of stock he holds, as shown on the records of the corporation, multiplied by the number of directors to be elected. The stockholder may group, or cumulate, his votes and cast them all for one candidate, or he may distribute them among two or more candidates.

curb exchange. The name, previous to 1953, of the AMERICAN STOCK EXCHANGE operating at 86 Trinity Place, New York, N. Y. It was originally organized before the Civil War, and for many years conducted its trading in the open street—hence the term. In 1921 the curb exchange opened its own building.

curb stock. See CAPITAL STOCK.

currency. Anything that serves as a medium of exchange, whether of general or limited acceptability. Hence, besides *cash* or MONEY, this term includes checks drawn on bank accounts, postal money orders, express checks, and other similar instruments which, while not enjoying the general acceptability of money because they usually require identification of maker or indorser, are nonetheless important as media of exchange in the business world. Indeed it is by means of bank checks rather than money that most business transactions are carried out. See (33).

currency bond. See BOND.

current asset. An asset which is temporary in character and hence will be transformed or converted into cash within a relatively short period of time, usually a year. In financial statements current assets are usually listed according to the degree of liquidity; for example, cash, ACCOUNTS RECEIVABLE, BILLS RECEIVABLE, and INVENTORY. Sometimes called *floating asset.* See ASSET.

current liability. A liability which is due within a comparatively short length of time, usually less than a year. See LIABILITY.

current ratio. In a BALANCE SHEET, the proportion of total CURRENT ASSETS to total CURRENT LIABILITIES. If the current assets

109

are $6,000 and the current liabilities $4,000, the current ratio is 1½ to 1. Current ratio is frequently used as one test to determine CREDIT RATING. See RATIO.

Current Tax Payment Act. An act of Congress, 1943, which requires certain employers to deduct legally stipulated percentages from the gross total of employees' wages and salaries at the time such wages or salaries become due and payable, and to remit the amounts deducted to the Internal Revenue Service of the Department of the Treasury. The deductions thus made on behalf of any employee constitute a credit against that employee's federal income-tax liability and are considered as such when the employee executes his formal tax return for any tax period. The deductions are sometimes improperly called a *withholding tax.* Actually, they are simply a means of keeping tax payments current; that is, of collecting a tax liability as soon as it becomes such.

current yield. The annual return on an investment expressed as a percentage of the principal sum. Thus, if the return is $20 per annum on an investment of $1,000, the current yield is 2 per cent. See YIELD.

custodian account. An arrangement whereby a bank, in return for a fee, provides for the safekeeping of securities and the collection of income and principal therefrom. The bank also executes purchase and sales orders as directed by the owner of the securities, rendering him an account of all transactions and providing him with such other services as may be called for in the custodian agreement. See ACCOUNT.

customers' net debit balances. The net amount outstanding at any time which customers have borrowed from broker members of a securities exchange such as the New York Stock Exchange in order to purchase stocks—normally covered by suitable collateral.

customhouse. The building where import and export duties are paid. If it is located in a seaport, vessels are entered and cleared at the customhouse.

customs. See CUSTOMS DUTY.

customs broker. An individual who, in return for a fee, handles for importers the details of clearing goods through the customs. Such brokers are licensed by the U. S. Treasury Department.

customs duty. A tax levied upon goods transported from one political jurisdiction to another, especially a tax on goods imported from a foreign country—normally distinguished from a TARIFF, which means a comprehensive schedule of such duties. See (27).

customs union. An agreement between two or more political jurisdictions to abolish customs duties and other trade restrictions among themselves, and to adopt a common policy regarding trade with political jurisdictions outside of the union. Sometimes referred to as *tariff union.*

cutback. As applied to labor relations, the laying off of workers because of a sudden cessation of work.

cutthroat competition. Intense competition which results in losses and which is often intended to eliminate one or more business rivals, the losses being recouped later by relatively high prices. Such competition, when entered into with an intent to create a monopoly or from sheer malice, may be illegal. Also called *rate war.* See COMPETITION.

cybernetics. The study of control and communication functions in animals and in electro-mechanical and electronic systems. The term was first used in 1947 by Norbert Weiner, Professor of Mathematics, The Massachusetts Institute of Technology, and by Dr. Arturo Rosenblueth, then of Harvard Medical School. It is derived from the Greek word meaning "steersman" and from the Latin corruption of the word meaning "governor."

cyclical fluctuations. More or less periodic variations in a time series frequently indicative of a BUSINESS CYCLE. There are various statistical methods for estimating cyclical fluctuations in a time series. The diagram on page 112 shows the cyclical fluctuations of the data given under TIME SERIES. The curve may be computed by calculating the SECULAR TREND using the LEAST-SQUARES METHOD, ascertaining the SEASONAL FLUCTUATIONS, and correcting the trend values accordingly. The results are then subtracted from the original data and the differences are expressed as percentages of the corrected trend values. The curve is finally smoothed by means of a five-item MOVING AVERAGE.

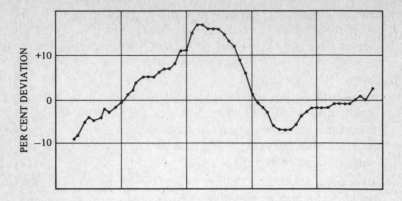

cyclical unemployment. Unemployment attributed to the deflationary phase of a business cycle. See UNEMPLOYMENT.

D

Danbury Hatters' case. A case, *Loewe* v. *Lawlor*, 208 U.S. 274 (1908), in which the Supreme Court ruled that a general boycott instituted by a labor organization against the product of an employer prevented him from engaging in interstate commerce and was therefore a violation of the Sherman Antitrust Act. The decision thus applied the Sherman Act to the activities of labor organizations when such activities affected directly and substantially the flow of commerce among the states. The provisions of the Clayton Act subsequently modified this ruling.

Daniel Ball, The. A case, 10 Wall. 557 (1871), in which the Supreme Court extended federal jurisdiction to all waterways such as lakes and rivers which are in fact navigable or can be made so and hence can serve as arteries of commerce between the states or with foreign nations.

datmation. The transmission of data by a COMPUTER. The word is formed from the two words "data" and "automation."

Dawes plan. A plan, put into effect in 1924, which fixed the amount of reparations owed by Germany to the Allied and associated nations under the terms of the Treaty of Versailles and sought to facilitate their payment. The plan included: (*a*) progressively higher payments by Germany each year for a period of 5 years and payments thereafter on the basis of a prosperity index; (*b*) stabilization of German currency and a balanced budget; (*c*) a foreign loan to Germany; (*d*) international control of Germany's financial affairs; and (*e*) the eventual withdrawal of Allied troops from occupied German territory. The plan was named for General Charles G. Dawes, chairman of the committee that formulated the plan. In 1929 it was superseded by the YOUNG PLAN.

day loan. A bank loan to a stockbroker to finance a day's business. If by the end of the day (4:00 P.M.) more funds had been required than were provided by the loan, an additional "overnight" loan is made to take care of the debit balance. This is sometimes called *overcertification.* The temporary loan is settled the following morning by cash, by a CALL LOAN, or by a loan in some more permanent form. See LOAN.

days of grace. See GRACE PERIOD.

Dayton-Goose Creek Ry. Co.* v. *United States. A case, 263 U.S. 456 (1924), in which the Supreme Court upheld the so-called "recapture provisions" of the Transportation (Esch-Cummins) Act of 1920. These stipulated that half the earnings in excess of a fair return be set up as a separate fund by each railroad and the other half be remitted to the Interstate Commerce Commission for a general railroad revolving fund. The Court stressed that the recapture provisions constituted the heart of a plan for the general betterment of the railroads which Congress had set up in the act and pointed out that what was recaptured was not a taking of property since the railways were entitled only to a fair return and not to the excess. The Court also rejected the argument that the recapture provisions interfered with the power of the states to fix returns on intrastate commerce, asserting that, in the Transportation Act, Congress had to treat the railways of the country as a unit and that, in so doing, its power extended to the necessary incidental control of intrastate commerce.

deadheading. 1. As used in the transportation industry, the movement of empty cars, buses, or trucks to a given destination, or the practice of furnishing free transportation to employees of a transportation company. **2.** As applied to labor relations, the promotion of a junior employee in preference to another who has seniority rights but is deemed incapable of filling the higher position satisfactorily.

dead rent. A fixed annual sum paid for a mine or a quarry, in addition to payment of royalties which vary in amount according to the yield. See RENT.

dead time. Time lost through no fault of the employee and for which he is usually paid at the full rate. Time lost because of machine breakdowns or delays in delivery of material are examples.

dear money. 1. A term used to describe a condition when the general price level is low. At such a time a relatively large quantity of goods or services exchanges for a relatively small quantity of money; hence, money is dear, or its value is high compared with the value of goods and services. **2.** The existence of high interest rates. See MONEY.

death rate. The number of deaths per 1,000 persons in any given area during the period of a year. This is called the *crude death rate.* If corrections are made to allow for differences in the composition of the population, for example the number of people in various age groups, the crude death rate becomes a *refined death rate.* The number of deaths per 1,000 children 1 to 10 years of age would be a refined death rate. See RATE.

death sentence. As applied to legislation regulating public-utility companies, a provision of the PUBLIC UTILITY HOLDING COMPANY ACT, passed by Congress in 1935, which required individual public-utility holding companies to simplify corporate structures by eliminating complicated networks of subsidiary and operating companies servicing extensive geographical areas.

debasement. As applied to coinage, the reduction of the amount of precious metal contained in the standard MONETARY UNIT.

debenture bond. See BOND. See also SUBORDINATED DEBENTURE.

debenture certificate. 1. A customhouse document authorizing a rebate on duties paid on imported goods destined to be exported. **2.** A document which authorizes the payment of money granted as a BOUNTY to an exporter of certain domestic goods. See CERTIFICATE.

debenture stock. See CAPITAL STOCK.

debit. An entry on the left or "debit" side of an account in double-entry bookkeeping. An account may be said to have a debit balance if the amounts debited are in excess of the amounts credited.

Debs case. A case, 158 U.S. 564 (1895), growing out of the Pullman Strike of 1894. Because of alleged interference by strikers with the United States mails and interstate commerce, the United States secured a writ from the federal circuit court in Chicago enjoining the strikers from interfering with these federal interests. Eugene Debs, as leader of the strikers, refused to obey the injunction, was subsequently held in contempt, and punished by fine and imprisonment. On Debs' appeal to the Supreme Court, that body declared that the federal government could use the entire strength of the nation to protect its interests, and that this broad authority included the lesser authority of securing injunctive relief from the courts. The decision was a factor in the subsequent demand of organized labor for a statute which would restrict the courts' power to issue injunctions in labor disputes and to try persons without a jury in cases of contempt. This demand led to the enactment in 1932 of the ANTI-INJUNCTION *(Norris-LaGuardia)* ACT.

debt. Whatever is owed to one person or organization by another. The obligation may involve money, goods, or services. See (21).

debt ceiling. A stipulation by Congress that the total debt of the United States shall not exceed a certain maximum, this limitation having the effect of preventing the Treasury from issuing and selling regular government obligations, even if authorized by statute, if their issuance should expand total debt beyond the maximum. From time to time, in recent years, Congress has raised the ceiling. See also DEBT LIMIT.

debt limit. As applied to public finance, a constitutional or legislative provision sometimes imposed upon a state or a municipal government limiting its authority to borrow funds to a certain specified sum, to a fixed per cent of the assessed value of the taxable property within its jurisdiction, or in some other manner restricting its borrowing capacity. See DEBT CEILING.

debt monetization. The procedures by which United States government SECURITIES are made to increase the CURRENCY in circulation. Debt monetization occurs in several ways: *(a)* DEPOSIT CURRENCY is credited to the government by certain COM-

MERCIAL BANKS in payment for government securities purchased by them; *(b)* CHECKS in payment of government securities purchased by the FEDERAL RESERVE BANKS in OPEN-MARKET OPERATIONS are deposited in federal reserve banks to the credit of MEMBER BANK RESERVES, which adds to the capacity of member banks to create deposit currency or to draw FEDERAL RESERVE NOTES; *(c)* the PROCEEDS of LOANS, supported by government securities, made to member banks by federal reserve banks are credited to member bank reserves, which also adds to the capacity of member banks to create deposit currency or federal reserve notes; *(d)* the amounts represented by the limited quantity of government securities that the federal reserve banks purchase directly from the United States Treasury are credited to the government's deposit account.

These operations are affected by legislation by Congress and regulations by the BOARD OF GOVERNORS of the FEDERAL RESERVE SYSTEM which determine BANK RESERVES.

debtor. One who owes a debt—the opposite of creditor.

debtor nation. A nation whose international trade and finance is such that the total amount which its government, private business, and banks owe to foreign creditors exceeds the sum due from foreign debtors. In other words, a nation which chronically has a debtor position in its BALANCE OF PAYMENTS.

debt service. Payment of the interest on a debt and of such installments of the principal as are legally due. Normally, the term is used in connection with a public debt.

decentralization. As applied to industry: **1.** the establishment of factories away from large cities and at some distance from one another—the policy applying to a single company or to an industry in general. **2.** A technique of organization in large business enterprises whereby units of the business representing separate products, common functions, or stages of process are given a large measure of autonomy, only general guidance and major decisions affecting the enterprise as a whole being reserved for central management.

deciles. See QUARTILES.

declining-marginal-efficiency-of-capital theory. The theory emphasized by Keynesian economists that when, at a given rate of consumption, more and more productive plants and equipment are established, the rate of return on new and existing capital equipment declines. Also referred to as the *falling-rate-of-profit theory*. See MARGINAL EFFICIENCY OF CAPITAL.

decreasing costs. Costs which, under a given set of conditions, decrease, per unit of product, as the total production increases. The savings brought about by mass production, by interchangeable parts, and by division of labor have resulted in a condition of decreasing costs. See COST.

decreasing returns. See DIMINISHING RETURNS.

dedication A gift of private property to some political jurisdiction; for example, a right of way or a park. The owner thereby relinquishes forever the right to the property in question.

deductible clause. In an insurance contract, a provision making the insured liable for the initial, usually modest, portion of any loss sustained by the insured (for example, $100 in the case of an automobile collision policy) thus reducing the cost of the insurance.

deductive method. A process of logical reasoning starting with a premise generally accepted as true and arriving at one or more conclusions based on such a premise. This method was widely used by the CLASSICAL SCHOOL and later challenged by the HISTORICAL SCHOOL. The usefulness of the method depends upon the validity of the basic assumptions or premises, and many times these have been found to be faulty. When properly used, however, the method has a recognized place in scientific investigation.

deed. A written document setting forth an agreement, particularly an agreement involving the transfer of property, the document having been duly signed, sealed, and delivered. Commonly the term refers to a document transferring the ownership of real property.

defalcation. Misappropriation of money or property, especially by an agent or officer holding such money or property in trust—EMBEZZLEMENT.

Defense Production Act. An act of Congress, 1950, which authorized STAND-BY CONTROLS for the nation's economy during the

Korean War, some of which were placed in effect during the late summer of 1950 and were subsequently lifted. Powers under this legislation are confided to the Business and Defense Services Administration of the Department of Commerce.

deferred annuity. An annuity which begins only after a specified period of time has elapsed following its purchase or other arrangements for its payment. Deferred annuities are often provided for in life-insurance policies. See ANNUITY.

deferred bond. See BOND.

deferred demand. Demand necessarily postponed because of a scarcity of goods and services. See DEMAND.

deferred income. See UNEARNED INCOME.

deficiency supply bill. An appropriation for a legally approved project or purpose made after the enactment of the annual budget or the regular appropriation bills.

deficit A deficiency usually expressed in money. On books of account it is the amount necessary to balance an asset and liability statement when the liabilities exceed the assets.

deficit financing. Large-scale expenditure of borrowed funds to meet some unusual or emergency situation requiring such expenditure or making such expenditure desirable. The term is used popularly to describe a governmental policy of alleviating a business depression by heavy expenditure of funds secured by expanding the public debt. This is often called *compensatory spending* because it is argued that the policy of government borrowing and spending may increase general purchasing power to such an extent as to compensate for the decline of private borrowing and spending to which the depression may have been attributed.

definitive. A term used to denote a permanent stock certificate or bond issued to replace an existing document because of some change in the corporation involved, particularly a change affecting the corporation's financial structure.

deflation. A decrease in the general price level; or the converse, an increase in the value of money in terms of goods and services. Deflation may occur when the quantity of MONEY or DEPOSIT CURRENCY in circulation is small compared with the quantity of goods and services offered, or when fear of the future or some other cause curtails consumer spending materially, thus reducing the velocity of circulation. See DISINFLATION.

deflationary gap. A statistical phrase denoting the amount by which the theoretical volume of spending necessary to maintain full employment or to absorb all available goods and services at prevailing prices exceeds actual private spending and government expenses.

degressive taxation. A form of PROGRESSIVE TAXATION in which rates increase as the base amount taxed increases, but in which each addition to the tax rate is less than the preceding one. A tax system in which a rate of 1 per cent is applied to a base of $1,000, 2½ percent to a base of $10,000, 3¾ per cent to a base of $100,000, and 4¼ percent to a base of $1,000,000 is an example.

del credere agreement. An agreement sometimes entered into by exporters with an agent in a foreign country. Such an agent guarantees payment for all goods sold to a buyer and receives an extra commission for this service.

delinquent tax. A tax that remains unpaid after the date when payment is due. In most cases penalties are imposed for short- and long-term delinquency. In the case of a delinquent property tax, the resulting tax lien on the property in question may, after a prescribed interval, be foreclosed and, through such proceedings, the property may revert to the taxing authorities. See TAX.

demand. 1. The quantity of an economic good that will be bought at a given price at a particular time. Demand in this sense is sometimes called *market demand*. For example, if at a particular time 100 units of an economic good can be sold at $5 and 200 units at $4, it is said that the market demand for the good is 100 at $5 and 200 at $4. **2.** The term may also be defined as the quantity of an economic good that will be bought at all possible prices at a particular time, often referred to as the total, or *schedule demand*. In the following table the schedule demand for a good is indicated for various prices at two different periods:

Price	First-period Demand	Second-period Demand
$5	100	200
4	200	300
3	300	400
2	400	500
1	500	600

It will be noted that, during the interval between the first and second periods, the total or schedule demand increased; that is, there was an increased demand for the good at all prices. These two schedule demands are represented by lines a—a′ and b—b′ in the appended diagram. See (12).

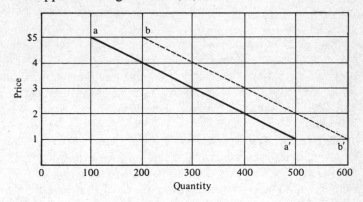

demand-and-supply curves. A graphic representation of the maximum buying and minimum selling prices offered and acceptable to traders in a specific commodity at a particular time and place, and the resulting market price. In the graph on page 122, which indicates a market price of 12, the horizontal axis represents quantities, and the vertical axis, prices, as follows:

Quantity Demanded	Prices	Quantity Offered
5	10	1
4	11	2
3	12	3
2	13	4
1	14	5

121

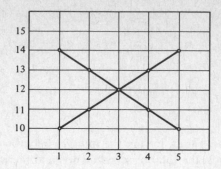

demand bill See BILL.

demand deposit. A bank deposit subject to withdrawal at any time—the usual type of deposit in a commercial bank. See BANK DEPOSIT.

democratic socialism. A somewhat vague term by which is meant a policy of reconciling a modified degree of socialism, particularly national economic planning, market control, and some nationalization of industry, with parliamentary political processes and the maintenance of traditional civil liberties. See SOCIALISM.

demonetization. 1. The removal of certain currency from circulation. **2.** The discontinuance of the monetary unit of a nation the value of which was previously defined in terms of a precious metal. The STANDARD MONEY made of that metal is then said to be demonetized, but it may continue to circulate as FIDUCIARY MONEY. **3.** Reduction in bank holdings of government bonds and other securities which, when purchased by commercial banks, serve to increase the value of DEPOSIT CURRENCY and of paper currency such as federal reserve notes.

demurrage. A charge made by a transportation company for holding freight cars or lighters beyond a stipulated period while being unloaded.

denominational value. The face value of coins, paper money, and securities of various kinds. See VALUE.

Department of Agriculture. One of the more important administrative units of the federal government with a secretary of cabinet rank, created February 9, 1889. Traditionally, its prime objective has been the conduct of educational and research activities of immediate benefit to the farm community. In recent decades, however, the department has acquired additional responsibilities of a regulatory and enforcement nature. It now has direct or indirect responsibility for the administration of many federal agricultural-aid programs, among them programs for the stabilization and extension of agricultural markets, the extension of various forms of credit to the agricultural community, the administration of agricultural price-support policies, the promotion of land-resource conservation, and of other programs to assist farmer and rancher. Some of the principal subsidiary units are AGRICULTURAL RESEARCH SERVICE, Agricultural Stabilization and Conservation Service, COMMODITY CREDIT CORPORATION, SOIL CONSERVATION SERVICE, FARMERS HOME ADMINISTRATION, and Forest Service.

Department of Commerce. A major administrative unit of the federal government, with a secretary of cabinet rank, which received its present title in 1913 when activities affecting the interests of labor were taken from it and set up within a separate DEPARTMENT OF LABOR (*q.v.*). It exerts jurisdiction over the census, patents, the Environmental Science Services Administration (Weather Bureau, Coast and Geodetic Survey, National Environmental Satellite Center, etc.), the Bureau of Standards, the Maritime Administration, and various other units having to do with the promotion of foreign and domestic commerce, development, and the promotion of tourism.

Department of Defense. A federal administrative department with a secretary of cabinet rank, set up in 1949 in succession to the National Military Establishment. It coordinates, but does not merge, the non-cabinet departments of the Army, Navy, and Air Force. Because of its direction of the armed forces and procurement for them, its responsibility for recruiting and training armed forces personnel, its intelligence activities, its support of weapons research and development, and its activities relating to national security and military strategy, it is often responsible for the expenditure of more than half of the national budget. Hence it exerts a profound influence on national business and general economic conditions.

Department of Health, Education, and Welfare. A federal department, with a secretary of cabinet rank, created in 1953, which has brought together under one administrative roof a variety of educational, social security, medical research, and public health activities. Together these require an annual expenditure that probably exceeds that of any other civilian administrative department. Its major units are the Social Security Administration, the Rehabilitation Services Administration, the Office of Education, the Public Health Service with its National Institutes of Health, and the Food and Drug Administration.

Department of Housing and Urban Development. A federal department created in 1965, with a secretary of cabinet rank, which has taken over responsibility for various governmental housing programs, including those of the FEDERAL HOUSING ADMINISTRATION and the FEDERAL NATIONAL MORTGAGE ASSOCIATION. In addition, it has initiated various programs for regional, metropolitan, and urban development.

Department of Justice. A major administrative unit of the federal government, created June 22, 1870, the head of which, the attorney general, has cabinet rank. The department has certain supervisory powers over federal prosecuting agencies and provides representation in courts in cases in which the federal government is a party. It has an ANTITRUST DIVISION which prepares and tries antitrust and similar cases and determines upon appeals in such cases and a Civil Rights Division, established in 1957, to enforce federal election laws and to enforce the rights of citizens guaranteed by the Constitution or federal statute. It also supervises the Immigration and Naturalization Service.

Department of Labor. A major administrative unit of the federal government, with a secretary of cabinet rank, created by Congress March 4, 1913, by dividing the erstwhile Department of Commerce and Labor into two separate departments. Among its more important subsidiary units are the WOMEN'S BUREAU and the BUREAUS OF LABOR STATISTICS, EMPLOYEES' COMPENSATION, EMPLOYMENT SECURITY, and LABOR STANDARDS.

Department of State. The first administrative department of the federal government, created in 1789. Its head enjoys the status of senior member of the President's cabinet. Although it has some domestic responsibilities, its primary functions are those of advising the President on foreign policy, supervising the nation's diplomatic and consular establishments, and administering the nation's many and complex activities affecting other nations, including many aspects of American citizens' contacts with foreign states, especially trade, cultural, and business contacts. The department's economic activities are numerous and varied. They embrace foreign aid, development programs in other states, foreign communications, economic policy relating to other nations and international organizations, and policies and programs relating to international trade and investment, grants, and technological assistance.

Department of the Interior. A major administrative unit with a secretary of cabinet rank, created March 3, 1849. Among the more important of its somewhat miscellaneous subsidiary units are the UNITED STATES FISH AND WILDLIFE SERVICE, the Bureau of Mines, the BUREAU OF RECLAMATION, the National Park Service, the BUREAU OF LAND MANAGEMENT, and the BONNEVILLE POWER ADMINISTRATION.

Department of the Treasury. The second of the principal executive departments to be created in the federal government, on Sept. 2, 1789. With the possible exception of guarding the person of the President through its Secret Service, seemingly exceptional duties of this department, such as the regulation of the narcotics traffic, registering and licensing ships in domestic and foreign commerce, administering export controls, preventing counterfeiting, and investigating theft of federal property, are all directly or indirectly related to its principal functions. These include the imposition and collection of taxes and customs duties; enforcement of revenue and fiscal legislation; the receipt, custody and disbursement of federal funds and the maintenance of appropriate accounting procedures; management of the public debt; and the coining and printing of money. In addition, Treasury officials make recommendations on tax, borrowing, monetary, and other fiscal policies, as such matters may relate to general economic conditions and the needs of the government, and on international currency and exchange problems, particularly on problems of international monetary equilibrium and on national balance-of-payments problems. Some of the department's more important administrative units or officials are: Bureaus of Customs, of the Mint, and of the Public Debt; Comptroller of the Currency; Fiscal Service; Internal Revenue Service; and Treasurer of the United States.

Department of Transportation. One of the more recently created (1966) executive departments of cabinet rank in the federal government. It is responsible for developing a coordinated national transportation policy embracing all media except waterborne transport (although the Coast Guard is under the department in time of peace). To that end the Federal Aviation Administration, the Bureau of Public Roads, and many other relevant existing agencies or activities were transferred to the newly created department. It is also responsible for enforcing transportation safety measures and for improving standards of safety and comfort for those using the nation's highways and air and rail facilities. Supervision of the enforcement of safety regulations, many of which were formerly confided to other agencies, and departments and of newer regulations concerned especially with standards of safety and comfort in automotive vehicles and highway construction programs, rests chiefly with the National Transportation Safety Board, one of the department's principal units.

depletion allowance. A deduction from taxable income derived from a WASTING ASSET. The Internal Revenue Code of the United States permits the calculation of depletion allowances either on the basis of a percentage of the gross income from the property in question, or on a per-unit-of-product basis. Depletion differs from DEPRECIATION in that the asset subject to depletion cannot be replaced. Thus a mine or an oil field cannot be replaced in the sense that a factory or a machine can.

depositary. 1. The recipient of deposits of money, or other property, as a bank. **2.** A DEPOSITORY (*q.v.*).

deposit bank. A bank chartered by a state of the United States in which federal funds were deposited following withdrawal of such funds from the second BANK OF THE UNITED STATES. See WILDCAT BANKING ERA.

deposit currency. A bank loan placed to the credit of a customer's deposit account in lieu of cash, also called DERIVATIVE DEPOSIT and *check currency*. Prudence dictates that an individual bank limit the amount of its deposit currency not to exceed its EXCESS RESERVES (*q.v.*) since the funds borrowed may be promptly withdrawn. The banking system as a whole, however, may expand its total deposit currency by a multiple of its total reserves because deposit currency withdrawn from one bank eventually becomes a PRIMARY DEPOSIT (*q.v.*) in some other bank. This primary deposit increases the second bank's excess reserves which may, in turn, be used to create more deposit currency. If the demand for bank loans is sufficient, this process may be repeated throughout the banking system until there are no more primary deposits to support additional deposit currency. At that point the total deposit currency in the banking system is in excess of its total BANK RESERVES (*q.v.*) by an amount depending upon the RESERVE RATIO (*q.v.*). See CURRENCY. See also DEBT MONETIZATION, NET FREE RESERVES, NET BORROWED RESERVES. Example:

	Original primary deposits in checking account	Deposit currency created (bank loans)	Bank reserves (Assumed deposit ratio 20%)
1st Bank	$100.00	$80.00	$20.00
2nd Bank	80.00	64.00	16.00
3rd Bank	64.00	51.20	12.80
4th Bank	51.20	40.96	10.24
Other banks	204.80	163.84	40.96
Total		$400.00	$100.00

deposit insurance. 1. Public insurance of individual deposits up to $15,000 in member banks of the Federal Reserve System, and in most approved non-member state banks, by the FEDERAL DEPOSIT INSURANCE CORPORATION; and in federal savings and loan associations, as well as in such state-chartered savings and loan associations as apply for insurance and are approved, by the FEDERAL SAVINGS AND LOAN INSURANCE CORPORATION. **2.** Protection against loss of public funds deposited in a commercial bank by special collateral hypothecated by the bank. See INSURANCE.

depository. A place for holding and safeguarding property, such as a safe-deposit vault or warehouse.

deposit slip. A printed form supplied by banks to their depositors and filled in by them when making deposits. The form provides spaces for recording the amount of bills (paper money), specie, and the amount of each check.

depreciation. In accounting, calculation, by one of various standardized methods, of the decline in value of an asset.

depression. A fairly lengthy period of low business activity when prices are low, purchasing power is sharply curtailed, and unemployment is high.

derivative deposit. A bank deposit created by a loan. So called because the deposit is derived from the credit operations of the bank rather than from a deposit by a customer. See BANK DEPOSIT. See also DEPOSIT CURRENCY.

derived demand. The demand for a commodity which grows out of the desire to satisfy the demand for some other commodity. The demand for a house, for example, may create a demand for lumber, bricks, and many other things needed to build the house. See DEMAND.

descriptive economics. Economic studies which explain and describe existing economic phenomena without necessarily attempting to make logical deductions as to their cause and effect. See ECONOMICS.

descriptive labeling. See GRADE LABELING.

destructive competition. Competition that forces prices to so low a level that satisfactory service or commodities cannot be offered the public, and sufficient revenue cannot be realized by the competitors properly to maintain their properties. Destructive competition is likely to develop when there are only a few competitors, when their fixed expenses are high compared with their variable expenses, and when a slight reduction in the selling price will attract a large volume of business. Such conditions exist frequently in local public-service companies and often lead to a NATURAL MONOPOLY (*q.v.*). See COMPETITION.

devaluation. 1. As applied to a monetary unit, a reduction in its metallic content as determined by law. In 1934, for example, the gold content of the United States dollar was reduced from 25.8 to $15\frac{5}{21}$ grains $\frac{9}{10}$ fine. **2.** The lowering of the value of one nation's currency in terms of the currencies of other nations. Such values or exchange rates are often determined arbitrarily irrespective of whatever actual values exist, and may, therefore, be changed at will.

development. **1.** Planned expansion and modernization of a nation's economy, especially the planned creation of the technical aspects of an industrial economy. See UNDERDEVELOPED AREA. **2.** The procedure of advancing an invention or a new design to the point of making it a commercially marketable product or process.

devise. A gift of real property provided for in a will.

diagonal expansion. Expansion of a business enterprise by developing new products which can be manufactured by using the equipment already employed in manufacturing its product or which contain much the same raw materials as the established product. The discovery of by-products is frequently the cause of diagonal expansion.

differential duty. A customs duty imposed at different rates upon identical commodities according to the source of those commodities or according to some other factor unrelated to the nature of the commodities themselves. Sometimes called *discriminating duty* or *preferential duty.* See CUSTOMS DUTY.

diffusion theory of taxation. The theory that the burden of any kind of tax is ultimately distributed throughout the population by means of price changes or by some other method of passing a tax, in whole or in part, on to other persons, by the person who actually pays it to the government.

digital computer. An electronic device capable of processing discrete or discontinuous data such as a sequence of arithmetical or logical operations, the processing usually being accomplished by the automatic conversion of decimal notation to some form of BINARY NOTATION. Unlike a desk calculator, which is operated manually, each step being in accord with the sequence of a problem, a digital computer can perform a sequence of operations automatically, relying on data and instructions which have been stored in it. See COMPUTER, PROGRAM.

Dillon Round. Agreements reached at Geneva, Switzerland, on January 16, 1962, for a series of reciprocal tariff reductions involving particularly the United States and EUROPEAN FREE TRADE ASSOCIATION and EUROPEAN ECONOMIC COMMUNITY states. Despite the EEC's increasing self-sufficiency in agricultural production, the agreements guaranteed continuation of duty-free American agricultural imports at about two-thirds of the then existing level. So-called because Douglas Dillon, at the time U.S. Secretary of the Treasury, headed the American delegation, See KENNEDY ROUND.

diminishing productivity. See DIMINISHING RETURNS.

diminishing returns. The condition which exists when, in successively applying equal amounts of one or two factors of production (land, labor, or capital) to the remaining factor or factors, an added application yields a lesser increase in production than the application just preceding. Also called *decreasing returns.* The condition may be illustrated by the following table.

Land and Capital Constant

Labor (Number of Men)	Total Production (Bushels)	Production Increase (Bushels)
1	10	10
2	21	11
3	32	11

Point of Diminishing Returns

4	42	10
5	51	9
6	59	8

Sometimes the term is restricted to cases where land is the constant factor. The term *diminishing productivity* is then used to describe cases where capital or labor is the constant factor. In any case there is some ideal relationship among the factors of production that will produce optimum returns. See also PROPORTIONALITY, LAW OF.

diminishing utility, law of. See MARGINAL UTILITY.

Dingley Tariff. The United States Tariff Act of 1897. It increased protective rates, removed raw sugar from the FREE LIST, and reincorporated the RECIPROCITY PRINCIPLE.

direct cost. See VARIABLE COST.

directed economy. See CONTROLLED ECONOMY.

direct financing. Raising capital without resort to UNDERWRITING (*q.v.*). Customary means used are selling capital stock or evidence of indebtedness to customers, employees, and existing stockholders, or reinvesting profits.

director. As applied to business corporations, a person elected to serve on the managerial board, called the *board of directors,* of a corporation. The laws of some states require a director to hold capital stock in the corporation. See (5).

director of internal revenue. The official in charge of one of the district offices of the Internal Revenue Service of the United States Treasury Department. To facilitate the collection of internal revenue, there are more than 60 district offices in the United States.

direct production. The satisfaction of a human want without the intervention of capital goods of any kind. The construction of shelter from stones, snow, or the boughs of trees without the use of tools is direct production. The term is used in contradistinction to INDIRECT, *roundabout,* or *capitalistic* production. See PRODUCTION.

direct reduction mortgage. A mortgage that is completely liquidated by a series of equal monthly payments for interest and amortization charges during its term. This type of mortgage came into common use during the 1930's. See MORTGAGE.

direct strike. A strike by employees against their own employer because of allegedly unsatisfactory wage scales or other grievances. See STRIKE.

direct tax. A tax, the burden of which cannot be easily shifted or passed on to some other person by the person on whom it is levied. The term is used in contradistinction to INDIRECT TAX. It is usually very difficult to determine when a tax is direct. A tax on a mortgage, for example, may seem to be a direct tax but might conceivably be shifted to the borrower in the form of a higher interest rate. Personal income, inheritance, and poll taxes are fair examples of direct taxes. See TAX.

disability benefits. Payments made to assist those who have become partly or totally incapacitated as a result of accident or illness or other cause. Most states of the United States have long had WORKMEN'S COMPENSATION LAWS. Under the federal government's social-security legislation, states with an appropriate plan may receive federal assistance in making "public assistance payments" to incapacitated persons. Such assistance may be extended to needy disabled persons 18 years of age or over on the same basis that aid is extended to the needy aged, to the blind, and to needy and dependent children. Some private companies have agreed in labor contracts to provide disability benefits for their employees.

disagio. A charge made for exchanging a currency for a depreciated foreign currency.

disaster relief program. Any of several programs under which the federal government of the United States may respond to appeals for emergency, economic, financial, or other aid from areas which have been stricken by flood, drought, fire, or other natural disasters.

discount. 1. A deduction made from a debt or charge, such as an amount deducted from a bill for prompt payment. **2.** The amount deducted from the face value of a promissory note or similar commercial paper for cashing it prior to the date of maturity. **3.** The difference between the face value of a bond and the market price when the face value is the higher.

discount house. See COMMERCIAL CREDIT COMPANY.

discounting the news. An explanation frequently given for an advance or decline in security prices preceding good or bad news. Presumably a sufficient number of traders anticipate the news and make decisions which are reflected on the security markets before the news becomes generally public.

discount loan. See INSTALLMENT INTEREST.

discount market. An indefinitely defined financial center where individuals, banks, and financial institutions of various kinds buy and sell commercial and financial paper. For example, a time DRAFT (*q.v.*), accepted by a bank, is considered a prime bill for funds seeking short-term employment and hence can be converted into cash immediately at a discount from its face value when offered in the discount market. See MARKET.

discount rate. The percentage of discount charged by banks and similar institutions for purchasing loans or commercial paper in advance of the date of maturity and providing the owner with the net proceeds (face value less the discount charge). See RATE.

discount store. A cut-rate store; one which maintains a consistent policy of underselling its competitors.

discriminating duty. See DIFFERENTIAL DUTY.

discrimination. 1. Unequal treatment of persons by other persons, especially as respects access to educational facilities, places of public amusement and accommodation, employment opportunities, and the like. **2.** Arbitrary or unreasonable classification of persons by government contrary to prevailing constitutional guarantees such as those of due process or equal protection under the law.

discriminatory taxation. 1. Taxation designed to favor certain industries. Excise taxes on margarine, for example, have been used to protect dairy interests. Likewise, special taxes on corporations, chartered outside a state in which they are doing business, have benefited local industry, and special taxes on CHAIN STORES have benefited independent merchants. **2.** Any exemption or allowance in a tax system which appears to have little or no justification in equity or public policy and hence is held to favor the beneficiary unjustly at the expense of other taxpayers. **3.** Taxes which are regressive, that is, impose a relatively heavier burden upon persons of low income than upon persons of high income.

disguised unemployment. 1. The condition said to exist in a densely populated country with a nonmonetary, agrarian economy when, with no change in production techniques, a material reduction in the agricultural working force would cause no reduction in the total volume of farm output. Although no one is idle, large numbers are engaged in tasks that could be equally well performed by fewer workers. Technically expressed, the MARGINAL PRODUCTIVITY (*q.v.*) of labor is zero. **2.** Generally, any condition in an industry or government department where more individuals are placed on the payroll than are actually required or can be profitably or efficiently employed. See UNEMPLOYMENT.

dishoarding. Taking something out of storage and putting it to use; for example, taking money from a safe-deposit box and investing it. The term is often applied to the act of reducing a stock of goods that was intended, when accumulated, to exceed normal future needs.

disinflation. A term recently coined to indicate a planned reduction in the general PRICE LEVEL, so administered that the economy is benefited by increased purchasing power and not harmed by drastic DEFLATION.

disintermediation. A sudden and pronounced shift of savings from federal SAVINGS AND LOAN ASSOCIATIONS and MUTUAL

SAVINGS BANKS—which are considered as intermediary institutions between savers and borrowers—into higher yielding short-term (especially government) securities.

disinvestment. A diminution of CAPITAL GOODS. The term is used to designate either an absolute diminution in the total supply of capital goods such as occurs when producers fail to renew worn-out items or when INVENTORIES are reduced, or a diminution in a particular stock of capital goods caused, for example, by the sale of a capital item. It is sometimes called *negative investment.*

dismal science. A term of derision applied to political economy by Thomas Carlyle.

dismissal wage. A sum of money paid to an employee who is dismissed from employment. The payment may be made in one lump sum or at intervals over a period of time. Also called *severance wage* and *terminal wage.* See WAGE.

disposable personal income. The income remaining to persons after deduction of personal taxes and all other payments to governments—the total of all individual savings and consumption expenditures. See INCOME.

dissaving. Expenditure in excess of income.

distribution. 1. The apportionment of the total income of society among the factors of production. As thus defined, distribution is one of the main topics customarily included in the study of ECONOMICS. Among the subjects included under "distribution" are INTEREST, PROFIT, RENT, and WAGES. Sometimes called *functional distribution.* **2.** The apportionment of the total income of a society among individuals. Sometimes called *personal distribution.* **3.** The diffusion of commodities through the ordinary channels of trade. Also called *physical distribution.* See (12).

disutility. The ability of a good to cause discomfiture or pain. For example, while one increment of a commodity, such as water, may save a life, and successive increments may satisfy wants ranging in intensity from the more to the less essential, a time arrives when an added increment is not wanted, and after such a point has been reached, further increments may cause distress or disutility.

diversification. 1. As applied to the purchase of securities, the investment of a capital sum in various kinds of securities, in different localities, and in different industries, in order to minimize risk. **2.** As applied to industry and trade, the manufacture or marketing of unrelated products.

dividend. A payment to the stockholders of a corporation from earnings. See (21).

dividend payment ratio. The per cent of earnings paid in preferred and common stock dividends during a specified length of time. See RATIO.

divisional bond. See BOND.

division of labor. A plan of production whereby each of several workers or groups of workers, in succession, performs only one or a very limited number of operations on a product until it is finally completed, a common feature of contemporary mass production procedure. See LABOR.

documentary bill. See BILL.

dole. Relief in cash or IN KIND given by a government body to unemployed workers or to families in needy circumstances.

dollar deficit. See DOLLAR GAP.

dollar exchange. A bill of exchange drawn abroad and payable within the United States in dollars; or one drawn within the United States in dollars and paid abroad in currency of equal value.

dollar gap. In any given period, the amount by which imports from the United States into any foreign area, and other dollar debits in such area, exceed that area's exports to the United States and other dollar credits. Also called *dollar deficit.*

domestic bill See BILL.

domestic exchange. Negotiable instruments such as checks or drafts used to settle debts within a country. See EXCHANGE.

domestic industry. See HOUSEHOLD SYSTEM.

domestic system. An economy prevalent in the 16th and 17th centuries in which merchants supplied materials and sometimes tools and machines to workers who produced goods at home and turned the finished products over to the merchants. Also called *home industry. See* ECONOMIC SYSTEM.

donated stock See CAPITAL STOCK.

double budget. A popular term for any plan to segregate capital and nonrecurring items in a budget from recurring items of income and expense. See BUDGET.

double entry. A system of BOOKKEEPING which provides two entries, a debit and a credit, for each transaction. Debit entries record increases of assets or of expenses or reductions of liabilities or of income; credit entries record increases of liabilities or of income or reduction of assets or of expenses. In double-entry bookkeeping the sum of the debits must always equal the sum of the credits.

double liability. The liability assumed by a stockholder of a corporation when the stock that he owns may be assessed up to an amount equal to its face value to pay the debts of the corporation. Once especially characteristic of bank stock in the United States. See LIABILITY.

double standard. See BIMETALLISM.

double taxation. The levy and collection, within one fiscal period, of two taxes both of which are calculated on the same tax base. Double taxation may occur because two competing tax jurisdictions assess the same tax base, or because the same tax jurisdiction assesses the same tax base twice. In the United States the first condition exists when both federal and state taxes are imposed upon estates and inheritances or upon incomes. The second condition may be said to exist when federal income taxes are levied upon corporation profits, once when earned by the corporation in question, and again when received by the stockholders in the form of dividends. The result of such double taxation is the same as though one tax were imposed equal in amount to the two that are imposed. A levy on the same tax base by state and federal governments, though double taxation in fact, is not so recognized in legal theory because the taxing authorities are constitutionally separate and independent entities. The term is often used to indicate an alleged injustice as, for example, when a person living in one state owns property in another and is compelled to pay taxes on the property to both states, one of them claiming jurisdiction over the property because of the property's situation, the other because of the residence of the owner of the property. Such situations, which create double taxation within the United States, may also exist internationally and result in *international double taxation* by the action of two or more sovereign states.

Dow-Jones averages. The arithmetic mean or average of closing prices of 30 representative industrial stocks, 15 public utility stocks, and 20 railroad stocks, and a composite average of all 65 computed at the end of each trading day on the New York

Stock Exchange; also, similar averages for 6 groups of bonds. Adjustments are made for stock splits, distribution of rights, and other such changes by equating the theoretical average price of the stocks after a change with their average before a change. The equating is effected by dividing the total theoretical price after a change by the average price before a change and using the resulting quotient as a divisor to compute the average theoretical price after the change. Example:

Prices before change			Theoretical prices after stock C split of 3 to 1	
Stock	Prices		Stock	Price
A	$ 5.00		A	$ 5.00
B	10.00		B	10.00
C	15.00		C	5.00
Total	$30.00		Total	$20.00

$$\text{Average} \quad \frac{\$30.00}{3} = \$10.00$$

$$\frac{\text{Total price after change}}{\text{Average price before change}} \quad \frac{\$20.00}{\$10.00} = 2, \text{ New divisor}$$

$$\frac{\text{Total after change}}{\text{New divisor}} \quad \frac{\$20.00}{2} = 10 \text{ Adjusted theoretical average after change which equals the average before change.}$$

down period. A period in which a factory is shut down for repairs and maintenance.

downtown. A term used to designate, rather indefinitely, the relatively old main business district of any sizable town or city. Originally used only when referring to a generally recognized business center in a specific town or city, the term has become generalized, particularly when differentiating older business centers from new SHOPPING MALLS located on the outskirts of the more populous areas.

Dow theory. The conception that, besides daily fluctuations, the prices of securities, traded in the stock exchange, follow a certain pattern indicated by a primary trend and a secondary reaction or reactions within a primary trend. The theory holds that the behavior of the primary trend indicates changes in its direction. See DOW-JONES AVERAGES.

draft. A written order for a definite sum of money, originating with a creditor and naming a debtor, customarily forwarded to a bank for collection. Upon receipt of a draft, the bank presents it to the debtor for payment. If paid the original document is retained by the debtor as a receipt. *Sight drafts* are payable at once. *Time drafts* are payable at some future time specified on the document.

drawback. A refund made for duties or internal taxes collected on imported goods which, not being intended for domestic consumption, are reshipped to other nations.

drayage. A charge made for carting goods from one place to another.

drummer. A salesman, usually one who solicits trade for a merchant by showing samples; so called because he "drums up" trade.

dry farming. In general, all phases of land use under semiarid conditions. Water is brought to the semiarid regions by irrigation, and various methods of conserving moisture are used. For example, the moisture may be allowed to accumulate one season for the use during the following one. Thus, a crop is produced every other season.

dual pay system. A method of computing the wages of employees in transportation companies by the mile and also by the hour, the employee being entitled to receive wages according to whichever calculation yields him the greater sum.

dual purpose (or leverage) fund. See SPLIT INVESTMENT COMPANY.

dummy directors. See DUMMY INCORPORATORS.

dummy incorporators. Usually at least three persons who, in the course of the formation of a new corporation, act temporarily as the incorporators and directors, later resigning and assigning their interest to the real owners. Also known as *dummy directors*. The practice is one of convenience to the real owners as it relieves them of the necessity of attending personally to all the details necessary to the formation of a new corporation.

dumping. 1. In general, selling a product at a low price in order to dispose of inventories or to gain an advantageous market position. In international trade the practice may be pursued by a MONOPOLY or near monopoly when a large volume of production materially lessens the unit cost of the product, and when, because of the large production, the price of the product would be materially reduced if sold entirely in the domestic market. By restricting the supply offered in the home market and thus gaining the maximum price on that part of the supply, the producer may sell the balance of the supply abroad at a lesser price and still gain larger gross sales and conceivably more profits than he would gain if the entire supply were sold at home. **2.** Specifically, in the United States, selling imported goods at prices less than the cost of production.

duopoly. The condition that exists when only two producers offer identical or nearly identical products. Although there is some element of COMPETITION in the fact that neither producer controls the entire supply, and the action of one producer can materially influence the other's price, the resulting situation approximates a MONOPOLY and is sometimes called a *partial monopoly.* An OLIGOPOLY results in a similar situation although it is less monopolistic. See MONOPOLISTIC COMPETITION.

duopsony. The condition that exists when there are only two buyers for identical or nearly identical products offered by numerous producers. See also MONOPOLISTIC COMPETITION.

Duplex Printing Co.* v. *Deering. A case, 254 U.S. 443 (1921), in which the Supreme Court implied that provisions of the Clayton Antitrust Act which purported to remove labor activities from the operation of the Sherman Antitrust Act were largely illusory. The court held that the Clayton Act merely restated existing law on the subject; that it was merely "declaratory of the law as it stood before."

Dutch auction. An auction in which the seller offers goods at a relatively high initial price and then successively lowers his prices until the goods are sold.

duty. A tax imposed on the importation, exportation, or consumption of goods. In the United States the term has come to mean a CUSTOMS DUTY.

dynamic economics. See GENERAL EQUILIBRIUM.

E

eagle. As applied to money, a United States $10 gold coin, first placed in circulation in 1794. None was coined between 1805 and 1837. In 1933 all gold coins were required to be surrendered to the United States Treasury in return for other forms of money. The $20 gold coin was called a double eagle, the $5 gold coin a half eagle, and the $2.50 gold coin a quarter eagle.

early vesting. See INSTANT VESTING.

earmarked gold. Gold owned by the central bank of one country and stored in the central bank of another country. Such gold is not considered a part of the monetary reserve of the country where it is stored but is held subject to ultimate disposition by the owning central bank.

earned income. Income which is received in return for services rendered or as the result of trading or some other similar business transaction. The term is used in contradistinction to UNEARNED INCOME. See INCOME.

earned surplus. Profits of an enterprise that remain undistributed and which have been gained through the regular operations of the enterprise in question. See SURPLUS.

earning-capacity standard. As applied to the valuation of a business enterprise, the fixing of its value by finding a principal sum which, at an assumed rate of interest, will yield an amount equivalent to the earnings of the enterprise. Virtually identical with CAPITALIZED-VALUE STANDARD. See VALUATION.

earnings. See PROFIT.

easement. Any one of a number of rights which may be possessed by one person in the real property of another.

Eastern States Retail Lumber Assn.* v. *United States. A case, 234 U.S. 600 (1914), in which the Supreme Court, relying on its ruling in the DANBURY HATTERS' CASE (*q.v.*), declared that a black list of certain wholesalers, circulated among retailers to persuade them not to deal with the black-listed wholesalers, was a conspiracy in restraint of interstate commerce and thus came within the interdiction of the SHERMAN ANTITRUST ACT.

ecclesiastical corporation. A corporation created for religious purposes, the members of which are usually churchmen or ecclesiastical persons. See CORPORATION.

econometrics. A subdiscipline which utilizes mathematical techniques in testing and applying economic theories. See ECONOMICS.

economic. Pertaining to any action or process which has to do with the creation of goods and services designed to satisfy human wants. More specifically, the term is used to characterize the relative efficiency of a process of production, of an administrative organization, or of the application of science and technology to satisfy man's material wants. See (12).

economic abundance. The condition that exists when the price structure and general purchasing power are such as to keep the productive facilities of an economy operating at capacity. Occasionally the term is used to describe a hypothetical condition when all wants are satisfied. See ECONOMIC.

Economic and Social Council. An agency of the United Nations which deals with economic, humanitarian, educational, and related functions entrusted to the United Nations, and which coordinates the activities of various specialized agencies such as the INTERNATIONAL LABOR ORGANIZATION and similar bodies. See also UNITED NATIONS.

Economic Commission for Africa. See REGIONAL ECONOMIC COMMISSIONS OF THE UNITED NATIONS.

Economic Commission for Asia and the Far East. See REGIONAL ECONOMIC COMMISSIONS OF THE UNITED NATIONS.

Economic Commission for Europe. See REGIONAL ECONOMIC COMMISSIONS OF THE UNITED NATIONS.

Economic Commission for Latin America. See REGIONAL ECONOMIC COMMISSIONS OF THE UNITED NATIONS.

Economic Cooperation Administration. See EUROPEAN RECOVERY PROGRAM.

economic democracy. 1. A society which seeks to maximize economic opportunity for all who seek to employ their talents gainfully and to guarantee at least a minimum income—one above an officially defined poverty level—to all individuals or families. **2.** The transfer of ownership and management of productive enterprise to the workers or their duly elected representatives. See ECONOMIC.

economic determinism. 1. The idea that social evolution is the result of economic forces. **2.** Defined more narrowly, especially in accordance with Marxian theory, the term suggests that the entire cultural, moral, and legal patterns of social organizations and their value systems are determined by the system of control exerted over the wealth-producing resources of that society. See ECONOMIC.

economic equality. The goal of a society which seeks to overcome extremes of wealth and poverty and achieve equality of economic opportunity for the great mass of its citizens. See ECONOMIC.

economic friction. The condition that obtains when obstacles of a social or psychological nature prevent the normal operation of economic forces. Custom, prejudice, likes, and dislikes are examples of such obstacles. See ECONOMIC.

economic good. Anything external to man that is inherently useful, appropriable, and relatively scarce. The term is used in contradistinction to FREE GOOD. Economic goods may be either material or immaterial. Thus, the services of a teacher or lawyer are considered economic goods quite as logically as the books that they use. As thus defined the term is more comprehensive than the term WEALTH, the latter, as defined in this dictionary, being restricted to material economic goods. See GOOD. See also ECONOMIC.

economic growth rate. The rate—a percentage of change in the real gross national product—by which the country's total production of goods and services increases (or declines) annually. In the United States the rate is based on the Department of

Commerce estimates formulated in 1958 dollars. See ECONOM-IC. See also RATE.

economic harmonies. The forces that are alleged to contribute to the welfare of society as a whole when each individual pursues his own self-interest. According to Adam Smith such forces were supernatural. Thus, he says that man is "led by an invisible hand to promote an end (the good of society) which was no part of his intention." See ECONOMIC.

economic history. A systematic literary reconstruction of events and forces that have molded the evolution of an economic institution in order to provide a better understanding of that institution's background and, if the institution has survived, of its current goals. See ECONOMIC.

economic imperialism. The extension of the sovereignty or influence of a nation over foreign territory and peoples for the purpose of obtaining raw materials, creating markets for finished products, or seeking profitable investment opportunities. See ECONOMIC.

economic independence. See ECONOMIC SELF-SUFFICIENCY.

economic interpretation of history. History written from the point of view that economic conditions and events and especially the economic motivations of individuals and organizations exert a predominant influence in shaping mankind's institutions and civilizations. See ECONOMIC. See also ECONOMIC DETERMINISM.

economic law. A generalization expressing a constant relationship among particular economic phenomena. Because of the complexity of such phenomena and the impossibility of isolating the effects of any one economic force from the effects of multitudinous other such forces operating in society, economic laws are either very general in scope as, for example, the LAW OF SUPPLY AND DEMAND or GRESHAM'S LAW; or they are generalizations expressing varying degrees of probability. The term is often misused, being applied to some popular nostrum or unproved assertion or to some generalization to which there are many obvious exceptions. See ECONOMIC.

economic liberalism. See CLASSICAL SCHOOL.

economic man. A hypothetical man moved only by economic motives. This was a concept created by the English economists of the Classical school and subject to criticism because of the broad generalizations based upon this restricted premise. The German Historical or Realist school of economic thought particularly opposed the concept as devoid of any practical application. See ECONOMIC.

economic mobilization. Any effort to focus the productive energies of a nation upon some major objective such as national defense or the successful prosecution of a war. The effort may be voluntary in some respects. Normally, however, the government must intervene with legislation affecting production, credit, prices, employment, etc. See ECONOMIC.

economic nationalism. See SELF-SUFFICIENT NATION.

Economic Opportunity Act. An act known as the Anti-Poverty Act, passed in 1964, which authorizes ten separate programs to assist the poor and coordinates their administration under the OFFICE OF ECONOMIC OPPORTUNITY (*q.v.*). The broad aim is to combat illiteracy, unemployment, and the conditions that lead to chronic poverty. Funds appropriated to secure the purposes of this measure finance the Job Corps (which offers the poor training and experience in various callings) and also various other programs, in both urban and rural areas, to ameliorate the condition of the poor.

economic planning. Any attempt to exercise forethought with reference to an economic operation and to anticipate the scope, character, and results of such an operation. Currently the phrase signifies governmental direction of economic activity. It may imply determination by some supreme governmental authority of both the kind and quantity of economic goods to be produced in a nation. It may also be used to indicate some measure of foresight and action exercised by the government in a capitalistic society particularly to offset disastrous depressions. The construction of public works to provide employment, the reduction of taxation to increase private purchasing power, or the use of the public debt to influence credit are examples of such limited *planning*. See ECONOMIC.

economic rent. A theoretical amount paid for the use of land, representing the difference in the productivity of one plot of land and the productivity of the poorest land similarly situated and used for the same purpose, the assumption being that equal increments of capital and labor have been expended on each. Thus, if the poorest land can produce 25 bu. of grain per acre, and a better piece of land can produce 50 bu., the economic rent for the better land, in terms of money, is 25 times the market price of the grain per bushel. "Productivity" may also be expressed in different degrees of fertility, in varying distances to market, or, particularly in the case of urban land, in relative desirability of location, either for business or for living purposes. Also called the *Ricardian theory of rent.* See RENT.

economic royalist. A man of wealth; a member of the plutocracy. President Franklin D. Roosevelt used the term in a disparaging sense in his 1936 acceptance speech in which he identified men of wealth as opposed to his policy of improving the economic status of the rank and file. See ECONOMIC.

economics. That body of knowledge which treats of the creation and appropriation of goods and services for the satisfaction of human wants. Some authorities emphasize the social aspects of such activities by including in the definition of economics the communal problems or social phenomena involved in the process of getting a living. Economics customarily includes the topics CONSUMPTION, DISTRIBUTION, EXCHANGE, and PRODUCTION. See (12).

economic sanctions. In international affairs, coercive efforts of an economic nature, such as economic boycotts, trade restrictions, arms and credit embargoes, etc., to which nations may resort collectively in order to compel another nation or group of nations to observe international obligations; e.g., trade restrictions and embargoes imposed in 1935 upon Italy by the League of Nations because of the Italian invasion of Ethiopia, or similar measures voted against Rhodesia by the UN Security Council, December 16, 1966. See ECONOMIC.

economic scarcity. The condition that exists when purchasing power, available at prevailing prices, is insufficient to keep the existing productive facilities for consumer goods working at capacity. Occasionally the term is used to describe the fact that, in a price economy, goods are necessarily distributed according to ability to pay, there never being enough goods or ability to acquire them to satisfy all wants. See ECONOMIC.

economic self-sufficiency. The production within a particular geographical area of everything that is consumed within that area. The area may be a farm, a community, a nation, or any other limited territory. Complete self-sufficiency is impossible, even for countries of considerable territorial extent and diversified resources, except on the basis of a relatively low LEVEL OF LIVING. Also referred to as *economic independence.* See ECONOMIC.

economic system. The nature of economic life as a whole, proposed or actual, with particular reference to the ownership and use of property and the extent of government regulation and controls. See (11).

economic union. An agreement between two or more nations involving the pursuance of common economic policies in such matters as customs duties, fiscal and monetary regulations, internal taxation, and related subjects. See ECONOMIC.

economic warfare. Economic activities designed to embarrass an enemy in time of war; for example, acquiring control of the supply of essential materials in neutral countries, bringing pressure upon those countries to restrict their trade with the enemy, or blockading the enemy territory to prevent the entrance of essential supplies. See ECONOMIC.

economic wealth. See WEALTH.

economist. A person learned in the science and practice of economics.

Edge Act. An act of Congress, 1919. It amended the FEDERAL RESERVE ACT so as to permit federal incorporation of organizations desiring to engage in international banking operations. Such organizations are sometimes called *Edge banks.*

Edge banks. See EDGE ACT.

educational tariff. A system of tariff duties that protects a new home industry, presumably until that industry is able to compete effectively with imported products. See TARIFF.

effective demand. The desire to buy coupled with the ability to pay. When the word "demand" is used in economic writings, effective demand is usually assumed. See DEMAND.

efficiency engineer. One whose profession it is to study production methods and controls with a view to eliminating waste and establishing more effective procedures.

elastic demand. Demand which increases or decreases in relatively large volume as prices increase or decrease. In general, the demand for luxuries is elastic. See DEMAND.

elastic money. Money the quantity of which can be increased or decreased as general economic conditions may require. In the United States FEDERAL RESERVE NOTES may be regarded as an elastic money. Their issue is related to the volume of REDISCOUNTS. Federal reserve notes are retired when the issuing bank deposits them with the FEDERAL RESERVE AGENT, and when so deposited they cannot be reissued except upon compliance with the conditions of an original issue. See MONEY.

elastic supply. Supply which increases or decreases in relatively large volume with a relatively slight change in price. See SUPPLY.

electronic data processing. The manipulation of information by machines capable of performing various sequences of logical and arithmetical operations through the use of vacuum, gas, or phototubes and other devices governing the behavior of currents of free electrons. See (7).

eleemosynary corporation. A corporation conducting charitable or alms-giving activities exclusively. See CORPORATION.

eligible paper. As applied to sec. 13 of the FEDERAL RESERVE ACT of 1913, PROMISSORY NOTES, BILLS, and other SECURITIES acceptable for REDISCOUNT or for purchase by the FEDERAL RESERVE BANKS.

eligible security. A security in which, under the law, banks, charitable institutions, trustees, etc., may invest funds committed to their care. See SECURITY.

embargo. Any prohibition imposed by a government upon commerce or freight. In 1807, for example, the United States government restricted the carrying of goods, destined for foreign ports, to certain approved ships. The term may also be applied to the refusal of transportation companies to accept or move freight in case of a strike or because of undue traffic congestion.

embezzlement. Appropriation for personal use of property belonging to another. It differs from theft in that the misappropriated property is legally in the custody of the guilty party, whereas in theft its possession is acquired illegally.

eminent domain. The right of a government, apart from its taxing power and police authority, to appropriate private property for the use of the public upon the payment of compensation ascertained according to law.

emolument. Remuneration in the form of a salary, fee, or perquisite of some kind.

Empire preference. A term sometimes applied to a system of tariff preferences and concessions affecting trade between the United Kingdom and the Commonwealth countries and British colonies, and also trade among the Commonwealth countries. The system began in the 19th century with preferential tariffs on United Kingdom imports from some British possessions, and became essentially reciprocal after 1919, and more especially after 1931, when the United Kingdom abandoned free trade. The preference system was extended following the OTTAWA AGREEMENTS (*q.v.*) of 1932.

employers' associations. Various kinds of local, state, and national organizations of employers, designed to promote their joint interests in matters other than those having to do with any particular trade or business. Employers' associations sometimes seek to resist the policies and activities of labor organizations in one way or another. Other associations attempt to further the principle of COLLECTIVE BARGAINING. Some carry on propaganda campaigns by means of advertising, newspaper articles, and even textbooks. Employers' associations should not be confused with TRADE ASSOCIATIONS (*q.v.*).

employers' liability insurance. Insurance covering employers' liability occasioned by industrial accidents to their employees, either under common law rules or WORKMEN'S COMPENSATION LAWS. See INSURANCE.

employers' liability laws. See WORKMEN'S COMPENSATION LAWS.

employment. Gainful engagement in an occupation, business, trade, or profession. For statistical purposes, both regular, long-term employment and casual, temporary employment are included.

Employment Act of 1946. An act of Congress, February 20, 1946, which seeks to maintain high levels of employment and production. To secure these ends, the act directs the President to make an annual report to Congress on the general economic condition of the nation and include in such report his recommendations for remedial legislation. To assist the President in preparing this report and to provide him with expert advice on economic conditions, the act set up a COUNCIL OF ECONOMIC ADVISERS (*q.v.*).

employment agency. Essentially an employment clearing establishment which recruits personnel for an employer or finds jobs for the unemployed. It may be operated for private profit, on a cooperative basis, or as a governmentally organized and financed body.

emporium. A commercial center, place of trade, or store where a variety of merchandise is sold.

enclosures. See AGRICULTURAL REVOLUTION.

end money. A reserve fund set aside for use in the event that the actual costs of a project exceed estimates. The term is used with particular reference to the production of motion picture films.

endogenous change. As applied to economics, an alteration in economic life due to a cause that is in itself essentially economic in character. OVERPRODUCTION owing to lack of PURCHASING POWER is a case in point. See also EXOGENOUS CHANGE.

endorsement. See INDORSEMENT.

endowment fund. A fund the principal of which remains intact, only the income being used. See FUND.

endowment plan of life insurance. A plan according to which a life insurance company agrees to pay a stipulated sum of money upon the death of an insured person or when he reaches a certain age, usually 65 or 70 years, in return for a fixed annual premium for a maximum number of years, usually from 15 to 30 years. See LIFE INSURANCE.

end product. The product that results after a series of changes in form or assembly, and which is then ready for use directly or indirectly to satisfy a human want.

Engel's law. The assertion that the lower the family money-income, the greater the percentage of that income spent for food; and that the percentage of family income spent for food is therefore the best measure for determining levels of living. Engel's law has frequently been interpreted to include other types of expenditure, but there is some question as to the validity of this broader interpretation.

entail. A legally prescribed order of succession applied to inherited lands. The owner of the land at any particular time is not permitted to change the order, or to terminate it by sale or by any other of the usual means of transferring title.

enterprise. In economics, a business undertaking involving risk, especially as to funds ventured, and initiated with the hope of making a profit.

entrepot. A place for the storage of goods in transit, i.e., goods intended for reshipment or re-export.

entrepreneur. A person who, in the course of production, assumes the responsibilities of organization, management, and risk.

entrepreneurship. See MANAGEMENT.

Environmental Science Services Administration. A unit in the U.S. Department of Commerce which brings together the Weather Bureau, the Coast and Geodetic Survey, the National Environmental Satellite Center, the Environmental Data Service, and Institutes for Environmental Research. These divisions provide research, observational, informational, and other services, in such fields as meteorology, cartography, oceanography, electromagnetic properties of the atmosphere, telecommunications, and related matters.

equalization fee. A fee collected from some or all participants in a project, the proceeds then being distributed in such a manner that those who gained the least from the project, or suffered the most, receive a disproportionately large share.

equalization of assessments. The adjustment of locally assessed valuations of real properties over a considerable area, such as a county or a state, with a view to establishing a more equitable division of the total tax burden within the area. See also ASSESSMENT.

equation of exchange. A mathematical expression of the modern version of the QUANTITY THEORY OF MONEY. As formulated by Irving Fisher, the equation is: $P = \dfrac{MV + M'V'}{T}$. P represents the general PRICE LEVEL, or the average price of all goods and services exchanged within a given period of time. M represents the amount of MONEY IN CIRCULATION, and M' the amount of money substitutes, such as CREDIT, in circulation during the same period of time. V represents the velocity of money circulation, and V' the VELOCITY OF CIRCULATION of money substitutes during the period, that is, the number of times that a unit of money or a money substitute changes hands. T represents the volume of trade, or the total number of units sold during the period. This is frequently called the cash-transactions type of equation because involved in the velocity of circulation is the CURRENCY turnover among all individual spenders, and included in the volume of trade are all the units sold even if sold over and over again in the course of their progress toward final CONSUMPTION.

In contrast to the above cash-transactions type of equation, the income-flow type limits V to EXCHANGES of finished products involving both money and money substitutes, and T to units which constitute only final goods and services. M represents both money and money substitutes in use. The income-flow equation thus indicates the income VALUE of money in contrast to the transaction value of money. It may be written:

$P_y = \dfrac{MV_y}{T_y}$, the y distinguishing it from the cash-transactions

type of equation shown above.

Another version of the equation of exchange is the cash-balance type. This is similar to the income-flow type except that there is a different measure for velocity. Velocity is measured by the average length of time that cash balances—both money and money substitutes—are held idle. It may be indicated by K, and expressed as a period of time, usually a fraction of a year. Thus if $K = \frac{1}{12}$, cash balances are being held in sufficient volume to purchase goods and services for $\frac{1}{12}$ of a year, or 1 month. There is a reciprocal relationship between K and the V used in the other two equations. When K is high, V is low because currency is being held idle and not circulated. Conversely, when K is low, V is high because currency is being circulated instead of being held idle. The cash-balance type of equation thus indicates the value of money in terms of the demand for, and the supply of, cash balances. It may be written:

$P_y = \dfrac{M_y}{KT_y}.$

equimarginal principle. See MARGINAL RATE OF SUBSTITUTION.

equipment trust bond. See BOND.

equity. 1. That part of the law of England created in the English Chancery courts between the 12th and 15th centuries; also, a part of the civil law in the United States. **2.** The net investment in a business enterprise; also, by extension, that portion of a mortgaged property or good or service purchased on the installment payment plan which the nominal owner has amortized. **3.** A stock, as distinguished from a bond or other security.

equity capital. Funds which the owners have personally invested in an enterprise, as distinguished from borrowed funds. See CAPITAL.

equity trading. The practice of increasing the earnings of an enterprise by borrowing funds at a rate of interest less than the rate of profit which can be earned by such borrowed funds when applied to the normal operations of the enterprise. A corporation may, for example, be assured of a 6 per cent return on any and all funds invested or applied to its operations. Its existing capital and surplus amount to $100,000 and its total profit would thus be $6,000. But if it can borrow $100,000 at 4 per cent, total profit can be increased by an additional 2 per cent on the amount borrowed, or $2,000.

Erdman Act. An act of Congress, 1898. It provided for the conciliation and arbitration of labor disputes between the railroads and such of their employees as were engaged in the operation of interstate trains. The act also made it a misdemeanor for any employer to require an employee to agree not to become a member of a labor union. This latter provision was declared unconstitutional by the Supreme Court in 1908. See also *ADAIR v. UNITED STATES*.

escalator clause. 1. A clause frequently inserted in leases during a period of public RENT CONTROL, allowing the landlord to raise the rent under certain legally recognized conditions. **2.** Generally, any clause in a contract which permits a change upward in the obligations incurred, in case certain events transpire, for example, a clause in a sales contract permitting a higher price before delivery if there has been a general price rise, or a clause in a labor-management contract which calls for an increase in wages as the cost-of-living index advances or because of some other circumstance.

escape clause. **1.** A provision in a labor contract which allows employees a certain length of time, usually about 15 days, prior to the date when the contract goes into effect, in which to resign from the union if they wish to do so. Otherwise they must remain union members in good standing as a condition of continued employment. **2.** In bilateral or multilateral commercial agreements, a clause permitting a signatory nation to suspend tariff or other concessions if they threaten to produce serious harm for competitive domestic production.

escheat. Transfer of title to property to the state for want of heirs or to public authority for failure, after a protracted period, to identify the owner.

Esch-Cummins Act. An act of Congress, 1920. It provided for the division of the country into railroad rate districts and for the establishment of rates that would make it possible for the railroads, collectively in each district, to earn a fair return. It also provided for the disposition of earnings in excess of a FAIR RETURN and for the valuation of all railroad properties. The act permitted the consolidation of railroads under certain conditions. Also known as the *Transportation Act* of 1920. See also RECAPTURE OF EARNINGS.

escrow. Property placed by one person in the hands of a second person, usually a trust company, for delivery to a third person upon the fulfillment by the latter of certain specific obligations.

essential industry. A term used in the United States during World War II to indicate an industry considered necessary to the successful prosecution of war.

establishment. A vague term indicating a societal culture as a whole; or some particular culture trait or complex such as an institution, law, group of laws, custom or belief; or intellectual or political leaders whose values and opinions are dominant in a culture.

estate. Specifically, the nature and extent of a person's ownership of real property. The term is frequently broadened, however, to include personal property.

estate tax. A tax, usually progressive in character, levied upon the gross estate of a deceased person prior to its division. The term should not be confused with an INHERITANCE TAX. See TAX.

Euclid v. Ambler Realty Co. A *zoning case,* 272 U.S. 365 (1926), in which the Supreme Court established the constitutionality of comprehensive zoning ordinances; that is, legislation restricting the use of land in designated areas for business, industrial, or residential purposes.

Eurobonds. See EURODOLLARS.

Eurodollars. Claims held by Europeans for United States dollars. The claims arise when, through the purchase of a BILL OF EXCHANGE or some similar transaction, a foreign bank debits the account of a United States bank and credits a dollar deposit account. These deposit accounts (Eurodollars) are extensively used abroad for financial transactions such as short-term loans, the purchase of dollar CERTIFICATES OF DEPOSIT, or the purchase of dollar bonds, called *Eurobonds,* often issued by United States companies for the benefit of their overseas operations. See FOREIGN EXCHANGE (*q.v.*).

Euromarket. See EUROPEAN ECONOMIC COMMUNITY.

Euromart. See EUROPEAN ECONOMIC COMMUNITY.

European Atomic Energy Community. One of the two 6-state (France, Italy, German Federal Republic, Belgium, the Netherlands, and Luxembourg) European Communities created by the Rome Treaty of 1957. Known popularly as Euratom, it was established to develop nuclear fuel and power for civilian purposes in the 6 contracting states. Its formerly separate executive body, or Commission, was merged in 1967 into a 14-man EUROPEAN COMMISSION common to it and to the EUROPEAN ECONOMIC COMMUNITY and the EUROPEAN COMMUNITY FOR COAL AND STEEL.

European Commission. The 14-man managerial body of three European Communities, the product of a merger in July, 1967, of the former High Authority of the European Coal and Steel Community and of the two Commissions of the EUROPEAN ECONOMIC COMMUNITY and the EUROPEAN ATOMIC ENERGY COMMUNITY.

European Community for Coal and Steel. The first of the 6-state (France, Italy, German Federal Republic, Belgium, the Netherlands, and Luxembourg) supranational Communities. It was created by the so-called *Schuman Treaty* (after Robert Schuman, French Foreign Minister) at Paris, March 19, 1951, to establish a common market for coal and steel among the contracting states. It became a viable precedent for the two subsequent Communities created by the Rome Treaty of 1957, the EUROPEAN ATOMIC ENERGY COMMUNITY (*q.v.*), or Euratom, and the EUROPEAN ECONOMIC COMMUNITY (*q.v.*), or Common Market. Its chief agency, the High Authority, was merged with the Commissions of the other two Communities in 1967 to form a common 14-man EUROPEAN COMMISSION.

European depository receipt. See AMERICAN DEPOSITORY RECEIPT.

European Economic Community. An association of 6 European countries (France, Italy, German Federal Republic, Belgium, the Netherlands, and Luxembourg), created by the Rome Treaty of 1957, for the purpose of eventually abolishing tariff barriers within their borders, establishing common import duties for products originating elsewhere, and establishing other common economic policies. On July 1, 1968, all remaining tariffs among the 6 states were abolished, and intra-Community free trade was instituted. In 1967, the special EEC Commission was merged into a 14-man EUROPEAN COMMISSION to serve this and the other two 6-state European Communities (the EUROPEAN ATOMIC ENERGY COMMISSION and the EUROPEAN COMMUNITY FOR COAL AND STEEL. Also known as *Common Market, Euromarket, Euromart.*

European Free Trade Association. A group of 7 European nations (the United Kingdom, Portugal, Switzerland, Sweden, Norway, Denmark, and Austria) known more familiarly by the acronym EFTA, created in 1959 to counter the formation of the EUROPEAN ECONOMIC COMMUNITY (*q.v.*) or Common Market. At the end of 1967, EFTA announced it had achieved its principal aim of establishing free trade among the contracting states, each such state maintaining its commercial policy and tariffs towards all non-EFTA states. Also known as *Outer Seven.*

European Monetary Agreement. An agreement among states of the ORGANIZATION FOR ECONOMIC COOPERATION AND DEVELOPMENT, 1958, which set up a fund upon which member states could draw for short-term balance-of-payments assistance, and provided an arrangement for settling international accounts under which a central bank is assured of payment in dollars, gold, or equivalent, in clearing credit balances held by it against other member states' central banks. As successor to the EURO-PEAN PAYMENTS UNION, it operates with a board of management under the Council of the Organization for Economic Cooperation and Development, the Bank for International Settlements acting as agent.

European Payments Union. An organization composed of the United States and 17 European nations which participated in the EUROPEAN RECOVERY PROGRAM. It was set up at the council meeting of the Organization for European Economic Cooperation (OEEC) in Paris, July, 1950. Its purpose was to provide a clearing agency for the trade balances of the European members, to stimulate multilateral trade and discourage bilateralism. Operations were suspended in December, 1958, when EPU was replaced by the new arrangements developed under the EUROPEAN MONETARY AGREEMENT (*q.v.*).

European Recovery Program. A plan for the economic rehabilitation of Europe, first outlined by General George C. Marshall (1880-1959), American Secretary of State, at Harvard University on June 5, 1947. The plan called for a survey of Europe's resources and needs by the European countries themselves, definite procedures for coordinated self-rehabilitation, and a detailed report to the United States setting forth the assistance needed. The plan envisaged American financial aid either as a loan or gift or both, provided that the European nations made effective use of existing resources and sought to overcome political divisions and trade barriers. Between 1948 and 1951, when the program was officially terminated, 17 European states had received about $12 billion of American aid through the *Economic Cooperation Administration* of the United States government. Also called the *MARSHALL PLAN*.

ever-normal granary. See AGRICULTURAL ADJUSTMENT ACT (SECOND).

excess condemnation. The acquisition by public authority of private real property under the power of EMINENT DOMAIN when the need is not essential or imminent or where condemned property exceeds actual need; for example, the acquisition of property for aesthetic purposes. Excess condemnation is not

authorized in most of the states of the United States. See also
CONDEMNATION.

excess profits tax. A tax designed to reduce the profits made by
virtue of abnormal consumer demands, particularly in wartime.
In the United States the first general excess profits tax was
enacted in 1917 and repealed in 1922. An excess profits tax was
again enacted in 1940, materially amended in 1941, 1942, and
1944, and repealed as of December 31, 1946. See TAX.

excess reserves. As applied to banking, the difference between
total and legally required reserves. Excess reserves permit expansion of a bank's loans. See RESERVES.

exchange. 1. The acceptance of one thing for another. Exchange
is one of the main topics customarily considered in ECONOMICS.
Among the subjects included under this main topic are CREDIT,
FOREIGN EXCHANGE, MARKETS, and MONEY. 2. A marketplace
especially for securities or staple commodities. See (6).

exchange control. Government regulations relating to the
buying and selling of foreign exchange. During recent years
such regulations have taken many forms. For some of the more
common, see BLOCKED EXCHANGE, CLEARING AGREEMENT, EX-
CHANGE STABILIZATION FUND, MULTIPLE CURRENCY SYSTEM, RA-
TIONING OF FOREIGN EXCHANGE, STERLING AREA. See also
CONTROL.

exchange rate. A price of one national currency in terms of
another. Thus, at any time, a BILL OF EXCHANGE, payable in
some foreign currency, may cost a few cents more or less per
dollar depending upon whether or not the United States dollar
is at a premium or at a discount in terms of that currency. The
exchange rate may be fixed by the nation involved, or it may
be the rate on a free or uncontrolled international market. See
RATE.

exchange stabilization fund. In the United States, a fund created
by the profits which accrued to the government from the devaluation of the dollar in 1934. The fund was used to buy and sell
foreign exchange and thereby promote a more stable equilibrium between the value of the dollar and foreign currencies.
See FUND.

excise tax. Generally, any tax levied internally upon some phase
of the production and distribution of goods or services, but

157

occasionally applied to a CUSTOMS DUTY. Also called *consumption tax*. See TAX.

ex dividend. Without dividend. When a dividend is declared by the board of directors of a corporation, it is declared payable to stockholders of record as of a certain future date. Stock sold between the record date and the date of the dividend payment is sold ex dividend since the seller will receive the dividend.

executive. Any person or body carrying on administrative work involving forethought, planning, decisions as to policy, and considerable discretion as to ways and means by which such work shall be accomplished.

Executive Office of the President. A term which embraces various offices subject to direct control of the President. They include such agencies as the White House office, COUNCIL OF ECONOMIC ADVISERS, BUREAU OF THE BUDGET, OFFICE OF ECONOMIC OPPORTUNITY, COUNCIL FOR URBAN AFFAIRS, and the OFFICE OF EMERGENCY PREPAREDNESS.

Executive Peace Corps. See INTERNATIONAL EXECUTIVE SERVICE CORPS.

executor. A person named in a will to carry out its provisions.

ex interest. Without interest. The value of a bond after deduction of accrued interest from the date of the last interest payment to the date of sale. The price of the bond includes this interest, but the buyer recovers the interest when the next interest payment is made.

ex officio. Literally, by virtue of an office. The term is used to identify certain duties or prerogatives which fall to the holder of an office by virtue of his office, but which are not a part of the regular duties of such office. For example, the president of a corporation, although not a regular member of the corporation's finance committee, might take part in the deliberations of that committee as an ex officio member.

exogenous change. As applied to economics, an alteration in economic life due to a cause that is essentially noneconomic in character. A scarcity of wheat because of a drought is a case in point. See also ENDOGENOUS CHANGE.

expediter. In industry, one whose duty it is to see that the proper materials are in the designated places at the right times, and that deliveries are made in accordance with prearranged time schedules.

expendable. Usable to the point of total destruction in the ordinary course of service.

expense account. An allowance, in cash or kind, supplied to executives or other employees of private enterprises or to government officials for travel, entertainment, and other activities ostensibly essential to the execution of their respective assignments. Often a blanket cash allowance is provided the individual for which no accounting is required and which is thus virtually a salary supplement. See ACCOUNT.

export. To ship merchandise abroad, particularly to foreign countries; hence, merchandise so shipped.

export association. See WEBB-POMERENE ACT.

export bounty. A government subsidy paid on certain exports in order to develop an industry or to increase a country's foreign trade. See also BOUNTY.

Export-Import Bank of the United States. A public corporation created by executive order of the President February 2, 1934, and given a statutory basis in 1945. The bank makes or guarantees loans to encourage trade between the United States and its insular possessions and with foreign countries. Its authorized capital is $1 billion. See BANK.

export license. Authority from a government to export a specific quantity of a particular commodity. Such authority must often be secured when governments place limited EMBARGOES or related restrictions upon exports.

export tax. A duty on merchandise exported from a country. In the United States it is prohibited by the Constitution. See TAX.

expropriation. The exercise of the sovereign right of a government to appropriate individual or corporate property rights. Normally, this is done with compensation to existing owners, as under EMINENT DOMAIN, but it may and does take place without compensation, or with inadequate compensation.

ex rights. A term describing corporate stock offered without the privilege of purchasing a limited number of shares of a new issue of such stock. STOCK RIGHTS (*q.v.*) are issued to the stockholders of record as of a certain date. A person buying the stock of the corporation after this date will not receive the stock rights. The stock is therefore offered ex rights. The term is used in contradistinction to CUM RIGHTS.

extended. **1.** A term applied to an obligation when a period of time for its settlement beyond the date of its maturity has been granted. The term *overextended* is frequently used to indicate liabilities high in proportion to current assets. **2.** Extension of coverage in an insurance policy; e.g., a fire insurance policy that provides the beneficiary coverage for damage by windstorm or other disasters caused by nature.

extended bond. See BOND.

extension bond. See BOND.

Extension Service. A cooperative activity of U.S. Department of Agriculture personnel, specialists in the LAND-GRANT COLLEGES and universities, state and *county agricultural agents, 4-H Club agents,* and *home demonstration agents,* who provide farmers and ranchers and their households, and marketing and consumer groups, with current agricultural production and marketing information, and supply them with the results of research and with cultural information about rural life.

extensive cultivation. The use of relatively small amounts of capital and labor on relatively large amounts of agricultural land.

external public debt. That portion of the public debt owed to nonresident foreign creditors. External public debt is usually made payable in the currency of the country of the creditor, as to both interest and principal. In recent times none of the public debt of the U.S. has been external. See DEBT.

extractive industry. **1.** An industry which takes materials from the earth or water directly and thereby depletes the natural resources. **2.** An industry which produces or uses extracts; for example, the tanning or dyeing industries. See INDUSTRY.

extrapolation. An estimate of an unknown value outside or beyond the range of a series of known values. For example, from the present record of population growth in the United States, an estimate might be made of the population, say 10 years hence.

F

Fabian socialism. A term generally applied to a school of social-ism which supports collectivist doctrines but rejects the con-cept of class struggle. Fabian socialists believe in bringing about the socialist state by evolution and compromise with other political parties working for reform. The term was origi-nally applied to the members of the Fabian Society, organized in England in 1889. See SOCIALISM.

face value. The principal sum stated on a stock or bond or other financial document. See VALUE.

factor. As used in commerce, a firm or other organization which, under a continuous contract with a client, purchases his accounts receivable, with or without recourse, advances funds on open credit or on the security of inventories or fixed assets, and offers auxiliary services in such areas as marketing, sales analysis, and management. Before 1930, factoring was confined largely to the textile industry where it was customarily com-bined with selling services. Currently, it is being used by an increasing number of concerns in various lines of business.

factorage. The commission received by a FACTOR (*q.v.*).

factor cost. A term used by the U.S. Department of Commerce to indicate the MARKET PRICE of a commodity less all items in its cost other than those of the FACTORS OF PRODUCTION employed in its manufacture. INDIRECT TAXES, for example, such as EXCISE TAXES and SALES TAXES, not being payments for any specific factor of production, are excluded from the concept of factor cost. Likewise, DEPRECIATION and business TRANSFER PAYMENTS, not being essential payments for a factor of production, are excluded. DIRECT TAXES, on the other hand, are part of factor costs. SOCIAL INSURANCE contributions, for example, are a direct consequence of the employment of the labor factor. The NATIONAL INCOME is computed on a factor-cost basis. Factor cost is also a useful index to resource distribution in the economy, the total of such costs for each industry indicating the extent to which the available factors of production are absorbed by that industry. See COST.

factor reversal test. A method for determining the mathematical validity of an INDEX NUMBER (*q.v.*) constructed on the basis of a WEIGHTED AVERAGE. Separate index numbers are computed for the value change and for the quantity change from the base period to some other period designated hereafter as the first time period, and these are multiplied one by the other. If the product equals the ratio of the total values (that is, the sum of all the quantities times the prices) in the first time period to the total values in the base period, the index is considered a valid one mathematically. Example:

price index (See FISHER'S IDEAL INDEX) $= 3.65$

quantity index:

$$\sqrt{\frac{q_1 p_0}{q_0 p_0} \times \frac{q_1 p_1}{q_0 p_1}} = \sqrt{\frac{190}{106} \times \frac{1{,}145}{234}}$$
$$= \sqrt{1.7924 \times 4.8931} = \sqrt{8.7704} = 2.96$$
$$2.96 \times 3.65 = 10.80$$

Ratio of first time total values to base period total values

$$\frac{p_1 q_1}{p_0 q_0} = \frac{1{,}145}{106} = 10.80$$

See also TIME REVERSAL TEST.

factors of production. The various agents, broadly classified, that combine to produce additional wealth. LAND, LABOR, and CAPITAL are generally recognized as factors of production. Frequently a fourth, called MANAGEMENT, is added. Also called *agents of production.*

factory system. An economy in which workers are brought together under one roof and supplied tools, machines, and materials with which they work in return for wages. See ECONOMIC SYSTEMS.

faculty principle of taxation. See ABILITY-TO-PAY PRINCIPLE OF TAXATION.

Fair Deal. A term used by President Harry S. Truman to characterize the program presented in his message to the 81st Congress on January 5, 1949. The program included higher taxes, inflation curbs, and various measures which the President had proposed earlier, but which had been rejected or ignored by the 80th Congress.

fair-employment practices legislation. Statutes such as the New York State Ives-Quinn bill (1945) which created a permanent special state commission charged with the task of eliminating discrimination in employment because of race, creed, color, or national origin. Recent federal civil-rights legislation accomplishes the same purpose.

fair, international trade. A special market or trade exhibition usually arranged under public or semipublic auspices at which manufacturers and traders display their products in an endeavor to stimulate sales. Fairs, which attracted traders from a relatively wide area, were popular during the Middle Ages. They provided an important large-scale market. As business grew and markets became more numerous and continuous, however, fairs declined. Since World War II there has been a revival of fairs in important trade centers in Europe and North America, but they serve chiefly as international exhibitions of wares rather than markets.

Fair Labor Standards Act (*Wage and Hour Law*). An act of Congress, 1938, which established for most employees engaged in or producing goods for interstate commerce a minimum hourly wage and provided for one and a half times the regular hourly wage rate for hours worked in excess of 40 per week. The act also prohibited the employment of children under 16 years of age (with certain exceptions) in establishments producing goods for interstate shipment, and regulated HOMEWORK in specified industries. Amendments have since tightened the provisions against the employment of children. Also known as *maximum-hour legislation.* See *United States* v. *Darby Lumber Co.*

fair labor standards case. See UNITED STATES V. DARBY LUMBER CO.

fair price. A price that yields a fair return on capital invested or that includes a sufficient markup on goods or services sold to insure a reasonable profit margin for the entrepreneur. See PRICE.

fair return. A rate of return on the invested capital of transportation companies and public utilities which is based on a fair valuation of assets, criteria for which have been suggested by the courts beginning with the case of *Smyth* v. *Ames,* 169 U.S. 466 (1898). See VALUATION.

fair-trade practices acts. Statutes of various states of the United States permitting *resale price agreements* in which the retailers are required to maintain specified prices on certain commodities. Such agreements were originally held invalid by the courts as, for example, in the BEECH-NUT PACKING CASE; but state legislation subsequently validated them, and Congress passed the MILLER-TYDINGS ACT (*q.v.*) in 1937 to exempt such agreements from the provisions of the SHERMAN ANTITRUST ACT. In May, 1951, in the Schwegmann case (*Schwegmann Brothers* v. *Calvert Distillers Corp.,* 341 U.S. 384), the Supreme Court held that the Miller-Tydings Act affected only those retailers who signed price agreements and did not control the action of non-signers who were presumably free to "cut" prices. To remedy this loophole thus revealed for nonsigners, Congress passed the McGuire Act (July, 1952). Because of adverse judicial decisions in various states and the unsympathetic attitude of the federal courts, many manufacturers, finding it impractical to enforce minimum resale prices, began gradually, after 1958, to abandon "fair-trade" pricing.

falling-rate-of-profit theory. See DECLINING-MARGINAL-EFFI-CIENCY-OF-CAPITAL THEORY.

family industry. See HOUSEHOLD SYSTEM.

Fannie Mae. See FEDERAL NATIONAL MORTGAGE ASSOCIATION.

Fansteel case. A case, *National Labor Relations Board* v. *Fansteel Metallurgical Corp.,* 306 U.S. 240 (1939), in which the Supreme Court ruled that sit-down strikers were not entitled to reinstatement in their former positions of employment, under the terms of the National Labor Relations (Wagner-Connery) Act. The decision explained that to reinstate the strikers would encourage the use of force instead of legal means in seeking remedies for disputes.

farm bloc. A term sometimes used to identify those senators and representatives in the United States Congress who represent agricultural regions and consistently support measures favorable to the agricultural interests.

Farm Bureau. See AMERICAN FARM BUREAU FEDERATION.

Farm Credit Administration. An autonomous agency of the executive branch of the federal government, the general purpose of which is to provide a comprehensive credit system for agriculture, including long-term, intermediate, and short-term credit to farmers, ranchers, and to certain farmers' organizations. In each of the 12 districts into which the United States is divided, the Farm Credit Administration conducts its operations through four local credit agencies, viz., a FEDERAL LAND BANK, a FEDERAL INTERMEDIATE CREDIT BANK, a production credit corporation, and a BANK FOR COOPERATIVES. Necessary coordination is secured through the farm credit board of each district, members of which are ex officio directors of each of the four credit institutions located in the district.

Farmers Home Administration. A unit of the U.S. Department of Agriculture. It provides certain types of credit to farmers who cannot obtain loans through the ordinary channels at prevailing rates and terms.

Farmers Union. See NATIONAL FARMERS UNION.

farm subsidies. Sums paid or loaned, under certain conditions, to producers of specialized farm products when the market price falls below the per cent of AGRICULTURAL PARITY (*q.v.*) or if excess acreages are diverted to pasturage or to uses recommended by conservationist policy; or if such payments are deemed necessary to stabilize a market or to carry out international commitments.

farm surpluses. Under United States farm legislation, products purchased by the United States government, or taken as security for agricultural loans, in order to maintain prices. The products are stored in government depositaries awaiting eventual disposal. Some of the products involved are: wheat, cotton, corn, rice, peanuts, butter, honey, barley, cottonseed, tobacco, rye, mohair, soybeans, sorghum grain, and flaxseed.

fascism. In its economic aspects, a plan by which the institution of private property and the private production of goods and services is retained but is made subject to extensive control by government, particularly as respects management and new capital expansion. Under fascism, moreover, labor loses its freedom to organize and bargain collectively, these activities falling under the direct control of the state. See ECONOMIC SYSTEM.

favorable balance of trade. A condition in the international trade of a given country when the money value of its merchandise exports exceeds the money value of its merchandise imports for a particular period of time. The term originated in the theories of the MERCANTILIST SCHOOL (*q.v.*) and should not today be considered synonymous with "desirable balance of trade." Also called *active trade balance.* See also BALANCE OF TRADE.

featherbedding. As applied to labor relations, labor union rules allegedly made to provide easy jobs or to require that more workers be assigned to a given task than necessary.

Fed. A nickname for the FEDERAL RESERVE SYSTEM.

Federal Advisory Council. A body of 12 advisers, representing each of the 12 federal reserve districts of the United States, which makes recommendations to the Board of Governors of the FEDERAL RESERVE SYSTEM on matters within that board's jurisdiction and on general economic and business conditions.

Federal-Aid Highway Acts. Various acts of Congress, including those of 1916 and 1921, which have authorized the expenditure of federal funds to assist the states in the construction of main trunk and tributary highways. In 1956 the federal government entered upon an ambitious program for the construction of a system of so-called "interstate highways" and the receipts of certain special federal tax revenues, particularly taxes upon fuels and commodities used in transportation, were to be used to defray the cost of this program. Administration of the program rests with the Bureau of Public Roads of the Department of Transportation.

Federal Aviation Administration. Formerly an independent agency of the United States government, created in 1958, and now a part of the Department of Transportation. The FAA promulgates safety regulations for air commerce and for the inspection of aircraft. It administers legislation and appropriations for the construction and expansion of airports, the examination and rating of airplane crews, the installation and maintenance of landing devices on airfields, and the development of federally supported research into more advanced airplane design and performance. It also investigates airplane accidents, and prescribes rules for air traffic.

Federal Communications Commission. An autonomous, 7-member, federal agency created in 1934 to regulate the services, accounting procedures, and rates of telephone and telegraph companies. It licenses and assigns frequencies to radio and television broadcasting stations and networks, and engages in engineering research on electronic equipment, including its use to promote safety at sea and to facilitate communication by satellite.

Federal Crop Insurance Corporation. A public corporation, operating under the U.S. Department of Agriculture, which insures growers of certain staples against loss from natural and other hazards. See CROP INSURANCE.

Federal Deposit Insurance Corporation. A public corporation created by the United States government in 1933 to insure deposits in banks and thereby protect depositors against loss in case of a bank's failure. Deposits up to $20,000 are insured in all banks which are members of the FEDERAL RESERVE SYSTEM and may be insured in other banks if the application of such banks for insurance is approved by the FDIC. Occasionally it acts as RECEIVER of closed banks and may purchase bank assets or make other disposition of the property of closed banks in order to conserve the assets.

Federal Farm Loan Act. An act of Congress, 1916, which divided the continental United States into 12 districts and provided for a FEDERAL LAND BANK in each district and for the organization of federal land bank associations.

Federal Food, Drug, and Cosmetic Act. An act of Congress, 1938, which extended and supplemented previous federal consumer legislation, particularly the PURE FOOD AND DRUGS ACT OF 1906. It provided somewhat more effective regulations for identifying the quality and composition of packaged goods and more adequate safeguards against the misuse of dangerous drugs. Some of the regulatory provisions of the earlier legislation were extended to include cosmetics.

Federal funds market. Interbank borrowing and lending of BANK RESERVES. Some banks may, at times, be deficient in reserves while others have a surplus. Interbank loans, made on a day-to-day basis, correct such conditions. See MARKET.

Federal Home Loan Bank Act. An act of Congress, 1932, which provided for a system of regional banks to serve as a source of credit for member home-financing and thrift institutions. See also FEDERAL HOME LOAN BANK SYSTEM.

Federal Home Loan Bank Board. Since 1955 an autonomous three-member agency. It supervises the administration of the FEDERAL HOME LOAN BANK SYSTEM and the FEDERAL SAVINGS AND LOAN INSURANCE CORPORATION.

Federal Home Loan Bank System. Twelve regional banks created under the authority of the FEDERAL HOME LOAN BANK ACT of 1932 to provide credit for the banks' member home-financing and thrift institutions. SAVINGS AND LOAN ASSOCIATIONS, federally chartered, are required to become members of a regional federal home loan bank. Other eligible member institutions are building and loan and savings and loan institutions, homestead associations, savings and co-operative banks, and insurance companies. Each member institution subscribes to the capital stock of its regional federal home loan bank. The federal home loan banks may issue bonds, debentures, or other obligations to provide credit resources.

Federal Housing Administration. A unit of the U.S. Department of Housing and Urban Development which insures private lending institutions against loss on loans secured by residential mortgages and on loans advanced for repairs, alterations, and improvements which may be secured by collateral.

federal intermediate credit bank. One of 12 banks, operating under the FARM CREDIT ADMINISTRATION, authorized by Congress in 1923 to provide short-term loans to farmers and ranchers. The bank makes loans to, or rediscounts paper for, banks for cooperatives and other local institutions such as production credit associations, state and national banks, and livestock loan companies. Operating funds are derived principally from the public sale of collateral trust debentures which are obligations of the banks but not of the United States government. See BANK.

federal land bank. A bank created in 1916 and administered by the FARM CREDIT ADMINISTRATION (*q.v.*). The bank's primary purpose is to provide long-term, first-mortgage loans to farmers and agricultural corporations and, with certain limitations, to livestock corporations. There is a federal land bank in each of the 12 farm credit districts. Loans are negotiated through cooperatives known as federal land bank associations. Land bank operations are financed from the public sale of consolidated federal farm loan bonds. See BANK.

federal land bank association. A local cooperative association of farmers and ranchers which secures long-term loans for farmers from one of the 12 federal land banks. The borrowing farmer must secure the association's approval of his proposed loan and its indorsement of the mortgage he offers as security. He must also purchase stock in the association (sometimes directly in the land bank) equal to 5 per cent of his loan, this stock being retired when the loan is repaid. Purchase of the stock makes the borrower a member of the association, able to cast one vote at all stockholders' meetings.

Federal Maritime Commission. A 5-member federal board which exercises regulatory power over rates and services of

169

water-borne carriers and applies various statutory requirements affecting commerce on the high seas and navigable waters. See also MARITIME ADMINISTRATION.

Federal Mediation and Conciliation Service. An autonomous federal agency created by the Labor-Management Relations (Taft-Hartley) Act of 1947 to replace the Conciliation Service of the Department of Labor. It offers its conciliation services in any important labor dispute affecting interstate commerce or may intervene in any labor dispute upon request of either party.

Federal National Mortgage Association. A public corporation, popularly called *Fannie Mae,* chartered originally in 1938 and now part of the Department of Housing and Urban Affairs. It lends funds, secured by mortgages, to public and private agencies for the construction of low rental housing units. Its principal aim is to maintain the liquidity of the mortgage market and to that end, from time to time, it purchases or guarantees mortgages. It also is responsible for the management of its own rather sizable mortgage portfolio. Under the Housing and Urban Development Act of 1968, the agency became a "government-sponsored" private corporation.

Federal Open Market Committee. A committee which regulates the open-market operations of the federal reserve banks and thereby seeks to stabilize the money market. Generally called *Open Market Committee,* it is composed of the Board of Governors of the FEDERAL RESERVE SYSTEM, and the presidents of five FEDERAL RESERVE BANKS. The president of the New York bank serves as a permanent member of the Committee. The presidents of the other banks rotate as members, 4 being elected each year by the reserve banks.

Federal Power Act. An act of Congress, 1935, which includes the provisions of the Federal Water Power Act of 1921 and amendments. This consolidated legislation extends the authority of the FEDERAL POWER COMMISSION to improve the navigability of rivers, develop and utilize federal water-power resources, and regulate the rates, services, and various activities of public utilities engaged in the interstate distribution of electric power.

Federal Power Commission. A 5-member autonomous agency of the United States government which seeks to improve navigation and develop water power on navigable waters and on federally owned power sites licensed by the commission for private exploitation; to regulate and fix the wholesale rates of utility companies which furnish electricity interstate; to construct facilities for carrying gas interstate and to regulate its local sale; and to control the issuance of securities by power and gas companies.

Federal Prison Industries, Inc. A 6-member public corporation controlled by the Department of Justice which supervises vocational training and industrial enterprise in federal penal and correctional institutions.

Federal Reserve Act. An act of Congress, 1913, which created the FEDERAL RESERVE SYSTEM (*q.v.*) and changed banking in the United States from a decentralized system to one relatively centralized.

federal reserve agent. An appointee of the Board of Governors of the FEDERAL RESERVE SYSTEM who maintains a local office for the Board of Governors on the premises of a particular reserve bank and who also is designated as chairman of the board of directors of that reserve bank.

federal reserve bank. A bank chartered and supervised by the United States government, which acts as a source of credit and as a depositary of reserves, and which performs other services for national and other banks that are members of the FEDERAL RESERVE SYSTEM. It also issues federal reserve notes, which are the principal form of national currency, and acts as a fiscal agent of the United States government. There are 12 federal reserve banks, one in each of 12 federal reserve districts into which the nation is divided. The capital stock of each federal reserve bank is owned by the member banks in its district. National banks are required by law to be members; other banks may be members upon approval of an application. In respect to many of their activities, the federal reserve banks are supervised by a Board of Governors of the Federal Reserve System. See BANK.

171

federal reserve bank float. CREDIT extended by FEDERAL RESERVE BANKS on uncollected deposits. The federal reserve banks do not give immediate credit for CHECKS, DRAFTS, etc., deposited. Credit is given, however, at the end of a period estimated to be sufficient to effect collection even though actual collection has not been made at that time. The financial statements of the federal reserve banks reflect federal reserve bank float in the difference between the balance of uncollected items and the balance of deferred availability items.

federal reserve bank note. A form of United States paper money issued before 1935 by the federal reserve banks and secured by United States bonds and TREASURY NOTES authorized to be used for that purpose. Federal reserve bank notes have been retired from circulation. See NOTE.

federal reserve city. A city in which one of the 12 federal reserve banks is situated. These cities are Atlanta, Ga.; Boston, Mass.; Chicago, Ill.; Cleveland, Ohio; Dallas, Tex.; Kansas City, Mo.; Minneapolis, Minn.; New York, N.Y.; Philadelphia, Pa.; Richmond, Va.; San Francisco, Calif.; and St. Louis, Mo.

federal reserve notes. The principal, and virtually the only, paper currency in circulation in the United States. Federal reserve notes are issued in various denominations by the FEDERAL RESERVE SYSTEM through the reserve banks and are secured by United States government securities and eligible commercial paper. The notes are full legal tender. See NOTE.

Federal Reserve System. Virtually the entire banking system of the United States, which includes 12 federal reserve banks, one located in each of 12 federal reserve districts, some 24 reserve branch banks, all national banks and such state-chartered commercial banks and trust companies as have been admitted to membership. Member banks comprise about 45 per cent of all commercial banks of the country and these hold about 80 per cent of the time and demand deposits of such banks. Operating through the 12 reserve banks, a FEDERAL OPEN MARKET COMMITTEE (*q.v.*), a Federal Advisory Council, and especially a BOARD OF GOVERNORS OF THE FEDERAL RESERVE SYSTEM (*q.v.*), the System exerts a major influence upon the country's monetary and credit policies and its commercial banks.

federal savings and loan association. See SAVINGS AND LOAN ASSOCIATION.

Federal Savings and Loan Insurance Corporation. A PUBLIC CORPORATION of the United States government, administered by the FEDERAL HOME LOAN BANK BOARD, which insures the safety of deposits in all federally chartered SAVINGS AND LOAN ASSOCIATIONS and such state-chartered associations as apply for insurance and are approved. The corporation guarantees the safety of deposits up to $15,000 for each depositor in an insured institution.

federal tax immunity case. A case, *Helvering* v. *Gerhardt,* 304 U.S. 405 (1938), in which the Supreme Court reversed the old rule that the salaries of state employees were immune from federal taxation and sustained the application of the federal income tax law to the salaries of employees of the Port of New York Authority.

Federal Trade Commission. A 5-member, quasi-judicial agency of the United States government, created in 1914, which, under various statutes, is charged with the responsibility of discouraging unlawful conspiracies or combinations in restraint of interstate commerce and preventing unfair or deceptive acts or practices in the pricing, advertising, and distribution of various commodities and services. In carrying out these responsibilities, the commission may, under certain circumstances, act directly, or it may institute proceedings in the courts. It has power to seek injunctions in U.S. district courts to stop unfair advertising; to issue cease-and-desist orders in cases of conspiracy to restrain trade (orders which only the courts can set aside following an appeal by the affected party), and to secure voluntary compliance by companies to stop trade practices deemed to be unfair.

Federal Trade Commission Act. An act of Congress, 1914, which established the FEDERAL TRADE COMMISSION (*q.v.*) and empowered it to prevent unfair methods of competition, boycotts, and price-fixing arrangements. The act was amended by the WHEELER-LEA ACT (*q.v.*) which authorizes the commission to control false advertising of foods, drugs, and other commodities and to prevent unfair or deceptive trade practices. The Commission's jurisdiction was also extended by other legislation, including the Clayton Act, the Wool Products Labeling Act, and the Lanham Trade-Mark Act.

federal trust funds. Funds of the federal government which are set apart from the general fund and are earmarked to finance expenditures for special purposes. Among the principal trust funds are the Social Security Trust Fund and the Interstate Highway Construction Trust Fund. See FUND.

Federal Water Pollution Control Administration. See POLLUTION CONTROL.

fee. A payment for particular services or for a privilege. For example, a payment to a physician for professional services, payment to a government agency for a license, or a sum paid for admission to a museum.

fellow-servant doctrine. A common-law doctrine that reduced an employer's responsibility for an injury to an employee if that injury could be shown to have been caused by the act of another employee. WORKMEN'S COMPENSATION LAWS have generally modified this doctrine.

feudal system. The system of political, social, and economic relationships which existed in Europe and elsewhere during the Middle Ages, from approximately the 9th to the 14th or 15th centuries. The system was characterized by the existence of manors ruled by lords and worked by vassals who received protection and subsistence in return for their labor and service.

fiat money. Inconvertible paper money in support of which there is no reserve of specie. Governments issuing such money usually give it the quality of full legal tender. See MONEY.

fiat standard. See MANAGED MONEY.

fidelity bond. A contract in which one person guarantees a second person against defalcation by a third person holding a position of trust. Fidelity bonds sometimes name a position of trust instead of identifying the person holding that position; but this simply means that any person holding that position is covered by the fidelity bond.

fidelity insurance. A type of insurance by which an employer protects himself against financial loss due to the dishonesty of an employee. A FIDELITY BOND is the instrument of such insurance. See INSURANCE.

fiduciary. A person who holds property in trust for the benefit of others. Guardians and trustees act in the capacity of a fiduciary.

fiduciary money. Money not fully secured by gold or silver—also called *credit money*. All money currently in circulation in the United States is fiduciary money. See MONEY.

fiduciary standard. A monetary system in which the monetary unit is defined in terms of paper money. The latter may be made full legal tender but is not redeemable in any precious metal or other commodity. Also a monetary system based on a precious metal and the coinage thereof, but in which the face value of the coins is very little more than a substance on which to stamp an arbitrary value. See MONETARY SYSTEM.

fifo. A method of inventory and cost-of-sales valuation in which the individual items are valued according to the cost of earlier acquisitions. It is assumed that the first items purchased or produced are the first items sold. The costs of articles sold or used, therefore, may not be current costs but those of an earlier date, whereas the costs of the items remaining in the inventory are at the latest purchase price. The term is an abbreviation of "first in, first out." See also LIFO.

final good. A product sold to an ultimate purchaser. It is the value of final goods that is recorded in the GROSS NATIONAL PRODUCT. See GOOD.

final utility theory of value. The theory that explains value on the grounds of final or MARGINAL UTILITY (*q.v.*). Thus, a product like water, although a prime necessity of life, is low in value because the quantities available are normally without limit for all practical purposes. Diamonds, on the other hand, although of little functional use, assume a high value because their quantity is limited.

finance bill. See BILL.

financial investment. Expenditure for ownership, part ownership, or other interest in some existing capital asset or assets, for example, the purchase of a SEASONED SECURITY on the stock

market. The term is used in contradistinction to REAL INVEST-
MENT. See INVESTMENT.

financial statement. A presentation of financial data obtained
from accounting records. See (1).

fine. 1. As applied to precious metals, a term meaning pure metal. **2.** A penalty imposed by a magistrate upon an offender,
requiring him to pay a certain sum of money to the government. The payment may be in place of, or in conjunction
with, other forms of punishment.

fink. A member of a labor union who reports to his employer on
the activities of the union and his fellow employees. When
discovered, a fink is usually expelled from the union. The LA-
BOR-MANAGEMENT RELATIONS (TAFT-HARTLEY) ACT of 1947,
however, permits unions to expel members only for failure to
pay union dues or fees.

first-lien bond. See BOND.

fiscal. Having to do with money and credit, particularly public
finance. For certain uses of the term see FISCAL MONOPOLY,
FISCAL POLICY, FISCAL YEAR.

fiscal monopoly. A government monopoly conducted for revenue
purposes. Commodities such as salt and tobacco, for
example, are sometimes reserved for sale by the government,
the profits derived therefrom being used for public purposes.
See MONOPOLY.

fiscal policy. The government's policy toward taxation, public
debt, public appropriations and expenditures, and similar matters; also, the intended effect of such policy upon private business and the economy of the nation at large.

fiscal year. Any 12 months selected as an accounting period. A
fiscal year may or may not correspond with the calendar year.
The fiscal year of the U.S. government, for example, ends
June 30 of each year.

Fisher's ideal index. An index number compiled by a formula
devised by Irving Fisher (1867–1947), American economist,
and independently by others, the formula being designed to
construct an index number free from the bias inherent to some
extent in index numbers compiled by other methods. The formula is:

$$\sqrt{\frac{\Sigma p_1 q_0}{\Sigma p_0 q_0} \times \frac{\Sigma p_1 q_1}{\Sigma p_0 q_1}}$$

when

p_0 = price at base period,
q_0 = quantity at base period,
p_1 = price at first time period,
q_1 = quantity at first time period.

Commodity	Price, Period B[1]	Quantity, Period A[1]	Price times quantity	Price, Period B[1]	Quantity, Period B[1]	Price times quantity
A	$8.00	9	$72.00	$8.00	8	$ 64.00
B	9.00	8	72.00	9.00	9	81.00
C	1.00	90	90.00	1.00	1,000	1,000.00
Totals			$234.00			$1,145.00

Commodity	Price, Period A[1]	Quantity, Period A[1]	Price times quantity	Price, Period A[1]	Quantity, Period B[1]	Price times quantity
A	$9.00	9	$ 81.00	$9.00	8	$ 72.00
B	2.00	8	16.00	2.00	9	18.00
C	0.10	90	9.00	0.10	1,000	100.00
Totals			$106.00			$190.00

For tests to determine the mathematical validity of an index number, see FACTOR REVERSAL TEST, TIME REVERSAL TEST.

An example showing how an index number may be calculated from the formula follows:

$$\sqrt{\frac{234}{106} \times \frac{1,145}{190}} = \sqrt{2.2075 \times 6.0263} = \sqrt{13.303} = 3.65.$$

In customary usage, 365 is said to be the price index number for period B.[1] See INDEX NUMBER.

five percenter. A popular term, used in a disparaging sense, to identify persons who, for a fee of 5 per cent or more, use their alleged influence with public officials to secure federal government contracts for their business clientele.

five-twenty bond. A popular name for certain United States bonds issued from 1862 to 1865. They were redeemable after 5 years, payable in 20 years, and yielded 6 per cent interest. See BOND.

fixed asset. An asset of such a nature that it is used directly or indirectly to produce goods or services and is not for sale in the regular course of business. Examples are land, buildings, and machinery. See ASSET.

fixed capital good. A capital good which is relatively durable. The term is used in contradistinction to CIRCULATING CAPITAL GOOD. See GOOD.

fixed cost. A cost which does not necessarily increase or decrease as the total volume of production increases or decreases. Interest on borrowed capital, expenses of maintenance, and fire insurance are examples. Also called *indirect, overhead,* and *supplementary cost.* See COST.

fixed liability. A liability which is not due for at least a year from the time it is incurred. Also known as *long-term liability.* See also LIABILITY.

fixed shift. In an enterprise where a 24-hour interval is divided into two or three shifts or working periods, the practice of keeping the same employees on a particular shift instead of interchanging employees in such a way that over a period of time they will have taken a turn on each of the shifts. See SHIFT.

flexible schedule. As applied to labor relations, a plan by which the number of hours of employment per day or the number of work days per week may be varied, provided such variations do not exceed the maximum period of employment fixed by law or in a labor contract for a given interval of time.

flexible tariff. A tariff system which permits administrative officers or a tariff commission a measure of discretion in fixing the amount of a customs duty when temporary or abnormal conditions change the competitive relationship between foreign and domestic products. A flexible tariff has been applied particularly for the control of DUMPING. See TARIFF.

flight of capital. See FLIGHT OF THE DOLLAR.

flight of the dollar. A popular phrase to indicate the purchase of foreign securities with dollar exchange, the real purpose being to escape the adverse consequences of INFLATION, DEVALUATION, or some related economic circumstance. Under similar conditions the same trend could affect the CURRENCY of any country. A more generalized phrase is *flight of capital.*

floating asset. See CURRENT ASSET.

floating debt. A debt consisting of short-term obligations. The term is used in contradistinction to long-term or FUNDED DEBT in the United States. It is frequently applied to that part of the PUBLIC DEBT held in TREASURY BILLS or other short-term obligations. The difference between a floating debt and a funded debt is not always clear. See DEBT.

floating exchange rate. Fluctuation in the rate of exchange of a national currency, when its value is no longer fixed in terms of gold or of some other national currency such as the United States dollar. Member countries of the INTERNATIONAL MONETARY FUND are obligated to correct such fluctuations exceeding 1 per cent by appropriate foreign exchange transactions. See RATE.

floor trader. A member of an organized stock exchange who, unlike a broker, buys and sells on his own account and executes his own orders on the floor of the exchange. He may act in the capacity of a dealer or jobber in securities.

flotsam. Goods or equipment floating on the high seas as a result of a wreck or similar disaster and subject to salvage rules.

flow chart. 1. A graphic device (See diagram A) depicting hypothetical movements of money, goods, or some other element in the economy from one point to another. Thus, diagram A shows an imaginary flow of money from productive enterprise to ultimate consumers, and from thence back to productive enterprise by way of expenditures or investments. 2. A graphic representation (See diagram B) of the major steps in automatic data processing required to convert input data into some predetermined form. Thus in diagram B, the input is a succession of due dates of bills, notes, or some other such documents. Each due date is processed to determine whether or not payment or other action is overdue. If payment is overdue, an appropriate notice is printed before the next succeeding due date is processed; if it is not overdue, the next succeeding due date is processed immediately.

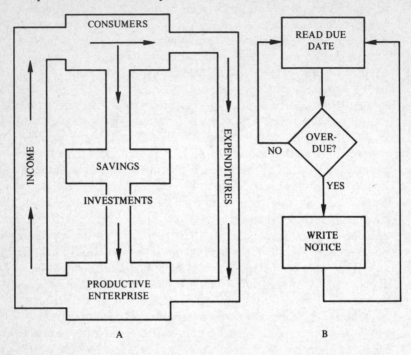

A   B

fluid savings. Savings that have not been invested or spent. See SAVING.

Food and Agriculture Organization of the United Nations. A specialized agency of the UNITED NATIONS consisting of more than 110 states. By serving as a clearinghouse and making appropriate recommendations to member states, the organization hopes to raise nutritional and living standards, better the conditions of rural populations, and promote more efficient and orderly production of food and agricultural staples throughout the world.

Food and Drug Administration. A unit of the U.S. Department of Health, Education, and Welfare which administers various laws seeking to protect consumers against impure or adulterated food products, dangerous drugs, poisons and pesticides, and fraudulent or misleading branding or labeling of products.

Its enforcement agents seek voluntary compliance with the findings of investigators but may cite violators for prosecution. The unit also conducts research to detect toxic or dangerous ingredients in foods, drugs, cosmetics, etc.

food stamp plan. A public subsidy plan authorized by the Food Stamp Act of 1964, administered by the Consumer and Marketing Service of the U.S. Department of Agriculture, and designed to increase the demand for surplus commodities above that required by the normal channels of trade. Through state welfare agencies, food coupons are sold to participating households to the extent of the amount of money they normally spend for food. The food coupons enjoy a higher monetary value than the money with which they are bought and hence can purchase more food at those retail stores approved by the Service than could be bought with the original money exchanged for the stamps.

forced loan. A loan made because of some exigency; for example, a loan that cannot be collected at maturity and which is therefore renewed, or the payment by a bank of an OVER-DRAFT which is later converted into a formal loan. See LOAN.

forced sale. A sale made necessary by the action of a creditor; for example, a sale made under compulsion of FORECLOSURE.

Fordney-McCumber Tariff. The United States *Tariff Act of 1922.* It raised many duties to meet altered competitive conditions abroad, due to World War I, and provided for a FLEXIBLE TARIFF.

foreclosure. As applied to mortgages, a sale under a judgment held when a mortgagor fails to make payments on the debt secured by a mortgage, the right of redemption being retained by the mortgagor. If the mortgagor fails to redeem the property upon notice, he is forever barred from exercising any such right.

foreign bill. See BILL.

foreign corporation. 1. In the United States, a private corporation doing business in one state but chartered in another state. **2.** A private corporation chartered in a foreign country and doing business within the United States. See CORPORATION.

foreign exchange. The process of settling debts between persons or establishments located in different countries; also the instruments used in the process of settling such debts. These instruments, known as BILLS OF EXCHANGE, are claims for payment in a foreign currency. Any person owing money abroad may buy such exchange and use it to settle his obligation. The foreigner to whom the obligation is owed and who receives the purchased bill may cash it and receive the currency of his own country. Or a person wishing to collect a debt owed by a foreign debtor may sell a bill of exchange and receive for it the currency of his own country or a credit to a dollar deposit account, while the foreign debtor pays the amount involved in the currency of his country. Such transactions are handled by banks conducting international operations. See EXCHANGE.

Foreign Investors Tax Act. An act of Congress, 1966, a principal purpose of which was to establish a tax ceiling (30 per cent) for overseas investors in American securities, the objective being to stimulate foreign investment in the United States and thus help reduce the deficit in the United States international account.

Foreign Securities Act. See JOHNSON ACT.

Foreign Service officer. A public representative of the United States abroad, with the rank of ambassador, counsel of embassy, attaché, diplomatic secretary, consul general, consul, or vice consul.

foreign-trade zone. An area in or adjacent to a port of entry, for storing and transshipping imported goods to foreign ports without payment of duties and without the intervention of customs officials, except under certain conditions. In the United States foreign-trade zones are operated as a public utility by private corporations under the supervision of the Foreign-Trade Zones Board of the Department of Commerce. Also called *free port.*

foreign valuation. For the application of tariff schedules (or exemptions) by customs officers in the United States, the market value, or equivalent, of goods imported into the United States. See VALUATION.

Forest Service. See NATIONAL FORESTS.

forms of business organization. The various ways in which business enterprises may be organized. See (4).

form utility. Satisfaction of a human desire as the result of the alteration of the shape, structure, or composition of some good. When goods are manufactured, a form utility is created. Wood made into a desk is an example. See UTILITY.

Fort Knox. A United States Army reservation in Kentucky where the federal government maintains its Gold Bullion Depository and the bulk of the nation's gold, most of which is held as security for the gold certificate account of the FEDERAL RESERVE BANKS, i.e., gold-certificate credits to the federal reserve banks on the books of the Treasury. The gold stock also includes EARMARKED GOLD, and gold in the Treasury's general fund. See STERILIZED GOLD.

forward exchange. A foreign bill of exchange bought or sold at a stipulated price and payable at some future date. By purchasing or selling forward exchange, an importer or exporter can protect himself against the risk of exchange fluctuations. See EXCHANGE.

forwarding agent. A person or a business whose function it is to collect merchandise and to ship or deliver it as directed.

4-H Club agent. See EXTENSION SERVICE.

Fourierism. See PHALANSTERY.

fractional currency. Any form of currency of a value less than the standard monetary unit; in the United States, any coin of a value less than $1. See CURRENCY.

frame of reference. As applied to the social sciences, limits of related thoughts, attitudes, meanings, and similar concepts within which some given intellectual activity takes place.

franchise. A special privilege conferred by government; for example, the privilege of operating an omnibus service on the streets of a city. The term is sometimes used to indicate a privilege granted by a private organization as, for example, the grant of exclusive territory to a sales agent by a private corporation.

franchise tax. A tax levied on some special privilege extended by the government to a private enterprise. See TAX.

franking. The privilege of sending material through the United States mails free of charge, granted by the United States government to the President, Senators, Representatives, the Courts, administrative departments, and other agencies and individuals.

Frazier-Lemke Act. An act of Congress, 1935, which established a MORATORIUM on farm mortgage foreclosures, permitting the owners to pay rent for a 3-year period.

free and clear. The absence of any liens or other legal encumbrances on property.

free banking system of New York. A system established in 1839 in New York State, authorizing the issuance of bank notes backed by approved securities deposited with the state government. A similar plan was later applied to the NATIONAL BANKS.

free capital good. A capital good which can be used for a variety of purposes. The term is used in contradistinction to SPECIALIZED CAPITAL GOOD. See GOOD.

free coinage. A regulation by which the government is obligated to accept for coinage unlimited quantities of a specified metal or metals under conditions prescribed by law. The term should not be confused with GRATUITOUS COINAGE. See COINAGE.

free competition. See COMPETITION.

freedom of contract. The right of an individual under law to determine his obligations toward others and his rights to property by contract as opposed to the determination of such relations and rights by law or governmental regulation. The phrase has a special significance in employer-employee relations where governmental regulation and legally enforced collective bargaining have largely ousted the concept of contract between individual employer and employee.

Freedom Shares. A name given United States *savings notes* first issued in 1967. They mature in 4½ years and those issued after June 1, 1968 yield 4.74 per cent annual interest payable upon maturity. Freedom Shares are available to purchasers of E savings bonds on a dollar for dollar basis, up to $350 face value per calendar quarter and $1,350 per calendar year.

free enterprise. See CAPITALISM.

free good. Anything external to man which is inherently useful and which is in such bountiful supply that as much of it as is desired can be had without conscious effort. The term is used in contradistinction to ECONOMIC GOOD. Fresh air, climate, and sunshine are examples of free goods. It should be noted, however, that indispensability is not necessarily an attribute of a free good. Water in cities, for example, although indispensable, is not a free good because its distribution requires conscious effort. Nor are things that are distributed gratuitously designated as free goods if conscious effort on the part of someone is necessary to acquire them. See GOOD.

free list. As applied to a customs tariff, a list of goods not liable to the payment of duties.

free market. A market in which buyers and sellers are at liberty to trade without restrictions as to prices or quantities, and in which there is no compulsion either to buy or to sell. See MARKET.

free port. See FOREIGN-TRADE ZONE.

free silver. The unrestricted coinage of silver. See FREE COINAGE.

free trade. As applied to international trade, the absence of export and import duties, quantitative restrictions, and regulations which are clearly designed to reduce or prevent such trade.

frequency curve. See FREQUENCY DISTRIBUTION.

frequency distribution. A classification of statistical data into class intervals according to size or magnitude with the number of items (frequency) applicable to each class interval. Sometimes called *frequency table.* The following is a frequency distribution of the weekly earnings of 200 employees.

Class Interval	Frequency
40–40.99	5
41–41.99	8
42–42.99	20
43–43.99	30
44–44.99	50
45–45.99	40
46–46.99	25
47–47.99	12
48–48.99	5
49–49.99	5

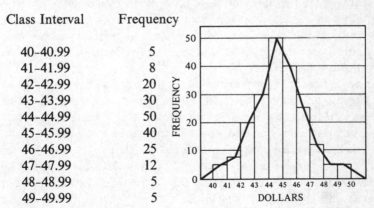

When displayed graphically, using the X axis for class intervals and the Y axis for frequencies, a frequency distribution is called a *column diagram* or *histogram.* When the midpoints of the class intervals at the various frequency levels are joined with straight lines, the resulting broken line is called a *frequency polygon.* A histogram and a frequency polygon derived from the above frequency distribution are shown in the appended diagram. A frequency polygon is customarily made more regular or smoothed out either by inspection or mathematically, as, for example, by a MOVING AVERAGE. The resulting curve is called a *frequency curve.* Frequency distributions are used extensively in economic analysis, as, for example, in comparing one array of statistics with another. The characteristics of a frequency distribution are described by various statistical measurements, the more commonly used of which are as follows. Calculated averages measuring central tendency: ARITHMETIC MEAN, GEOMETRIC MEAN, HARMONIC MEAN. See also WEIGHTED AVERAGE. Positional averages measuring central tendency: MEDIAN, MODE. Measurements showing absolute dispersion, variability, or scatter: MEAN DEVIATION, PROBABLE ERROR, QUARTILE DEVIATION, RANGE, STANDARD DEVIATION. Measurements showing relative dispersion: COEFFICIENT OF VARIATION. For other measurements, see KURTOSIS, SKEWNESS. See also NORMAL CURVE OF DISTRIBUTION.

frequency polygon. See FREQUENCY DISTRIBUTION.

frequency table. See FREQUENCY DISTRIBUTION.

frictional unemployment. Unemployment caused by imperfections in the technical functioning of the labor market. Lack of information regarding where work is available or time consumed in changing jobs are causes of frictional unemployment. See UNEMPLOYMENT.

fringe benefit. Compensation (or the equivalent) received by employees other than regular wages for time actually spent on a job. Examples of fringe benefits are wages paid for holidays and vacations, and sums paid in insurance and pension plans, medical services, and recreational activities.

Frothingham* v. *Mellon. A case, 262 U.S. 447 (1923), in which an individual taxpayer sought to enjoin the federal government or its agent from disbursing funds under a federal grant-in-aid of a state program for maternal and child welfare, alleging that such a program was a state and not a federal responsibility under the Tenth Amendment. The Supreme Court ruled that the suing taxpayer's interest was so negligible and remote that he lacked standing as a party in interest and that the case was essentially moot. In 1968, however, the Court specifically overruled this concept that an individual taxpayer lacked sufficient interest to sue and held that a taxpayer would not be prevented from seeking a judicial ruling that the First Amendment barred federal aid to private and parochial schools offered under the terms of the Education Act of 1965. Various suits were subsequently begun on which the courts have still to rule (1968).

frozen. As used in business terminology, the word suggests that the conversion of something of value into money is difficult or virtually impossible. Thus, frozen assets or capital are assets or capital that cannot readily be converted into money, or at least cannot be so converted without considerable loss. The term is used in contradistinction to LIQUID. See ASSET, CAPITAL.

full employment. The condition which exists when all who are able and willing to work can find remunerative employment. Time consumed in vacations, changing jobs, and similar periods without work cause a certain amount of unemployment at all times. As long as this does not exceed 3 to 4 per cent of the labor force, however, full employment is said to exist.

full-paid stock. See CAPITAL STOCK.

full stock. See CAPITAL STOCK.

function. As applied in economic analysis, a variable the value of which depends upon another variable. Thus, the increase of a sum of money at a fixed rate of interest is a function of time. The general mathematical expression for a functional relationship is $y = f(x)$, meaning that y is a function of x.

functional distribution. See DISTRIBUTION.

functional finance. See COMPENSATORY FISCAL POLICY.

functions of money. The various ways in which money may be used, or the service it renders in the economy. The use of money as a medium of exchange is the principal function. It is also used as a standard of value; that is, as a means of measuring and of comparing values when no exchange is made or contemplated. Further, money is used as a standard of deferred payments when an obligation is assumed at one time to be paid at some future date. It is used as a means of storing value when received as the result of a sale and not immediately used for a purchase. Finally, it is used as a reserve against various forms of currency such as DEPOSIT CURRENCY and thus performs an important function in the creation of credit.

fund. Money, or its equivalent, set aside for a specific purpose the nature of which is usually indicated in the name of the fund. See (21).

fundamental disequilibrium. A term used in Art. IV, sec. 5 of the Articles of Agreement of the INTERNATIONAL MONETARY FUND to indicate a substantial and persisting variation between the PAR EXCHANGE RATE of a national currency and its PURCHASING-POWER PARITY (*q.v.*) with the currencies of other nations. For example, in June, 1949, the British pound was valued at $4.03, but British wholesale prices had risen approximately 6 per cent during the previous year, while prices in the United States had declined in like proportion. Hence, a commodity which cost $20.15 in the United States and £5 in Britain in 1948, in 1949 cost $18.94 in the United States and £5, 6s in Britain. The change placed traders in Britain at a disadvantage because importers in the United States and other HARD MONEY nations tended to reduce their British purchases. With the consent of the International Monetary Fund, the pound sterling was accordingly devalued from $4.03 to $2.80, the devaluation being in excess of the actual disparity in the purchasing power of the two currencies, presumably to avoid another devaluation of the pound at a later date, a hope which proved vain since the British pound was devalued to $2.40 in 1967.

funded debt. 1. A debt represented by a formal written agreement between the borrower and a trustee for the lenders, in which the borrower agrees to pay stipulated amounts at specified times and places until the debt is extinguished. The agreement may, and usually does, provide for some sort of security for the debt. **2.** A debt created by the sale of an issue of long-term securities, the proceeds from which have been used to liquidate one or more issues of short-term securities. The term is used in contradistinction to FLOATING DEBT. See DEBT.

futures. 1. As applied to international trade, the purchase or sale of FOREIGN EXCHANGE on the basis of a rate quoted as of some future date. **2.** As applied to trading on the commodity exchanges, see HEDGING.

G

gain sharing. A bonus system according to which additional wage increments paid to workers for increased production become progressively smaller as production increases.

Gantt chart. A device which displays in graphic form various production data essential to managerial operations. For example, it can show a comparative record of production planned with production completed at any particular time, or a comparative record of the accomplishments of employees with established standards or with each other, or the comparative periods of idleness and activity of machines. The chart was developed by Henry Laurence Gantt (1861–1919), an American management engineer.

garnishment. The prerogative of a court, increasingly limited by law, to require an employer to pay part or all of the wages of a debtor employee to a court officer for the benefit of a creditor.

General Accounting Office. A federal agency, created in 1921 and directly responsible to Congress, which performs general auditing and accounting functions as respects the federal government's financial operations. It is also responsible for settling all claims in favor of or against the government, and for investigating all matters relating to the collection, disbursement, and use of public funds. In this latter connection the agency's head, the Comptroller General, has power to render binding decisions concerning the legality of contemplated or actual expenditures by government agencies.

General Agreement on Tariffs and Trade. An international agreement, usually identified by its acronym GATT, which has acquired a more or less permanent character and an administrative structure at Geneva, Switzerland, for the discussion and determination of international commercial policy. It originated in a trade conference of 23 nations held at Geneva in 1947 to discourage a growing trend toward bilateral trade agreements and encourage more liberal commercial policies especially among key industrial nations. During the 1950's and particularly the 1960's, GATT conferees were responsible for various initiatives to liberalize trade, including the DILLON ROUND (*q.v.*) and the KENNEDY ROUND (*q.v.*). The developing nations sometimes regard GATT as a club of the more advanced nations and criticize it as insensitive to their needs; for their world trade forum, these developing states favor the UNITED NATIONS CONFERENCE ON TRADE AND DEVELOPMENT (*q.v.*).

General Assembly of the United Nations. A principal organ of the UNITED NATIONS consisting of more than 125 states which have equal voting power. It examines and makes recommendations on policies relating to maintenance of peace and the promotion of general welfare. It receives reports from all other agencies of the United Nations and exercises a degree of supervision over most of their activities. Regular meetings are held annually, and special meetings may be called when necessary.

general equilibrium. As applied to theoretical economic analysis, the concept of a balance among interdependent economic forces, each activated by individual decisions based upon SELF-INTEREST. Assuming free COMPETITION, PRIVATE PROPERTY, and FREEDOM OF CONTRACT, forces of SUPPLY and DEMAND acting upon ECONOMIC GOODS are held to be equated at prices that offer the greatest number of traders maximum satisfactions and that are mutually consistent with one another in that respect. A price change in one commodity or service may engender price changes in innumerable other directly and indirectly related commodities and services with resulting maladjustments; but equilibrium, in the sense described, tends eventually to be restored. Actually, general equilibrium is never absolute in a developing economy because of changes in consumer demands and dispositions to spend, save, and invest; new technological developments; shifting competitive relationships; depletion of existing resources and discovery of new ones, and other factors. The concept is supplementary to that of *partial or particular equilibrium* which considers the economics of specific economic goods. The study of general equilibrium, considered in the light of the effects of change-producing factors on the economy as a whole, consequent disequilibriums, and the processes by which simultaneous adjustment tends to restore a new equilibrium, is called *dynamic economics,* as opposed to *static economics,* which is the study of a particular economic relationship under certain prescribed conditions assumed to be constant.

general equilibrium theory of international trade. An explanation of the conditions giving rise to international trade, the condition being, fundamentally, an established difference in exchange ratios among the trading nations. Thus, if two commodities x and y exchange in the ratio of 3 to 1 in nation A, and 2 to 1 in nation B, commodity x will be exported from nation A to nation B. Differences in exchange ratios are caused, by varying conditions of supply and demand in the nations concerned. Conditions of supply depend upon natural resources and the natural aptitudes and acquired skills of the people, or other factors that establish ABSOLUTE or COMPARATIVE ADVANTAGE in production; demand depends upon tastes expressed in buying dispositions as well as upon a nation's purchasing power, this being influenced, in turn, by the distribution of the NATIONAL INCOME. The theory holds that equilibrium prevails when the value of the exports just equals the value of the imports. The theory is an extension of the concept of GENERAL EQUILIBRIUM to international trade.

general fund. Monies available for expenditure that are not earmarked for any specific program or project. See FUND.

general property tax. See PROPERTY TAX.

General Services Administration. An autonomous federal agency created in 1949 by the Federal Property and Administrative Services Act. It constructs and maintains public buildings, manages public property, stockpiles critical and strategic materials, publishes certain official documents and provides a depositary for certain public records, acts as a supply procurement and transportation agency for all units of government, and renders other logistic and maintenance services.

general strike. Work stoppage in all industries everywhere. The term is frequently used to designate a strike only in certain strategic industries or a general work stoppage in a certain geographic area. It may and sometimes has been directed against government. In the writings of such Anarcho-Syndicalists as Georges Sorel, the concept became an ideological rallying cry and a major tactical weapon in a political struggle between capital and labor. See STRIKE.

general tariff. See SINGLE-SCHEDULE TARIFF.

genetic industry. An industry engaged directly in increasing the supply of some form of plant or animal life. Farming and cattle raising are examples. See INDUSTRY.

gentlemen's agreement. As applied to industry, an informal, often a mere verbal, agreement between two or more industries to divide markets, maintain prices, restrict output, or engage in other related practices designed to reduce competition. Such agreements are now generally outlawed.

geometric mean. A calculated average computed by first finding the product of the numbers to be averaged and then finding whatever root of this product is indicated by the total quantity of numbers to be averaged. The mathematical formula is:

$$M_g = \sqrt[n]{a_1 a_2 a_3 \cdots a_n}$$

when

$$M_g = \text{the geometric mean,}$$
$$a_1, a_2, a_3 \cdots a_n = \text{the numbers to be averaged.}$$

In contrast to the ARITHMETIC MEAN, the geometric mean is suitable for averaging ratios. It is therefore frequently used in the computation of INDEX NUMBERS that record ratios of change in prices and other data. Its advantage for such use can be illustrated in the following frequently cited example:

Commodity	Price First Year	Price Second Year
A	100	1,000
B	100	10
Arithmetic mean	100	505
Geometric mean	100	100

In the first case it would seem that there had been a substantial increase in prices from the first to the second year. In the second case the two changes, being equal ratios in opposite directions, have canceled each other. See AVERAGE.

geometric progression. See PROGRESSION.

George-Deen Act. See SMITH-HUGHES ACT.

George-Ellzey Act. See SMITH-HUGHES ACT.

George-Reed Act. See SMITH-HUGHES ACT.

German Alliance Insurance Co. v. *Lewis.* A case, 233 U.S. 389 (1914), in which the Supreme Court construed a state statute (Kansas), regulating the rates of fire-insurance companies, as consistent with the due process clause of the 14th Amendment. The Court's decision was based on the theory that the fire-insurance business was semimonopolistic in character, that it affected the public welfare so vitally as to require regulation, and that, in effect, the business presented a justification for public regulation no different than is presented by transportation, grain elevators, and other enterprises held to be clothed with a public interest and hence subject to public control.

ghetto. 1. Historically, a part of a city to which persons of certain races were restricted. **2.** Currently, a blighted urban area inhabited by minority groups, in part because they lack the means to command better housing and a better environment, in part because they are the victims of discrimination that prevents economic advance and social mobility.

Gibbons v. *Ogden.* A case, 9 Wheaton 1 (1824), in which the Supreme Court was called upon for the first time to outline generally the boundaries of the commerce power of Congress under the Constitution. Speaking through Chief Justice Marshall, the Court declared that the power over foreign and interstate commerce was a regulatory power; that it comprehended every species of commercial intercourse between the United States and foreign nations; that, in the case of commerce among the several states, the regulatory power of Congress did not stop at the external boundary line of any state of the Union but was applicable within the interior of a state; and that this power embraced every commercial transaction that was not carried on wholly within the boundaries of a single state. The decision also specifically included navigation within the term "commerce."

G. I. Bill of Rights (*Servicemen's Readjustment Act*). An act of Congress, 1944, which, with subsequent amendments, provided allowances to veterans of World War II and subsequent conflicts while unemployed and allowances for subsistence and tuition while attending school or college, and guaranteed loans for the purchase of homes, farms, and businesses.

gift. A voluntary transfer of property, without consideration, from one person to another.

gift tax. In the United States, a tax levied upon the value of a gift after certain specified exemptions, the rate of the tax increasing as the amount of the gift increases. Under federal law an individual may give away to one or more persons a total of $30,000 which is tax free to both donor and recipient. In addition he may make gifts to individuals not exceeding $3,000 to any one person in any one year. This is also tax free for both donor and recipient. See TAX.

gilt-edge security. A security in which the factor of risk is reduced to a minimum; for example, a United States government bond. See SECURITY.

give-up. A part of a stockbroker's commission paid, by arrangement with his customer, to a second broker for services rendered the customer by the second broker, the services having no relation to the transaction yielding the commission thus shared.

Glass-Steagall Act. See BANKING ACT.

going business. A vague term generally indicating an enterprise that, over a period of years, has been profitable, well managed, and financially responsible, and holds prospects for continued prosperity in the foreseeable future.

going value. The anticipated exchange value of some good or service or of some enterprise predicated on the assumption that existing economic conditions are inherently relatively stable, and on the further assumption that market conditions will not be adversely influenced by important technological changes, panics, wars, or some other unforeseen circumstances. See VALUE.

going wage. The established or accepted local or national rate of compensation for a particular type of work. See WAGE.

gold bond. See BOND.

gold-bullion standard. A monetary system in which the monetary unit is defined in terms of gold, that metal being accepted by the mint at a stipulated price, but not for coinage. All forms of money are redeemable in gold bullion, but redemption can be demanded only for relatively large amounts at one time. When money can be redeemed in gold bullion only for export purposes, the system is sometimes called the *international gold-bullion standard.* See MONETARY SYSTEM.

gold certificate. A form of United States paper money, representing gold bullion and fully secured thereby, in circulation from 1865 to 1933. Thereafter, until 1955, gold certificates were issued, in revised form, only to federal reserve banks for reserve purposes. Since then, the reserves have been indicated only by a bookkeeping record called INTERDISTRICT SETTLEMENT FUND. See CERTIFICATE.

gold clause. A term used in the United States to identify a clause in a contract which defines a money obligation in terms of a dollar of a specified weight and fineness of gold. In February, 1935, the Supreme Court delivered opinions in certain cases involving contractual obligations containing gold clauses. The Court upheld the power of Congress, previously exercised, to invalidate the gold clauses of private contracts. See also GOLD-CLAUSE CASES.

gold-clause cases. Cases in which the Supreme Court passed upon the power of Congress to abrogate the gold clause in private and public contracts; that is: (*a*) upon the power of Congress to require a private creditor to accept existing legal tender in payment of a contractual debt even though the contract called for payment in gold of a certain weight and fineness; and (*b*) to require holders of United States bonds to accept payment in existing legal tender even though the bonds called for payment of gold of a certain weight and fineness. In *Norman* v. *Baltimore and Ohio R.R. Co.* 294 U.S. 240 (1935), the Court held that Congress could abrogate the gold clause in private contracts on the theory that the terms of any such contract are always potentially subject to regulation by the constitutional power of government, including the established constitutional power of Congress to control the currency. On the issue of the government's refusal to honor the gold clause in its own bonds the Court, in *Perry* v. *United States,* 294 U.S. 330 (1935), held that Congress was controlled by its own promise to pay which it had given under its constitutional authority to borrow on the credit of the United States, and that hence it could not dishonor its pledges to its creditors. At the same time the Court could find no actual contractual damages resulting to the holder of the gold bonds from the government's decision to pay in existing legal tender and consequently refused to sustain the bondholder's plea for payment in gold or its equivalent. See also GOLD CLAUSE.

gold cover. 1. A legal requirement, such as existed until recently for United States federal reserve notes, that a specific percentage of the value of an issue of paper currency must be backed by an actual gold reserve. The cover for federal reserve notes was 25 per cent. **2.** Generally, the gold reserve of any state or international agency which, for practical purposes, is a reserve against its currency or similar obligations. See GOLD-COVER REPEAL ACT.

Gold-cover Repeal Act. An act of Congress, 1968, which repealed the existing requirement that the United States paper currency (federal reserve notes) be backed by a gold reserve of 25 per cent of the value of the currency outstanding. The act freed $10.4 billion in gold reserves for international exchange transactions and international fortification of the dollar.

gold-exchange standard. A monetary system that permits the redemption of its money in BILLS OF EXCHANGE (*q.v.*) on some gold-standard country in which bank deposits are carried, these being regarded a part of the monetary reserves of the monetary system in question. In this way, it is possible, if the GOLD STANDARD (*q.v.*) is maintained anywhere, for a nation, not itself on the gold standard, to keep its money on a par with gold without maintaining at least the full amount of gold reserves usually required to attain that end. By pursuing the same plan of redeeming its money in BILLS OF EXCHANGE, a nation can keep its money on a par with the money of some other nation even though neither is on the gold standard. Also called *indirect* *foreign-exchange standard* and *irredeemable foreign-exchange standard.* See MONETARY SYSTEM.

gold points. In exchange transactions between traders in gold-standard countries, the rate immediately above and below the MINT PAR OF EXCHANGE value of gold at which it becomes as cheap to export or import gold and pay for its transportation as to buy or sell BILLS OF EXCHANGE; hence, the limits in terms of gold beyond which the price of bills of exchange will not fluctuate.

Gold Pool. Seven representatives of central banks of the United States, the United Kingdom, Belgium, Italy, The Netherlands, Switzerland, and the Federal Republic of Germany, who, operating primarily through the Bank for International Settlements of Basle, have sought to maintain equilibrium in the price of gold by buying and selling on the markets within certain minimum and maximum levels, the primary aim being to keep the price of gold on the world market consistent with the gold price of the dollar. In 1968 these same bankers established the TWO-TIER GOLD PRICE.

gold price. See TWO-TIER GOLD PRICE.

Gold Reserve Act. An act of Congress, 1934, which authorized the DEVALUATION of the dollar in terms of gold by from 50 to 60 per cent at the discretion of the President and ordered the acquisition by the Treasury of all gold held by the federal reserve banks in return for GOLD CERTIFICATES. It abolished the coinage of gold and prohibited the redemption of money in gold. An EXCHANGE STABILIZATION FUND was created out of the premium resulting from the dollar's devaluation.

gold standard. The use of gold as the basis of a monetary system and as a standard of value for its currency. Traditionally, a monetary system on the gold standard defined its monetary unit in terms of gold of a certain weight and fineness, permitted the free and unlimited coinage of gold, made gold coins legal tender, permitted them to circulate freely and to be exchanged freely with any other form of legal currency, and maintained the value of all other forms of money at a par with gold coins. See MONETARY SYSTEM.

Gold Standard Act. An act of Congress, 1900, which defined the United States dollar as 25⁸⁄₁₀ grains of gold ⁹⁄₁₀ fine, provided that all forms of United States money should be maintained at parity with the gold dollar, created a reserve fund of approximately $150,000,000 in gold for the redemption of United States notes and treasury notes, and specified other regulations for the maintenance of a gold reserve.

Gompers v. Bucks Stove and Range Co. A case, 221 U.S. 418 (1911), in which the Supreme Court established, among other things, that when a labor boycott causes a substantial reduction in the movement of goods in interstate commerce, a violation of the Sherman Act is indicated. The decision of the Court in the DANBURY HATTERS' CASE (*q.v.*) was thus strengthened.

good. As used in economic theory, anything external to man, either material or immaterial, that satisfies a human desire. It should be noted that, unlike the use of the term in popular speech, there is no legal, moral, or ethical connotation in its technical use. A dangerous and harmful drug may satisfy a human desire; so may fresh air. This technical use of the term, of course, in no way justifies the illegal or condones the immoral or unethical. It simply delineates, in part, the scope of economic study. See (12).

good faith. Observance of honorable intent in business relations and avoidance of any attempt to deceive or mislead in assuming and discharging contractual obligations.

good will. As used in an asset and liability statement, the value imputed to a name or reputation. Presumably an established name or favorable reputation assures a certain amount of continuing business which a new establishment would not enjoy. This probability of continued business is an asset, and its value is usually considered when a GOING BUSINESS is sold.

government depositary. A bank, or similar institution, which accepts deposits of public funds and in which the government maintains an account. The FEDERAL RESERVE BANKS act as depositaries of the federal government and as fiscal agents. Certain approved commercial banks are designated by the Treasury as depositaries for receiving taxes and the proceeds of securities sold to the public. Such deposits are known as *tax and loan accounts.*

Government Printing Office. A federal agency, responsible to

Congress, which provides the services of printer and binder to all governmental units and sells government documents to the public.

grace period. A period of time—usually 3 days—after a debt falls due, during which the debtor may occasionally be permitted to delay fulfillment of his obligation without incurring a penalty or other liability. Commonly referred to as *days of grace.*

graded tax. A system of local taxation so designed as to impose an increasingly heavy burden upon land values and a decreasing burden upon improvements. Either the assessed valuation or the tax rate may be used to effect the differential. The object of such a tax is to encourage building and to discourage the holding of unimproved land over a long period of time. See TAX.

grade labeling. The labeling of consumer goods in accordance with certain standards, presumably established by an authoritative body. A term, letter, or number is used to designate a certain quality, size, or other characteristic essential in judging the product and the price asked for it. The term is used in contradistinction to *descriptive labeling* which, presumably, describes a product but without reference to any recognized authoritative standards.

graduated tax. A form of progressive tax in which the rate of tax per unit of the tax base increases progressively as the number of units increase. See CHAIN-STORE TAX, PROGRESSIVE TAXATION, TAX.

Grain Futures Act. An act of Congress, 1922, which provided for federal supervision of operations in grain futures, particularly the control of false or misleading information designed to influence prices of grain futures.

Grain Standards Act. An act of Congress, 1916, which standardizes grades for grains and provides for federal supervision over all grain-inspection systems.

Grange. See NATIONAL GRANGE ORDER OF THE PATRONS OF HUSBANDRY.

Granger cases. See *MUNN V. ILLINOIS.*

granger legislation. Laws favoring agricultural interests enacted in many western states of the United States between 1870 and

199

1890. The laws resulted from the organized efforts of farmers to curb monopolistic and discriminatory practices on the part of railroads, warehouses, grain elevators, and the like, by bringing the rates and services of such enterprises under public control. See also MUNN V. ILLINOIS.

grant. **1.** A donation of funds by government or by a private philanthropic institution to a public or private body or individual to finance a research, educational, or charitable enterprise. **2.** A legal transfer of land or real property.

gratuitous coinage. Under a system of free coinage, a governmental policy of manufacturing metal into coins without cost to the owner of the metal. See COINAGE.

gratuity. A voluntary payment given usually in return for some service rendered; a tip.

Graves* v. *New York* ex rel. *O'Keefe. See STATE TAX IMMUNITY CASE.

graveyard shift. The shift working from 12 midnight until 8 A.M., when three shifts, each working 8 hours, are employed in an enterprise. See SHIFT.

gray market. Sources of supply where scarce commodities can be purchased for immediate delivery at a premium considerably above the normal market price. Gray-market operators speculate on future demands. The important distinction between their activities and those of BLACK-MARKET operators is that the latter are illegal. See MARKET.

greenbacks. A form of fiduciary paper money, first issued by the United States Treasury in 1862, the total eventually reaching $450 million. It was expected that the greenbacks would be retired soon after the Civil War, but such plans met with strong opposition. Some greenbacks were retired under the provision of the Resumption Act of 1875, but more than $346,000,000 worth were left in circulation, and subsequent legislation provided for the constant reissue of greenbacks. In 1900, under the GOLD STANDARD ACT (*q.v.*), a gold reserve of approximately $150,000,000 was provided to insure the redeemability of the greenbacks, and it is estimated that there are about $300 million still technically in circulation.

Green* v. *Frazier. A somewhat novel case, 253 U.S. 233 (1920), in which the Supreme Court reviewed a series of statutes of North Dakota authorizing that state's government to become the proprietor and operator of a variety of business establishments. These included a bank, warehouses, flour mills and food processing and distributing plants, normally not deemed to come within the scope of governmental enterprise in the United States. The Court was petitioned to declare these statutes contrary to the due process clause of the 14th Amendment of the United States Constitution because taxes levied to support the proposed activities and the incidental property which the state might acquire were alleged to be for a nonpublic purpose. In its decision, in which it declined to identify any constitutional bar to this collectivistic program, the Court gave particular weight to the special character of North Dakota's economy and to the fact that the state's program had the sanction of its constitution, its legislature, and its people.

Gresham's law. The well-known fact that when two or more kinds of money of unequal exchange value are in concurrent circulation, each being available for payments, the one of inferior value tends to drive the one of higher value out of circulation. Named for Sir Thomas Gresham, English financier (1519–1579).

grievance. In labor relations, dissatisfaction with conditions of employment, especially objections to interpretation of provisions of a labor agreement applicable to working conditions and wages.

gross income. The term may refer to the total receipts of an enterprise or it may refer to the total receipts less certain expenses. Modern income or profit-and-loss statements customarily group expense accounts into certain broad classifications such as cost of goods sold, selling expenses, operating expenses, etc. In such statements the term "gross income" is frequently used to indicate the amount remaining after the total "costs of goods sold" only has been deducted from the total sales. Other expenses are then deducted until the NET INCOME is finally computed. In the accounts required of some public-utility companies, the term is used to indicate the amount remaining after all the expenses have been deducted except debt charges and a few other items. See INCOME.

gross interest. A price paid for the use of capital which includes a sum to cover the risk involved and a sum to cover the administration costs incurred in making the loan. The customary price paid for the use of capital is gross interest but is customarily referred to as merely INTEREST. See INTEREST.

gross national debt. The total national debt outstanding, including duplications and that part of the debt held by governmental units in trust, in investment, or in sinking funds. See DEBT.

gross national product. A statement of the distribution, at market prices, of the goods and services produced in the national economy during a given year. Distribution is shown in terms of consumer purchases, government purchases, gross private domestic investments, and exports of goods and services. See Appendix B, items 11 to 15 inclusive. See also NATIONAL INCOME, NATIONAL INCOME AND PRODUCT ACCOUNT.

gross national products deflator. A statistical measure—essentially a price index or a combination of price indexes—which reveals changes, up or down, in the price level over a period of years according to constant values and for a larger economic segment than is usually embraced by other price indexes. It is used particularly in estimating, in constant dollars, the growth (or decline) of the physical volume of the gross national product.

gross profit. See PROFIT.

ground rent. A price paid for the use of land without improvements, including the right to occupy and improve it. See RENT.

group banking. See CHAIN BANKING.

group insurance. Life, medical, accident, or other insurance often purchased on a group basis by a business concern to cover its employees. See INSURANCE.

group medicine. Any cooperative or voluntary plan for securing certain medical services to members of a specific group or association, such services often embracing periodic medical examinations as well as medical care in case of illness. Such a plan may take the form of medical insurance for employees placed through an employer, or it may take the form of special arrangements between medical practitioners and particular groups of persons who pay for medical care collectively.

Group of Ten. Key financial and industrial countries (United States, Canada, United Kingdom, German Federal Republic, Italy, Belgium, The Netherlands, Sweden, Japan, France) which, in the late 1960's, assumed leadership in providing a more flexible international system of monetary reserves and urged internal financial discipline upon member countries, particularly upon the United States and United Kingdom whose currencies are regarded as reserve currencies in international finance. Nine of this group (France abstaining) were responsible at the Stockholm Monetary Conference, March 30, 1968, for recommending the creation of the so-called SPECIAL DRAWING RIGHTS (*q.v.*).

growth stock. The stock of a corporation whose retained earnings and earning prospects are such as to insure an appreciable and constant increase in the stock's market value over a considerable period of time, the rate of increase in value being greater than that enjoyed by the general run of corporate shares.

Grundy tariff. See HAWLEY-SMOOT TARIFF.

guaranteed annual income. Any of a variety of plans—e.g., the NEGATIVE INCOME TAX (*q.v.*)—under which government would provide income supplements, graded according to need and family size, in order to raise total family income to a minimum level which economists and welfare workers consider to be above the poverty level. Such an income guarantee would differ from prevailing welfare payments, which it would largely supersede, by eliminating penalties to recipients for income from gainful employment and, indeed, by encouraging recipients to seek gainful employment. See INCOME.

guaranteed annual wage. See ANNUAL WAGE.

guaranteed bond. See BOND.

guaranteed stock. See CAPITAL STOCK.

guaranteed-wage plan. Generally a labor contract in which employees are guaranteed employment or a stated amount in wages during a specified period of time. In some studies the term is limited to agreements which guarantee a minimum of three months employment during a one-year period, or the equivalent in wages.

guaranty savings bank. A type of savings bank located in New Hampshire having some features of the mutual savings bank and some features of the stock savings bank. There are two classes of depositors, regular and special. The regular depositors are paid a stipulated amount of interest; the special deposi-

203

tors are paid all net earnings not held as reserves, in excess of the payments to the regular depositors. The feature of having two classes of depositors distinguishes a guaranty savings bank from other types of savings banks. See BANK.

Guffey Coal Act. An act of Congress, 1937, designed to secure conservation and better utilization of coal and to stabilize the soft-coal industry by the creation of a bituminous coal code. The code aimed to promote fair competition, establish minimum prices, and improve labor relations. Companies subject to the act but refusing to accept the code were subjected to an ad valorem tax on their products. The act expired April 26, 1943.

guild. 1. Historically, an association of tradesmen or artisans which controlled production of a particular commodity or service and regulated the admission of members. See (24). **2.** Another name for a labor union or professional association.

guild socialism. Social ownership of the means of production, with industrial operations managed by workers organized into associations comparable to medieval guilds. Local guilds would be federated in national guilds, which would be represented in a guild congress. The guild congress would concern itself with the overall direction of industry and would supplement but not replace existing political assemblies. Guild socialist theories were advanced by G. D. H. Cole and other British intellectuals in the early part of the 20th century. See SOCIALISM.

H

half stock. See CAPITAL STOCK.

hallmark. An impression made upon gold- and silverware, required by the British public assay office, indicating the degree of fineness of the metals used. The custom was introduced as early as 1300 by the English Guild of Gold and Silver Smiths and was enforced by royal command.

Hammer v. Dagenhart. See CHILD-LABOR CASES.

handicraft economy. An economy that appeared with the growth of towns in the 14th and 15th centuries when artisans pursued crafts or trades, usually in their home or small shop, for the purpose of producing goods for the market. See ECONOMIC SYSTEMS.

hard money. 1. Metal coins in contrast to paper money. **2.** A national money with relatively stable value both internally and in international exchange. See MONEY.

hard sell. Extremely aggressive selling practice. Examples are: constant repetition of a phrase or slogan in a radio or television program; scare headlines or extravagant therapeutic claims in newspaper and magazine advertising; and conspicuous outdoor billboards which obstruct attractive landscape views.

harmonic mean. A calculated average computed by finding the reciprocal of the ARITHMETIC MEAN of the reciprocals of the numbers to be averaged. The mathematical formula is:

$$\frac{1}{H} = \frac{\dfrac{1}{r_1} + \dfrac{1}{r_2} + \dfrac{1}{r_3} \cdots + \dfrac{1}{r_n}}{N}$$

when

H = the harmonic mean,
$r_1, r_2, r_3 \cdots r_n$ = the numbers to be averaged,
N = the total quantity of numbers.

In economic computation the harmonic mean is used in averaging such data as time rates and rate-per-dollar prices. For example, suppose the average price per unit is required when a commodity sells for 10 for $1.00 in one store, 20 for $1.00 in another store, and 25 for $1.00 in a third store. The arithmetic mean of 10, 20, and 25 is 18.334, the average number of units sold per dollar, and $1.00 divided by 18.334 is 5.454 cents, the apparent price per unit. But if the arithmetic mean of the unit price is computed (10, 5, and 4 cents), the average price per unit is 6.33 + cents. If, however, the harmonic mean of 10, 20, and 25 is computed, the result is 15.797 +, the average number of units sold per $1.00, and the unit price is 6.33 + cents, the same as the arithmetic mean of the unit prices. The computation is as follows:

$$\frac{1}{H} = \frac{\dfrac{1}{10} + \dfrac{1}{20} + \dfrac{1}{25}}{3} = \frac{0.1 + 0.05 + 0.04}{3} = \frac{0.19}{3} = 0.0633 + .$$

$$\frac{1}{H} = 0.0633 + . \quad H = 15.797 + .$$

$$\frac{1.00}{15.797} = 6.33 + \text{ cents.}$$

See AVERAGE.

harmonic progression. See PROGRESSION.

harmonies. As applied to economic theory, the doctrine that economic life is governed by forces that are essentially in accord with one another and that operate to assure the ultimate welfare of mankind. Although these forces are frequently found in apparent conflict owing to temporary disarrangement, harmony is ultimately restored. The idea is found early in the history of economic thought in the concept of the NATURAL ORDER and in more systematic and comprehensive form, although with some contradictions, in Adam Smith's (1723-1790) development of LAISSEZ FAIRE. Later pronouncements of the CLASSICAL SCHOOL, notably in the MALTHUSIAN THEORY OF POPULATION, and in the Ricardian theory of rent (ECONOMIC RENT) left the doctrine of harmonies somewhat impaired. It was reasserted by various adherents of the OPTIMIST SCHOOL, especially Henry C. Carey (1793-1879), the American publicist and economist, and Claude Frédéric Bastiat (1801-1850), a French economist. The latter went beyond the original conception in his emphasis upon divine guidance. The present-day theory of GENERAL EQUILIBRIUM may be said, perhaps, to express scientifically the idea inherent in the doctrine.

Harper v. Virginia State Board of Elections. See POLL TAX.

Hatch Act. An act of Congress, 1887, which authorized the establishment of agricultural stations in connection with the LAND-GRANT COLLEGES and universities for the purpose of conducting original research in agricultural science. It was supplemented by legislation passed in 1906 and in 1925.

Hawes-Cooper Act. An act of Congress, 1929, removing goods made by convict labor from the protection of the Supreme Court ruling that states cannot impose taxes or police regulations upon goods in interstate commerce so long as such goods remain in the packages in which they were originally shipped. See also ORIGINAL-PACKAGE CASES.

Hawley-Smoot Tariff. The United States Tariff Act of 1930. It raised the rates on more than 1,000 articles but contained a provision that permitted the President to alter the rates up or down within limits of 50 per cent on advice of the UNITED STATES TARIFF COMMISSION which was to investigate differences in cost production of dutiable or equivalent articles abroad. Effective reductions in this tariff did not occur until after 1934 when, in pursuance of the TRADE AGREEMENTS ACT of 1934 and similar subsequent legislation, the United States inaugurated the policy of reducing tariffs on the basis of reciprocity. The tariff was nicknamed the *Grundy Tariff* after Joseph

Grundy, president of the Pennsylvania Manufacturers Association, who was the chief lobbyist.

headright. **1.** A grant of land awarded to an immigrant who agreed to fulfill certain conditions regarding settling on and developing the land, as in the colony of Virginia in 1619 and in Texas in 1839. **2.** The right of a member of an Indian tribe to share in the income of a tribal trust fund, such as that obtained from the sale or lease of oil or mineral rights.

head of family. Any person maintaining a family unit who, under tax regulations, may enjoy special exemptions or be given special consideration.

head tax. **1.** A tax levied upon immigrant aliens entering at any port of the United States. **2.** See POLL TAX, TAX.

health insurance. A system of insurance against financial loss due to illness. Some contemporary governments provide such insurance, and some protection is afforded to limited numbers of persons in low-income groups by fraternal orders, labor-union benefit funds, and employers' relief funds. Casualty and life insurance companies offer such insurance on a profit-making basis. See INSURANCE. See also MEDICAID, MEDICARE.

heat pipe. A heat conductor, at present in the development stage, consisting of a pipe containing a wick which, by capillary action, moves heated vapor in one direction and cooled liquid in another. It is said to be many times more effective than other means of heat transmission.

hedge fund. A partnership of individuals who pool funds for investment. Unlike an INVESTMENT COMPANY, these essentially private groups are not rigidly controlled and exercise considerable trading latitude such as SELLING SHORT and BUYING ON MARGIN. See FUND.

hedging. A method of selling for future delivery, whereby dealers and processors protect themselves against a declining market price between the time they buy a product and sell or process it. For example, a miller, buying a quantity of wheat to convert into flour, will sell a similar quantity of wheat, which he does not own at the time, at the same price or near the same price as the wheat he buys for processing. He will agree to deliver this extra lot of wheat at the time that his flour is ready for market. If at that time, the price of wheat, and hence of flour, has gone down, he will lose on his flour, but he can buy wheat at the current low price and deliver at a profit the order previously sold for future delivery. If, on the other hand, the price of wheat, and hence of flour, has gone up, he will make an extra profit on his flour. This extra profit he will have to sacrifice, however, by purchasing wheat at the current high price in order to make good his contract to sell. In either event his manufacturing profits are protected. Contracts for future delivery are called *futures.*

hedonistic principle. The idea that although every individual wishes to avoid effort, the desire for well-being and wealth stimulates an attempt to attain them however repugnant the effort expended in so doing may be. Sometimes called *law of self-interest.*

Helvering v. Davis. See SOCIAL-SECURITY CASES.

Helvering v. Gerhardt. See FEDERAL TAX IMMUNITY CASE.

Hepburn Act. An act of Congress, 1906, which (*a*) provided that railway rates determined by the INTERSTATE COMMERCE COMMISSION should become effective within 30 days of their announcement, and should remain in force unless suspended by a court; (*b*) required individual railways to establish joint tariffs; (*c*) made a uniform system of accounting mandatory for railways; and (*d*) extended the jurisdiction of the Commission to cover pipelines, and express and sleeping-car companies.

Hepburn v. Griswold. See LEGAL-TENDER CASES.

hidden inflation. The condition that exists when, because of deterioration of the quality of a service or the deterioration of the quality or the reduction of the size or content of a product, less value is offered for the same amount of money. See INFLATION.

hidden tax. A tax of an indirect nature which is incorporated in the price of goods and services and which is therefore not apparent as such when paid. For example, a CUSTOMS DUTY may increase the price of imported products without the consumer being cognizant of how much of the price is due to the payment of those duties. See TAX.

higgling. The process of bargaining. Buyers attempt to buy at as low a price as possible, and sellers attempt to sell at as high a price as possible. This necessitates a certain amount of bargaining until, for any one product in any particular market, a price is established at which trading takes place.

hire purchase. See INSTALLMENT BUYING.

highway. A publicly constructed and maintained way for the transport of goods and persons. Major systems of hard-surface highways date from Roman times. With certain historic exceptions, highway construction in the United States was a primary responsibility of the states until well into the 20th century, and several of the states have recently built major arterial toll roads. The federal government initiated systematic assistance for highway construction through grants-in-aid in 1916. Forty years later it inaugurated a vast ($33.4 billion, subsequently generously supplemented, especially in 1968) program of interstate north-south, east-west, continental freeways for which the principal financial outlay was federal, although the states provided necessary supplementary funds and were responsible for actual construction.

histogram. See FREQUENCY DISTRIBUTION.

Historical school. A school of economic thought that first came into prominence in Germany during the middle part of the 19th century. It was a reaction against the abstract and deductive methods of the Classical economists. The writers of the Historical school insisted that economists should turn to history to discover the realities of economic life, and emphasized the evolutionary aspect of economic laws. See SCHOOLS OF ECONOMIC THOUGHT.

hoarding. Deliberate accumulation of goods, currency, or the supply of some service beyond normal needs. Money saved and placed in a safe-deposit box is hoarded. Stocks of goods beyond the normal inventory requirements of a business or beyond the immediate future needs of a household are likewise hoarded. See PROPENSITY TO HOARD.

hold-back pay. Wages withheld by an employer, usually for the period necessary to calculate the pay roll. Thus, employees may be paid on Saturday for all work up to Thursday night of a given weekly period.

holding company. A corporation which holds a sufficient quantity of the stock of some other corporation, usually an operating company, to permit it to direct its affairs. Sometimes referred to as a *controlling company.* See COMBINATION, COMPANY.

holding the line. A phrase frequently employed to indicate fiscal or monetary policies used to prevent or discourage prices from rising beyond a current level. Freezing prices, checking bank credit, increasing bank reserves, increasing the discount rates, and imposing restrictions on consumer loans, are among the measures commonly used.

holograph. A will or other legal instrument handwritten by the person from whom the instrument proceeds.

Home Building and Loan Association v. Blaisdell. A *mortgage-moratorium case* arising out of state laws passed during the depression of the 1930's. The Supreme Court ruled, 290 U. S. 398 (1934), that such laws, extending a mortgagor's right to redeem foreclosed property beyond the time limit stipulated when the mortgage was made, were a proper exercise of the state's police power required by the circumstances of an economic emergency and that the laws did not violate the contract clause (Art. I, Sec. 10) of the Constitution.

home demonstration agent. See EXTENSION SERVICE.

home economics. A general term covering a variety of subject matter, including household skills such as cooking, sewing, child care, budgeting, and consumer purchasing for the home, and sometimes training for gainful employment in certain special fields such as dietetics. See ECONOMICS.

home industry. See DOMESTIC SYSTEM.

homestead. An owner-occupied house and adjacent property which, under the laws of some states, cannot be sold to satisfy a judgment for a creditor.

Homestead Act. An act of Congress, 1862. It granted 160 acres of public lands free to settlers after 5 years of residence or at $1.25 per acre after 6 months of residence.

homestead-aid benefit association. See BUILDING AND LOAN ASSOCIATION.

homework. As applied to some industries, the practice of supplying materials to workers so that they perform certain operations in the production of a commodity at home. Such workers are generally paid on a PIECEWORK (*q.v.*) basis.

Hoosac Mills case. A case, *United States* v. *Butler,* 297 U. S. 1 (1936), in which the Supreme Court invalidated the first Agricultural Adjustment Act. The Court asserted that, under the Constitution, the government had no power to enforce commands on the farmer to secure compliance with the price and production-quota objectives of this statute, regulation of agriculture being outside the scope of the delegated power of Congress and reserved, by the 10th Amendment to the Constitution, to the states. As a consequence, the Court continued, Congress could not secure compliance of the farmer through the use of the taxing and appropriatory power. In the Court's opinion this meant that the processing tax, provided for in the act, was not a bona fide revenue measure but part of a plan of regulation, itself unconstitutional, and that the appropriation of the proceeds of this tax could not be sustained under the general welfare clause of the Constitution since the phrase "general welfare" did not comprehend the use to which these proceeds were to be put. See AGRICULTURAL ADJUSTMENT ACT (first). The court later reversed this decision. See AGRICULTURAL ADJUSTMENT ACT CASE (second).

Hoover moratorium. A proposal made on June 20, 1931, by President Herbert Hoover and subsequently ratified by Congress, that a moratorium of 1 year be declared on all reparation payments from the defeated powers of World War I, and on all inter-government debts created by loans made among the Allied and Associated Powers during and immediately after World War I. It had the practical effect of suspending payments indefinitely. See INTERALLIED DEBTS.

horizontal expansion. Expansion of a business establishment by absorbing or constructing additional facilities to take care of an increased volume of the activity in which the establishment is already engaged.

horizontal labor union. See CRAFT UNION.

hot money. A term applied to various kinds of money transactions that are either illegal or questionable from the standpoint of the welfare of a particular nation's economy. It is sometimes applied to short-term international capital movements which result solely from the fact that the interest rate is temporarily more attractive in the country to which the funds are exported.

Such operations are often embarrassing to a country's financial structure because they complicate the problem of maintaining equilibrium of the BALANCE OF PAYMENTS. See MONEY.

hot-oil case. A case, *Panama Refining Co.* v. *Ryan,* 293 U. S. 388 (1935), in which the Supreme Court invalidated a portion of the National Industrial Recovery Act under which the President had sought to prohibit the movement in interstate and foreign commerce of petroleum or petroleum products in excess of production or marketing quotas fixed by the laws of the oil-producing states of the United States. The purpose of the President's action under the law had been to assist in stabilizing production and prices in the petroleum industry. The Court ruled that the authority under which the President had acted constituted a delegation of legislative power to the executive and was therefore unconstitutional.

household system. An economy in which the clan, tribe, or family, as an economic unit, produces the goods required for home consumption. Also called *domestic industry, family-industry.* See ECONOMIC SYSTEM.

Houston East and West Texas Ry. Co. v. United States. See SHREVEPORT CASE.

hypothecate. The act of pledging and depositing property to secure a loan. The property in question is then said to be hypothecated.

hypothesis. A tentative statement setting forth an apparent relationship among observed facts. See INDUCTIVE METHOD.

I

idle money. A term usually referring to inactive bank deposits. The deposits are said to be inactive when the ratio between a bank's reserves and deposits permits of additional loans which are not made, or when the deposits do not show continuously fluctuating balances characteristic of active checking accounts. See MONEY.

illegal strike. 1. Work stoppage by union members not authorized by union officials or not voted upon in accordance with union regulations. Sometimes called a *quickie, outlaw,* or *wildcat strike.* **2.** Any strike called in violation of the conditions set forth in the LABOR-MANAGEMENT RELATIONS (TAFT-HARTLEY) ACT of 1947. See STRIKE.

illth. Consumer goods and services that are injurious to the individuals who consume them and to society as a whole.

immigrant remittances. Funds sent by immigrants to their country of origin for the benefit of relatives and friends. Such remittances are an invisible item of trade and have the same effect on the balance of payments of the country from which the remittances are sent as an import of merchandise from the country to which the remittances are sent; that is, they contribute toward a deficit balance.

immigration. The migration of people into a country for permanent settlement, the usual objective being expanded employment opportunities. Under post-1965 immigration policy, which continues to limit total admissions, the United States, in determining whom to admit, gives preference to professional people, people with special skills, close relatives of American residents or citizens, and certain political refugees.

impacted area. A local area in the United States in which construction of federal installations, military and civil, has removed so much property from tax rolls that the federal government provides special appropriations for the local schools to compensate for lost tax revenue.

impair investment. An investment which does not create a new capital asset; for example, the purchase of existing securities from other holders, or loans for the purpose of consumption. See INVESTMENT.

impartial chairman. As applied to labor relations, an arbitrator appointed jointly by labor and management to assist in the settlement of any disputes that may arise in reference to a specific labor contract. See also ARBITRATION.

imperfect competition. The situation said to exist when, because of peculiar conditions of the market or advantages held by certain buyers or sellers, prices can be abnormally influenced by one or more traders. In the retail trade, for example, imperfect competition is the rule because the market is scattered and the buyers cannot always estimate quality accurately. Monopolistic or semimonopolistic advantages held by certain traders also create imperfect competition. See COMPETITION.

impersonal account. A ledger account bearing a title which is not a personal name; for example, cash account, bank account, captial account. See ACCOUNT.

import. To receive merchandise from abroad, particularly from foreign countries; hence, merchandise so received. See also INVISIBLE ITEMS OF TRADE.

import duty. An ad valorem or specific tax levied upon goods imported into a country, the tax base usually being the wholesale value of the goods in the exporting country. Compare AMERICAN SELLING PRICE.

import license. Authority from a government to import a specified quantity of a particular commodity. Such authority must often be secured when imports are subject to an IMPORT QUOTA.

import quota. A specified maximum amount of a commodity permitted to enter a country within a certain period of time.

impost. A tax, especially an import duty.

imprest fund. A definite sum of money set aside for cash expenditures and renewed from time to time to the extent of the exact amount of the signed receipts obtained when the cash expenditures are made. An imprest fund is frequently used for petty-cash expenses and withdrawals. It is easily audited, as the sum of the cash on hand and the receipts for payments should always equal the total amount of the fund. See FUND.

improved good. An economic good (commodity), usually imported, which is eventually processed or assembled in some other product and hence increased in value. See GOOD.

imputed. A generic term used in economics to denote an estimated value when no cash payment is made such as would establish a value. For example, an enterprise might calculate *imputed interest* on its invested capital when no interest as such is paid. *Imputed rent* might be estimated for a dwelling owned and occupied by the owner. An *imputed cost* to an INDIVIDUAL PROPRIETORSHIP might be the estimated labor of the proprietor.

imputed cost. See IMPUTED.

imputed interest. See IMPUTED.

imputed rent. See IMPUTED.

inactive stock. See CAPITAL STOCK.

incentive. A material or intangible motivational factor which stimulates to more vigorous action or greater efficiency.

incentive taxation. A tax plan which, by modifying the structure of an existing system of taxation, changing its rates, shifting its incidence, or by other appropriate change, is expected to stimulate investment or business activity generally.

incentive wage system. A system of wage payments which encourages increased production with some sort of bonus or premium wage payment. See WAGE.

incidence of taxation. The point where the burden of a tax actually rests, irrespective of how or against whom it is formally levied. For example, the incidence of a sales tax almost invariably rests on the consumer, although the seller is the one formally taxed and it is he who remits the tax to the government. Frequently called *shifting of taxation.*

income. 1. As used in theoretical economics, the money return or other material benefit arising from the use of wealth or from the services of free human beings. See also DISPOSABLE PERSONAL INCOME, NATIONAL INCOME, PSYCHIC INCOME. **2.** As used in accounting, the term is a broad one indicating, in general, the receipts of an enterprise or of an individual. See (1).

income and expenditure equation. A mathematical expression of the relation, under conditions of equilibrium, between the national income on the one hand and consumer expenditures and investment on the other. The equation is:

$$Y = C + I$$

when

Y = the national income,
C = consumer expenditures,
I = investments.

This equation is useful because of its implied relation to savings and the general level of economic activity. For if

$$Y = C + I,$$

and

$$S \text{ (savings)} = \dot{Y} - C,$$

then

$$Y = C + S,$$

and

$$I = S.$$

To maintain the national income, and hence the general level of economic activity, all collective savings must therefore be invested. For conditions under disequilibrium, see PROPENSITY TO INVEST. See also KEYNESIAN ECONOMICS.

income bond. See BOND.

income maintenance. See NEGATIVE INCOME TAX.

income statement. See PROFIT-AND-LOSS STATEMENT.

income tax. In the United States a federal, state, or local tax levied upon corporate income or individual income, such as wages, rents, interest, dividends, royalties, profits, commissions, etc. The tax is levied on amounts in excess of certain exemptions and deductions, and the rate is usually steeply progressive. Capital gains taxes, though subject to separate rules, are

usually incorporated administratively in the income tax. See
TAX.

income-tax case. A case, *Pollock* v. *Farmers' Loan and Trust Co.,*
157 U. S. 429 (1894); 158 U. S. 601 (1895), in which the Supreme
Court held unconstitutional the Income Tax Law of 1894.
The issue involved in the Court's decision was whether a federal income tax was a direct tax within the meaning of Art. I,
sec. 3, of the Constitution which requires that direct taxes be
apportioned among the states according to population. The
Court decided that an income tax was a direct tax, and that
since the law of 1894 had not apportioned its burden among
the states according to population, the law was void. The decision stimulated agitation for a constitutional change which
would make it unnecessary to apportion income taxes, and this
agitation culminated in the adoption of the 16th, or "income-
tax," Amendment to the Constitution in 1913. In substance this
amendment declares that Congress may levy and collect taxes
on income from any source without apportioning them among
the several states according to population.

inconvertible money. See IRREDEEMABLE MONEY.

incorporation. See CORPORATION.

increasing costs. Costs which, under a given set of conditions,
increase, per unit of product, as the total production increases.
So far as poorer and deeper mines have to be used to meet a
constant or increasing demand, the coal-mining industry may
be said to be operating under a condition of increasing costs.
See COST.

increasing misery, theory of. See MARXIAN LAW OF CAPITALIST
ACCUMULATION.

increasing returns. **1.** Usually the condition which exists as long
as each equal amount of one or two factors of production
(land, labor, or capital) successively applied to the remaining
factor or factors yields a greater increase in production than the
application just preceding. This is a common situation before
the condition of DIMINISHING RETURNS (*q.v.*) begins to operate.
2. The term is also used to describe the condition that exists
when output is increased without adding to any factor of production. Division of labor, or economies brought about by purchasing in large quantities, or increased productivity on the

part of labor may bring about increasing returns as thus defined.

increment. An increase, a gain, or something added. See also UNEARNED INCREMENT.

indemnity. 1. As applied to trading, an option to buy or sell a definite quantity of a commodity at a stated price within a specified length of time. **2.** A guarantee against possible loss. **3.** A payment for damages.

indent. An order from a buyer to a middleman importer to import certain specified goods at a stated price. The importer may accept or refuse the indent within a specified length of time, usually about 6 weeks. The term is sometimes more generally applied to any order for foreign merchandise.

indenture. 1. A formal documentary agreement between two or more persons—so called because of the custom, now obsolete, of placing the copies of an agreement together, before delivery to the interested parties, and tearing an irregular edge on one side. Matching of the edges of any two documents at a later date was considered proof of the identity of the original documents. **2.** Historically, the contract by which an apprentice was bound to a master, or an individual, in return for passage, was bound to service of a master. See INDENTURED SERVANT.

indentured servant. 1. A person who, during the latter part of the 17th century, received his passage to America in return for a definite term of service in the colonies. He also received his maintenance during that period of service. **2.** Any person so bound by contract.

independent treasury system. A system, begun in 1840, of handling funds and financing the United States government independently of banks. The system was introduced because of the bank panic of 1837, at which time the United States Treasury lost large sums deposited in state banks. The system was suspended in 1841, re-established in 1846, and finally terminated in 1920. Also called *subtreasury system.*

independent union. A labor union that is not affiliated with a national or international labor organization. See LABOR UNION.

index number. A figure which discloses the relative change, if any, of prices, costs, or similar statistical phenomena between one period of time and some other period of time selected as the *base period*. The latter period is usually assigned the index number of 100. There are numerous methods of calculating an index number. See (10).

indifference curve. A graphic representation of the various combinations of two commodities or services that will yield equal satisfaction to a given consumer. An indifference curve is shown in the diagram on page 221. Quantities of commodity y are plotted on the Y axis, and quantities of commodity x are plotted on the X axis. The consumer starts with a stock of $35y$. He sacrifices $5y$ to gain $1x$. It is a matter of indifference to him whether he has $35y$, or $30y$ and $1x$; in other words, $35y$ yields him the same satisfaction as $30y$ and $1x$. With $1x$ now in his possession, he is willing to sacrifice 2 more of y to gain another x. It is a matter of indifference to him whether he has $35y$, or $30y$ and $1x$, or $28y$ and $2x$, etc., according to the following *indifference schedule*. The last two columns in this schedule contain the figures plotted on the chart.

Sacrifices of y	Gains of x	Total stock of y	Total stock of x
		35	0
5	1	30	1
2	1	28	2
5	3	23	5
3	2	20	7
7	6	13	13
5	5	8	18
3	5	5	23
2	6	3	29
2	7	1	35

See also INDIFFERENCE MAP.

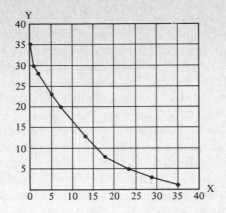

indifference map. A graphic representation of a number of IN-
DIFFERENCE CURVES (*q.v.*). An indifference map is shown in
Diagram 1 on page 222. Quantities of commodity *y* are plotted
on the *Y* axis, and quantities of commodity *x* are plotted on the
X axis. If a given consumer starts with 35*y*, he may be willing
to sacrifice 5*y* in order to gain 1*x*, then to sacrifice 2*y* to gain
another *x,* as shown in indifference curve *A* in Diagram 1. But
if instead of 35*y* the consumer starts with some other quantity,
say 50, or 10, or 83*y*, the indifference curve will be different;
that is, it will differ according to the initial quantity possessed
and the resulting exchange dispositions. A larger stock of *y,* for
example, might prompt the consumer to sacrifice more of *y* to
gain his first *x,* whereas a smaller initial stock of *y* might make
him unwilling to sacrifice even 5*y* for 1*x*. It is possible, therefore, to construct an indefinite number of indifference curves
applicable to one consumer and two commodities. A group of
these curves on one chart is the indifference map. Each indifference curve, proceeding from left to right, represents a higher
scale of satisfactions because of the increased quantities
involved.

An indifference map makes it possible to forecast with some
degree of accuracy the quantities of each of the two commodities that a consumer will purchase, given the consumer's income and the prices of the commodities. Assume, for example,

that the consumer's income is $150 for a given period of time, that the market price of *y* is $7.50 per unit, and the price of *x* is $5 per unit. If the entire income were spent on *y*, 20 items could be bought; if spent on *x*, 30 items could be bought. These quantities are plotted on axis *Y* and axis *X*, respectively, and a straight line is drawn connecting them, as shown in the appended Diagram 2. This straight line shows the various combinations of the two commodities that can be bought with $150 at established prices, regardless of which combinations yield the greatest satisfaction. At point *B*, however, the straight line is tangent to an indifference curve. Point *B* on the indifference curve indicates a combination of the two commodities that will yield at least as much satisfaction as any other combination represented by any other point on that indifference curve. Also, this curve is the farthest to the right of any that can be tangent to the straight line. The possible combinations indicated by this curve, therefore, offer greater satisfactions than those indicated by any curve to the left of it. Hence, point *B* discloses not only the amount of each commodity that can be bought with the stipulated income but also the amount of each that will be bought at that income to yield the maximum amount of satisfaction. The amounts are 8*y* and 18*x*. See also PRICE CONSUMPTION CURVE.

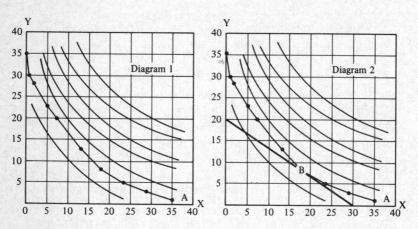

indifference schedule. See INDIFFERENCE CURVE.
indirect cost. See FIXED COST.

indirect exporting. The process of exporting through a middleman such as an export merchant. Many producers, wishing to reach a foreign market but too small to maintain an export department, use this means of developing their foreign trade.

indirect foreign-exchange standard. See GOLD-EXCHANGE STANDARD.

indirect production. The making of a tool, a machine, or any other kind of capital good that will, in turn, assist in making a product used directly to satisfy a human want. The tool or the machine in question does not directly satisfy the want but facilitates the production of something else that does; in other words, it facilitates the production of a consumer good. Sometimes called *roundabout* or *capitalistic production.* The term is used in contradistinction to DIRECT PRODUCTION. See PRODUCTION.

indirect tax. A tax, the burden of which can be fairly readily shifted or passed on to someone else by the person who is required by law to pay the tax to the government. The term is used in contradistinction to DIRECT TAX (*q.v.*). Most EXCISE TAXES are indirect taxes. See TAX.

individualism. As applied to economic life, the enjoyment by individuals and groups of the rights of freedom of contract and private property. The term implies PRIVATE ENTERPRISE and LAISSEZ FAIRE as opposed to COLLECTIVISM and STATE SOCIALISM. See also FREEDOM OF CONTRACT, PRIVATE PROPERTY.

Individualist school. See CLASSICAL SCHOOL.

individual proprietorship. A form of business organization in which one individual owns and manages, assumes all the risks of, and derives all the profits from, an enterprise. Usually referred to as *proprietorship.* See FORMS OF BUSINESS ORGANIZATION.

indorsed bond. See BOND.

indorsement. A signature customarily written on the back, but sometimes on the face, of a negotiable instrument. An indorsement guarantees payment or establishes transfer of legal title. Also spelled *endorsement.* See (21).

induced consumption. Increased consumer spending resulting from new CAPITAL FORMATION. Additional employees in the capital goods industries are the first recipients of increased income; as a proportion of these earnings is spent, employees in the consumer goods industries become recipients, resulting in additional consumption, etc. See CONSUMPTION. See also MULTIPLIER PRINCIPLE.

induced investment. New CAPITAL FORMATION resulting from an increase in the rate of consumer spending. The extent of the new capital formation depends upon such factors as the excess plant capacity (if any) in existence, the amount of capital required to produce one unit of consumer product, individual estimates of the duration of the increased consumer spending, etc. See INVESTMENT. See also ACCELERATION PRINCIPLE.

inductive method. As used in economics, a process of logical reasoning, starting with observed facts and arriving at a generalization, setting forth an apparent relationship among those observed facts. Such a generalization is called a HYPOTHESIS; when repeatedly verified it is called a THEORY. The usefulness of the inductive method depends upon the validity of the basic observations. When properly used, however, it has a recognized place in scientific investigation. Sometimes it is called the *realistic method.*

industrial bank. A financial organization which makes relatively small loans on co-maker promissory notes, usually two or more co-makers being required. Also called *Morris Plan bank.* Most industrial banks have now become commercial banks and have dropped the term "industrial." As commercial banks they engage in conventional loan practices. See BANK.

industrial bond. See BOND.

industrial democracy. A term first used to indicate democratic government within labor unions. More recently, it has come to mean limitation upon the absolute control of management resulting from such practices as collective bargaining, employee stock ownership with full voting rights, and profit sharing. Rather vaguely, the term implies a limited form of socialization.

industrial life insurance. Life insurance, issued in policies of small amounts averaging less than $250, and usually calling for the payment of weekly or monthly premiums by the person insured. See LIFE INSURANCE.

industrial relations. The relations between employers and employees. Since the beginning of the 20th century, demands of employees for a voice in the determination of wages and working conditions, and the growing public control over employer-employee relationships, have created a specialized field of study generally known by this term. Referred to also as *labor relations.*

industrial-relations court. A court organized to adjudicate or arbitrate labor disputes. One, known as the *Kansas Industrial Court,* existed in Kansas between 1920 and 1925 for the settlement of disputes in certain industries. Most of the law establishing the court's jurisdiction was subsequently invalidated by the Supreme Court. See WOLFF PACKING CO. v. INDUSTRIAL COURT OF KANSAS.

industrial research. Research conducted by, or in the interests of, private industries to discover more efficient methods of production or to develop new and improved products. The term is sometimes applied to studies having to do with marketing methods, labor relations, and the like.

industrial revenue bond. See BOND.

Industrial Revolution. The conditions which existed during the latter part of the 18th and the early part of the 19th centuries when changes in the techniques of production brought about the replacement of the DOMESTIC SYSTEM by the FACTORY SYSTEM.

industrial-type farming. See PLANTATION SYSTEM.

industrial union. A labor union, the membership of which is made up of workers from an entire industry. A union of coal miners is an example. Also called *vertical labor union.* See LABOR UNION.

Industrial Workers of the World. An industrial type of labor union in the United States, founded in 1904, which sought to achieve the supremacy of the worker in society not by formal political means but by economic weapons such as the strike. Known popularly as Wobblies.

industry. Productive enterprise, especially manufacturing or certain service enterprises such as transportation and communications, which employs relatively large amounts of capital and labor. The term is often used in a collective sense referring, for example, to the production activities of an entire country or other area. It is also used to identify a special segment of productive enterprise, such as the steel industry. Normally "trading" is not included in the concept "industry," the phrase "commerce and industry" being used if reference is made both to industry as defined above and to buying and selling. See (5).

industry-wide bargaining. As applied to labor relations, negotiations carried on between employers and unions with a view to formulating uniform regulations and wage contracts for all workers in an industry, irrespective of the number or location of the different plants or companies concerned.

inelastic demand. Demand which increases or decreases in relatively small volume as prices increase or decrease. In general the demand for necessities is inelastic. See DEMAND. See also COEFFICIENT OF ELASTICITY.

inelastic supply. Supply which increases or decreases only slightly despite extensive changes in price. See SUPPLY. See also COEFFICIENT OF ELASTICITY.

infant industry. A term applied to newly established or relatively undeveloped manufacturing enterprises with particular reference to the argument, especially popular during the latter part of the 19th century in the United States, that such industries should be protected from foreign competition by import duties until such time as they could compete on an equal footing with foreign producers. See INDUSTRY.

inflation. A disproportionately large and relatively sudden increase in the general price level. Inflation becomes apparent when the quantity of money or deposit currency in circulation is large (when measured against some previous period) compared with the quantity of goods and services offered, or when, because of a loss of public confidence in the medium of exchange, a general and widespread attempt to convert money into commodities is precipitated. A normal increase in the price level after a period of depression is not generally regarded as inflation. See (12).

inflationary gap. A statistical phrase denoting the amount by which actual private spending and government expenses exceed the theoretical amount of spending necessary to maintain full employment, or exceed the theoretical amount of spending adequate to absorb all the available goods and services without appreciably raising the price level.

inherent vice. Deterioration of a commodity constituting the cargo of a ship, such deterioration being occasioned by the nature of the goods rather than through any negligence on the part of the carrier. Agricultural products, for example, are often subject to such deterioration.

inheritance tax. A tax, usually progressive in nature, levied upon the property which individual beneficiaries receive from an estate of a deceased person. The term should not be confused with an ESTATE TAX. See TAX.

injunction. An order, issued by a court applying equitable remedies, which requires an individual or organization to refrain from engaging in an activity identified in the order under penalty of contempt of court.

in kind. Value in goods or services as distinguished from value in money. Thus, payment in kind is payment in produce, commodities, or services.

inland bill. See BILL.

input and output analysis. An extension of the GROSS NATIONAL PRODUCT showing all transactions of individual enterprises with other firms within a given accounting period, inputs being what a firm buys, and outputs, what it sells. The entries must balance as the total expenditures of all groups equal the total receipts of all groups, and investments equal savings. Input-output calculations have been so extended during recent years as to require the most modern ELECTRONIC DATA PROCESSING.

inside director. A director of a corporation who enjoys a sizable stock interest and may be employed by the corporation. See DIRECTOR.

insolvency. The condition which exists when liabilities, other than those representing ownership, amount to more than the total assets. Thus, in the statement given below, non-ownership liabilities amount to $1,600,000 while the total assets amount only to $1,000,000. An insolvent condition therefore exists.

Assets		Liabilities	
Plant	$800,000	Capital stock	$400,000
Cash	200,000	Accounts payable	600,000
Deficit	1,000,000	Bonds payable	1,000,000
	$2,000,000		$2,000,000

installment bond. See BOND

installment buying. Conditional purchase of goods or services on credit, payment being made by the purchaser, usually after an initial down payment, at fixed intervals over a period of time, each installment payment including interest charges. Also called *hire purchase*. See also INSTALLMENT INTEREST.

installment interest. The interest on a loan payable in equal amounts at regular intervals over a period of time. The interest on such loans is usually either added to the principal (*add-on-loan*) or deducted from the principal (*discount loan*) at the time the loan is made, and the published or stated interest rate is computed accordingly. The principal amount of the loan is reduced, however, after each installment payment. If the dollar amount of the interest charged, therefore, is computed on the basis of the funds actually in the hands of the borrower after each installment payment, the resulting actual or true interest rate is considerably higher than the published or stated rate. The true interest rate may be computed according to the following equation:

$$X = \frac{2 (A \times B)}{C (N + 1)} \text{ when}$$

X = the annual true interest rate
A = the number of payments per year
B = the dollar amount of the published or stated interest
C = the amount actually received by the borrower
N = the total number of payments

Example: A loan of \$100 at a published or stated annual rate of interest of 4 per cent is repaid in 18 equal monthly installments.

Add-on-loan

$$\frac{2 (12 \times 6.00)}{100 (18 + 1)} = \frac{144}{1900} = .0757 \text{ True interest rate}$$

Discount loan

$$\frac{2 (12 \times 6:00)}{94 (18 + 1)} = \frac{144}{1786} = .0806 \text{ True interest rate}$$

See INTEREST. See also TRUTH-IN-LENDING ACT.

instant vesting. Giving employees the privilege of changing employment to another company within a given industry or region at any time without jeopardizing pension credits for which their former employer remains liable. If the right of transfer is conceded after five or ten years it is called *early vesting*. Also known as *portable pension*.

institutional economics. An approach to the study of economics which emphasizes the influences of the social environment on man's economic behavior. For example, Thorstein Veblen (1857-1929) argued that, in the course of social evolution, the institution of private property had subordinated the instinct of workmanship to the desire for the accumulation of private property. Accordingly, the struggle for property, prestige, and power tended to overshadow the kind of competition that reduces prices and makes for better quality. This tendency is manifested, according to Veblen, by monopoly, maintenance of price through limitation of production, and the extension of distribution control by producers over wholesale and retail agencies. See ECONOMICS.

institutional investor. A mutual fund, insurance company, bank, pension fund, or foundation which, for its revenue and growth, is chiefly concerned with the proper administration of an extensive securities portfolio. Because it deals in large blocks of securities, such an investor exerts a considerable influence on price levels in a security market.

institutionalism. The extension of the coercive authority of public institutions, or the extension of the influence of tradition, social values, and other noneconomic factors, over economic life.

instrument. A general term often applied to documents of various kinds; for example, a negotiable instrument or an instrument of credit such as a PROMISSORY NOTE. See (17).

instrumental capital. See CAPITAL GOOD.

insular bond. See BOND.

insurance. Protection against risk. To secure such protection private contracts are made according to which, for a consideration of a premium paid by one party called the insured, another party agrees to indemnify the insured, or other identified beneficiary, should he suffer losses specified in the contract. In the United States private insurance contracts may be regulated by

Congress under the interstate commerce clause of the Constitution. Beneficiaries of some private insurance, for example, group insurance provided by industry for employees, do not themselves contribute to the premiums. Likewise, beneficiaries of various kinds of social insurance provided by a government may or may not make direct contributions for the support of such insurance; when such contributions are made, they are usually supplemented by public funds. There are innumerable kinds of insurance, the names of which are often self-descriptive. See (25).

insurance case. A case, *United States* v. *South-Eastern Underwriters Association,* 322 U. S. 533 (1944), in which the Supreme Court effectively overruled an earlier decision, *Paul* v. *Virginia,* 8 Wallace 168 (1869), and held that insurance policies which establish contractual relations across state lines must be considered interstate commerce and hence potentially subject to congressional regulation. The case specifically held the SHERMAN ANTITRUST ACT applicable to interstate insurance business.

intangible asset. As used in accounting, an asset having no material substance and not representing anything material. Good will and patent rights are examples. See ASSET.

intangible property. 1. A right of interest of some kind; for example, a claim evidenced by ownership of a bond, or an interest in a business indicated by ownership of a share of stock. **2.** Any property the value of which cannot readily be obtained by an appraisal. See PROPERTY.

integration. The process of bringing together under single corporate management the production and marketing of a multiplicity of unrelated commodities and services.

Intelsat. A contraction of International Telecommunications Satellite Consortium in which more than 50 nations, including the United States as the principal member, cooperate to provide a world-wide satellite-relay telephonic, telegraphic, and television communication system. The consortium grew out of agreements originally signed by 18 nations in Washington in 1963 to invest in *Comsat,* or Communications Satellite Corporation, a privately chartered United States corporation which includes private shareholders, especially some 163 communications companies of which the American Telephone and Telegraph Company has the largest block of stock, and which serves as the managing agency for the Intelsat system. By 1968 some 5 satellites had been placed in orbit over the Atlantic and Pacific oceans. In the meantime, Comsat has sought to provide satellite relays for internal United States electronic communication and thus has raised broad questions about corporate control and public policy toward such communication.

intensive cultivation. The use of relatively large amounts of capital and labor on relatively small amounts of agricultural land.

Interallied debts. Debts arising out of the network of intergovernmental loans made by the principal Allied and Associated Powers during World War I and immediately after the cessation of hostilities. France and Great Britain had made loans early in the war to the lesser Allies. The United States later made loans to both France and Great Britain and to other allied states and thus became the principal creditor. Virtually none of the loans has been repaid. See DEBT. See also HOOVER MORATORIUM.

Inter-American Development Bank. The 21-nation western hemisphere credit agency, created in 1959 to make loans to both public and private agencies for economic development projects in Latin America. The bank's authorized capital for ordinary lending is in excess of $2 billion, a sizable percentage of which serves as a guarantee of the bank's own borrowings, that is, of its securities sold on the capital markets. An independently administered subsidiary fund for special operations makes available "soft loans," that is, loans for relatively unorthodox economic projects on which an interest rate less than the market rate is charged and which may sometimes be repaid in the borrowing country's own currency. See BANK.

interchangeable bond. See BOND.

interchangeable parts. The characteristic feature of a system of manufacturing in which any part of a machine can be interchanged with an identical part in any similar machine. Mass production is made possible by this emphasis upon interchangeable parts. Large quantities of individual parts are made with such accuracy and tested with such precision that they can be selected indiscriminately and assembled into a final product.

interdistrict settlement fund. Gold reserves of 12 federal reserve banks on deposit with the United States Treasury to clear debits and credits within the FEDERAL RESERVE SYSTEM. In its role as a clearing agent for its member banks, each federal reserve bank reports daily to the Treasury the total of the credits and debits which it has entered for each of the other 11 banks; and if at any time any bank's net debit balance falls below an allowed minimum, the Board of Governors of the Federal Reserve System requires it to deposit additional reserves. See FUND.

interest. 1. A sum paid or calculated for the use of capital. The sum is usually expressed in terms of a RATE or percentage of the capital involved, called the *interest rate.* For theories of interest see AGIO THEORY OF INTEREST, LIQUIDITY-PREFERENCE THEORY OF INTEREST, LOANABLE-FUNDS THEORY OF INTEREST, MARGINAL UTILITY THEORY OF INTEREST. 2. A group of individuals of enterprises having a common aim. 3. The equity of a shareholder in a corporation or of a partner in a business. See (21).

interest bond. See BOND.

interest equalization tax. A federal tax on new American foreign investments; that is, on the purchase of foreign securities by Americans. It was first levied in 1963 to offset higher interest rates outside the United States which attract such investment, the purpose being to hold down the debit increase in the United States international account and inhibit the outflow of gold and exchange. Under the FOREIGN INVESTORS TAX ACT of 1966 (*q.v.*), loans made by American branch banks abroad were exempted from the tax. In 1967 the tax, with some modifications, was extended to 1969. See TAX.

interest rate. See INTEREST.

Intergovernmental Maritime Consultative Organization. A specialized agency of the United Nations, consisting of some 50 states including the United States, which is concerned with securing observance of the Convention for Safety at Sea which maritime states signed at London in 1960, and other sea safety regulations, and with the observance by maritime states of international regulations concerning the pollution of harbors and the high seas, especially by petroleum products. It is also concerned with promoting liberal national maritime policies.

interim bond. See BOND.

interlocking directorate. The condition which exists when one person serves as a director of two or more companies. Under federal law in the United States the term applies if each of the companies of which the person is a director has combined capital, surplus, and undivided profits of at least $1,000,000, if all of them are engaged in interstate commerce, and if they are natural competitors. See also DIRECTOR.

intermediate good. See CAPITAL GOOD.

internal improvement. Any new capital construction of a public nature, such as highways, canals, bridges, or dredged harbors, carried out at public expense.

internal public debt. That portion of a nation's public debt owed to persons residing within the nation incurring the debt. See DEBT.

internal revenue. In the United States, federal income from all taxation other than customs duties.

Internal Revenue Service. A branch of the U. S. Department of the Treasury which supervises the assessment and collection of all internal revenue taxes.

International Atomic Energy Agency. A specialized agency of the United Nations, located in Vienna and established in 1957, consisting of some 90 states of which the United States is one. It maintains its own laboratory facilities for nuclear research and encourages research and technical collaboration among member states on the peaceful uses of nuclear power.

International Bank for Reconstruction and Development *(World Bank).* An international credit and development agency, one of the specialized agencies of the United Nations, with more than 100 members including the United States. Located in Washington, D. C., the bank was created in December, 1945, on the basis of a plan developed a year earlier at the United Nations Monetary and Financial Conference held at Bretton Woods, N.H. The bank's broad purpose is to promote the economic development of member countries. To that end it insures or otherwise guarantees private loans and, when no private source of capital is available, it provides loans based on its resources and credit. Primarily its loans are used to finance public works, and to modernize the economic infrastructure of a country. Its own lendable funds come mainly from the sale of the bank's securities on the world capital market. In addition to extending credit, the bank provides expert technical, fiscal, and managerial advice to developing countries. In order to extend its assistance to the less conventional, financially more risky, projects of vital importance to developing countries, the bank, in 1960, created the INTERNATIONAL DEVELOPMENT ASSOCIATION (*q.v.*). See BANK.

International Chamber of Commerce. A world trade organization founded at Atlantic City, N.J., in 1920, with headquarters in Paris. Membership, derived from more than 70 countries, consists of chambers of commerce, trade and industrial associations, and individual business firms and corporations. It acts as a clearing house for the exchange of views on international economic policies and seeks to assist in solving international economic problems and to promote world trade. In 1946, it was granted consultative status by the Economic and Social Council of the United Nations.

International Civil Aviation Organization. A specialized agency of the United Nations which formulates policies and recommends procedures for its more than 110 member states, its aim being to develop international civil aviation with proper regard for safety standards, efficiency, economy, and adequacy of service, and equality of opportunity for each state to participate in international air transport. The organization, established on a provisional basis in June, 1945, acquired definitive status on April 4, 1947, after 26 states had ratified the Convention on International Civil Aviation which had been drafted at an international aviation conference in Chicago in 1944.

international commodity agreement. See COMMODITY AGREEMENT.

International Confederation of Free Trade Unions. An international labor organization, established in London in 1949, to counter the communist-dominated WORLD FEDERATION OF TRADE UNIONS. The AMERICAN FEDERATION OF LABOR AND CONGRESS OF INDUSTRIAL ORGANIZATIONS is an institutional member.

International Cotton Advisory Committee. Representatives of the principal cotton-producing and consuming countries who set up a permanent organization in 1939. By means of annual meetings, and a standing committee in Washington, D.C., this group of representatives provides statistical information on cotton production and markets and seeks to further international stabilization of cotton prices.

International Court of Justice. A tribunal of 15 judges from various nations, established under the UNITED NATIONS charter at The Hague in 1946 to adjudicate such justiciable civil disputes as states may voluntarily bring before it and to advise the principal organs of the United Nations on legal questions. Enforcement of the court's judgments is a responsibility of the Security Council but such judgments have occasionally not been enforced. Customary international law and treaty are the chief sources of applicable law in the court. All member states of the United Nations are ipso facto parties to the court's statute and nonmembers may become parties as determined by the GENERAL ASSEMBLY and SECURITY COUNCIL of the United Nations.

International Development Association. An auxiliary credit agency of the INTERNATIONAL BANK FOR RECONSTRUCTION AND DEVELOPMENT *(World Bank),* capitalized at $1 billion, with a membership of some 90 states, which was established in 1960 to handle requests for SOFT LOANS to developing countries to be repaid over a longer time interval than ordinarily, and sometimes to be repaid in the borrowing state's own currency.

international double taxation. See DOUBLE TAXATION.

international economics. That part of the study of economics which treats of international trade, finance, foreign exchange, and similar subjects. See ECONOMICS.

International Executive Service Corps. A nonprofit organization which offers private industry in economically underdeveloped countries the temporary consulting services of volunteer American business executives, normally retired, in such areas as management, production, marketing, and finance. An enterprise receiving the services pays the out-of-pocket expenses of the volunteers, who receive no other remuneration, and the recipient enterprise also pays the corps a fee comparable to the level of such fees prevailing in the area where the enterprise is located. The corps receives financial assistance from government foreign-aid funds and from private industry and founda-

235

tions. Sometimes called the *Executive Peace Corps* or *Paunch Corps.*

International Finance Corporation. An affiliate of the INTERNATIONAL BANK FOR RECONSTRUCTION AND DEVELOPMENT *(World Bank)* established in 1956 to assist private industrial and mining companies to establish themselves especially in developing countries. The corporation provides loans or invests directly in the companies, insures loans provided them by other lending agencies, and participates with other lenders in meeting investment demand. Its staff also provides technical, financial, and managerial appraisal of industrial enterprises or projects for other organizations. Operating capital is secured from the corporation's own paid-in-share capital, from the sale of loans and equities in its portfolio, and from borrowings from its parent, the World Bank.

international gold-bullion standard. See GOLD-BULLION STANDARD.

International Harvester case. A case, *United States* v. *International Harvester Co.,* 274 U.S. 693 (1927), in which the Supreme Court enunciated substantially the same doctrine as was developed (*q.v.*) in the UNITED STATES STEEL CASE (*q.v.*), viz., that the mere size of a corporation is not prima-facie evidence of violation of the antitrust statutes. The Court consequently refused to order the dissolution of the International Harvester Company even though it was a combination of producers of over 80 per cent of the agricultural implements manufactured in the United States.

International Labor Organization. A specialized agency of the United Nations with over 100 member nations, including the United States, financed by the member governments. It was originally established as an autonomous part of the League of Nations following World War I. Its purpose is to further the interests of labor in the various member nations and particularly to eliminate substandard working conditions and increase social security.

International Monetary Fund (IMF). A specialized agency of the United Nations with more than 100 members, including the United States. Plans for the IMF were first elaborated in July,

1944, at the United Nations Monetary and Financial Conference held at Bretton Woods, N.H. By encouraging member countries to avoid unilateral currency devaluations and the imposition of exchange restrictions, the IMF seeks to stabilize international exchange and expand trade on an orderly basis. It also assists in establishing par values for the currencies of member countries and in formulating standards for the convertibility of such currencies. According to the terms of the fund's Articles of Agreement, member countries may draw upon its supply of gold and foreign currencies, originally contributed by member countries, when such withdrawal is required to correct temporary maladjustments in their balance of payments. The fund has thus become a major instrument in the creation of a world monetary system. To provide even greater liquidity in that system, on October 3, 1969, the member countries agreed upon a plan for SPECIAL DRAWING RIGHTS (*q.v.*) to be administered through the fund. See FUND.

International Patents Bureau. A quasi-public body in Geneva, Switzerland, which administers international patent treaties, including the Paris Convention to which the United States is a subscriber. One of its major current projects is the compilation of a world patent index which would supply information as to what was being patented anywhere in the world and by whom, and would identify duplicate patents of an invention of a machine or process. Unless protected by treaty, patents are good only in the country which issues them.

International Rubber Study Group. A group of representatives of the rubber industry, set up in London in 1944, and expanded in 1947 to extend representation to some 30 rubber-producing and rubber-consuming countries. By means of position papers and bulletins of various sorts, it advises governments and the public on the world position of synthetic and natural rubber, that is, on production, markets, prices, and inventories.

International Statistical Institute. An independent, nongovernmental professional association, founded in London in 1885. Through constituent national statistical societies, and directly, it seeks to promote statistical education throughout the world and to improve statistical methods and procedures.

international stock. See CAPITAL STOCK.

International Telecommunication Union. A specialized agency of the United Nations, located in Geneva, Switzerland, and consisting of more than 120 states, including the United States, which grew out of the International Telegraph Union established at Paris in 1865. Through its staff, and special boards and committees, it examines and records radio frequencies, issues recommendations on technical, operational, and financial questions affecting the international use of telephone and telegraph, and informs on the observance by signatory states of various telecommunications conventions. International aspects of the performance of broadcasting satellites also fall within its jurisdiction.

international transit. The privilege of uninterrupted and free passage over a state's territory by trains, planes, and automobiles, usually secured by formal agreement between states.

international union. In the United States, the term means a labor union which has members in Canada as well as in the United States. See LABOR UNION.

international unit. A term sometimes applied to a statistical unit for measuring levels of living in various countries. In using it statisticians sometimes allow it to equal the average purchasing power of one dollar in the United States in the period 1925–34.

International Wheat Agreement. A multi-nation production and price-stabilization arrangement for world trade in wheat which arose out of the KENNEDY ROUND (*q.v.*) of trade agreements. In the United States the minimum prices for various grades of wheat established by this agreement will average 20 cents per bushel less than under an earlier agreement. The agreement was submitted to the United States Senate for ratification early in 1968.

interpolation. As applied to statistics, a method of estimating an intermediate unknown value in a series of numbers by reference to the known values in the series, or by reference to an associated series, the INCREMENTS of which are proportional to the increments of the series for which an intermediate value is desired. For example, the method is frequently used in calculating logarithms. Suppose log 801.4 is desired and log 801.0 is known to be 2.9036, and log 802.0 to be 2.9042, then

802.0 − 801.0 = 1.0   difference between numbers for which logs are known.

2.9042 − 2.9036 = .0006   difference between their logs.

801.4 − 801.0 = 0.4   difference between the number for which the log is wanted and the lesser number for which the log is known.

Hence:

$$\frac{0.4}{1.0} \times 0.0006 = .00024, \text{ and}$$

$$2.9036 + 0.00024 = 2.90384, \log \text{ of } 801.4$$

interstate commerce. As interpreted in American constitutional law, commerce among the various states, including all aspects of the transportation of goods and persons across state boundaries, and intrastate transportation if it adversely affects interstate transportation; also, more recently, agriculture, manufacturing, marketing, and economic undertakings in general if, as is almost inevitable, these activities transcend state boundaries.

Interstate Commerce Act. An act of Congress, 1887, the first of many federal statutes regulating interstate transportation. This original act forbade pools by rail carriers, prohibited special rates, rebates, and other practices considered discriminatory to shippers, and required railways to publish rate schedules. It also created the Interstate Commerce Commission and invested it with limited authority to control abuses among railways. The commission was authorized to require reports from railways, investigate complaints, and to issue cease and desist orders when a violation of law occurred. Many subsequent statutes have considerably amended the provisions of the Interstate Commerce Act, enlarged the authority of the commission which it created, and extended its jurisdiction to interstate carriers other than railways. These subsequent statutes or parts of them are often cited as part of the original Interstate Commerce Act. See also INTERSTATE COMMERCE COMMISSION.

Interstate Commerce Commission. An independent federal administrative agency created by Congress in 1887. Under the

INTERSTATE COMMERCE ACT of that year and various subsequent statutes, the commission has been authorized to pass upon the rates charged by various interstate carriers including railway, express, motor-coach, and sleeping-car companies, oil pipe lines, and certain interstate and coastal navigation lines. Its activities also include the prescription of uniform statistical and accounting practices among carriers, valuation of certain carrier property, introduction of devices and practices to insure greater safety and convenience for the traveler, the supervision of arrangements for consolidations and pooling arrangements among carriers, passing upon requests of carriers to discontinue service, and authorizing the issuance of securities by carriers.

interstate trade barriers. State laws in the United States which restrict passage of goods and services from one state to another. Regulations regarding interstate trucking, quarantine laws directed against plant diseases and insects, and DISCRIMINATORY TAXATION have all been used to keep out "foreign" competition; that is, competition emanating from the borders of a particular state. Whatever their ultimate intention, measures such as quarantine regulations are and can be defended as state inspection or health regulations, permitted under the federal Constitution, and regulatory or fiscal measures are often defended as efforts to introduce a degree of equality between a particular state's taxpayers and nonresidents who use the state's highways and other public works financed by local taxation.

intrastate commerce. In American constitutional theory, commerce deemed to be wholly within the borders of any one of the states of the United States.

intrinsic value. A property or capacity that is assumed to be inherent in an object. Thus it is often said that because bread has a capacity to satisfy hunger, it has an inherent or intrinsic value. From the standpoint of economic analysis, however, if more bread were produced than was wanted, the excess would have little or no value. Modern economics considers, therefore, that the value of any object depends upon its relation to unsatisfied wants rather than upon any inherent quality. See VALUE.

invention. A new and useful art, machine, process, or substance, including a distinct and new form of plant. See also PATENT.

inventory. An itemized list of a stock of goods showing quantities and, usually, values.

inventory control. The regulation of quantities of materials on hand in such a way as to assure current needs while avoiding excess reserve stocks, the calculation being based on the rate of withdrawals and the time necessary for replacement. In cases where a large number of items are involved, the computation is frequently done by an AUTOMATIC DATA PROCESSING SYSTEM. See CONTROL.

inventory valuation adjustment. An addition to, or a deduction from, the BOOK VALUES of nonfarm business inventories used by the United States Department of Commerce in computing the NATIONAL INCOME and the NATIONAL ACCOUNT. Only changes in the physical volume of inventories expressed in terms of current market prices are desired, but, depending upon the method used in valuing inventories of nonfarm enterprises, changes in the total value of those inventories from one accounting period to another may reflect price changes instead of, or in addition to, changes in physical volume. Some adjustment is called for, therefore, in order to isolate the changes in physical volume. Farm income is measured without regard to inventory profits and losses; hence no inventory valuation adjustment is necessary.

investment. The exchange of money for some form of property, such as securities or real estate, which, it is expected, will be held over a considerable period of time. Reasonable safety of principal and relative permanency of possession are inferred in the term, in contrast to SPECULATION. See (21).

Investment Advisers Act. An act of Congress, 1940, which gives the Securities and Exchange Commission power to regulate the activities of investment counselors, requiring them to register with the Commission and outlawing statements misrepresenting or giving false information about securities, one possible penalty being revocation of registration.

investment banking. The purchase of large blocks of a security by a financial organization, usually known as an investment bank, and the resale of such securities, generally in small blocks, in expectation of a profit. Investment banks are often used in the distribution of new issues of securities. The word

241

"banking," as here used, is misleading in that it suggests the function of deposit. Investment bankers are not permitted to engage in deposit banking. See also BANK.

investment bill. See BILL.

investment company. An institution that invests its capital in securities, such capital being obtained by the sale of its own securities. The income from its investments is used to defray its operating expenses and as a profit to stockholders. Often called *investment trust.* Some companies diversify their holdings over a wide range of stocks and bonds; others concentrate in special situations. Many companies offer a periodic payment plan for the convenience of investors who wish to purchase the company's stock. See COMPANY. See also INVESTMENT COMPANY ACT.

Investment Company Act. An act of Congress, 1940, which gives the SECURITIES AND EXCHANGE COMMISSION authority to regulate investment companies. The act requires such companies to register with the commission and to refrain from certain practices deemed to be unfair to stockholders such as electing more than a stipulated percentage of directors who are affiliated with brokerage or banking houses, inside stock deals in which company officials have a personal interest, and accounting practices which fail to reflect the true worth of the company's holdings.

investment counselor. One who for compensation advises on the purchase and sale of securities. Under the provisions of the INVESTMENT ADVISERS ACT passed by Congress in 1940, individuals and firms acting as investment counselors are required to register with the SECURITIES AND EXCHANGE COMMISSION. They are not permitted to charge for their services on the basis of profits gained by their clients or to buy securities from, or to sell securities to, their clients.

investment portfolio. A list of BONDS, CAPITAL STOCK CERTIFICATES, PROMISSORY NOTES, and other SECURITIES owned by an institution or by an individual.

investment trust. See INVESTMENT COMPANY.

invisible hand. A term used by Adam Smith in setting forth the thesis that when each person acts in his own self-interest, the welfare of society is assured. Hence, according to Adam Smith, society is governed by an "invisible hand" which insures the social welfare, even though individuals seek their own interests. See also ECONOMIC HARMONIES.

invisible items of trade. Items, such as freight and insurance charges and the expenditures of travelers, which, though not recorded as exports or imports, must be considered along with exports and imports in determining the balance of payments between two or more countries. The expenditures of American travelers in England, for example, are equivalent, as far as international balances are concerned, to American imports from England, and, although sometimes referred to as invisible imports, they are not formally recorded as imports. See also BALANCE OF PAYMENTS.

invoice. An itemized list of goods, stating prices and quantities, compiled by a seller and sent to a buyer or consignee. See also CONSULAR INVOICE.

involuntary bankruptcy. See BANKRUPTCY.

involuntary servitude. Slavery, or any form of compulsory service by private individuals even if provided for by contract. In the United States the courts invalidated such servitude under the 13th Amendment.

iron law of wages. The theory that wages tend to equal what the worker needs to maintain a bare subsistence level of living. According to this theory, wages temporarily higher than the cost of subsistence will result in an increase in the number of workers; competition will then reduce wages to the subsistence level. Wages less than the cost of subsistence will reduce the number of workers; competition will then eventually advance the wages to the subsistence level. The iron law of wages was formulated by Ferdinand Lassalle, one of the early leaders in the German socialist movement, during the latter half of the 19th century. Sometimes called the *brazen law of wages* and *subsistence law of wages.*

irredeemable. Lacking any provision to reimburse or repay in money or in kind or to exchange for something of equal value.

irredeemable bond. See BOND.

irredeemable foreign-exchange standard. See GOLD-EXCHANGE STANDARD.

irredeemable money. Any kind of money that cannot be exchanged for standard money. All money in the United States has been irredeemable since 1933. Also called *inconvertible money.* See MONEY.

irrevocable letter of credit. See LETTER OF CREDIT.

irrigation. Bringing moisture to agricultural land by means of ditches, piping, or other artificial means.

issue. 1. A block of capital stock, bonds, or other securities sold by a corporation at one time and constituting a part of its obligations. **2.** To place in circulation as, for example, new currency.

itemized appropriation. An appropriation which specifies in detail what disposition is to be made of the funds appropriated. The term is used in contradistinction to LUMP-SUM APPROPRIATION. Sometimes called *segregated appropriation.* See APPROPRIATION.

J

jetsam. Anything thrown overboard to lighten a vessel and hence subject to proprietorship of the discoverer.

job action. A vague term used to identify such a trade-union tactic as refusal to perform certain normal duties of employment while continuing duties essential to the public's health and security, the purpose being to avoid an outright strike (which may be illegal) but still focus public attention on the union members' grievances and economic demands.

jobber. A merchant middleman who buys from an importer or manufacturer or some large wholesaler and sells to retailers.

job classification. In an industry or in the public service, a division of jobs into classes or categories according to skill and training required and remuneration.

job evaluation. See LABOR GRADE.

Johnson Act. An act of Congress, 1934. Otherwise known as the *Foreign Securities Act.* It made illegal the sale in the United States of securities of foreign governments that had failed to pay their debts to the United States government.

joint agreement. As applied to labor relations, an agreement between two or more employers and two or more labor unions, or between one employer and two or more labor unions, or between two or more employers and one labor union. See also LABOR UNION.

joint and several bond. See BOND.

joint costs. The production costs of two or more products which must of necessity be produced together. When cotton is processed, for example, the seeds are separated from the fiber, and the seeds may be used to produce an oil. The production costs of the fiber, therefore, cannot be considered apart from the production costs of the oil. Sometimes referred to as *joint supply.* See COST.

joint council. Collectively, delegates from several local unions of the same parent union who negotiate a common or joint agreement with employers in a geographic area.

joint demand. The demand that arises when two or more commodities must be used together, if at all, and hence are wanted simultaneously. The demand for rubber, steel, leather, and many other commodities by automobile manufacturers is a case in point. See DEMAND.

Joint Economic Committee. A congressional committee of senators and representatives which, prior to March 1 each year, following appropriate investigations and the hearing of testimony by economists and others, presents a report to Congress and the public on the state of the economy and comments on the President's economic reports to Congress. The Committee's report and recommendations may serve as guides in formulating the nation's future economic policy.

joint rate. As applied to railway traffic, a single, consolidated rate charged for carrying freight between two points not on the same railroad and arranged by agreement between the two or more railroads carrying the freight from consignment point to destination. When no joint rate exists, a COMBINATION RATE (*q.v.*) is used. See RATE.

joint return. A combined report of the income of husband and wife permitted by the income tax regulations of the United States and of certain states. See COMMUNITY-PROPERTY PRINCIPLE.

joint-stock company. A form of partnership the members of which are issued shares of transferable stock up to the amount of their investment. Although enjoying a legal personality like a corporation, it has important differences. Unlike a corporation, a joint-stock company can usually sue and be sued only through some designated officer; moreover, unlike stockholders of a corporation who enjoy limited liability, members of a joint-stock company are individually and collectively liable for the debts of the organization. See COMPANY.

joint-stock land banks. Banks originally established by the FEDERAL FARM LOAN ACT of 1916 and placed in liquidation by the Emergency Farm Mortgage Act of 1933. They issued farm loan bonds to the investing public and made loans to farmers, the loans being secured by farm mortgages. Unlike the FEDERAL LAND BANKS, the joint-stock land banks were not integrated into any unified system. Each bank was responsible for its own securities. See BANK.

joint supply. See JOINT COSTS.

journeyman. A skilled worker who has qualified as such by serving an apprenticeship. See also APPRENTICE.

Juilliard* v. *Greenman. See LEGAL-TENDER CASES.

junior-lien bond. See BOND.

junket. 1. A trip at public expense by an official, ostensibly to investigate economic or other conditions to support pending legislation or to provide a report on the administration of some public project. 2. Unnecessary travel by an employee at the expense of an employer.

jurisdictional strike. A strike caused by a dispute between two craft unions, the members of which are employed in the same undertaking. Thus, if carpenters are engaged to hang steel doors, as a part of some construction project, on the ground that the hanging of doors has always been a part of their work, the metal workers may strike because they consider the installation of metal materials wholly within their province. See STRIKE.

just compensation. A payment for property taken by the government, under EMINENT DOMAIN or similar proceeding, which reflects a fair market value for the property thus taken and includes compensation for incidental loss of value which may result as respects the remaining holdings of the property owner.

K

Kameralism. See CAMERALISM.

Kansas Industrial Court. See INDUSTRIAL-RELATIONS COURT.

Keating-Owen Act. An act of Congress, 1916, invalidated in *Hammer* v. *Dagenhart*, the first of the CHILD-LABOR CASES (*q.v.*), which excluded from interstate commerce goods made in factories, etc., employing minors under specific ages.

Kennedy Round. Protracted negotiations by principal industrial states held in Geneva, Switzerland, under the auspices of the GENERAL AGREEMENT OF TARIFFS AND TRADE which, in 1967, yielded agreements reducing prevailing tariff levels on industrial products by about one-third. So called because President Kennedy's sponsorship of the Trade Expansion Act of 1962 placed the United States in a posture to negotiate and hence made negotiations a practicable idea.

key industry. An industry which, because of its size, strategic location, the peculiar importance of its product, or some other characteristic, commands a dominating influence in the particular field of its operations or in the economy as a whole. See INDUSTRY.

Keynesian economics. Economic theories and policies advanced by the British economist John Maynard (Lord) Keynes (1883–1946) and his followers, or attributed to them. A schematic outline of the important contributions of the Keynesian

248

school is shown in the accompanying diagram. NATIONAL INCOME and employment depend upon REAL INVESTMENTS and consumer expenditures. Real investments depend upon the INTEREST rate and the MARGINAL EFFICIENCY OF CAPITAL. The interest rate is determined by LIQUIDITY PREFERENCE and the supply of cash as regulated by banking policy. The marginal efficiency of capital depends upon the capital's replacement cost and discounted future earnings. Consumer expenditures, in turn, depend upon income and the PROPENSITY TO CONSUME. Investments and consumer expenditures interact according to the ACCELERATION PRINCIPLE (*q.v.*) and the MULTIPLIER PRINCIPLE (*q.v.*). See ECONOMICS. See also INCOME AND EXPENDITURE EQUATION. One of Lord Keynes' major works was *The General Theory of Employment, Interest and Money* (1936).

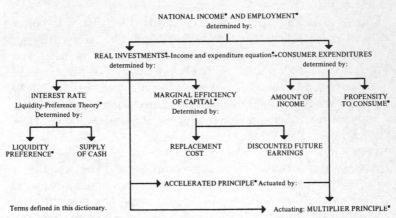

NATIONAL INCOME* AND EMPLOYMENT*
determined by:

REAL INVESTMENTS*-Income and expenditure equation*-CONSUMER EXPENDITURES
determined by: determined by:

INTEREST RATE
Liquidity-Preference Theory*
Determined by:

MARGINAL EFFICIENCY
OF CAPITAL*
Determined by:

AMOUNT OF
INCOME

PROPENSITY
TO CONSUME*

LIQUIDITY
PREFERENCE*

SUPPLY
OF CASH

REPLACEMENT
COST

DISCOUNTED FUTURE
EARNINGS

ACCELERATED PRINCIPLE* Actuated by:

Terms defined in this dictionary.

Actuating: MULTIPLIER PRINCIPLE*

Keynes's law of consumption. A principle of KEYNESIAN ECONOMICS that at every level of income a certain proportion of that income is spent for consumption goods, the proportion decreasing as the income increases. Although the law was formulated by John Maynard (Lord) Keynes (1883-1946), others have observed it in human behavior. See PROPENSITY TO CONSUME.

kickback. A payment by a worker to his employer, foreman or union representative in order to obtain or hold a job.

kiting. Issuing a check for a higher amount than there are funds on deposit to meet it and making up the deficiency, temporarily, by depositing another check, likewise in excess of deposits, but issued on some other bank. The procedure is considered prima facie evidence of fraudulent intent.

Knight case. An early antitrust case, *United States* v. *E. C. Knight Co.,* 156 U.S. 1 (1895), in which the Supreme Court refused to apply the SHERMAN ANTITRUST ACT to a merger of 4 sugar refineries in Philadelphia. The Court reasoned that the Sherman Act did not attempt to control monopoly as such but only monopoly in foreign and interstate commerce; that the merger complained of affected manufacture within a single state; and that the incidental results of such merger upon interstate commerce did not change the fact that it was a monopoly of manufacture and not a monopoly affecting interstate commerce which was involved. In later cases, involving application of the Sherman and other antitrust acts, this highly restrictive line of reasoning has been abandoned.

Knights of Labor. The Noble Order of the Knights of Labor, a labor organization founded in Philadelphia in 1869. Although based on CRAFT UNIONS, it adopted the plan of inclusive and direct membership after 1878. During the 1880's the organization reached the height of its power with a membership said to have been over 700,000. After 1893 it lost ground rapidly, being replaced by unions affiliated with the AMERICAN FEDERATION OF LABOR.

Knox* v. *Lee. See LEGAL-TENDER CASES.

kurtosis. A measure of the concentration of cases about the MODE of a frequency curve. A high concentration will cause a peak, and a low concentration a flat top. The measure is a comparison of any particular frequency curve with the NORMAL CURVE OF DISTRIBUTION. See also FREQUENCY DISTRIBUTION.

L

labor. One of the major factors of production consisting of manual or mental exertion for which wages, salaries, or professional fees are received. In popular speech the term is generally given a narrower meaning; that is, manual exertion only, or manual workers collectively. See (29).

labor agreement. See TRADE AGREEMENT.

labor dispute. As defined by federal law, a controversy between labor and management, or among employees, about wages and conditions of employment or concerning the representation of persons in COLLECTIVE BARGAINING. See LABOR.

labor exchange bank. A term used to denote various schemes advanced during the 19th century for the exchange of commodities on the basis of the amount of labor necessary to create them, and for currency and credit reforms that would do away with the use of precious metals for monetary purposes. Robert Owen, in 1832, arguing that gold and silver create artificial values, established an exchange in London where goods were traded on the basis of the labor hours necessary to produce them. Paper notes were issued for goods delivered, and these notes were accepted for goods purchase, Owen's idea being that such notes should become a common medium of exchange. Josiah Warren in the United States, and Benjamin Mazel in France, experimented with similar plans. In 1848 Pierre Joseph

Proudhon proposed that a bank be established in France to convert bills of exchange into a circulating medium, and that such currency be loaned to workers on merchandise collateral. All interest was to be eliminated, according to the plan, fees being charged to cover costs. A refinement of the labor-value exchange idea was introduced in 1871 by Johann Karl Rodbertus, a German socialist, who recognized that different kinds of labor might create different value relationships. Accordingly, he proposed that each industry should establish a working day of a length determined by the amount of physical and nervous energy expended by the workers. Money might then be issued on the basis of a day's labor. Ideas centering around the concept of labor exchange banks were gradually submerged in the growth of socialism. See BANK.

labor force. As defined by the United States Bureau of the Census, and the Bureau of Labor Statistics, the labor force of the United States consists of all persons 14 years of age and over; not housed in institutions, who are gainfully employed and working at their employment, or who are gainfully employed but are temporarily not working, or who are working at least 15 hours a week without pay on a family farm or in a family business, or who are unemployed, or are members of the armed forces. See LABOR.

labor grade. The degree of skill and responsibility and the amount of experience or other special qualifications required for a particular job, and the wages paid for that job. In factories requiring a great variety of labor skills, jobs are frequently evaluated by means of a point system, the number of points indicating in general the degree of competency necessary to perform a particular job. Each job is then assigned a minimum and maximum wage. Also called *job evaluation*. See LABOR.

Labor-Management Relations (*Taft-Hartley*) Act. An act of Congress, 1947. It amends the NATIONAL LABOR RELATIONS (*Wagner-Connery*) ACT of 1935 in many important respects. Among its provisions are those outlawing the CLOSED SHOP and imposing regulations upon the UNION SHOP, union welfare funds, and the CHECKOFF system. It specifies procedures for the handling of labor disputes threatening the national health and safety, denies foremen labor unions recognition under the law, bans strikes by government employees, and forbids industries or labor unions to make contributions for political purposes. It also provides for organizational and functional changes in the NATIONAL LABOR RELATIONS BOARD.

labor piracy. Any attempt to win workers away from other employers by offering higher wages or other benefits. See LABOR.

Labor Reform (*Landrum-Griffin*) Act. An act of Congress, 1959, which seeks to protect the rights of union members against exploitation by their leaders, and to make labor unions more accountable to the public for their actions. The act guarantees freedom of speech and a secret ballot to members of unions; limits the tenure of officers; requires periodic financial reports; outlaws secondary boycotts, that is, boycotts of employers doing business with employers against whom employees have a grievance; and establishes certain limitations upon so-called organizational picketing or picketing arising out of a demand for union recognition.

labor relations. See INDUSTRIAL RELATIONS.

laborsaving machinery. Machinery, usually of an automatic or semi-automatic nature, performing operations that would otherwise be performed by hand. The term implies that the labor necessary for the construction, maintenance, and operation or supervision of the machine is less than would be required to produce by hand whatever the machine will produce during its lifetime.

labor theory of value. The theory that the basis of value of an economic good is the amount of human labor expended in producing it. The theory does not deny that UTILITY or the power to satisfy a human want or desire is a basic condition of all value, but it contends that the cause of value, as distinct from the condition, is as above defined. The theory was taught by Adam Smith, and later expounded by Ricardo and others. It was accepted by Karl Marx and expanded into the SURPLUS LABOR AND VALUE THEORY.

labor union. An organization, incorporated or otherwise, consisting of employees. Generally called a *union*. The organization acts in the collective interests of the employees in negotiating with employers, particularly in matters of wages and working conditions. See (29).

La Follette Seamen's Act. An act of Congress, 1915. It established minimum standards for working conditions of crews on American merchant ships, and regulated their wage scales and the payment of their wages.

laissez faire (*laisser faire, laissez passer*). "Let things proceed without interference." The term originated among the PHYSIO-CRATS in France possibly as early as the first half of the 18th century, and was later developed by Adam Smith as a rule of practical economic conduct. He applied the principle of *laissez faire* to foreign trade and advocated the withdrawal of the restrictions favored by the MERCANTILIST SCHOOL. In domestic affairs, too, the principle was expressed in the assertion that the individual is most productive when allowed to follow his own self-interest without external restrictions.

land. One of the major factors of production consisting sometimes of a FREE GOOD, but usually of a material ECONOMIC GOOD which is supplied by nature without the aid of man. The term may include not only the earth's surface, both land and water, but also anything that is attached to the earth's surface. Thus, all natural resources in their original state, such as mineral deposits, wildlife, timber, and fish, are land within the technical meaning of the term; so also are sources of energy, outside of man himself, such as water, coal deposits, and the natural fertility of the soil. The technical meaning of the term is so much broader in scope than that usually given it in popular speech that some economists substitute the word *nature.* See FACTORS OF PRODUCTION.

land bank. An association of landowners in colonial America. Members pledged mortgages on their land to the association and received in return a form of currency called "bills of credit." See BANK. See also FEDERAL LAND BANK, JOINT-STOCK LAND BANKS.

land grant. A gift of public land by the United States government, often made in the past, to promote homesteading, to assist education, or to accomplish some other useful purpose.

land-grant bond. See BOND.

land-grant college. An institution of higher learning that benefited from land grants made by the United States government to the states in 1862 under certain stipulated conditions. See also MORRILL (LAND-GRANT COLLEGE) ACT.

land patent. A legal instrument giving title to the recipient of a LAND GRANT.

Landrum-Griffin Act. See LABOR REFORM ACT.

land tax. See PROPERTY TAX.

land-value tax. A tax on the value of land exclusive of all buildings and other improvements, the value being the appreciation due to population increase and general economic development of the community for which the landowner, as such, is in no way responsible. It is the UNEARNED INCREMENT, or ECONOMIC RENT, that is taxed in whole or in part. The tax is similar in some respects to a CAPITAL-GAINS TAX except that the appreciation of land value at any particular time is arrived at through APPRAISAL instead of being realized through a sale. See TAX.

large-scale production. See MASS PRODUCTION.

Laser technology. An abbreviation for "Light Amplification by Stimulated Emission of Radiation." The resulting beams of concentrated light are used in metallurgy, welding, spectroscopy, and many other fields.

Latin Monetary Union. An agreement entered into originally by France, Italy, Belgium, and Switzerland in 1865, and later by Greece, according to which the silver content in most of the coins of these nations was made uniform and hence the coins were interchangeable. Post-World War I inflation and restrictions on the use of the precious metals caused the members of the Union to disregard the agreement and the Union was effectively dissolved in the middle 1920's.

lawful money. In general, any kind of money which has the quality of legal tender. In a more restricted sense, any money authorized by, or under, the law which may or may not enjoy the quality of full legal tender. Since 1933, all legally authorized moneys in the United States have had the quality of full legal tender. See MONEY.

lay corporation. Any corporation organized for purely secular purposes, profit-making or otherwise, hence any corporation other than an ecclesiastical corporation. See CORPORATION.

lead time. The elapsed time between the initiation of some economic activity and its completion; for example, the elapsed

255

time between the purchase of an article and its delivery or between the inception of a new or modified product and its production.

leakage. As applied to economic analysis. an informal term indicating any influence which prevents new CAPITAL FORMATION from exerting its full effect upon the NATIONAL INCOME. According to the so-called MULTIPLIER PRINCIPLE (*q.v.*), the greater the marginal PROPENSITY TO CONSUME, the greater the contribution of new capital formation to the magnitude of the national income. Leakages decrease this contribution by decreasing the marginal propensity to consume. Examples are: high marginal PROPENSITY TO SAVE, payments on debts, an increase of imports over exports, an increase in the general PRICE LEVEL.

lease. A contract for the possession of specified property for the life of the party to whom the property is conveyed or for a period specified in the contract. See also NET LEASE.

leaseback. A transaction involving the sale of assets such as real estate or equipment, the purchased property then being leased to the original owner for a term of years. The prime purposes of the transaction are to provide the seller with more liquid assets for the expansion of his business and to permit him to charge off the rental on his tax return as a business expense. Occasionally, if the sale is made to a charity such as a foundation and the property is leased back, there may also be the more questionable objective of giving the original owner rental terms more favorable than the market because the charity, being tax-exempt, can offer more favorable terms.

leased life insurance. The sale or assignment of a life insurance policy to a leasing company, which company then leases the policy to its original owner in consideration of a fee presumably lower than the cost of the original coverage. See LIFE INSURANCE.

least-squares method. A mathematical procedure for computing the average relationship between 2 variables. Values which express this relationship most accurately are those that equal the minimum sum when the squares of their deviations from the original values of the two variables are added. The equations for obtaining this minimum sum are:

$$\Sigma(y) = Na + b\Sigma(x)$$

and

$$\Sigma(xy) = a\Sigma(x) + b\Sigma(x^2)$$

when

x and y = the variables,
N = the number of pairs of variables,
a and b = constants.

Two equations are secured by substituting the original values of x and y as above indicated. These equations are then solved simultaneously for a and b, the generalized equation for the average relationship being:

$$y = a + bx.$$

The least-squares method is used extensively in economic computations for estimating secular trend and for calculating the relationship between two or more variables for comparative purposes. For examples, see SCATTER CHART, SECULAR TREND.

legacy. See BEQUEST.

legal asset. An asset in the hands of an executor of an estate that can be used to discharge a debt under common law. See ASSET.

legal interest. A rate of interest determined by law which is applied in the absence of any specific agreement. See INTEREST.

legal person. A term frequently applied to a corporation, which is permitted to own property, to sue, to be sued, and to exercise many of the rights accorded to natural persons.

legal rate. The maximum interest rate allowed under the law. See RATE. See also LEGAL INTEREST.

legal reserves. See BANK RESERVES.

legal security. A security which, in the United States, is identified by state and federal laws as a permissible investment for certain fiduciary institutions. See SECURITY.

legal tender. Money which, according to law, must be accepted in payment of any obligation expressed in terms of money. It should be noted, however, that a seller is under no compulsion to accept legal tender in exchange for his goods if he does not wish to do so unless he expresses the exchange in terms of money or the business is one regulated by law.

legal-tender bond. See BOND.

legal-tender cases. A series of cases, *Hepburn* v. *Griswold,* 8 Wallace 603 (1870); *Knox* v. *Lee* and *Parker v. Davis,* 12 Wallace 457 (1871); and *Juilliard* v. *Greenman,* 110 U.S. 421 (1884), in which the Supreme Court established the constitutionality of the power of Congress to issue irredeemable paper money, such as greenbacks, and make them legal tender. In the first of these cases, that of *Hepburn* v. *Griswold,* the Court invalidated provisions of federal statutes, passed during the Civil War, which would have made such paper money a legal tender for debts contracted before the legislation. But in the subsequent cases, this earlier decision was overruled, and the power of Congress to issue paper money and make it a legal tender for any debts, whensoever contracted, was supported without qualification.

Leisy* v. *Hardin. See ORIGINAL-PACKAGE CASES.

lending authority. Authority given by law to an administrative agency to make loans.

Lend-Lease Act. An act of Congress, 1941. It authorized the President to supply munitions to any country, the defense of which was necessary to the defense of the United States, on terms which were deemed satisfactory to him. The act was later amended to include foodstuffs and other products.

letter of credit. A document, usually issued by a bank, in which the issuer agrees to accept drafts, under conditions set forth in the document, to be charged against credit previously established. The main types of letters of credit may be classified according to the extent of the liability assumed by the bank issuing a letter, and again by the use to which the letter is put.

Widely used terms indicating the bank's liability are as follows: *confirmed letter of credit,* a letter in which the payment of all drafts drawn against it is guaranteed; *irrevocable letter of credit,* one that cannot be canceled until a certain stipulated period of time expires; *revocable letter of credit,* one that may be canceled at any time; *straight letter of credit,* one that is confirmed and irrevocable; *unconfirmed letter of credit,* one for which credit has been established, but for which the issuing bank does not itself guarantee payment.

There are also terms indicating the use of letters of credit. A *circular letter of credit* is one not directed to any particular person, concern, or bank. When the beneficiary wishes to use it, he must find some agency willing to negotiate a draft. An *open letter of credit* contains no special stipulations. It is used, for example, when payments are desired without any documents being submitted with the draft drawn against the letter. A *revolving letter of credit* is one in which credit is automatically renewed as drafts are drawn against it. It is used frequently to facilitate payments by purchasing agents traveling abroad. A *traveler's letter of credit* is directed to any one of a number of correspondent banks, a separate list of which is given to the beneficiary. He may then call upon any bank named on the list, identify himself by a signature card given him by the issuing bank, and draw on the credit previously established. A record of the amount drawn is then noted on the letter of credit.

letter of lien. A document signed by a buyer, stating that certain goods are held by him in trust for the seller. An agreement of this kind is sometimes used, particularly in foreign trade, to assure the seller that he will be paid for the goods shipped to the buyer. When the buyer pays for the goods, the agreement becomes null and void. Also called *letter of trust.*

letter of marque. A license issued by a government to the owners of private ships in time of war permitting them to attack enemy ships and to seize those ships and such property as may be contained in them. Now virtually obsolete.

letter of trust. See LETTER OF LIEN.

letters patent. An instrument issued by a government which grants some right or conveys some title to a private individual or organization.

level of living. The actual degree of material well-being enjoyed by a person or a group. Also called *plane of living.*

liability. A debt or obligation stated in terms of money. Net worth is an obligation of an enterprise to the owners, although payable, in the case of a corporation, only through declaration of a dividend or liquidation. Liabilities are a part of a BALANCE SHEET. The other part consists of ASSETS. See (1).

Liberal school. See CLASSICAL SCHOOL.

liberty bond. A United States government bond issued during 1917 and 1918 to finance American participation in World War I and for loans to nations allied with the United States in that war. See BOND.

license. A right to engage in certain activities for which permission is necessary. Thus, public authorities may require that a license be secured by those engaged in certain occupations or professions, or an owner of a patent may grant a license for the manufacture of the patented article.

lien. A claim on property to secure the payment of a debt or the fulfillment of some contractual obligation. The law may permit the holder of the lien to enforce it by taking possession of the property.

life annuity. An annuity which ceases at the death of the person receiving the annuity payments. See ANNUITY.

life estate. Ownership and use of property for the lifetime of a person named in a will or identified by the law.

life insurance. Insurance which, in return for premiums paid in accordance with the terms of an appropriate contract, provides for a cash payment or the equivalent to beneficiaries named in the contract upon the death of the insured or upon the attainment by the insured of a certain age. See (25).

lifo. A method of inventory and cost-of-sales valuation in which the individual items sold or used are valued at the cost of the most recent acquisitions. It is assumed that the last items purchased or produced are the first items sold. The costs of articles sold or used, therefore, are current costs, whereas the costs of the items remaining in the inventory, if not currently purchased, are those of an earlier date. The term is an abbreviation of "last, in, first out." See also FIFO.

limited-dividend corporation. A corporation upon which a limitation has been placed as respects the maximum amount of dividends on its capital stock. Presumably, after the creation of the necessary and desirable surplus and reserves, such a corporation's prices might be reduced to the point where earnings were just enough to meet the maximum dividend requirements and to maintain reserves. See CORPORATION.

limited liability. The legal condition which exists when a stockholder cannot be held personally liable for the debts of a corporation beyond the amount that he has already invested in the enterprise. See LIABILITY.

limited partnership. A type of partnership business organization that limits the personal liability of inactive partners to their investment in the enterprise. See FORMS OF BUSINESS ORGANIZATION.

limited-payment plan of life insurance. A plan according to which a life-insurance company agrees to pay a stipulated sum of money upon the death of an insured person in return for annual premiums of a fixed amount from the insured person during a maximum number of years, usually about 30. See LIFE INSURANCE.

limping standard. A modification of the gold monetary standard according to which certain silver coins are treated as standard money to the extent that they are made unlimited legal tender and are not required by law to be redeemed in gold. See MONETARY SYSTEM.

line of regression. See SCATTER CHART.

linseed oil industry case. A case, *United States* v. *American Linseed Oil Co.,* 262 U.S. 371 (1923), involving a situation not unlike that in the LUMBER INDUSTRY CASE (*q.v.*) and a somewhat similar decision by the Supreme Court. Relying on the antitrust statutes, the Court enjoined the practice of the linseed oil industry of exchanging information on prices, sales, and related matters and of requiring individual enterprises in the industry to post bonds to assure their adherence to published price schedules.

liquid. As used in business terminology, the word indicates the relative ease with which something of value can be converted into money. Thus, a liquid asset, or liquid capital, is property that can be converted readily into money without appreciable loss in value. Property which is 100 per cent liquid is cash or its equivalent. The word is used in contradistinction to FROZEN. See ASSETS, CAPITAL.

liquidation. As generally used in business, the conversion of assets into cash. To liquidate securities, for example, means to sell securities. In terminating a business the term includes not only the process of converting the assets into cash but also the payment of the indebtedness and the distribution among the owners of the business of whatever remains. The term may also refer merely to the process of ascertaining the true values of things.

liquidity preference. The preference exhibited by savers as to the degree of liquidity of their savings; that is, as to whether they prefer to hold savings in completely liquid form, as in cash, or to convert them into relatively less liquid form, as in some investment. See KEYNESIAN ECONOMICS.

liquidity-preference theory of interest. A Keynesian theory that attributes the rate of interest to the demand and supply of money and money substitutes, the demand being determined by LIQUIDITY PREFERENCE and the supply by banking policy. In the appended diagram a liquidity-preference SCHEDULE is indicated by the solid line *AA'*. According to this schedule, when the interest rate is high, little cash is demanded by the economy because liquidity preference is weak; when the interest rate is low, more cash is demanded because liquidity preference is strong. The supply curve is indicated in the diagram by the straight line *SS'*. Demand and supply are equated at the point *O*, or at *y* rate of interest. If for some reason liquidity preference strengthens, indicated by the dotted line *BB'*, while the supply of cash remains the same, the interest rate will rise to point *x*. This new interest rate will, in turn, be affected by the sale of securities in order to realize cash. This will depress security prices and hence advance the interest rate. Conversely, if liquidity preference weakens, indicated by the dotted line *CC'*, while the supply of cash remains the same, the interest rate will decline to point *z*. This lower interest rate will be affected by a demand for securities in order to invest cash. This will advance the price of securities and hence reduce the interest rate. Changes in liquidity preference can be offset in varying degrees by banking policy which can encourage an increase or a decrease in the supply of cash as liquidity preference strengthens or weakens, respectively. This can be illustrated in the diagram by imagining the straight line *SS'* moved to the right until point *O* on that line touches *BB'*, or to the left until point *O* touches *CC'*. See also DEPOSIT CURRENCY, KEYNESIAN ECONOMICS.

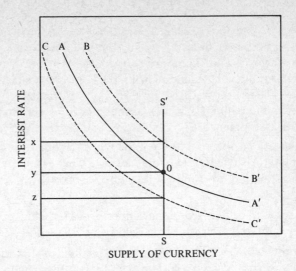

SUPPLY OF CURRENCY

listed security. A security which is admitted by a recognized stock exchange organization for trading on that exchange. See SECURITY.

listed stock. See CAPITAL STOCK.

list price. A price, usually published, which makes no allowance for trade or other discounts, rebates, or commissions. See PRICE.

little steel. A popular term which usually refers to all American steel-producing plants other than those of the United States Steel Corporation.

loan. As generally used in business, a sum of money borrowed from a commercial bank at the prevailing rate of interest. When bonds are sold by a borrower or when a borrower pledges a mortgage as security, the term may be qualified as *long-term loan* or *mortgage loan.* The term generally refers to a money transaction, the terms *hire, rent,* or *lease* customarily being used when goods are borrowed. However, the borrowing of a stock certificate to cover SELLING SHORT is a business loan not in terms of money. See (21).

loanable-funds theory of interest. The theory that interest rates are determined by the supply of, and the demand for, funds available for lending. The supply of such funds is determined mainly by the extent of savings and the net increase in DEPOSIT CURRENCY; and the demand, by the opportunities for new CAPITAL FORMATION and the desire to increase cash balances. The theory has much in common with the LIQUIDITY-PREFERENCE THEORY OF INTEREST, inasmuch as both recognize the part played by the banking system and the importance of the preference for cash balances for speculation and security purposes.

loan interest. A price paid by one person to another for the use of capital. Also called explicit interest. The term is used in contradistinction to imputed interest. See INTEREST. See also IMPUTED.

loan shark. An unlicensed moneylender, so called because of the excessive interest frequently charged by such a lender.

localization of labor. The tendency for skilled and semiskilled workers to congregate in certain regions because some characteristic of nature, such as climate or soil, favors a particular industry or trade—for example, labor devoted to citrus fruits in Florida, mining in Pennsylvania, and the raising of beef cattle on the Great Plains. This is sometimes called *regional division of labor*. See LABOR.

local rate. As applied to railway traffic, a rate charged for carrying freight between two points on the same railroad. See RATE.

Lochner v. New York. A case, 198 U.S. 45 (1905), in which the Supreme Court held unconstitutional a state statute (New York) fixing the maximum working day in bakeries at 10 hours. In its opinion the majority of the Court suggested that such a statute arbitrarily and unreasonably limited freedom of contract protected by the 14th Amendment to the Constitution, that it exceeded the police power of the state, and that it was without due process. It was in his dissenting opinion in this case that Mr. Justice Holmes uttered his famous dictum that the 14th Amendment did "not enact Mr. Herbert Spencer's Social Statics," an opinion which presaged a more favorable judicial verdict on regulatory statutes of this type in later cases. See BUNTING V. OREGON.

lockout. An attempt by an employer in an industrial dispute to bring employees to terms through the economic pressure created by shutting down the operation of a plant or other establishment, thereby denying employment to the workers.

Loewe v. Lawlor. See DANBURY HATTERS' CASE.

logistics. 1. Basically, the art of numerical calculation, derived from the Greek *logistikos.* **2.** In the 19th century, the word came into use in military terminology referring principally to the quartering, transporting, and supplying of troops. The meaning has been broadened in current usage to refer to the science and practice of providing the means for the conduct of military operations. It deals with personnel, materiel, facilities, and services and embraces all activities necessary to establish and maintain fighting forces, from the mobilization of the civilian industrial economy to the deployment of men and weapons in combat with an enemy.

London Economic Conference. An international conference held in London from June 12 to July 27, 1933, to consider world monetary and credit policies, the stabilization of world commodity prices, international capital movements, restrictions on international trade, commercial treaty and tariff policies, and the stimulation of production and world trade. It failed in its primary objective of securing agreement to stabilize major national currencies.

long and short haul. A term referring to a practice, once common among American railroads, of charging higher rates between points relatively close together, and served by only one railroad, than between points farther apart but served by competing railroads. The practice is now illegal.

long-term liability. See FIXED LIABILITY.

Lorenz curve. A graphic device, showing cumulative percentage relationships between two variables. It is customarily employed in displaying the extent of equality or inequality in the distribution of money income in an economy. The diagram on page 266 shows a Lorenz curve depicting a hypothetical distribution of DISPOSABLE PERSONAL INCOME among SPENDING UNITS, as follows:

Lorenz curve

Total spending units, per cent	Cumulative	Total disposable personal income, per cent	Cumulative
15	15	2	2
21	36	11	13
23	59	19	32
18	77	21	53
11	88	16	69
8	96	16	85
4	100	15	100

The dotted line represents complete equality; that is, 10 per cent of the spending units receive 10 per cent of the disposable personal income, 20 per cent of the spending units receive 20 per cent, etc. The broken line represents complete inequality; that is, 20 percent of the spending units receive no income; 40 per cent receive no income, etc., until one remaining spending unit receives 100 per cent of the income. The heavy solid line represents the actual distribution as specified above.

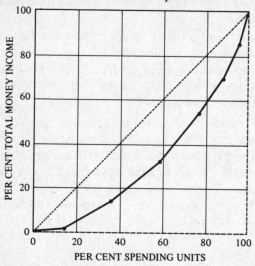

loss leader. A term applied to an article sold in retail trade below cost in order to attract buyers for other merchandise.

lucrative capital. See CAPITAL.

Luddite. A term applied to certain workmen in England who early in the 19th century conducted a campaign, accompanied in some cases by violence, against the introduction of laborsaving machinery. The term is said to be derived from the name of one Ned Lud who, somewhat earlier, had been particularly aggressive in destroying machines.

lumber industry case. A case, *American Column and Lumber Co. v. United States,* 257 U.S. 377 (1921), in which the Supreme Court held certain practices in the lumber industry to constitute a restraint of trade and a violation of the antitrust statutes. These practices included circularization among various companies in the industry of statistical information on production, sales, and shipments, and requests for curtailment of output to prevent overproduction in the lumber industry.

lump-sum appropriation. An appropriation, especially one by a legislative body for some governmental unit. The appropriation contains no specific instructions as to how the funds appropriated shall be spent. The term is opposed to ITEMIZED APPROPRIATION. See APPROPRIATION.

luxury tax. A tax imposed upon articles not considered essential to a normal standard of living and usually high in price. See TAX.

M

McCray v. United States. See OLEOMARGARINE CASE.

McCulloch v. Maryland. A case, 4 Wheaton 316 (1819), in which the Supreme Court established the constitutionality of the Second Bank of the United States. Chief Justice Marshall, speaking for the court, upheld the constitutional power of Congress to charter such a bank by establishing that this power was derived from other powers expressly confided to Congress by Art. I, Sec. 8 of the Constitution. He thereby gave judicial blessing to the doctrine that Congress had implied as well as express powers. The Chief Justice also established the principle that no state of the United States might tax the instrumentalities of the federal government, such as the branches of the Bank of the United States, at issue in the case, because such a power in the hands of the states might effectively challenge the supremacy of the federal government. Among its other practical effects, this part of the decision resulted in exempting the income from federal securities and the salaries of federal employees from state taxation, a rule which has since been relaxed somewhat. See *Graves* v. *New York* ex rel. *O'Keefe.*

McFadden Act. An act of Congress, 1927, which expanded the power of national banks to lend money on mortgages, gave them limited power to act as investment institutions, encouraged the consolidation of state banks with national banks, and allowed national banks to open new offices or branches within the corporate limits of the city in which they were located.

McKinley Tariff. The United States Tariff Act of 1890. It increased the import duties on wool and woolens, higher-grade cottons, other textiles, and many less important items. Some duties were made practically prohibitory. The duty on sugar was replaced by a bounty of 2 cents per pound for 14 years, granted to domestic sugar producers.

McNary-Haugen Bill. A bill which proposed to advance the prices of agricultural products in the domestic market by selling surplus products abroad for whatever they would bring. Farmers suffering losses from such exports were to be reimbursed from fees collected from all beneficiaries of the plan. The bill was vetoed twice by President Coolidge (1927). See also EQUALIZATION FEE.

macroeconomics. Economic studies or statistics that consider aggregates of individuals or groups of commodities; for example, total consumption, employment, or income. The term is used in contradistinction to MICROECONOMICS. See ECONOMICS.

maintenance. The upkeep of machinery, equipment, or other property. It is considered not as a capital cost but as a current business expense.

maintenance of membership. As applied to labor relations, a provision in a labor contract in which the management agrees that union workers must remain in good standing with the union in order to retain their jobs. See also UNION SECURITY CLAUSE.

make-work fallacy. The fallacious belief that accidental or deliberate destruction of wealth or inefficient or uneconomic application of labor is beneficial to the economy because it creates or prolongs employment. For example, when a period of unemployment is expected, workers may deliberately slow down their work in order to make their jobs last longer. They may succeed temporarily in prolonging their period of employment by forcing the employer to pay higher labor costs. If such a situation is continued over a period of time, however, it is evident that the amount of wealth created by the workers would be so reduced that the employer could no longer afford to pay their wages, and unemployment would follow anyway.

Moreover, if such a policy were pursued over an extended period, it would result in a general decline in living standard.

malfeasance. The performance of an illegal act, especially by a public official.

malpractice. Failure to exercise a professional duty in accordance with accepted professional standards, such failure resulting in loss or injury to others.

Malthusian theory of population. The theory that population increases faster than the means of subsistence. First formulated by Thomas Robert Malthus in an essay published anonymously in 1798 and revised in a second edition published in 1803 under his own name. Malthus claimed that population increased by GEOMETRIC PROGRESSION while the means of subsistence increased in ARITHMETIC PROGRESSION. Human beings were destined, therefore, to misery and poverty unless population growth was checked. Population growth might be slowed by what Malthus called preventive checks (moral restraint, late marriages, celibacy). If these were not exercised, positive checks (famines, wars, plagues) would reduce the population to the point of subsistence.

managed money. A monetary system in which an attempt is made by government to regulate the amount of money in circulation in such a way as to accomplish some specified objective such as the stabilization of prices. The paper money under such a system is inconvertible; it may or may not be partially secured by coins or bullion. Sometimes called *fiat standard*. See MONETARY SYSTEM.

management. The organization and coordination of the factors of production—land, labor, and capital—for maximum efficiency, often itself considered one of the factors. Collectively, those who direct an enterprise. Also called *entrepreneurship*.

management company. As applied to mutual funds, a company that manages and sells for a fee or commission the shares of OPEN-END *(mutual)* INVESTMENT COMPANIES. See COMPANY.

management science. See OPERATIONS RESEARCH.

management stock. See CAPITAL STOCK.

Manchester school. See CLASSICAL SCHOOL.

man-hour. In quantitative economics, a convenient unit (one hour by one employee) for measuring the time spent on some operation. It is used, for example, to measure productivity and costs.

manifest. A complete inventory of the cargo of a ship, together with the value, origin, and destination of each item. The term is also applied to carloads of mixed freight, contents of storage warehouses, and loads on long-distance trucks.

man-land ratio. The relationship which exists at a particular time and place between the total number of people, the natural resources, the stage of technological development, and the level of living. Thus, as long as the natural resources are sufficient and technological progress continues, population may increase, the standard of living may advance, or both may occur. Should natural resources become depleted, and progress in technological development cease, increased population will cause a decrease in the level of living. See RATIO.

Mann-Elkins Act. An act of Congress, 1910. It gave the Interstate Commerce Commission limited power to regulate the rates and operations of telegraph, telephone, and cable companies. This authority, considerably enlarged, has since been transferred to the FEDERAL COMMUNICATIONS COMMISSION.

manorial system. A medieval system of land tenure, the principal feature of which was a large estate owned by a feudal lord and maintained by dependent cultivators who provided services and dues in return for protection and parcels of land used for their maintenance.

marginal. As used in theoretical economics, the condition that exists when a minimal increment or decrement occurs in certain variables. See (12).

Manpower Administration. A part of the Department of Labor which coordinates federal programs for employment security and apprenticeship training, supervises the national network of employment and work-training agencies operated by the United States Training and Employment Service, and establishes standards for State unemployment insurance plans.

manpower control. Direction by the government as to the distribution of manpower available for employment, the purpose being to secure the most effective use of available skills in meeting some major national objective such as production for defense or war. See CONTROL.

marginal borrower. A borrower at a given rate of interest who will refuse to borrow if the rate of interest is advanced. See MARGINAL.

marginal buyer. A buyer at any given price who will refuse to buy if the price is advanced. See MARGINAL.

marginal cost. Whatever amount the production of one additional unit adds to the total costs of production. If the total cost of producing five units is $100 and the total cost of producing six units is $115, the marginal cost is $15. See COST, MARGINAL.

marginal desirability. See MARGINAL UTILITY.

marginal disutility of labor. The increment of labor effort which just equals the MARGINAL UTILITY to the worker of the compensation received for that increment. See MARGINAL.

marginal efficiency of capital. A statistical term denoting the discount necessary to equate the expected future earnings derived from the most profitable capital asset that can be added to an existing stock of capital goods, with the COST of reproducing that added capital asset. Thus, if for a given capital asset the replacement cost is $10,000, its life is 5 years, and the annual earnings for those 5 years are, respectively, $2,000, $3,000, $2,000, $2,500, and $2,500, the marginal efficiency of capital is 6.3 per cent. This is computed by means of the following equation:

$$A = 2,000(1 + i)^{-1} + 3,000(1 + i)^{-2} + 2,000(1 + i)^{-3} + 2,500(1 + i)^{-4} + 2,500(1 + i)^{-5}$$

when

A = the replacement cost,
i = the marginal efficiency of capital.

The equation is solved by substituting different values for i, tabulating the resulting values of A, and then interpolating. Thus, at $i = 5$ per cent,

$$2,000 \times 0.95238095 = 1,904.76190$$
$$3,000 \times 0.90703948 = 2,721.08844$$
$$2,000 \times 0.86384760 = 1,727.69520$$
$$2,500 \times 0.82270247 = 2,056.75618$$
$$2,500 \times 0.78353671 = \underline{1,958.84178}$$
$$10,369.14350$$

Repeating for 6 per cent and 6½ per cent, the results are:

i, per cent	*A*
5	10,369.14
6	10,086.80
6½	9,946.62

By interpolation for $10,000, i = 6.3 per cent. See MARGINAL. See also KEYNESIAN ECONOMICS.

marginal land. Land which will just repay the cost of products grown on it at the market prices prevailing for such products. See MARGINAL.

marginal lender. A lender or investor at a given rate of interest who will refuse to lend or invest if the rate of interest is reduced. See MARGINAL.

marginal producer. A producer who, at a given market price for his product, is able just to meet his costs of production. See MARGINAL.

marginal product. Whatever is produced by virtue of the addition of a single increment of a variable factor of production. For example, if 10 bu. of grain are produced on a given piece of land, and a unit of 25 lb. of fertilizer increases the yield to 14 bu., the marginal product is 4 bu. See MARGINAL.

marginal productivity. The ability of one additional increment of a variable factor of production to increase the total product. The term is generally used in conjunction with some particular factor of production; thus, the marginal productivity of land, labor, capital, or management means, in each case, the ability of one additional increment of the factor in question to increase the total product. See MARGINAL.

marginal-productivity theory of wages. The theory that wages tend to equal the value of the product that would be lost if one less worker were employed. An employer, it is asserted, cannot afford to pay a worker more than the value of the additional product produced because of the worker. If that amount is acceptable to the worker, he may be employed. And since all workers, according to the theory, are interchangeable, the amount paid to the marginal worker will determine the wages of all the workers. The theory assumes perfect competition, complete mobility of labor, and full employment among the workers engaged in any particular kind of work.

marginal propensity to consume. See PROPENSITY TO CONSUME.

marginal propensity to save. See PROPENSITY TO SAVE.

marginal rate of substitution. As applied to consumers, the quantity of one commodity or service that a given consumer feels he must acquire to compensate him exactly for the loss of one unit of some other commodity or service. When applied to money, the marginal rate of substitution is the price that a given consumer may be willing to pay for a specified quantity of some commodity or service. Also called *equimarginal principle.* See MARGINAL.

marginal revenue. The amount which the sale of one additional unit of product will add to the total income. If, for example, the total income received from the sale of 30 units is $30, and the total income received from the sale of 31 units is $30.50, the marginal revenue is 50 cents. See MARGINAL.

marginal seller. A seller at any given price who will refuse to sell if the price is reduced. See MARGINAL.

marginal trading. See BUYING ON MARGIN.

marginal utility. The least utility attributed to any one item of a supply of goods. In the diagram shown below, for example, the four vertical lines marked A, B, C, and D represent four items exactly alike. The marginal utility, as long as there are four items, is represented by 1. If one item is removed, leaving only three, the marginal utility is then represented by 2, etc. In general, the greater the number of items, the less the marginal utility. This is sometimes called the *law of diminishing utility,* or the *law of satiety*. The extent to which the marginal utility lessens with each additional item depends upon the individual concerned and the objects considered. Also called *marginal desirability*. See UTILITY.

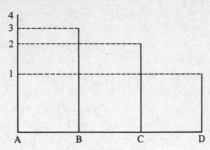

marginal utility theory of interest. The theory that interest rates are determined by the desire of individuals to equalize the MARGINAL UTILITY estimates of their present possessions with the marginal utility estimates of future possessions. For example, under certain assumed conditions, the immediate ownership of a dwelling, when none is possessed, may, for a given individual, offer such a high marginal utility that he is willing to pay a premium for it; that is, he is willing to borrow and pay interest and thus sacrifice the marginal utility of some possession that he might otherwise acquire in the future when the loan must be repaid. Conversely, to another individual the present estimate of the future marginal utility of, say, an automobile may be greater than his estimate of the marginal utility of any immediate new possession or added increment to any present possession. He is therefore willing to lend and thereby receive interest which, together with the return of the principal, will enable him to purchase the automobile at some future time. In those psychological attitudes involving what economists call marginal utility, it is contended, is to be found an explanation for prevailing interest rates. The theory is an amplification of the AGIO THEORY OF INTEREST.

margin of cultivation. That stage in the cultivation of land which results in a revenue just sufficient to pay the cost of production. The margin may be extensive or intensive. It is extensive when additional increments of capital and labor are applied to relatively poor land, and intensive when such increments are applied to better grades of land at a point when DIMINISHING RETURNS have set in. See also MARGINAL LAND.

Maritime Administration. A unit of the U.S. Department of Commerce which exercises regulatory powers over merchant ship construction with federal funds, private leasing of publicly built vessels, and subsidies to private maritime carriers.

market. 1. The area within which buyers and sellers are in communication with one another and within which exchanges take place. The communication sometimes takes place face to face, and the market, then is a very restricted area. On the other hand, the communication may be by telephone, telegraph, cable, or radio, in which case the market may be world-wide. See (6). **2.** The estimated or realized demand for a product or service. **3.** The process of preparing and distributing a product or service to the consumer.

market demand. See DEMAND.

marketing agreement. An agreement among the producers of certain agricultural commodities (or a large percentage of such producers) to limit the volume of shipments of such commodities to the market. The agreement is usually undertaken in conjunction with acreage limitations, for which producers are compensated by government subsidies for conservation practices. This is one means by which the U.S. Department of Agriculture tries to stabilize prices of agricultural commodities and equate supply with demand. Producers may also receive various kinds of AGRICULTURAL PRICE SUPPORTS *(q.v.)*.

market price. Under conditions of pure competition, the price at which the quantity of a good offered by the sellers just equals the quantity that will be taken by the buyers in a particular market at a specific time. For example, under the conditions noted below, at a market price of 8 cents, the sellers offer 300 and the buyers will take 300. At 9 cents the sellers offer 400, but the buyers will take only 200; hence, the price will be forced down. At 7 cents the sellers offer only 200 while the buyers will take 400, therefore the price will be bid up. At 8 cents equilibrium is established. Also called *market value.* See PRICE.

Prices	Quantities Offered by Sellers	Quantities That Buyers Will Take
10	500	100
9	400	200
8	300	300
7	200	400
6	100	500

markets, law of. The assertion that the greater the number and variety of commodities offered for sale, the greater the market for each one. If, for example, a trader barters his wares, he is more likely to dispose of all that he has if the market offers him an abundance of things and a wide variety in exchange. This is another way of saying that general overproduction cannot occur as long as all human wants are not satisfied. The law was formulated by J. B. Say during the 19th century.

market value. See MARKET PRICE.

markon. See MARKUP.

markup. 1. The difference between the price at which a product is sold and its cost at the point of sale, usually expressed as a percentage. The percentage may be based on the cost or on the selling price. Thus, if the cost is $10.00 and the selling price $15.00, the markup, based on the cost, is 50 per cent; if based on the selling price, it is 33⅓ per cent. When the markup is expressed in dollars and cents, it is sometimes called a *markon*. **2.** An increase of a previously lower selling price.

Marshall plan. See EUROPEAN RECOVERY PROGRAM.

Marxian law of capitalist accumulation. A generalization advanced by Karl Marx (1818-1883) and by certain of his disciples to the effect that as CAPITALISM develops, CAPITAL GOODS increase in amount and productivity, ownership becomes concentrated in fewer sources and eventually in the state, and workers become increasingly subject to exploitation and unemployment. During the early stages of capitalist development, according to the argument, surplus value is spent in capital goods rather than in CONSUMER GOODS, and this relative disparity between expenditures on capital, as opposed to consumer goods, continues even as production increases, the trend being aided by the effect of competition. Moreover, so the argument runs, the corporate form of business organization tends to eliminate the small producers in favor of the larger ones. This augments the number of workers and reduces the number of employers. The increase in the amount and concentration of capital goods makes necessary the expenditure of an increasing percentage of money capital on plant, equipment, and raw materials. Increased productivity, on the other hand, decreases the demand for labor. Unemployment results, causing a decrease in the total amount of wages paid. The end result is an accumulation of poverty together with an accumulation of capital goods.

Proponents of this law predict that when the process reaches its conclusion and all industry is in the hands of a few or perhaps only one huge trust, stockholders will be divested of their property in favor of state ownership for the benefit of the workers. Thus, say the proponents of this view, the PROLETARIAT will divest the BOURGEOISIE of their property, just as a few centuries ago the bourgeoisie allegedly divested the artisans of their tools and established the factory system. Also called *appropriation, law of; increasing misery, theory of.* See also SURPLUS LABOR AND VALUE THEORY.

Marxian School. Economic and social theories advanced by Karl Marx (1818–1883), German social philosopher and reformer, and various of his disciples. So-called laws of history are invoked, for example, the SURPLUS LABOR AND VALUE THEORY and the MARXIAN LAW OF CAPITALIST ACCUMULATION, which make "inevitable" the decline of capitalism, the eventual dominance of the proletariat or working class and, in time, the establishment of a classless society. Some of Marx's followers, notably Eduard Bernstein, have rejected many of the more orthodox ideas and have developed a more "gradualist" conception of capitalist decay and of the advent of a socialist society. Others, for example, Russian Leninist Communists and Chinese Maoist Communists, have sought to maintain Marxian orthodoxy. See SCHOOLS OF ECONOMIC THOUGHT.

Massachusetts trust. A business organization which conducts its affairs through a trustee, according to a declaration or agreement of trust. As such, it is neither a CORPORATION nor a

PARTNERSHIP. Contributions of capital are made to the trustees who carry on the business, certificates being issued to the contributors as evidence of their contributions, and earnings being paid them as dividends are paid to the stockholders of a corporation. The contributors may enjoy LIMITED LIABILITY, but they have no control over the management of the enterprise. So called because the plan originated in Massachusetts. Sometimes called *common-law trust.*

mass picketing. Picketing by large numbers of people before the entrance of the establishment being picketed. It is done for its dramatic effect and sometimes to make entrance to the establishment difficult. See PICKETING.

mass production. The production of goods in large quantities usually by means of machinery and frequently by reliance on interchangeable parts and division of labor. Also called *large-scale production.* See PRODUCTION.

mathematical economics. Economic principles and arguments expressed, in part, by mathematical symbols. Use of such symbols is thus a method of economic analysis; it does not constitute a special school of economic thought. The use of graphs and mathematical symbols to supplement an explanation in words is common practice. The use of mathematics as a general tool in economic reasoning is much more limited. See ECONOMICS.

mature economy. A term used by a few economists to describe the condition of a nation's economy when there is a decline in the rate of population growth and a decrease in the proportion of national income devoted to new capital investment, relatively more national income being spent for consumer goods.

maturity. As applied to securities and commercial paper, the date when payment of the principal is due.

maximum and minimum tariff system. A system of tariff legislation which provides two schedules—minimum and maximum—for particular articles, the purpose being to permit a country's trade negotiators to impose penalties or grant concessions, within the discretionary area thus allowed by legislation, in the course of trade negotiations with another country. See TARIFF.

maximum-hour legislation. See FAIR LABOR STANDARDS ACT.

mean. See AVERAGE.

mean deviation. A statistical measure of the extent of absolute dispersion, variability, or scatter in a FREQUENCY DISTRIBUTION *(q.v.)* obtained by ascertaining the ARITHMETIC MEAN of the total deviations (disregarding plus and minus signs) from a central value such as the MEDIAN *(q.v.).*
Example with median = 2.53 given:

Class interval	Midpoint	Frequency	Deviations from median (disregarding plus and minus signs)	Total deviations (deviations times frequency)
−0.5 to 0.4	0	10	2.53 − 0 = 2.53	25.30
0.5 to 1.4	1	30	2.53 − 1 = 1.53	45.90
1.5 to 2.4	2	40	2.53 − 2 = 0.53	21.20
2.5 to 3.4	3	50	2.53 − 3 = 0.47	23.50
3.5 to 4.4	4	25	2.53 − 4 = 1.47	36.75
4.5 to 5.4	5	8	2.53 − 5 = 2.47	19.76
		163		172.41

$$\text{Mean deviation} = \frac{172.41}{163} = 1.0577.$$

The mean deviation is particularly well suited to economic analysis because, although it is influenced by every value in the series, undue weight is not given to the extremes.

means test. A formal investigation to determine whether an individual's resources are so limited as to warrant his receiving unemployment relief, public assistance, a college scholarship, or similar aid.

measured day rate. As applied to the compensation of an employee, a daily adjustment of wages based on a record of the employee's previous daily production over a period of time. See RATE.

median. As applied to a FREQUENCY DISTRIBUTION *(q.v.),* a positional average, indicating central tendency, secured by designating the midpoint. Its position thus being midway in the frequency distribution, one half of the cases are below it and one half above it. Likewise, the value of the median is such that one half of the cases are less than it, and one half are in excess of it. It is calculated by first ascertaining the class interval within which it is located, then finding its value within this class interval by interpolation.

Example:

Frequency distribution

Class interval	Midpoint	Frequency	Cumulative frequency to the third-class interval
−0.5 to 0.4	0	10	10
0.5 to 1.4	1	30	40
1.5 to 2.4	2	40	80
2.5 to 3.4	3	50	
3.5 to 4.4	4	25	
4.5 to 5.4	5	8	
		163	

$$\frac{163}{2} = 81.5.$$
$$81.5 - 80 = 1.5.$$

$$\text{Median} = 2.5 + \left(\frac{1.5}{50} \times 1 \right) = 2.5 + 0.03 = 2.53.$$

See AVERAGE.

mediation. A procedure for settling disputes, akin to CONCILIA-TION but somewhat more formal, often involving the use of a board or commission before which the disputants may appear with their attorneys. Mediation is conducted by a *mediator,* who is professionally qualified to examine impartially into a dispute, especially a labor dispute, and, by clarifying the issues and suggesting compromises and possible solutions, to provide the disputants with a better understanding of the issues and hopefully advance them towards a mutually satisfactory adjustment of the controversy.

mediator. See MEDIATION.

medicaid. A program providing medical assistance to aged low-income persons. The program is financed largely by the states and local governments although augmented by grants from the federal government. Within prescribed limitations, the states are permitted considerable latitude in determining those eligible for assistance and the kind and extent of the assistance available. See also MEDICARE.

medicare. A federal government program of health insurance for persons aged 65 and over, consisting of both hospital and medical insurance. The hospital insurance program covers most health-care services while the individual is hospitalized and provides certain supplementary out-patient services. The medical insurance program, part of the cost of which is borne by the insured, covers a major share of medical expenses such as doctor's fees, diagnostic tests, and similar services. See MEDICAID.

medium of exchange. See MONEY.

member bank. A term usually applied to a bank which is a member of the FEDERAL RESERVE SYSTEM. See BANK.

mercantile agency. An organization that supplies information regarding business concerns seeking CREDIT.

mercantilist school. Economists and economic theorists, especially influential during the 16th and 17th centuries, who taught that, in order to increase national wealth and prestige, a state should favor manufacture over agriculture, and by appropriate regulations, secure a favorable foreign trade balance, that is an excess of exports over imports, collecting the difference in the form of precious metals from the debtor countries. See SCHOOLS OF ECONOMIC THOUGHT.

merchant guild. A medieval merchant association that commanded a monopoly of town trade and became closely identified with municipal authority, sometimes to the point of merging with that authority. See GUILD.

merchantman. A transoceanic or coastwise commercial vessel carrying passengers or freight.

merchant marine. Commercial ships owned and operated either by the government or by the private citizens of a state.

merger. The absorption by one business enterprise of the assets and liabilities of another enterprise or of other enterprises which may have produced similar or dissimilar products, the absorbed enterprises being dissolved. Compare CONSOLIDATION. See COMBINATION.

merit rating. As applied to labor relations, a periodic appraisal of an employee's efficiency, responsibility, and other qualifications, frequently used as a basis for determining wage increases and promotions, sometimes to determine which employee shall be laid off in the event a plant is temporarily closed or work becomes slack, and less frequently to determine workers' unemployment compensation contributions.

microeconomics. Economic studies or statistics that consider particular individuals or single commodities; for example, the demand for wheat or for employment in the automotive industries. The term is used in contradistinction to MACROECONOMICS. See ECONOMICS.

middleman. A merchant, jobber, wholesaler, or some other such intermediary between the producer and the consumer.

middle way. See MIXED ECONOMY.

migrant worker. A worker without fixed abode who moves from one part of the country to another to take advantage of seasonal demand for his services particularly during harvest time on the farm and in the orchard. In the United States he is likely to belong to a racial minority or, as in the case of the so-called *wetback* or *bracero,* he may be a Mexican national who has entered the country illegally. Migrant workers usually lack the protection of legislation or of trade union membership and they are consequently exploited by being made the victims of substandard housing, poor working conditions, and relatively low pay.

milk-control case. A case, *Nebbia* v. *New York,* 291 U.S. 502 (1934), in which the Supreme Court upheld a New York State statute which regulated the retail price of milk as consistent with the due process clause of the 14th Amendment to the Constitution. Primary significance attaches to this case because the subject regulated, that is, the milk business, does not fall within the category of businesses, such as utilitieş, which were traditionally considered to be "affected with a public interest" and therefore subject to such regulation as was here attempted.

Indeed, the Court specifically indicated that in its opinion there existed no particular class of businesses affected with a public interest and suggested that the courts would determine in each case, as it arose, whether circumstances warranted regulation or whether the regulation was arbitrary and discriminatory.

Miller-Tydings Act. An act of Congress, 1937, which modified antitrust regulations to the extent of permitting minimum resale price agreements for trade-marked goods in interstate commerce, when also permitted by state law.

minimum rate. As applied to public-utility companies, the lowest rate that a company is permitted to charge for a specific commodity or service. Minimum rates are established by regulatory commissions. See RATE.

minimum wage. A wage established by law as the lowest which may be paid employees in one or more industries. See WAGE.

minimum-wage cases. 1. *Adkins* v. *Children's Hospital.* One of the early minimum-wage cases, 261 U.S. 525 (1923), to come before the Supreme Court in which that tribunal held unconstitutional a federal minimum-wage act the operation of which was limited to the District of Columbia. Applicable only to women and children in various industries for which a wage board prescribed minimum pay standards, the act was held to establish an uncertain yardstick for compensation and to discriminate arbitrarily against the employer; hence, it was deemed to go beyond the standards of due process prescribed by the 5th Amendment to the Constitution and to be an unreasonable interference with liberty of contract. **2.** *West Coast Hotel Co.* v. *Parrish.* A case, 300 U.S. 379 (1937), in which the Supreme Court ruled that legislative establishment of reasonable minimum-wage rates for women was a proper use of the police power of the state. Earlier minimum-wage decisions, such as the one in the Adkins case above, were thus overruled in recognition of the necessity for a broader interpretation of the police power of the states to meet changing economic needs.

minor coin. A coin made of base metal. See COIN.

mint. A place where bullion is made into coins, usually operated by or under the authority of the government.

mintage. Any charge made by a government for converting bullion into coins.

mint par of exchange. As applied to the GOLD STANDARD, the ratio between the weights of the pure metal in the MONETARY UNITS of two nations. Thus, before January 31, 1934, when Great Britain and the United States were both on the gold standard, the British pound contained 113.0016 grains of fine gold, and the United States dollar 23.22 grains. The mint par of exchange was, therefore, 4.8665, obtained by dividing the first figure by the second. Mint par of exchange was self-regulating, the value of gold being maintained by FREE COINAGE and a free market. With the passing of the gold standard, PAR EXCHANGE RATE *(q.v.)* has largely replaced the mint par of exchange.

mint price of gold. The price, determined by law, which a government pays for gold delivered at the mint. In the United States, the dollar is defined by law as $15\frac{5}{21}$ grains of gold $\frac{9}{10}$ fine or 13.714+ grains of pure gold. There being 480 grains to the troy ounce, the mint price of gold is, therefore, $\dfrac{480}{13.714}$ or $35 per fine troy ounce.

mint ratio. In a bimetallic monetary system, the ratio of weight of one metal in the monetary system to the weight of the other metal in that system. For example, in the American presidential campaign of 1896, the forces supporting Bryan's bimetallic program urged a mint ratio between silver and gold of 16 to 1. See RATIO. See also BIMETALLISM.

misfeasance. Improper or illegal exercise of a legal responsibility.

Mississippi bubble. A speculative trading and banking venture engineered in France, 1716-20, by John Law, Scottish economist. Having secured from the French crown the right to establish a bank which eventually became the Bank Royale with the privilege of issuing paper money granted by the government, Law set up a company to exploit trading and other privileges granted him in the Mississippi Valley area. Subsequently the company and bank acquired a virtual monopoly over colonial trade, the tobacco concession, banking, and the issue of notes and coins, the latter having little to support them other than the assets of the Law enterprises. France experienced a speculative orgy especially in the shares of the bank and trading company. This was succeeded by a panic during which the Law bank reduced the value of its paper money and eventually made its notes inconvertible. Law thereupon left the country.

mixed economy. An economic system in which can be found some of the characteristics of both CAPITALISM and SOCIALISM as well as some measure of CONTROL and regulation by the central government, often called the *middle way.* See ECONOMIC SYSTEM.

mode. As applied to a FREQUENCY DISTRIBUTION *(q.v.),* a positional average, indicating central tendency, secured by designating the most common measure or value. As such, it is the point on the X axis corresponding to the maximum ordinate. It can be derived only approximately from a frequency distribution. The class interval with the greatest frequency is selected. This is called the "modal class." The equation for the mode is then:

$$Mo = l + \frac{f_2}{f_2 + f_1} \times i$$

when

Mo = mode,
f_1 = frequency of class next below the modal class,
f_2 = frequency of class next above the modal class,
i = class interval,
l = lower limit of modal class.

Example:

Class Interval	Frequency
− 0.5 to 0.4	10
0.5 to 1.4	30
1.5 to 2.4	40
2.5 to 3.4	50*
3.5 to 4.4	25
4.5 to 5.4	8

*Modal class.

$$Mo = 2.5 + \frac{25}{25 + 40} \times 1 = 2.5 + 0.385 = 2.885.$$

See AVERAGE.

modified union shop. A shop in which, upon the consummation of a labor agreement, the status of the existing employees in reference to their labor-union membership, or nonmembership, remains unchanged, but in which new employees are obligated to join the labor union. See SHOP.

modular housing. Units of prefabricated houses that can be joined horizontally or vertically to form a contiguous connected unit.

monetary policy. As distinguished from FISCAL POLICY *(q.v.)*, the actions of governments relating to currency revaluation, credit contraction or expansion, and rediscount policy; also, regulations relating to bank reserves or to the purchase or sale of government securities. More particularly, any of the above actions which affect directly the volume of currency and credit and hence the stability of the economy.

monetary reserves. The amount of bullion held by the government or by the banks as security for fiduciary or credit money in circulation. For example, it is estimated that there is still in circulation in the United States about $300 million in GREEN-BACKS secured by about half their face value in bullion. See RESERVES.

monetary sovereignty. A right, said to inhere in any sovereign nation, to safeguard its economy against severe deflation, unemployment, or imbalance in its foreign payments, despite formal pledges of cooperation which it may have given to such organizations as the INTERNATIONAL MONETARY FUND.

monetary system. A general term embracing the policies and practices affecting a particular nation's money. Although characteristically concerned with the definition of STANDARD MONEY, the term may include regulations governing COINAGE and emission of MONEY, MONETARY RESERVES, and LEGAL TENDER, requirements and regulations affecting the value of different types of PAPER MONEY and COINS in terms of the standard money, etc. There are innumerable kinds of monetary systems in use and proposed. See (33).

monetary union. See LATIN MONETARY UNION, SCANDINAVIAN MONETARY UNION, TRIPARTITE CURRENCY AGREEMENT. See also STERLING BLOC.

monetary unit. A specified amount and quality of a commodity selected as standard money and designated by a name. In the case of the United States the commodity selected is gold, and the amount and quality specified is 15⁵⁄₂₁ grains ⁹⁄₁₀ fine. The name of the unit is the dollar.

money. Anything generally accepted in exchange for other things within more or less definite areas; hence, a customary *medium of exchange.* Money is also customarily used as a measure of, and a means of storing, value. Historically, commodities used as money were relatively scarce and universally wanted. Many articles possessing these prerequisites have been used as money, but the precious metals, in addition to these qualities, have been found to possess other characteristics which greatly facilitate their use as money. They are easily recognized, uniform in quality, easily divisible, and they encompass a relatively high value within a small space. An ideal money should also have stability of value in addition to these other characteristics, but no money has yet been devised to meet this requirement satisfactorily. The value of modern coins rests to a large extent upon the credit of the government issuing them rather than upon their intrinsic value, and this is true to an even greater extent of modern paper money. It should be noted that money as here defined is one form of CURRENCY *(q.v.).* Some authorities, however, use the term "money" in the more general sense and the term "currency" in the more restricted sense. See (33).

money capital. See CAPITAL.

money in circulation. In the United States, coins and paper money circulating outside of the United States Treasury and the federal reserve banks.

money market. An indefinitely defined financial center where foreign and domestic BILLS *(q.v.),* foreign currency, and bullion are bought and sold. See MARKET.

money order. An order purchased by a person wishing to make a remittance to some distant point. It is sent to the payee, who may subsequently cash it at the place of payment specifically identified. A money order is usually cashable at any bank, upon identification. Money orders are generally named according to the agency that sells them (bank, express company, postal), according to the means of their transmission (cable, telegraph), or according to their destination (domestic, foreign, international).

money wage. The amount of wages paid in money. The term is used to emphasize the fact that what can be bought with the wages depends upon the PRICE LEVEL. See WAGE.

monometallism. A monetary system in which the monetary unit is legally defined in terms of but one metal, that metal being accepted in unlimited quantities for coinage and made unlimited legal tender. Also called *single standard.* See MONETARY SYSTEM.

monopolistic competition. The condition that exists in a market when the operations of one or a few buyers or sellers can materially affect the market price. See COMPETITION.

monopoly. Usually the condition which exists when there is a single control over all the supply of a product, thus permitting the release of the supply at such a rate as will yield the most profitable price. The monopolist cannot dictate the schedule demand for his product. He can only discover it. But he can dictate the schedule supply. This enables him to offer for sale the particular quantity of his product that, according to the schedule demand, will yield him the most profitable price. This price may be relatively high or low depending upon the nature of the product and the nature of the schedule demand. See (4).

monopsony. See BUYER'S MONOPOLY.

moonlighting. Regular employment during the day or week in more than one job, a practice made possible by the shorter legal working day and the staggered hours for some types of employment.

moratorium. A period, usually stipulated by law, during which the settlement of debts may be postponed.

more-favorable-terms clause. A clause in a labor contract in which the contracting labor union agrees that it will not grant more favorable terms in any future contracts with competitors of the contracting employer.

Morrill (Land-Grant College) Act. An act of Congress, 1862. It provided grants of public lands to the states, the revenue from which was to be used for education in agricultural and mechanical arts.

Morrill Tariff. The United States Tariff Act of 1861. Its purpose was avowedly protective. Existing duties were advanced. SPECIFIC DUTIES were restored on raw wool, cotton bagging, and other commodities.

Morris Plan bank. See INDUSTRIAL BANK.

mortgage. 1. A conditional conveyance of property as security for the payment of a debt or the performance of some other obligation. **2.** A contract specifying that certain property is hypothecated for the payment of a debt or for the performance of some other obligation. See (17).

mortgage bond. See BOND.

mortgagee. A person who grants a loan secured by a mortgage and to whom the mortgage is given. See also MORTGAGE.

mortgage-moratorium case. See *HOME BUILDING AND LOAN ASSOCIATION* v. *BLAISDELL*.

mortgagor. A person who gives a mortgage on his property as security for a loan. See MORTGAGE.

most-favored-nation clause. A provision in a commercial treaty binding the contracting nations to confer upon each other all the most favorable trade concessions that either may grant to any other nation subsequent to the signing of the agreement.

Motor Carrier Act. An act of Congress, 1935, which brings most trucks, buses, and other commercial motor vehicles operating in interstate commerce within the jurisdiction of the INTERSTATE COMMERCE COMMISSION and subjects the rate structure and the services of companies operating such vehicles to the commission's regulatory power.

moving average. A series of averages obtained by selecting a fixed number of successive items in a series, computing the average, then dropping the first item and adding the next succeeding one, computing the average of this second group, dropping the second item and adding the next succeeding one, computing the average of this third group, etc., throughout the series. The following is an example of a three-item moving average:

Items	Three-item moving totals	Three-item moving average
2		
6	9	3
1	15	5
8	12	4
3	12	4
1	15	5
11	24	8
12	27	9
4		

In economic computation, moving averages are frequently used in smoothing out irregular curves. See AVERAGE.

Mulford v. Smith. See AGRICULTURAL ADJUSTMENT ACT CASE (SECOND).

Muller v. Oregon. A case, 208 U.S. 412 (1908), in which the Supreme Court upheld the constitutionality of an Oregon statute limiting the workday of women employed in certain establishments to 10 hours. Apparently the Court differentiated this case from the situation in LOCHNER V. NEW YORK *(q.v.)*, decided a few years earlier, because it felt that women were less able to endure sustained labor than men and hence required special protection by law.

multicraft union. A craft labor union, the members of which include workers in several distinctly different kinds of trades and occupations. See LABOR UNION.

multilateral agreement. An agreement in which more than two parties participate.

multilinear tariff. See MULTIPLE TARIFF SYSTEM.

multiple-commodity reserve dollar. A plan designed to maintain a constant value ratio between gold and other commodities in terms of dollars. It proposes to establish a reserve of selected goods. Money would then be redeemable either in gold or in these reserve goods, and gold and the reserve goods could always be exchanged for dollars. Thus, it is claimed, a constant ratio would be maintained between the value of the commodities, the gold, and the dollar. See MONETARY SYSTEM.

multiple currency system. A form of exchange control. It involves the establishment by law of different foreign exchange values for the national currency, the applicable value in any exchange transaction depending upon the type of commodity purchased abroad for which exchange is desired. See also EXCHANGE CONTROL.

multiple expansion of credit. The process by which a loan made by one bank may, in the ordinary course of business transactions, become a deposit in another bank and be used by this second bank as a reserve for another loan. See DEPOSIT CURRENCY *(q.v.)*.

multiple tariff system. A system of differential customs duties, that is, a tariff which applies duties at different rates on the same imported commodity, the level of duty being determined by the importing country according to the commodity's country of origin. Also called *multilinear tariff*. See TARIFF.

multiplier principle. As applied to investments, an explanation, propounded especially by Keynesian economists, as to the way in which an increase or a decrease in new CAPITAL FORMATION can cause cumulative effects in the NATIONAL INCOME through consumer expenditures. For example, assume an increase in new capital formation of $4,000,000. This will normally yield a like increase in the national income in the form of wages, interest, profit, rent, etc. The recipients of this INCOME will spend it according to the existing marginal PROPENSITY TO CONSUME. Assuming this to be 65 per cent, then $2,600,000 will be spent for consumer goods. This will increase the income in the consumer goods industry by that amount. The recipients of that income, in turn, will, according to the assumption, spend 65 per cent of $2,600,000, or $1,690,000. And as this last amount becomes income, 65 per cent of it will be spent, and so on, according to the following table, based on the assumed increase in new capital formation.

Investment, $4,000,000
Marginal Propensity to Consume, 65 per cent

Income	Expenditure
$4,000,000.00	$2,600,000.00
2,600,000.00	1,690,000.00
1,690,000.00	1,098,500.00
1,098,500.00	714,025.00
714,025.00	464,116.25
464,116.25	301,675.56
301,675.56	etc.

Ultimately, the total increase in income will approach $11,428,571, in accordance with the following formula:

$$\frac{l}{1 - R}$$

when

l = the original increase in new capital formation,
R = the marginal propensity to consume.

Applying this to the above example, the results are:

$$\frac{\$4,000,000}{1 - 0.65} = \frac{\$4,000,000}{0.35} = \$11,428,571.$$

The multiplier is the ratio between the increase or decrease in income (Y) and the increase or decrease in new capital formation (I), or, in the above example:

$$\frac{\Delta Y}{\Delta I} = \frac{11,428,571}{4,000,000} = 2.8571.$$

A decrease in investments will, of course, have the opposite effect and will decrease the national income. The decrease in the national income from this cause will, it is held, equal the amount of the decrease in new capital formation times the multiplier. See also KEYNESIAN ECONOMICS, LEAKAGE.

municipal bond. See BOND.

municipal corporation. A corporation organized for the purpose of administering a political subdivision of a state, usually a city, village, or town but sometimes also a county. See CORPORATION.

municipal socialism. Ownership and operation of local utility services by a municipality. Examples are water supply, transportation facilities, gas, or electricity. See SOCIALISM.

Munn v. Illinois. The most important of the so-called *Granger cases* which involved judicial review of the efforts of midwest farming interests in the United States to reduce, through appropriate legislation, the rates charged by railways and warehouses for the transportation and storage of grain and other commodities. This particular case, 94 U.S. 113 (1876), involved an Illinois statute fixing maximum charges for grain storage in elevators, and the principal legal issue was whether such legislation deprived elevator proprietors of their property rights protected by the due process clause of the 14th Amendment to the Constitution. The Supreme Court's decision, upholding the regulatory statute, is noteworthy because it is based on the theory that there are certain businesses, like that of operating a grain elevator, which, though privately owned, are nonetheless businesses in which the "public has a direct and positive interest"; that is, they are businesses clothed with a public interest and, as such, are amenable to public control. The decision thus became one of the pioneer judicial precedents in the United States validating public regulation of the rates and services of what are commonly known as PUBLIC UTILITIES.

mutual company. Usually a corporation without capital stock, the profits, if any, after deduction of reserves, being available for distribution among the customers in proportion to the business done with the company. A MUTUAL SAVINGS BANK is a common form of mutual company. See COMPANY.

mutual fund. See OPEN-END INVESTMENT COMPANY.

mutualism. The economic ideas of Pierre Joseph Proudhon (1809-65), a French neoanarchist leader, and his followers. Proudhon objected particularly to unearned income payments and value appreciation arising from the private ownership of property. He believed that such payments as rent, interest, and profits were parasitical shares and should be abolished. Services rendered and received would, he argued, then be in balance on the basis of equality.

mutual loan association. See BUILDING AND LOAN ASSOCIATION.

mutual savings bank. A savings bank, the depositors of which are the owners, and the net earnings of which are available for distribution among the depositors. It is governed by a board of self-perpetuating trustees. See BANK.

N

narrow market. The condition that exists when the demand for or supply of a security or commodity is so limited that relatively small changes in supply or demand will cause wide fluctuations in the market price. Also called *thin market*. See MARKET.

National Academy of Sciences. A private agency, given a national charter in 1863, which is broadly concerned with the advancement of scientific research and development. Various committees of the Academy survey scientific problems and report to the public and to public agencies when requested to do so. There are two adjunct organizations, the National Research Council and the National Academy of Engineering.

National Advisory Council on International Monetary and Financial Policies. A special federal agency which coordinates the policies and operations of the United States representatives to the International Monetary Fund, the International Bank for Reconstruction and Development, the Inter-American Development Bank, and the Asian Development Bank, and of federal fiscal institutions like the Export-Import Bank of the United States insofar as these may deal with foreign loans, exchange, or monetary transactions.

National Aeronautics and Space Administration. An independent federal agency, created in 1958, to conduct research into the problems of flight, both within and beyond the earth's atmosphere, to plan and conduct such activities as might be required for the peaceful utilization of outer space, including the creation, testing, and operation of space vehicles, and to assist scientists in their research in relevant disciplines.

National Association of Manufacturers. An organization with a large direct membership and several hundred state and local associations, founded in 1895 to act as a spokesman for industrial management before the legislative and administrative agencies of the federal government, and to review pending legislative, administrative, and other public actions as these may affect the welfare of industry. The Association publishes various periodical bulletins and occasional studies.

national bank. A bank chartered under the NATIONAL BANK ACT of 1863 and subsequent legislation, and subject to the supervision of the Comptroller of the Currency, which engages in general commercial banking. Until 1935, such a bank also had the privilege of issuing notes as paper currency, based on federal bonds; but all national bank notes have been retired. See BANK, COMMERCIAL BANK, NATIONAL BANK ACT.

National Bank Act. An act of Congress, 1863, at first called the *National Currency Act.* It established a system of NATIONAL BANKS (*q.v.*). Subsequently, in 1866, a federal tax of 10 per cent on state bank notes drove such notes out of circulation and had the effect of making the national banks the only banks of issue at the time. See also *VEAZIE BANK* v. *FENNO.*

National Bureau of Standards. A unit of the U.S. Department of Commerce which has custody of the national standards of physical measurement. Separate institutes within the Bureau conduct research on the quality and performance of materials for industry and government and supply both of these constituencies with quantitative and technical information on the uses of advancing technology.

National Currency Act. See NATIONAL BANK ACT.

national debt. The debt of a central government as distinct from the debts of the political subdivisions of the nation and the debts of private persons corporate and natural. The national debt plus the debts of local governments of a country comprise its PUBLIC DEBT. See DEBT.

297

National Defense Education Act. An act of Congress, 1958, the aim of which is to strengthen the nation's defense posture by expanding the number of trained personnel in certain subjects and disciplines. It authorizes loans and grants for students, especially in the sciences, and for the improvement of laboratory and instructional facilities in schools and colleges, the strengthening of education in mathematics, the sciences, and foreign languages, and the improvement of facilities for guiding and counseling students.

national economy. The economic life of a nation. The term implies that the economic life of a nation forms a unified whole—a not entirely tenable idea in view of the impact of extra-national influences.

National Farmers Union. A general farm organization, usually known as the *Farmers Union,* founded in Point, Texas, in 1902 and now composed of more than 200,000 farm families and various related subsidiary groups, whose principal aim is to secure parity of income for farm families in America. To secure its objectives, it seeks to influence government policies and conducts local educational programs. Through subsidiaries it has property interests in insurance and fertilizer companies.

national forests. The wooded preserve of the public lands of the United States, almost 200 million acres in extent, which is administered by the *Forest Service* with the aims of preserving as far as possible a natural ecological balance over wide areas, of supplying forest products for commercial purposes, of providing recreational areas, and of maintaining wildlife resources.

National Grange Order of the Patrons of Husbandry. One of the earliest American farm organizations, founded in 1867. It was originally conceived as a secret organization and has always retained its ritual service. Its object is to improve rural life, foster the processes of democracy, and crystallize an informed public opinion concerning national affairs. It is claimed that there are at least 800,000 dues-paying members, and several thousand local granges, perhaps half of which own their own halls. These halls are often community centers where regular meetings are held to further the objects of the organization. Popularly known as the *Grange.* Also called *Patrons of Husbandry.*

national income. The total earnings of labor and property in the nation's economy during a given year. These earnings arise from the production of goods and services, and measure the total FACTOR COSTS of the goods and services produced. National income is used to chart trends in economic activity (prosperity, recessions, and depressions), to compute the rate of the nation's economic growth, and, with the use of INDEX NUMBERS, to estimate changes in the level of living of the population. See Appendix B, items 1 to 10, inclusive. See INCOME.

national income accounts budget. A federal budget which, unlike the customary ADMINISTRATIVE BUDGET, includes social security, highway, and other autonomously financed programs. Also, unlike the administrative budget it is compiled on an ACCRUAL BASIS (*q.v.*). See BUDGET.

national income and product account. A combined statement of the NATIONAL INCOME and the GROSS NATIONAL PRODUCT. In order to balance one with the other, depreciation and other CAPITAL CONSUMPTION ALLOWANCES, TRANSFER PAYMENTS, and certain indirect business taxes, such as sales, customs duties, business property taxes, etc., which are excluded from the national income but included in gross national product, must be deducted from gross national product, while subsidies, less current surplus of government enterprises, must be added to it. There is always a slight statistical discrepancy. See Appendix B, items 16 to 20 inclusive.

National Industrial Recovery Act. An act of Congress, 1933, which provided for CODES OF FAIR COMPETITION, COLLECTIVE BARGAINING, and other measures designed to promote recovery from the economic depression then in existence. The code provisions of the act were declared unconstitutional by the Supreme Court in 1935. See also SCHECHTER CASE.

National Institutes of Health. Various units of the U.S. Public Health Service concerned with advancing knowledge about certain degenerative and infectious diseases both by pursuing research programs themselves and by funding such programs in universities and medical schools.

national insurance. See SOCIAL INSURANCE.

nationalization. Ownership and operation by the central government of a nation of some enterprise previously a private or local-government undertaking.

National Labor Relations (*Wagner-Connery*) Act. An act of Congress, 1935, which guarantees the right of certain employees to full freedom in self-organization and in the designation of representatives of their own choosing for the purpose of collective bargaining, and makes unlawful unfair labor practices which abridge or deny the right of collective bargaining. Its provisions were subsequently (1947) amended by the LABOR-MANAGEMENT RELATIONS (TAFT-HARTLEY) ACT (*q.v.*).

National Labor Relations Act case. A case, *National Labor Relations Board* v. *Jones and Laughlin Steel Corp.*, 301 U.S. 1 (1937), in which the Supreme Court upheld as constitutional the National Labor Relations Act of 1935 (Wagner-Connery Act) as a valid exercise of congressional power. The Court declared that the act, in its provisions for collective bargaining and control over labor relations, sought to reach labor disputes which might burden or obstruct foreign or interstate commerce. In doing so, commented the Court, the act "must be construed as contemplating the exercise of control within the Constitutional bounds."

National Labor Relations Board. An independent federal agency consisting of five members, created by the NATIONAL LABOR RELATIONS (WAGNER-CONNERY) ACT of 1935 and continued, with certain changes, under the LABOR-MANAGEMENT RELATIONS (TAFT-HARTLEY) ACT of 1947. Among the board's duties are those of conducting elections among private employees to determine what labor organization shall represent them in collective bargaining and to certify labor organizations for collective bargaining. The board also investigates allegations of unfair labor practices by either unions or management; for example, the exaction of discriminatory or excessive fees by unions or employer discrimination against employees for union activity. If the board finds unfair practices, it may issue cease-and-desist orders and subsequently petition a federal circuit court of appeals to enforce them. Responsibility for instituting proceedings against management or labor unions for unfair practices vests in the board's general counsel who is appointed by the President and the Senate for a term of 4 years.

National Labor Relations Board v. ***Fansteel Metallurgical Corp.*** See FANSTEEL CASE.

National Labor Relations Board v. ***Jones and Laughlin Steel Corp.*** See NATIONAL LABOR RELATIONS ACT CASE.

National Mediation Board. An independent, three-member federal agency created in 1934 to carry out the provisions of the Railway Labor Act of 1926 and subsequent related legislation. The Board mediates disputes growing out of the interpretation of agreements between labor and management of interstate railway and air carriers or out of efforts to create such agreements. It also holds elections to identify and certify employee representatives to engage in collective bargaining with management. Certain disputes, especially those growing out of an agreement, are referred to one of four employer-employee panels of the *National Railroad Adjustment Board* which, if deadlocked, may be assisted in making an award by a referee appointed by the National Mediation Board.

national minimum. A social-security policy which sets a certain "floor," or minimum, to the level of living. The government attempts to assure this minimum to each individual through social insurance, relief, or some other means of public assistance.

National Monetary Commission. See ALDRICH-VREELAND ACT.

national product. See GROSS NATIONAL PRODUCT, NET NATIONAL PRODUCT.

National Railroad Adjustment Board. See NATIONAL MEDIATION BOARD.

National Science Foundation. An independent federal agency created in 1950 to promote education and research in the sciences. Various divisions, operating under a director and a 24-member board, commit sizable appropriations annually, in grants and contracts, to universities and comparable institutions, to support fellowships, scientific research projects, curriculum revision, scholarly exchange programs, information programs, teacher-training programs, and the improvement of laboratories and educational facilities.

National Security Council. A division of the Executive Office of the President, created by the National Security Act, 1947, to integrate civilian and military policies having to do with the nation's defense, thus providing more effective cooperation between the military services and the various other agencies of the federal government. The Council is composed of the President, the Vice President, the Secretary of State, the Secretary of Defense, and the Director of the Office of Emergency Planning.

national security exchange. Any securities exchange whose activities are interstate, that is, whose customers may live in more than one state or whose traded securities are those of corporations from more than one state, and which, in order to do business, must register with the SECURITIES AND EXCHANGE COMMISSION and comply with federal securities exchange regulations. See EXCHANGE.

National Transportation Safety Board. A 5-member board within the U.S. Department of Transportation which (*a*) examines into the causes of aircraft, pipeline, rail, marine, and highway vehicle accidents; (*b*) makes recommendations to reduce and prevent such accidents; and (*c*) reviews appeals from the suspension or revocation of certificates or licenses issued to carriers.

national union. In the United States, a labor union whose members are widely distributed throughout the nation but none of whom resides in a foreign country, and which therefore has no foreign locals. See LABOR UNION.

national wealth. The total money value at any particular time of all the material economic goods possessed by members of a given nation. For analytical and statistical purposes the national wealth may be said to consist of (*a*) reproducible assets such as structures; (*b*) nonreproducible assets such as land; (*c*) various goods—durable, semi-durable, and soft, plus inventories; and (*d*) monetary metals. For many nations the property within the nation owned by foreigners just about balances the property outside of the nation owned by nationals. In such cases the matter of nationality is ignored as it is, for example, in the statistics of the national wealth of the United States issued by the U.S. Bureau of the Census. Where no such balance exists, a distinction may be made between "national wealth" and "wealth within the borders," much of which may be held by nonnationals. See WEALTH.

National Woodwork Manufacturers Association* v. *N.L.R.B. A case, 368 U.S. 612 (1967), in which the Supreme Court held that carpenters who refused to hang pre-cut doors did not violate legislative prohibitions of secondary boycotts, such legislative prohibitions not having been intended to limit the right of union members to protect their existing jobs.

natural capital. See CAPITAL GOOD.

Natural Gas Act. An act of Congress, 1938, which, as amended in 1942, gives the Federal Power Commission considerable authority over interstate transportation and sale of natural gas. The commission's powers under the legislation include control of rates, the regulation of services, and the investigation of interstate compacts dealing with various aspects of the natural gas industry.

natural monopoly. 1. A monopoly due to natural conditions. For example, the natural conditions may be a peculiarity of soil within a small area enabling the owner or owners of that area to produce a product that cannot be grown elsewhere, or the existence of a limited supply of mineral wealth coming under the control of a single enterprise. **2.** A monopoly due to characteristics inherent in the business. The characteristics are usually those which make competition self-destructive and hence incompatible with the public interest. Such conditions have been met by subjecting such businesses to government control as in the case of PUBLIC-SERVICE CORPORATIONS. See MONOPOLY.

natural order. A conception of the physiocrats popular during the 18th century. According to this conception human societies were subject to laws of nature such as govern the physical world. It was necessary, therefore, that all human activities should be brought into harmony with these laws of nature. This, it was held, could be accomplished by seeking the greatest satisfactions with the least sacrifice; and when each member of society thus ordered his activities, the welfare of society as a whole was assured. It was in this conception of a natural order that the term *LAISSEZ FAIRE* originated.

natural resources. Wealth supplied by nature. Mineral deposits, soil fertility, timber, potential water power, and fish and wildlife are included in the concept. The term "natural resources" is identical with the formal economic concept of LAND.

natural rights. Individual rights which are believed to be beyond the province of the state to deny. The Declaration of Independence of the United States defines such rights as "life, liberty, and the pursuit of happiness."

nature. See LAND.

navicert. A document issued by a belligerent nation permitting specified commodities to be transported overseas by a neutral nation through a blockaded area to a named neutral port of destination. A cargo navicert names the commodities and certifies that the shipment is within the normal requirements of the neutral country to which it is consigned. A ship navicert specifies the cargo carried and certifies that permission has been granted for the vessel to make that specific voyage. The term is an abbreviation of "naval certificate."

near money. LIQUID assets held by individuals and organizations. United States BONDS, short-term bills, and various kinds of savings accounts are examples. The concept is significant in economic analysis because the possession of near money may influence buying and saving plans quite as much as does the possession of actual money. See MONEY.

Nebbia v. New York. See MILK-CONTROL CASE.

negative income tax. A proposed public subsidy to individuals, varying in amount according to the age and obligations of the recipient and the cost of living, payable to those whose personal income falls below the level for a minimum tax payment. Also called *income maintenance.* See TAX.

negative investment. See DISINVESTMENT.

negotiability. The quality possessed by a bank check, promissory note, or other legal instrument of value which permits legal title to it to be transferred from one person to another by INDORSEMENT and delivery, or by delivery without indorsement.

Neoclassical school. A school of economic thought based chiefly on the writings of the English economist, Alfred Marshall (1842-1924), and those who followed his ideas and elaborated upon his doctrines. The Neoclassical school represents a synthesis of the ideas of various schools of thought, with modifications and additions of its own. Thus it follows closely the findings of the CLASSICAL SCHOOL but emphasizes the limitations of some of the classical doctrines, notably that of *LAISSEZ FAIRE.*

It adopts the methods of the German HISTORICAL SCHOOL in considering the origin and development of economic forces but subjects these to critical analysis. It makes use of the conception of MARGINAL UTILITY developed by the PSYCHOLOGICAL SCHOOL and accepts MATHEMATICAL ECONOMICS as one method of presentation. Many modern ideas have been developed by writers of the Neoclassical school, including the NEOCLASSICAL THEORY OF VALUE, and various contemporary theories of money and foreign trade. Also called *Cambridge school.* See SCHOOLS OF ECONOMIC THOUGHT.

neoclassical theory of value. The theory which holds that the value of a particular commodity is determined by the interaction between the forces of demand expressed in a demand schedule and the forces of supply expressed in a supply schedule. Value is determined at a point of balance or equilibrium which is the point where the maximum number of exchanges takes place. See also MARKET PRICE, VALUE.

net borrowed reserves. As applied to banking, borrowings less EXCESS RESERVES (*q.v.*). See RESERVES.

net free reserves. As applied to banking, EXCESS RESERVES (*q.v.*) less borrowings. See RESERVES.

net income. As normally used in accounting practice, whatever remains from earnings and profits after all costs, expenses, and allowances for depreciation and probable losses have been deducted. Thus used, the term is usually synonymous with *net profits.* See INCOME. See also PROFIT.

net interest. See PURE INTEREST.

net lease. A LEASE requiring the tenant to pay the taxes and insurance and the cost of repairs, maintenance, alterations, and improvements on the leased property.

net national product. The GROSS NATIONAL PRODUCT less capital consumption allowances, such as depreciation, accidental damage to fixed capital, and capital outlays charged to current expense.

net price. The price after all deductions, allowances, and discounts have been made. See PRICE.

net product. A term used by the PHYSIOCRATS during the middle of the 18th century to indicate the difference between the value of new wealth and the value of the wealth used to create the new wealth. A net product existed, they believed, only in the case of agricultural production, industry being sterile, although essential to the economy. See also *TABLEAU ÉCONOMIQUE*.

net profit. See PROFIT.

net worth. In accounting, total assets minus total liabilities, the difference being what would accrue to stockholders or other owners in the event of liquidation.

New Deal. A general term applying to various measures, initiated during the administration of President Franklin D. Roosevelt, to promote national economic recovery and social security in the United States, following the advent of the economic depression of the 1930's. The more important of these measures sought to stimulate industry, improve the economic position of agriculture, regulate public-utility holding companies, reform the banking structure and devalue the currency, and provide direct unemployment relief, unemployment insurance, and old-age pensions.

Newlands Act. An act of Congress, 1913, which provided for a board of 4 full-time members to mediate, upon the board's own initiative or upon request, in the case of disputes between the railroads and their employees. The railroads had urged the creation of a single board to control wages and hours as well as rates and service. The act in question, however, although replacing the mediation and arbitration features of the ERDMAN ACT, gave the newly created mediation board no authority over rates and service.

***New York*, et al., v. *United States*, et al.** A case, 331 U.S. 284 (1947), in which the Supreme Court sustained an order issued by the INTERSTATE COMMERCE COMMISSION deducting 10 per cent from certain transportation rates of southern, southwestern, and western trunk-line railroads and adding 10 per cent to the same transportation rates in eastern territory. The court thus sustained the thesis that the Interstate Commerce Commission may require adjustments to overcome alleged regional discrimination in certain railroad rates and thereby promote greater equality in the treatment of shippers throughout the United States.

New York Stock Exchange. The principal security market in the United States, often called the big board. It is an unincorporated voluntary organization composed of more than a thousand members and traces its beginning back to 1790. Membership, or a "seat" on the exchange as it is called, is obtained by purchase from a retiring member or from the estate of a deceased member, and upon approval of a committee on admissions.

Noble State Bank **v.** *Haskell.* A case, 219 U.S. 104 (1911), in which the Supreme Court held that an Oklahoma plan to insure bank deposits was a legitimate exertion of a state's police power under the due process clause of the 14th Amendment, such insurance being essential to the integrity of savings and check currency and credit, and this integrity in turn being necessary for the well-being of business. The case foreshadowed federal legislation leading, among other things, to the creation of the FEDERAL DEPOSIT INSURANCE CORPORATION (*q.v.*).

nominal account. A term used in double-entry bookkeeping to indicate an account which is closed out at the end of an accounting period, and thus not carried over to the new accounting period. An EXPENSE ACCOUNT and a revenue account are examples. See ACCOUNT.

nominal price. A price in name only. The term may imply an amount so small as hardly to justify the term "price," or it may refer to an estimated price for a security or commodity that is not bought and sold often enough to establish a definite market price. See PRICE.

nominal yield. The rate of return specified on a security calculated on its par or face value. Thus "6 per cent" appearing on a preferred stock certificate the par or face value of which is $100 indicates a nominal yield of 6 per cent of $100, or $6. See YIELD.

nonassented or stock bond. See BOND, CAPITAL STOCK.

nonassessable stock. See CAPITAL STOCK.

nonclearinghouse stock. See CAPITAL STOCK.

noncontributory pension. A PENSION for the benefit of employees the entire cost of which is assumed by the employer.

noncumulative stock. See CAPITAL STOCK.

nonfeasance. Failure to perform an act which is required by law or which is required by accepted standards of professional conduct and responsibility.

Nonimportation Act. An act of Congress, 1806, which prohibited certain goods originating in any part of the British Empire from entering the United States.

nonimportation agreement. One of numerous agreements, made by American colonials at various times between 1768 and 1774, not to import commodities from England.

Nonintercourse Act. An act of Congress, 1809, which prohibited British and French ships or cargoes from entering American ports.

noninterest-bearing discount bond. See BOND.

nonrecourse loans. A loan, security for which is limited to the value of pledged collateral and for which, indeed, the only repayment may be the money equivalent which the lender obtains for the pledged collateral. The term is particularly applicable to the federal government's loans to farmers on surplus commodities, the farmers' obligation to the government lending agency being limited to the commodities pledged for the loan. See LOAN.

nonrecurring expense. An expense occasioned by some condition that is not regularly repeated in the ordinary course of business operations.

no-par-value stock. See CAPITAL STOCK.

normal curve of distribution. A mathematical concept consisting of a symmetrical bell-shaped curve exhibiting unique relationships between the ordinate of maximum value on the Y axis and other ordinates at various STANDARD DEVIATION (*q.v.*) distances from it, and therefore between the areas separated by the various ordinates and the total area beneath the curve. These relationships are shown in the diagram on page 309. The normal curve of distribution depicts fairly accurately many types of data in economic life and hence is used extensively in statistical analyses, particularly in statistical inference. Also called *normal curve of error* and *probability curve*. See also FREQUENCY DISTRIBUTION.

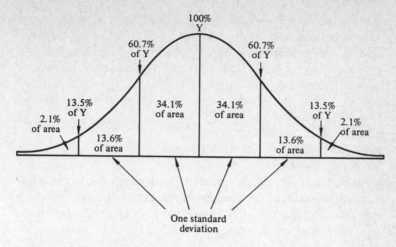

One standard
deviation

normal curve of error. See NORMAL CURVE OF DISTRIBUTION.

normal price. An equilibrium price to which the market price tends to return after temporary fluctuations either upward or downward. Normal price, therefore, suggests an average price over a relatively long period of time, whereas MARKET PRICE indicates a price at a given moment of time. See PRICE.

Norman* v. *Baltimore and Ohio R. R. Co. See GOLD-CLAUSE CASES.

Norris-LaGuardia Act. See ANTI-INJUNCTION ACT.

Northern Securities Co.* v. *United States. A case, 193 U.S. 197 (1904), in which the Supreme Court ordered the dissolution of the Northern Securities Co., a holding company which had been used for the purpose of bringing under single control two of the largest transcontinental railroad systems of the country. The injunction against the holding company was based upon the antitrust provisions of the Sherman Act.

***nostro* overdraft.** Literally, "our" OVERDRAFT. The term sometimes appears on a domestic bank's statements indicating that BILLS OF EXCHANGE have been sold in greater amount than purchased, and that, in consequence, the domestic bank is indebted to some foreign bank or banks to the extent indicated by the overdraft.

notary public. In the United States, an officer appointed under the laws of a state to administer oaths; to protest bank checks, promissory notes, and other such papers; and to authenticate copies of documents.

note. A credit instrument having general or limited negotiability, issued by an individual, a private corporation, or a governmental body, and consisting of a promise to pay a sum of money to a named creditor or to the bearer either on demand or at a specified time. See (17).

notes payable. See BILLS PAYABLE.

notes receivable. See BILLS RECEIVABLE.

NRA case. See SCHECHTER CASE.

nuisance tax. Any tax the revenue from which does not justify the inconvenience it causes those subject to the tax or which yields a disproportionately low return after costs of administration are deducted. See TAX.

O

obligational authority. Legal authorization given by a legislature to an administrative agency to make commitments to spend. The actual funds to be expended must be separately authorized.

obsolescence. The condition of being out of date. Obsolescence is caused by new inventions and improved processes for production or a change in the demand for the things produced. It is not the result of mere age or wear.

occupational level. A vocational grouping based on the existence of some characteristic common to the group. The common characteristic may be the degree of skill required, and the groups may be classified as skilled, semiskilled, and unskilled. Or the character of the work performed may provide the basis of classification. Thus, the United States census makes the following classification: professional, semiprofessional, farmers and farm managers, proprietors and managers, salesmen and saleswomen, craftsmen and foremen, operatives, domestic-service workers, protective-service workers, farm laborers and foremen, other laborers.

occupation money. Money used by military forces in occupied enemy territory. In most cases such money is issued in the MONETARY UNIT of the occupied country and is pure FIAT MONEY. It is used to make local purchases, to pay local labor, and to pay personnel when money that would be accepted locally is required. In the invasion of North Africa during November, 1942, however, the United States used what was known as the *yellow seal dollar* or *spearhead money,* and the British forces used the "military pound" known as the "British Military Authority note." The United States yellow seal dollars were charged against the War Department appropriation, but the British military pound was reported to have been a direct obligation of the British treasury. See MONEY.

occupation tax. 1. A fee exacted by the government when issuing a license to a person desiring to engage in a certain occupation or profession. **2.** Generally, any tax levied upon a particular occupation or calling. Sometimes called *privilege tax* or *license fee.* See TAX.

odd-lot broker. A stockbroker who buys and sells stock in lots of less than 100 shares.

Office of Business Economics. A unit of the U.S. Department of Commerce. It compiles statistics for gauging national and international economic activity; analyzes the United States balance of payments position, current business conditions, and future business prospects; and conducts economic research in cooperation with other government agencies, business organizations, and educational institutions. It publishes the official monthly journal, *Survey of Current Business.*

Office of Comptroller of the Currency. A unit of the U.S. Department of the Treasury which supervises the operations of all NATIONAL BANKS and examines them. Under the NATIONAL BANK ACT of 1863 which created this office, the Comptroller must report directly to Congress annually.

Office of Economic Opportunity. A broadly empowered federal agency, nominally part of the Executive Office of the President, established in 1964 to assist minorities, especially the black minority, in combatting delinquency and poverty and affirmatively to expand economic opportunities for them. It creates training and employment opportunities in conjunction with the Department of Health, Education, and Welfare, furnishes managerial expertise for small business and identifies opportunities for investment in such business, and assists in training personnel for the Job Corps, VISTA, local youth groups, and other welfare agencies.

Office of Education. A unit of the U.S. Department of Health, Education, and Welfare which prepares and disseminates statistical information on education; conducts research on curricula, educational administration, teaching methods, and allied subjects; and administers the distribution of very considerable federal appropriations for education from the pre-primary to the graduate level.

Office of Emergency Planning. A unit of the Executive Office of the President which advises on and makes plans for the organization of the government and of the nation's economy in time of war or other national emergency, including the utilization of manpower, materials, and transportation and communication facilities, and the setting up of economic controls and regulations.

Office of Science and Technology. A unit of the Executive Office of the President which advises the President on scientific and technological matters as they relate to national security and national policies, evaluates and coordinates the scientific programs of various government agencies, and encourages the development of national scientific resources.

Office of Tax Legislative Counsel. A unit of the U.S. Department of the Treasury which advises the Department on tax policy and drafts proposals for changes in the revenue laws which the Secretary or his spokesman may present to Congress.

Office of the Special Representative for Trade Negotiations. A federal agency, whose chief officer has the rank of ambassador and is directly responsible to the President, which coordinates and supervises foreign trade policy. The agency has been concerned with efforts to liberalize international trade as envisaged by the Trade Expansion Act of 1962 and provided the American negotiating team that brought about GATT trade reductions and liberalization policies incorporated in the DILLON ROUND (*q.v.*) and the KENNEDY ROUND (*q.v.*).

Office of the Treasurer of the United States. A part of the fiscal service branch of the U.S. Department of the Treasury which is responsible for the receipts and disbursements of public moneys, for the issue and redemption of United States paper money and coin, the payment of interest and principal on the national debt, and the safekeeping of securities deposited with

313

the federal government as collateral. Usually referred to as *Treasurer of the United States.*

official exchange rate. The price, in terms of its own currency, that the monetary authority of a given nation will pay for the currencies of other nations. This rate may often vary from the FREE MARKET exchange rate. See RATE.

offsets to savings. Ways of using liquid savings or creating expenditures which are equivalent to such use. For example, savings may be offset directly by investing them in new capital assets, by using them to replace worn-out capital assets, or through payments for increased business inventories. However, if savings remain liquid, they may be offset by indirect means; that is, other economic activities may have the same effect upon the economy as though the savings were actually used as explained above. For example, indirect means of offsetting savings are the creation of government expenses in excess of income, an increase of credit, or an excess of exports over imports. See SAVING.

offshore oil cases. Two *tidelands oil* cases, *United States* v. *Louisiana,* 363 U.S. 1 (1960), and *United States* v. *Florida,* 363 U.S. 121 (1960), in which the Supreme Court decided that only Texas and Florida had qualified under the terms of a federal statute of 1953 which extended to littoral states on the Gulf of Mexico the right to exploit subsoil mineral wealth, particularly petroleum, both within the traditional 3-mile maritime limit and also up to 10½ miles from the low-tide line, provided such states could prove historic justification for their claim to the more extended area of exploitation. Other littoral states, including oil-rich Louisiana, did not qualify. These were thenceforth restricted to the 3-mile area. In 1947 the Court had declared that the tidal oil-land rights inhered in the national government, but in the aforesaid statute in 1953, Congress had limited this federal authority.

ogive. As applied to statistics, a curve derived directly from a statistical array or obtained from a FREQUENCY DISTRIBUTION by using the X axis for class intervals and the Y axis for cumulative frequencies. If the ogive slopes upward from left to right it is called a "less-than ogive"; that is, each point on the curve indicates the number of cases on the Y axis that are less than the value, or other numerical designation, on the X axis. If the ogive slopes downward from left to right it is a "more-than ogive"; that is, each point on the curve indicates the number of cases on the Y axis that are more than the value, or other numerical designation, on the X axis. The following diagram shows a less-than ogive and a more-than ogive. Both are derived from the following frequency distribution:

Class interval	Frequency	Cumulative frequencies	
		Less than	More than
1 to 1.9	1	1	40
2 to 2.9	3	4	39
3 to 3.9	5	9	36
4 to 4.9	8	17	31
5 to 5.9	10	27	23
6 to 6.9	7	34	13
7 to 7.9	3	37	6
8 to 8.9	2	39	3
9 to 9.9	1	40	1

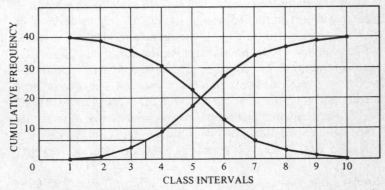

Ogives are sometimes used in economic analysis to approximate values that could otherwise be obtained only by mathematical interpolation. Thus, in the above frequency distribution, if it is desired to know the number of cases at, say, 3½, the number can be approximated at 6½ as shown on the diagram.

old-age (retirement), survivors' and disability insurance. A nation-wide system of social insurance, initiated by the basic Social Security Act of 1935 and developed in subsequent legislation, which is administered by several bureaus under the direction of the Commissioner of Social Security in the SOCIAL SECURITY ADMINISTRATION (*q.v.*). The system embraces retirement pensions for most of the older population (over 65 years of age), financial assistance for those who become disabled prior to retirement, and allowances for dependents in case of the death of the insured. The program is financed by taxes upon employer payrolls and upon the wages and salaries of employees and the incomes of professional people and the self-employed. The proceeds of such taxes purchase government obligations which are credited to two special trust funds. Technically, therefore, the resources of the program are government obligations, and the real support of the program depends upon the credit and solvency of the government. In a more fundamental sense, its support depends upon the current productive capacity of the nation. Separate provision is made under the MEDICARE (*q.v.*) program for health-care insurance although, administratively, this has been absorbed into the broader social security system.

Old Dearborn Distributing Co. v. Seagram Distillers Corp. A *resale price-maintenance case,* 299 U.S. 183 (1936), in which the Supreme Court sustained the provisions of fair-trade laws in certain states permitting manufacturers and dealers to enter into voluntary resale price-maintenance contracts. Normally, such contracts are limited to branded or trade-marked commodities. The Court ruled this practice a legitimate means of protecting the manufacturer's good will. The decision narrowed earlier decisions in which resale price-maintenance agreements were held to violate anti-trust statutes. See also BEECH-NUT PACKING CASE, FAIR-TRADE PRACTICES ACTS, MILLER-TYDINGS ACT.

oleomargarine case. A case, *McCray* v. *United States,* 195 U.S. 27 (1904), in which the Supreme Court supported as a valid revenue measure a virtually prohibitive federal tax of 10 cents per pound on oleomargarine if that product was artificially colored to resemble butter. The tax, although accepted by the Court as a revenue measure, was actually a regulatory measure enacted to favor the national dairy interests.

oligopoly. A market situation where sellers are so few that the supply offered by any one of them materially affects the market price, and each seller is able to measure, with a fair degree of accuracy, the effect of his price and production decisions upon similar decisions by his competitors. Also called *partial monopoly.*

one-thousand-hour clause. A clause in the Fair Labor Standards Act of 1938 which permits departure, for certain types of employment, from the basic 8 hours per day and 40 hours per week schedule fixed in the act, but limits any modified schedule to a maximum of 12 hours per day and 56 hours per week and stipulates, moreover, that the total working hours for any one employee during any 26 consecutive weeks may not exceed 1,000 hours.

open account. A term usually referring to a manner of supplying credit by charging goods and services to a customer's account, payment for which is to be made at some future time. The account is said to be open until all payments have been received. In bookkeeping any account may be said to be open, however, until it is balanced or closed by an entry which causes the sum of the debits to equal the sum of the credits. See ACCOUNT.

open commitments. See OPEN INTEREST.

open competition. A term used to describe a plan whereby members of a trade association exchange statistical information relating to production, stocks on hand, orders, shipments, prices, and other similar data. The Supreme Court, in 1921, characterized the term as a "misleading misnomer" in the LUMBER INDUSTRY CASE. See COMPETITION.

open contracts. See OPEN INTEREST.

open-door policy. A policy under which a nation opens its foreign trade to foreign nationals on equal terms; the same principle governs any internal commercial or other concessions which the nation may grant to foreigners.

317

open-end contract. An agreement whereby a supplier contracts to meet the requirements of a buyer for a specific product during a specified period of time, whatever those requirements may be. Since no definite quantity is mentioned, the contract is designated "open-end." See CONTRACT.

open-end investment company. An INVESTMENT COMPANY that sells and redeems its CAPITAL STOCK continuously, selling it at BOOK VALUE plus a sales charge, and redeeming it at book value or at a slight discount. Also called *mutual fund.*

open interest. As applied to commodity markets, the total number of futures contracts that remain undelivered at any specific time. Also called *open commitments* and *open contracts.*

open letter of credit. See LETTER OF CREDIT.

open market. In general, the condition which exists when trading is not restricted to any particular area or persons; specifically, as applied to securities, a market in which purchases and sales occur outside a formally organized STOCK EXCHANGE. See MARKET.

Open Market Committee. See FEDERAL OPEN MARKET COMMITTEE.

open-market operations. As applied to the federal reserve banks, the purchase and sale in the open market of various securities, chiefly obligations of the United States, and of bills of exchange and bankers' acceptances of the kinds and maturities eligible for discount by the federal reserve banks. Open-market operations are conducted by the banks subject to the direction of and under the regulations of the FEDERAL OPEN MARKET COMMITTEE with a view to accommodating commerce and business and to stabilizing the general credit situation of the country.

open-market paper. COMMERCIAL PAPER bought by and sold to financial institutions through brokers. For example, instead of borrowing directly from a bank, a business enterprise with a sufficiently high credit standing may issue PROMISSORY NOTES payable to itself and containing a BLANK INDORSEMENT, thus making the notes negotiable. The notes do not bear interest but are sold at a discount. They usually run from 4 to 6 months, common denominations being from $5,000 to $10,000. The issuer receives the face value of the notes less a discount and commission. The notes may be resold many times before maturity.

open mortgage. A mortgage which, having been pledged as collateral security for a loan, may be increased while serving as such collateral, thereby diminishing the security originally provided for each dollar of the loan. See MORTGAGE.

open price system. A concerted effort on the part of some or all of the individual units of an industry to keep one another informed concerning the past, present, and future prices of their products. See also OPEN COMPETITION.

open shop. A shop in which employment is offered without reference to membership or nonmembership in a labor union. See SHOP.

open union. A labor union whose membership is not restricted by prohibitive entrance fees or by race or sex discrimination. See LABOR UNION.

operating cost. See VARIABLE COST.

operating profit. As used in accounting, an increase in wealth resulting from the regular activities of an enterprise, as distinguished from any activities foreign to that business. For example, income or other gain from financial investments of a mercantile establishment would not be a part of the operating profits of that establishment. See PROFIT.

operating ratio. The per cent of revenue paid in operating expenses, including depreciation and excluding income taxes, during a specified period of time. See RATIO.

operations research. The application of mathematical and logical techniques to certain business problems with the object of discovering a best possible course of action. How to allocate working capital among the various departments of a retail store so as to maximize profits, how to use men and machines in a job machine shop to achieve the highest possible output and the least idle time, or how to manage the routing of freight cars so as to assure their greatest use, are problems amenable to operations research. The procedure followed is usually to express the problem in the form of a mathematical equation, the solution to which indicates the effectiveness of a given set of conditions. The method may involve a sampling process, the calculation of probabilities, linear programming, or some other such technique. The computations are frequently so involved or so lengthy as to require use of an AUTOMATIC DATA PROCESSING SYSTEM. Sometimes called *management science*.

opportunity cost. The most favorable price that can be commanded by a factor of production which thus tends to become the minimum cost at which that factor can be had by any entrepreneur. Tool makers, for example, may be able to sell their labor to automobile manufacturers as well as to many other manufacturers. The automobile manufacturers may be willing and able to pay more than the other manufacturers and the latter, in that case, will have to pay the opportunity costs thus set by the automobile manufacturers. See COST.

Optimist school. The economic ideas of Claude Frédéric Bastiat (1801–50), a French economist, and Henry C. Carey (1793–1879), an American, and their followers. In general, their writings defended the economic order existing at the time against the attack of socialists and others. The concept of ECONOMIC RENT was questioned, CAPITAL was defended, and the MALTHUSIAN THEORY OF POPULATION was denied. Proof was lacking, it was said, of any tendency of population to press upon food supply. Rent was regarded as a return from previously invested capital, and income from capital was defended on the ground that it was merely a return on past labor. See SCHOOLS OF ECONOMIC THOUGHT.

optimum population. As applied to economic life, the number of people in a given area at a particular time who, with the available capital, equipment, level of technological development, and natural resources, can produce the greatest per capita output in that area and at that time.

option. An agreement, often for a consideration, which permits one to buy or to sell something within a stipulated time in accordance with the terms of the agreement.

optional bond. See BOND.

optional dividend. A dividend which may be paid either in stock or in cash, according to the stockholder's preference. See DIVIDEND.

order. In economic and business affairs: **1.** A direction or instruction to deliver goods, or to render services, or to purchase goods or securities—an action which, with some limitations, legally commits the one who issues the request unless the request can be revoked before action is taken. **2.** The direction given on a check, note, or other negotiable instrument as to the identity of the payee.

order bill of lading. A negotiable bill of lading stating that goods are consigned to the order of a specified person who must indorse the bill of lading before the goods may be delivered to the buyer. This form of bill of lading is frequently used when it is agreed that payment shall be made upon delivery. The shipper consigns the goods to his own order, indorses the bill of lading, and attaches a draft. He then sends these documents to a bank, usually the bank where the buyer has a deposit account. Upon payment of the draft by the buyer, the bank delivers the bill of lading to him, and he may then claim the goods from the transportation company. See BILL OF LADING.

ordinary asset. As applied to income-tax computations in the United States, the term refers only to an asset regularly bought and sold in the ordinary course of the taxpayer's business. Thus, stocks and bonds would be an ordinary asset to a dealer in securities, but they would be a CAPITAL ASSET to a person engaged in some other occupation and who bought such securities for investment. See ASSET.

ordinary rent. See RENT.

ordinary stock. See CAPITAL STOCK.

Organic school. A term sometimes applied to those who draw an analogy between society and a biological organism. Thus, for example, the railroad system is identified with the arterial and venous system, telegraph wires with the nervous system, the stock exchange with the heart, etc. Such parallels were elaborated in great detail by Herbert Spencer. They are not generally considered of very much scientific value. See SCHOOLS OF ECONOMIC THOUGHT.

Organization for Economic Cooperation and Development. Originally an association of 17 European states (including the German Federal Republic), created April 16, 1948, and known until 1960 as the *Organization for European Economic Cooperation.* Its original purpose was to plan for European economic recovery from World War II on a cooperative basis. Subsequently the association was enlarged by the admission of non-European states, including Canada, the United States, and Japan, and reached a total membership of 21. Thus expanded, it acquired its present name and has been transformed into a general world planning body, promoting the stable economic growth of member countries, the expansion of world trade and investment, and the economic development of emerging nations. Its headquarters are in Paris.

Organization for European Economic Cooperation. See ORGANIZATION FOR ECONOMIC COOPERATION AND DEVELOPMENT.

Organization of American States. A regional agency within the UNITED NATIONS, made up of the republics of the Western Hemisphere. Its purpose is to maintain the peace and strengthen collaboration among the American states and to defend their sovereignty and independence. The Organization's principal administrative agency is the PAN AMERICAN UNION, Washington, D.C.

original-cost standard. In determining the value of an enterprise, the actual initial cost of its assets, as distinguished from the criteria of other valuation standards, such as REPRODUCTION-COST STANDARD OR PRUDENT-INVESTMENT-COST STANDARD (*q.q.v.*). See VALUATION.

original-issue stock. See CAPITAL STOCK.

original-package cases. Two cases, *Brown* v. *Maryland,* 12 Wheaton 419 (1827), and *Leisy* v. *Hardin,* 135 U.S. 100 (1890), in which was developed the so-called ORIGINAL-PACKAGE DOCTRINE in foreign and interstate commerce. In the first of these cases the Supreme Court declared that as long as commodities had not been removed from the containers in which they had been imported into the United States, no state of the United States could apply its taxing power or its police regulations to such commodities. In the second case, that of *Leisy* v. *Hardin,* substantially the same decision was made with respect to goods in interstate commerce having a domestic origin. Goods lawfully brought into one state of the United States from another state were held exempt from police or tax regulations of the state of destination as long as such goods remained in their original package and as long as Congress, by its silence, implied that the states were not to interfere with interstate commerce.

original-package doctrine. A ruling established by the Supreme Court that commodities in foreign or interstate commerce which had not been removed from the containers in which they had been imported or shipped interstate were not subject to the taxing power or police regulations of the states. The doctrine has been modified by Congress, particularly as respects alcoholic beverages and goods made by convict labor. See ORIGINAL-PACKAGE CASES.

Orthodox school. See CLASSICAL SCHOOL.

Ottawa agreements. Trade agreements made at the Imperial Economic Conference held at Ottawa, Canada, in 1932, to supplement and extend existing tariff and other trade preferences among the United Kingdom and Commonwealth countries. When the United Kingdom abandoned free trade between 1919 and 1931, the preferential duties and trade concessions which the Dominions had previously granted to the United Kingdom became effectively reciprocal for Dominion exports to the United Kingdom. Some of the Commonwealth Dominions made similar preferential trade agreements among themselves.

Outer 7. See EUROPEAN FREE TRADE ASSOCIATION.

outlaw strike. See ILLEGAL STRIKE.

outside director. A director of a corporation who enjoys no appreciable stock ownership and has no office in the corporation. See DIRECTOR.

overcertification. See DAY LOAN.

overdraft. The amount by which the face value of a check, acceptance, promissory note, or other similar commercial paper exceeds the funds on deposit to meet it. See *NOSTRO* OVERDRAFT.

overdraw. To issue a bank check for an amount in excess of the deposit in the bank on which the check is drawn.

overextended. See EXTENDED.

overhead cost. See FIXED COST.

overheating. Excessive economic activity which economic analysts fear may lead to inflation.

overinvestment theory of the business cycle. See OVERSAVING THEORY OF THE BUSINESS CYCLE.

overlying bond. See BOND.

overproduction. **1.** More than can be sold at any price. **2.** More than can be sold at a profitable price. Using the term in the sense of the first definition, it is possible to have overproduction in certain specific commodities but not in all commodities at one time, since, for all practical purposes, human wants are without limit. Using the term in the sense of the second definition, it is possible to have overproduction in certain specific commodities as well as general overproduction. See PRODUCTION.

oversaving. 1. More liquid savings than can be used in investment opportunities. **2.** The condition said to exist when invested capital, representing savings, produces more goods than can be sold at a profit. See SAVING.

oversaving theory of the business cycle. The theory which holds that, because of the unequal distribution of the national income, there is so much saving among the higher income groups that those savings, when invested, create more productive capacity than can be permanently and profitably employed. Production thus tends to exceed the ability of the mass of people to buy, prices fall to unprofitable levels, unemployment increases, and depressed conditions prevail until the surplus production is gradually absorbed. Also called *overinvestment theory of the business cycle*. See also BUSINESS CYCLE.

over-the-counter market. The purchase and sale of securities outside of the organized stock exchanges. See MARKET.

Owenism. The ideas of social reform advanced by Robert Owen (1771-1858), a British industrialist. Owen maintained that good wages and working conditions were not incompatible with business prosperity—a revolutionary doctrine for the time—and proceeded to demonstrate his contention at New Lanark, Scotland, where he established a model industrial village and pioneered in the establishment of a LIMITED-DIVIDEND CORPORATION. He advocated such reforms as the limitation of employment of children, a system of government factory inspection, and the establishment of an 8-hour working day. In 1839, in Hampshire, England, Owen founded one of his famous villages of cooperation where he proposed to develop a partly industrial and partly farming community and provide for the exchange of products surplus to each group on a mutually advantageous basis. While recognizing innate differences in individuals,

Owen believed that character was molded by environmental conditions and social institutions and thus anticipated the materialistic and deterministic views of Karl Marx and the so-called scientific socialists. See also LABOR EXCHANGE BANK, UTOPIAN SOCIALISM.

ownership utility. See POSSESSION UTILITY.

P

pace setter. As applied to labor relations, a particularly rapid and skilled worker whose production for a specified period of time establishes the basis on which piecework rates are calculated for all workers.

Packers and Stockyards Act. An act of Congress, 1921, which provided for federal supervision and regulation of packing and stockyard companies. Its principal aim was to end discriminatory practices by stockyards in favoring particular regions or ranchers and to assure fair business practices in the meat-packing industry.

paid-in surplus. Surplus of a business enterprise arising from sources other than profits. For example, paid-in surplus may be acquired from the sale of capital stock at a premium or from donations from stockholders or others. See SURPLUS.

paid-up stock. See CAPITAL STOCK.

Panama Refining Co. v. Ryan. See HOT-OIL CASE.

Pan American Union. The central organ and permanent General Secretariat of the ORGANIZATION OF AMERICAN STATES. It acts as advisor to the council of that organization, offers it technical and other assistance, and is the custodian of inter-American agreements.

panic. Widespread fear for the financial and economic stability of a country, accompanied by efforts quickly to convert assets, especially securities, into cash, by runs on banks by depositors, and by the unwillingness of entrepreneurs to undertake new ventures. Usually, it is an indication of a serious deflationary downturn in the economy.

paper gold. See SPECIAL DRAWING RIGHTS.

paper money. Documents issued by the government, or by governmental authority, to be used as money. Paper money may circulate by virtue of a government's mere fiat and nothing else; or it may represent metal coins or bullion, held in some depositary, up to the full amount of the paper's stated value. Between these two extremes, paper money may be secured in numerous ways and to a varying extent. See MONEY.

parallel standard. A monetary system in which two or more metals are coined and made full legal tender, but are not maintained at any fixed ratio one to the other. The value of each metal is subject to the forces of supply and demand, necessitating a new calculation whenever the value of a coin of one metallic content is expressed in terms of another coin of a different metallic content. The system is wholly impractical for a modern economy. See MONETARY SYSTEM.

Pareto's law. A generalization of Vilfredo Pareto (1848-1923), Italian sociologist and economist, to the effect that the NATIONAL INCOME tends to be distributed in the same proportion among consumers in any area of the world, regardless of differing institutions and systems of taxation. The universality and inevitability of the law would seem to be subject to serious question.

par exchange rate. **1.** The free market price of one national currency in terms of another. **2.** Under the regulations of the INTERNATIONAL MONETARY FUND, the value of the MONETARY UNIT of one member country in terms of another. Values are expressed in gold and par exchange rates are obtained from values so expressed. For example, prior to sterling devaluation in 1967 the pound sterling was valued at 2.48828 grams of fine gold and the dollar at 0.888671 gram of fine gold; hence one pound sterling equaled $2.80. Unlike the system using the GOLD STANDARD, the IMF regulations use gold merely as a unit of measure to avoid the necessity of expressing the value of each currency in terms of every other currency. The gold value assigned a currency, and hence its par exchange rate with other currencies, is determined by Fund officials in consultation with representatives of the nation involved, the normal practice being to accept the valuation suggested by the national representatives. See RATE. See also MINT PAR OF EXCHANGE.

parity. The condition of being equivalent. The term is used particularly in respect to public price policies for agricultural products, such policies being designed theoretically to equilibrate farm-income standards with the income standards of other sectors of the national economy. The term is also used to describe an exchange rate between the currencies of two countries which makes the purchasing power of one currency substantially equivalent to that of the other currency. See (3).

Parker v. Davis. See LEGAL-TENDER CASES.

Parkinson's laws. "Laws" formulated by Professor C. Northcote Parkinson, formerly of the University of Malaya, in quasi-satirical accounts of business and public administration procedures. The laws are: *(a)* Work (or at least activity) invariably expands so as to fill the time available for its completion. *(b)* Expenditure rises to meet income.

par-list bank. A bank which, although not a member of the FEDERAL RESERVE SYSTEM, participates in the CLEARINGHOUSE operations of the district FEDERAL RESERVE BANK by paying all CHECKS drawn on it without deductions for service or other fees. MEMBER BANKS are required thus to remit at par. Other banks that agree to do so are placed on a par list published by the Board of Governors of the Federal Reserve System. See BANK.

partial monopoly. See OLIGOPOLY, DUOPOLY.

partial or particular equilibrium. See GENERAL EQUILIBRIUM.

participating bond. See BOND.

participating certificate. 1. An instrument which identifies a partial owner interest in a security. **2.** A federal security sold in multiples of $5,000 and guaranteed by the FEDERAL NATIONAL MORTGAGE ASSOCIATION (Fannie Mae). According to the Participation Sales Act of 1966, the sale of such certificates is intended to transfer to private ownership some $11 billion of outstanding loans of various federal agencies. See CERTIFICATE.

participating preferred stock. See CAPITAL STOCK.

partnership. A form of business organization created through a contractual arrangement between two or more individuals, each of whom assumes full personal liability for the debts of the joint enterprise. See FORMS OF BUSINESS ORGANIZATION.

part-paid stock. See CAPITAL STOCK.

par value. As applied to stocks and bonds, the face value, if any, appearing on the stock certificate or on the bond instrument. In the case of stocks a par value is arbitrarily assigned at the time of original issue. Thus, if a corporation plans to raise $1,000,000 by a stock issue, it may issue 10,000 shares at a par value of $100 a share, or it may issue 20,000 shares at a par value of $50 a share. Par value is not significant and should not be confused with either MARKET PRICE or BOOK VALUE, both of which reflect an important condition. Par value means so little, in fact, that many stocks are issued with no par value. In the case of bonds the par value is usually $1,000. This, too, may be very different from the market price. See VALUE.

par-value stock. See CAPITAL STOCK.

passbook. A small account book issued by banks to depositors. Deposits and withdrawals are recorded in the book. Although still in use by SAVINGS BANKS, duplicate deposit slips, duly receipted, and monthly statements showing deposits and withdrawals have largely replaced passbooks in COMMERCIAL BANKS.

passive bond. See BOND.

passive trade balance. See UNFAVORABLE BALANCE OF TRADE.

patent. The right of exclusive proprietorship of an invention granted by a government to a person or organization for a term of years. In the United States patents are granted for any new and useful art, machine, process, or substance, including distinct and new forms of plants, for a term of 17 years. For designs, patents are granted for terms of 3½, 7, or 14 years, as requested by the inventor. Patent rights may be enforced through the courts.

Patent Office. A major unit of the U.S. Department of Commerce which has charge of all matters pertaining to the granting of patents and administers federal trade-mark laws. Through its various examiners and its Board of Appeals, the office passes finally upon the patentability of all inventions which may be submitted to it and determines the question of priority of invention when conflicting claims arise.

paternalism. A governmental policy of rendering welfare and protective services to the citizens; for example, supplying jobs to those who are unemployed, providing old-age assistance, or protecting citizens against unfair business practices.

Patrons of Husbandry. See NATIONAL GRANGE ORDER OF THE PATRONS OF HUSBANDRY.

patroon. A title given to any grantee of land in Dutch New Netherlands, now part of New York, who, during the second quarter of the 17th century, established 50 persons over 15 years of age in the colony and received as a reward a grant of 4 miles on the seacoast or 2 miles on a navigable river with no limit toward the interior.

Paul v. *Virginia.* See INSURANCE CASE.

Paunch Corps. See INTERNATIONAL EXECUTIVE SERVICE CORPS.

pauper. A person dependent upon public support for his subsistence. The condition, if formally established under the law, may impose legal limitations upon or grant certain privileges to the person so designated.

pawnbroker. One who makes small loans secured by personal property or valuable things other than securities.

pay-as-you-go. 1. The policy of requiring payment of income taxes as income is earned, achieved by requiring the employer, acting for the government, to make appropriate deductions from the wages or salaries of employees when they are paid, and by periodic payments on estimates of current income. **2.** The policy of some governments, especially in states of the United States, of financing capital improvements out of current income rather than out of the proceeds of borrowing.

payment bill. See BILL.

Payne-Aldrich Tariff. The United States Tariff Act of 1909. Though strongly protectionist, it nevertheless reduced rates for about 20 per cent of the imports. It allegedly introduced the principle of imposing such duties as would equalize costs of production at home and abroad, together with a reasonable profit, abandoned the RECIPROCITY PRINCIPLE, and adopted the MAXIMUM AND MINIMUM TARIFF SYSTEM.

payola. A slang term for money, gifts of merchandise, or other things of value offered to public entertainers or others who are in a position to use their calling to direct public attention to the alleged merits of some product or service, the purpose being to increase demand for such product or service. In the case of radio, television, or similar performers, comment on the product or service is ostensibly incidental to a given program or discussion, but is actually aimed at promoting the sale of the product or service in question.

payroll tax. Any tax levied against an employer which is based wholly or in part on the amount he pays in wages and salaries; for example, taxes paid by an employer to assist in financing various types of social insurance. See TAX.

Peace Corps. A service agency, operating under the U.S. Department of State, which recruits, trains, and assigns qualified volunteers for service in developing countries in the areas of agriculture, forestry, health, family counseling, and teaching. The volunteers receive little more than maintenance compensation and, where possible, live and work directly with the people they are assisting.

peasant movement. A term descriptive of the growing class consciousness and political activity of small farmer and peasant groups, particularly in Eastern Europe. Following World War I, reforms gave the peasants in many countries ownership of the land they cultivated and the political franchise. The aims of the movement differ from country to country; all such movements, however, maintain a belief in rural life based on small property holdings.

pecuniary exchange. Trade by means of money. The term is used in contradistinction to BARTER. See EXCHANGE.

pegging. The attempt to keep a market price at a certain figure or very close to that figure by freely buying or selling as circumstances demand.

peg point. A rate of pay for some key operation which serves as a base from which rates of pay for other operations are calculated.

pension. Payments at regular intervals to a person after he has retired from active work. Pensions are created in various ways. Frequently they are derived from a fund made up of contributions by the employer and the employee during the latter's period of employment. Payments by government to retired persons under a social security system may also be classed as pensions.

pension pool. A plan whereby private industries in a particular area create a common fund to finance pensions for their employees, permitting the employees to change from one plant to another within the area without losing the pension benefits accumulated previous to such a change. Also called *regional pension system.*

peonage. Compulsory performance of labor in payment of a debt, which may be required under a contract or under law. It is unconstitutional in the United States under the 13th Amendment as interpreted in *Taylor* v. *Georgia,* 315 U.S. 25 (1942).

peppercorn rent. A nominal rent, usually paid in kind, chiefly to give formal recognition to the legal rights of the landlord; so called because during the Middle Ages such rent was often paid in peppercorns. See RENT.

per capita. By the individual. The per capita national debt, for example, is the total national debt divided by the population.

percentiles. See QUARTILES.

per contra item. As applied to accounting, a balance in one account that is offset by a balance in some other account. For example, in bank statements an item designated as "Customers' Acceptance Liability" will often appear as an ASSET, and an item designated as "Acceptances Outstanding" as a LIABILITY. In this case the customers advance the funds to pay the ACCEPTANCES upon maturity. The asset thus offsets the liability. The bank merely guarantees payment.

per diem. By the day.

perfect competition. See COMPETITION.

peril point. A hypothetical limit beyond which reductions in a United States CUSTOMS DUTY could injure a domestic industry. The term was used in 1949 legislation which extended the TRADE AGREEMENTS ACT, and which provided that the peril points should be established by the UNITED STATES TARIFF COMMISSION and that the President should submit specific reasons to Congress if and when any customs duty was reduced below a point thus established.

permissive wage-adjustment clause. A clause in a labor contract permitting renegotiation of wage rates in case changes in general economic conditions, specified in the contract, such as changes in the cost-of-living index or changes occasioned by technological improvement, should occur during the life of the contract.

permit. Formal authority to exercise some right or privilege. For example, a permit is granted allowing the removal of goods imported into the United States after the duties have been paid.

perpetual bond. See BOND.

perquisite. Compensation or profit in addition to regular salary, such as a gift, bonus, tip, a special expense allowance, or free living quarters.

Perry v. United States. See GOLD-CLAUSE CASES.

personal account. A term used in double-entry bookkeeping to indicate an account carried in the name of a person or a company. See ACCOUNT.

personal distribution. See DISTRIBUTION.

personal finance company. An enterprise which makes a business of lending relatively small sums of money at relatively high rates of interest to individuals for personal needs. In most states such companies must be licensed. See COMPANY.

personal income. In government statistics, the NATIONAL INCOME less undivided profits, corporate taxes, and social security tax contributions, plus TRANSFER PAYMENTS from government or business including social security benefits and military pensions. It includes non-monetary items such as net rental income to home owner occupants, gratuitous services from financial intermediaries, and the value of food raised and consumed on farms. Personal income, thus defined, applies to non-profit institutions, private trust funds, and private health and welfare funds, as well as to individuals. See INCOME.

personal property. A right or interest in things other than real property; for example, such things as money, clothing, and household furnishings, as well as bonds, stocks, mortgages, and other evidences of interest or debt. See PROPERTY.

personal property tax. See PROPERTY TAX.

pet banks. A term used by political opponents of President Andrew Jackson to designate the STATE BANKS selected after 1833 as DEPOSITARIES for federal funds. On President Jackson's orders, such funds had been removed from the Second Bank of the United States, following Jackson's veto of a renewal charter for that institution in 1832. It was claimed, sometimes with justice, that the depositary state institutions were selected with an eye to partisan advantage rather than financial solvency.

petty cash. Money set apart for small cash disbursements. Petty cash is usually handled as an IMPREST FUND.

phalanstery. One of numerous voluntary associations, known as *phalanstère* or *phalange,* envisaged by the French social reformer, Charles Fourier (1772–1837). Each association was to provide housing for approximately 1,600 persons, be economically self-sufficient, and provide maximum opportunity for vocational and professional aptitudes. Fourier's ideas, which greatly influenced the later Marxians, were materialistic, deterministic, irrational, and essentially antistate. Also known as *Fourierism.* See also UTOPIAN SOCIALISM.

Phillips curve. A statistical device showing the relation between INFLATION and unemployment. The curve is named after A. W. Phillips, a professor at the London School of Economics.

physical distribution. See DISTRIBUTION.

physiocrats. A group of French statesmen and philosophers who, about the middle of the 18th century, made the first systematic attempt to form an economic science on a broad basis. They particularly emphasized LAND as a source of wealth. See SCHOOLS OF ECONOMIC THOUGHT.

picketing. As applied to industrial disputes, the stationing of striking workers at the entrances to factories or other establishments involved in a labor dispute to dissuade workers and others from entering the premises. See (29).

piecework. A wage schedule which computes wages by assigning a certain sum for each article produced or each operation completed, and sometimes used as a production incentive plan.

piggyback. 1. As applied to transportation, the carrying of one vehicle by another. Some automobile trucks are so constructed that the bodies can be lifted from the chassis and then placed on a flatcar and transported by rail. **2.** Two satellites, placed into orbit from a single rocket and separated after an interval of time, each following some predetermined path, are said to be launched piggyback fashion.

pit. A place on the floor of an exchange arranged in broad, circular steps to enable the traders better to see and hear one another. The term is often used in connection with grain trading as in the term "grain pit" which refers to the pit on the floor of the Chicago Board of Trade.

place utility. The accessibility of goods at a place where they are wanted to satisfy human desires. When goods are transported from a place where they are plentiful to a place where they are scarce, a place utility is created. California fruit obtainable in New York is an example. See UTILITY.

plain bond. See BOND.

plane of living. See LEVEL OF LIVING.

planning. See ECONOMIC PLANNING.

plantation system. An agricultural system comprised of large estates cultivated by laborers. In the United States, the system was firmly established in the southern states by 1840, with the typical proprietor and his managerial staff, employing the labor of slaves, devoting relatively large acreages to the production of certain staples such as tobacco, cotton, or sugar. In some respects the system is similar to the large-scale *industrial-type farming* which became common in the United States after 1950, which also comprises large tracts of land under single management but which depends heavily upon mechanization and scientific agriculture.

Plessy v. Ferguson. See *BROWN v. BOARD OF EDUCATION OF TOPEKA.*

Plumb plan. A proposal made by Glenn E. Plumb of the railroad brotherhoods, antedating enactment of the TRANSPORTATION (ESCH-CUMMINS) ACT of 1920 (*q.v.*), that the government, upon relinquishing the control of the railroads which it had exercised during World War I, purchase the railroads and lease them to representatives of unions and private management for operation.

plunger. Usually a speculator of some kind, especially a speculator in securities or commodities, who takes heavy risks and either profits greatly or loses disastrously.

plutocracy. Rule by the wealthy, or a government dominated by or strongly influenced by persons of wealth.

point. As applied to a market price, a specified amount considered as a unit or step in a price advance or decline. In the stock and bond market a point is 1 per cent of $100. In foreign exchange a point is one hundredth of 1 cent. Thus, if the dollar price of pounds sterling changes from 2.3867 to 2.3886 there is said to be a 19-point advance. In commodity markets such as those dealing in cotton, coffee, or sugar, a point is one hundredth of 1 cent per pound. An advance in the price of cotton of ¼ cent per pound would be described as a 25-point advance.

Point Four Program. A plan, known as the *Truman Plan,* suggested by President Harry S. Truman in his inaugural address of January, 1949, to share the scientific and technical knowledge and industrial know-how of the United States with the economically underdeveloped and undeveloped areas of the world and to promote productive investment in such areas. Funds for the program were to come from the United States and United Nations sources and from the beneficiary countries.

point of ideal proportions. That stage in the operation of a productive enterprise at which the most profitable relative amounts of the FACTORS OF PRODUCTION (land, labor, capital and management) are employed. See also PROPORTIONALITY, LAW OF.

point of indifference. That stage in the operation of a productive enterprise at which the cost of an additional increment of any FACTOR OF PRODUCTION (land, labor, capital, or management) merely equals the money return of the additional product created because of that increment.

policy. 1. A statement of principle, or a course of action to be followed with its attendant goals, usually formulated by a principal governmental officer or the leader of an enterprise and subsequently carried into effect by administrative staff and employees. **2.** An insurance contract.

political arithmetic. Political economy. The term was used in England during the latter part of the 18th century; for example, *Several Essays in Political Arithmetick* by Sir William Petty (1690).

political economy. Literally, the management of a free commonwealth. The Greek οἰκονομική denotes the management of a household, and πολισ, a city as a political unit. For many centuries discussions of production, trade, and finance were inextricably involved in considerations of monetary, fiscal, and commercial policies of governments. The term "political economy," therefore, was descriptive. But during the 19th century such matters began to be discussed more frequently apart from governmental policies, and the term "economics" began to be used. The publication in 1890 of Alfred Marshall's *Principles of Economics* had a great influence in bringing about the change, although the term "political economy" is still frequently used, particularly outside the United States; and it is reacquiring significance in view of the increasingly intimate involvement of government in economic life.

Pollock v. Farmers' Loan and Trust Co. See INCOME-TAX CASE.

poll tax. A local tax levied at a uniform rate upon all male and sometimes female adults. Since the tax is levied at a certain amount per head, it is also called a *capitation tax* or a *head tax.* Veterans, paupers, and disabled persons are usually exempt. In some states of the United States, payment of the tax is a prerequisite for obtaining an automobile driver's license, or for other privileges. The poll tax requirement for participation in elections was abolished in the United States, both for federal and local elections, by the 24th Amendment to the Constitution and by subsequent interpretative decisions by the Supreme Court, especially in *Harper* v. *Virginia State Board of Elections,* 383 U.S. 663 (1966). See TAX.

pollution control. An organized effort by administrators, scientists, and technicians, to keep land, water, and the atmosphere free of contaminants, such as smoke, oil, gas, and sewage, or to reduce their volume, the aim being to preserve, as nearly as possible, the natural ecological balance and to promote the health and well-being of human, plant, and animal life. A *Federal Water Pollution Control Administration* in the U.S. Department of the Interior was created to execute various recently enacted federal anti-pollution measures, particularly the Water Pollution Control Act. See CONTROL.

polymetallism. A theoretical monetary system in which more than two metals are made standard money and coined in some definite ratio one to another in the matter of weight and fineness. See MONETARY SYSTEM.

polypoly. A market situation where sellers are so few that the supply offered by any one of them materially affects the market price, but where, nevertheless, there is a sufficiently large number of sellers so that no one seller can effectively gauge the possible effect of his price or production decisions upon similar decisions of his competitors.

pool. A loose combination of business units for some specific and often temporary purpose, such as the division of markets, the maintenance of prices, and the combining of selling organizations. Pools were prohibited in the case of railroads by the INTERSTATE COMMERCE ACT of 1887, and in other fields, when in restraint of trade, by the SHERMAN ANTITRUST ACT of 1890 and subsequent anti-monopoly legislation. See COMBINATION.

population pyramid. In demography, a graphic device for displaying the composition of a population according to sex and age groups. The appended diagram shows a population pyramid. The vertical axis is divided according to age groups in 5-year intervals from 0 to 105. The bars extending to the right and to the left from the vertical axis represent the percentage of the total population in the various age groups. The bars to the left represent the male population, and those to the right the female.

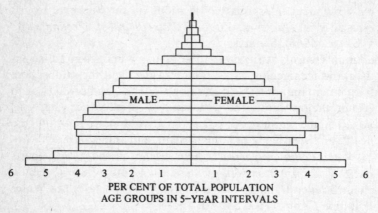

PER CENT OF TOTAL POPULATION
AGE GROUPS IN 5–YEAR INTERVALS

portable pension. See INSTANT VESTING.

Portal-to-Portal Act. An act of Congress, 1947, which invalidates all claims to portal-to-portal pay not covered specifically in labor contracts, and which places a 2-year limit on claims which might arise under existing federal minimum-wage laws. The act arose from a controversy over lawsuits brought by labor unions to recover back pay for uncompensated time claimed to be due under existing legislation. See PORTAL-TO-PORTAL PAY.

portal-to-portal pay. Compensation for an hourly rate employee, which embraces not merely the period during which the employee is actually engaged on an assigned task or operation but the entire period during which he is on the employer's premises or during which he is subject to the employer's direction. The term originally applied to coal mines where the portal or mouth of the mine is a definite place, and time must elapse until the employee is conveyed down the mine shaft to the site of actual operations. Compensation begins at the mouth of the mine. When the concept is applied to the building and grounds of a factory, the exact point where the employee comes under the direction of the employer cannot be so readily identified. If the employee is ordered to display identification credentials, the place where that order is given may be considered the portal, and compensated time might begin at that point. Or, if the employee arrives in an automobile and is told by a factory guard where to park it, the place where such direction is given might be considered the portal, and compensated time might begin at that point.

port authority. A commission or other agency, usually created by legislative action and enjoying a legal personality, which is given power to co-ordinate land and water traffic in and about a port. Its power, which may supersede that of other local jurisdictions, may extend to the construction and maintenance of bridges, tunnels, and other structures essential to the development of the port area. In the United States, because of federal control over navigable waters and because the area of a port may affect the territory of more than one state, the concurrence of Congress and of the legislatures of all states affected is necessary to the creation of such an authority; for example, the *Port of New York Authority*.

port of entry. In the United States, any place where a customs officer is stationed and authorized to administer customs regulations and to collect duties on imported materials.

Port of New York Authority. See PORT AUTHORITY.

possession utility. The satisfaction resulting from the actual possession of goods or services. In an exchange between two traders, two possession utilities are created; that is, each trader has greater satisfaction in the thing he received than in the thing he gave in the exchange. Also called *ownership utility.* See UTILITY.

postal savings. A service established in 1910 by the U.S. Post Office Department which enabled individuals to deposit money in certain post offices and to receive interest at a rate normally below that paid by savings institutions. The service was discontinued in 1966.

Post Office Department. A federal administrative agency of cabinet rank, created in 1789, and transformed into a quasi-independent federal corporation in 1970. In its operation of the mails and in carrying on certain related activities, such as money order and parcel post services, it is responsible for one of the most extensive and complicated enterprises in the nation, both as regards costs and the number of employees involved.

potential demand. Demand that is expected to become effective at some future time. Increased purchasing power, the stimulation of wants, or reduced prices may transform potential demand into EFFECTIVE DEMAND. See DEMAND.

potential stock. See CAPITAL STOCK.

poverty. A relative term indicating the absence of the comforts of life and an inadequate supply of the necessities. Sometimes the term is defined more precisely as that point at which deprivation makes impossible the maintenance of physical efficiency. In contemporary social welfare regulations in the United States, a statistical minimum income required for bare necessities is identified, and any family's income falling below that minimum (which usually varies regionally) is held to be below standard and prima facie evidence of a condition of poverty.

power of attorney. Authority granted to one person to act on behalf of another. A general power of attorney authorizes the agent to act for the principal in all matters. A special power of attorney limits the agent's acts to specific matters.

preclusive buying. Buying materials or services for the express purpose of denying their use to a competitor, or similar buying by a belligerent nation in wartime to prevent neutrals from selling goods or services to the enemy.

prefabricate. To produce standardized parts of a larger assembly in a factory, making possible the construction of a product elsewhere with only assembly operations. Standardized wall, floor, ceiling, roof, window and door sections for houses are frequently produced in a factory and shipped to the construction site where they are assembled to form a complete house.

preference stock. See CAPITAL STOCK.

preferential duty. See DIFFERENTIAL DUTY.

preferential shop. An establishment in which union employees are granted certain privileges not accorded to nonunion employees. For example, union employees may be the last to be laid off or the first to be re-employed after a layoff. See SHOP.

preferred stock. See CAPITAL STOCK.

premium. 1. Generally, an amount paid over and above a given figure. **2.** As applied to bond prices, the difference between the face value of a bond and the market price when the face value is the lower. **3.** As applied to insurance, a payment for protection against a risk. See (21).

premium for risk. The actual yield on an investment less the BASIC YIELD prevailing at the time. See PREMIUM.

premium pay. A sum which is paid in addition to the regular compensation because of unusual circumstances, such as overtime, Sunday, or holiday work; because the work is of a particularly hazardous or unpleasant nature; or because the employee receiving the premium possesses unusual ability or skill. See PREMIUM.

premium stock See CAPITAL STOCK, PREMIUM.

prepaid expense. In accounting, a payment for goods or services not yet received. As such, it is a charge deferred over a period of time until the benefit for which payment has been made is realized; for example, insurance or rent extending beyond the current accounting period.

prescription. The vesting of title to real property by virtue of long use.

price. Value expressed in terms of money. See (6).

price consumption curve. A curve placed on an INDIFFERENCE MAP (*q.v.*) indicating the demand by one consumer for a given commodity or service at different prices. In Diagram 1 on page 343, the price consumption curve is *A B,* as usual in an indifference map. Various quantities of *x* are plotted on the *X* axis. On the *Y* axis, however, the PURCHASING POWER or cash possessed by the consumer is plotted, and the spaces into which the *Y* axis is divided represent units of purchasing power. An income of $35.00 for a given period of time is assumed. Straight lines are drawn from point 35 on the *Y* axis to each main quantity division on the *X* axis, and prices are assigned for each quantity of *x* that will absorb the entire income if the entire income is spent for *x*. These various quantities and prices are as follows:

Price	Quantity	Income
$7.00	5	$35.00
3.50	10	35.00
2.33	15	35.00
1.75	20	35.00
1.40	25	35.00
1.16	30	35.00
1.00	35	35.00

On each straight line, then, may be plotted all the possibilities of purchasing various quantities of *x* at a specified price and of retaining some quantity of purchasing power or cash. Each straight line, however, is tangent to an INDIFFERENCE CURVE (*q.v.*), shown by dotted lines *a, b, c, d,* and *e* and shown only in part. This point of contact indicates just what quantity of *x* will be purchased at a specified price and just how much purchasing power will be retained by a given individual. The summary of these combinations, indicated by the price consumption curve, is as follows:

Price x	Quantity of x purchased	Total expended for x	Total purchasing power retained	Total income
$7.00	1	$ 7.00	$28.00	$35.00
3.50	4	14.00	21.00	35.00
1.75	12	21.00	14.00	35.00
1.40	20	28.00	7.00	35.00
1.00	30	30.00	5.00	35.00

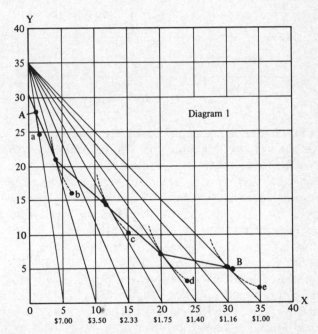

Diagram 2 on page 344 shows the above data in the form of a graph representing a schedule demand for commodity x on the part of one consumer. By combining such demand curves for all consumers, a generalized schedule demand curve can be obtained. See also DEMAND, DEMAND-AND-SUPPLY CURVES.

343

price control

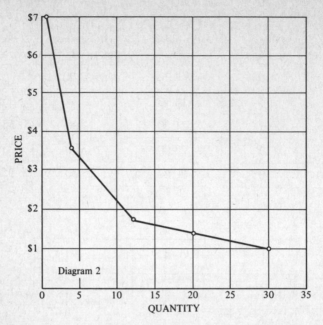

Diagram 2

PRICE

QUANTITY

price control. The fixing of prices by the government. During World War II, for example, the United States government fixed *ceiling* (or maximum) *prices* on many commodities and introduced a RATIONING system. The term may also apply to any effort by the government to influence the PRICE LEVEL—for example, by means of CREDIT CONTROL; or it may refer to efforts of private organizations to fix prices or to restrict the freedom of the market. Sometimes called *price fixing*. See CONTROL. See also PRICE-CONTROL LEGISLATION.

price-control legislation. Laws which fix prices or authorize the fixing of prices for the market, usually by establishing a ceiling or maximum price above which an article or a service cannot be sold. Federal legislation of this nature was enacted to cover rents in the District of Columbia following World War I. In World War II, the comprehensive Emergency Price Control Act of 1942 established the Office of Price Administration to determine ceiling prices. This Act expired on June 30, 1946. Another bill, providing for greatly modified controls to operate for a limited period, was then enacted; but virtually all federal price controls were discontinued by January, 1948. Modified price-control legislation was reinaugurated January 25, 1951, following the outbreak of the Korean War, and continued, with various amendments, into 1953. See also RENT CONTROL.

price-earnings ratio. The market price of a corporation's stock divided by its per share earnings, often abbreviated P/E. See RATIO.

price fixing. See PRICE CONTROL.

price leadership. The assumption that prices in a given industry are often determined by one, usually the largest, producer and that other producers in that industry tacitly accept the prices thus determined. Since no one producer is able to control the market in the industry, this pricing policy allegedly establishes a more favorable price for the producers than might be obtained under truly competitive conditions.

price level. The prices, usually at wholesale, of a selected list of representative commodities at a particular time, expressed in a composite figure called an INDEX NUMBER.

price loco. The price at the place where a purchase is made. See PRICE.

price rigidity. Relatively long-term insensitivity of prices of raw or manufactured goods to the inflationary influences of a depression or a recession.

price specie-flow theory. An explanation of the distribution, under relatively uncontrolled conditions, of the precious metals among nations, the causative factors allegedly being the impact of the precious metals upon the domestic PRICE LEVEL and the needs of trade. The theory holds that imports of the precious metals increase the money supply and hence advance the price level. Those countries receiving the precious metals therefore become good markets for commodity imports and poor markets for foreign buyers. Hence, they tend to develop an excess of imports over exports, and this eventually reverses their position as importers of metals. The excess of commodity imports is paid for by exporting the precious metals. Other countries which receive the precious metals in turn develop relatively high prices and an excess of commodity imports, and eventually become exporters of the precious metals. Thus, according to the theory, the precious metals tend to be distributed among

345

the nations automatically, in accordance with the needs of trade. The theory, originally formulated by David Hume (1711–1776), a Scottish philosopher and economist, became the basis of the international trade theory of the CLASSICAL SCHOOL. As national monetary supplies became less dependent upon the precious metals and central banking systems exerted an increasing influence upon the price level through the regulation of credit, the price specie-flow theory failed to offer any realistic explanation of distribution of the precious metals among nations.

price support. Governmental regulations, usually involving some form of public subsidy or financial aid to producers or distributors, designed to keep market prices from falling below a certain minimum level. In the United States, for example, agricultural prices are maintained by a complex system of outright subsidies, government purchase of commodities at prices higher than the market, or government loans to producers at prices higher than the market. By means of a stabilization fund used to purchase foreign exchange, and other devices, governments also often attempt to check serious declines in foreign-exchange rates.

price system. The system by which the kind and quantity of economic goods produced is determined by the price that consumers, collectively, are willing to pay, the actual allocation of those goods being determined by the ability of consumers, individually, to pay the price.

pricing out of the market. A popular phrase to describe a price structure so high that goods cease to sell in their usual market.

primary boycott. See BOYCOTT.

primary deposit. Money or the equivalent deposited in a bank by a customer, so called because it may be used to increase the bank's legal reserves. See BANK DEPOSIT.

primary money. See STANDARD MONEY.

prime bill. See BILL.

prime cost. See VARIABLE COST.

prime rate. The interest rate which is charged business borrowers having the highest CREDIT RATING. See RATE.

primogeniture. A preference in inheritance given to the eldest son or sometimes the eldest daughter; especially, under common law, the right of the eldest son to inherit all real property of his parent.

priority system. See RATIONING.

prior-lien bond. See BOND.

prior stock. See CAPITAL STOCK.

private bank. An unincorporated bank which, in the United States, operates under state laws. See BANK.

private corporation. A corporation created to conduct enterprises for private profit. The term includes quasi-public or public-service corporations. See CORPORATION.

private debt. The debt of private persons, corporate or natural, as distinct from the debt owed by a government or its subdivisions. See DEBT.

private enterprise. Economic activities carried on with the expectation of profit by private individuals acting either as individual entrepreneurs or through partnerships, associations, joint-stock companies, or corporations. The term is used to distinguish such activities from economic activities carried on by the government.

privateering. The wartime practice, common in the 17th and 18th centuries, of using private vessels, with government authority, to prey upon the merchantmen of the enemy. See LETTER OF MARQUE.

private property. The exclusive right of a person, natural or corporate, to control and enjoy an economic good, limited by law. In popular speech the term frequently refers to whatever is owned by individuals. See PROPERTY.

privilege tax. See OCCUPATION TAX.

probability curve. See NORMAL CURVE OF DISTRIBUTION.

probable error. As applied to a NORMAL CURVE OF DISTRIBUTION, a measure of dispersion, variation, or scatter such as, when pointed off on both sides of the ARITHMETIC MEAN, will provide a space that will include one-half the total number of cases. It may be computed from the STANDARD DEVIATION by multiplying the standard deviation by 0.6745. The name is derived from the custom of grouping, in a FREQUENCY DISTRIBUTION, measures obtained by various observers of a given astronomical or other scientific phenomenon in order to establish an index

347

indicating the reliability of the observations. It is seldom used in statistical analysis today.

proceeds. 1. The amount remaining after deducting the DIS-COUNT from the face value of a promissory note or similar commercial paper. **2.** A tax yield after deducting the costs of collection. **3.** Receipts from the sale of securities or other assets.

process effects. A term sometimes applied to the increase in consumer spending and private investment resulting directly from the spending on a public-works project.

processing tax. A tax such as the one which, under the terms of the first Agricultural Adjustment Act (1933), was levied upon millers, packers, and other processors of agricultural commodities, the returns from which were used to compensate farmers for the difference between the market price of the unprocessed commodity and the higher parity price authorized by law. The Supreme Court held this processing tax unconstitutional on January 6, 1936, (HOOSAC MILLS CASE) for the reason that it was not a tax as usually defined but a special burden levied upon one class of persons for the benefit of another class, and for the additional reason that this tax allegedly invaded the reserved powers of the states under the 10th Amendment to the Constitution. The second Agricultural Adjustment Act (1938) eliminated the processing tax and drew upon the general revenues of the government for the special financial benefits it provided farmers. See TAX.

procurement. As applied to industry or government, the procedure of identifying required materials and services, contracting for their purchase, and holding them for eventual use by the purchaser.

producer's capital. See CAPITAL GOOD.

production. The process of increasing the capacity of goods to satisfy human desires or of rendering services capable of satisfying human desires. In formal economics, of which production is one of the main topics, it is generally recognized that the utility or power of a material good to satisfy a human desire may be increased by the creation of (*a*) a TIME UTILITY, (*b*) a PLACE UTILITY, (*c*) a FORM UTILITY, or (*d*) a POSSESSION UTILITY. For specific purposes the term production is sometimes given a much more restricted meaning. As defined for federal income-tax purposes, for example, it means created, fabricated, manufactured, extracted, processed, cured, or aged. In popular speech, too, the term suggests a process of creating or changing the form of something. See (12).

production allocation program. Placing production plans for war materials required by the armed forces of the United States with private industry in order that a rapid transition from peacetime to wartime production may be effected in the event of an emergency. The program aims to provide an effective distribution of manufacturing load, to disclose possible shortages requiring remedial action, and to familiarize private management with its potential responsibilities.

production factors. Various indexes which measure production and data closely related thereto. Examples are: physical production, number of wage earners, wages paid, productivity per worker. The term should not be confused with FACTORS OF PRODUCTION.

productivity. The results obtained from resources expended. Productivity depends upon technological development, capital equipment, organization and management, working and living conditions, education and training, and many other factors. It is measured in various ways. For example, the number of articles produced or operations performed per worker per unit of time can be counted. The U.S. Department of Agriculture uses dollar-sales per hour to measure the productivity of retail sales clerks. Thus, in one way or another the productivity of specific operations, whole industries, groups of industries, sectors of the economy, or of the economy as a whole may be calculated periodically for comparative purposes. Changes in quality are not reflected in the statistical measurements, but might well be considered a part of the general concept.

profit. 1. As used in theoretical economics, the residual share of the product of enterprise accruing to the entrepreneur after all payments for capital (interest), for land (rent), and for labor including management (salaries and wages). Also called *pure profit* and *earnings*. **2.** As used in accounting, a broad term indicating an increase in wealth resulting from the operation of an enterprise. The term *gross profit* usually indicates the difference between the selling price and the cost price, such items as selling expenses and operating expenses being customarily deducted from the gross profits in order to arrive at the *net profit* or NET INCOME. See (1).

profit-and-loss statement. A condensed account of the operations of a business enterprise over a period of time, usually 1 year. Such an account sets forth the total sales, the cost of goods or services sold, and the gross profit or loss. The expenses of running the business are then listed under general classifications to arrive at net operating profit or loss. Other income is subsequently added and other expenses are deducted to show net profit or net loss. Also called *income statement*. See FINANCIAL STATEMENT.

profit sharing. A policy, in operation in some enterprises, of setting aside a percentage of the profits, on an annual or other basis, and then distributing the total as supplements to wages or other benefits paid employees.

profit-sharing bond. See BOND.

pro forma statement. A financial document presenting estimated figures for some contemplated business transaction or undertaking, or displaying hypothetical figures designed to show the form in which subsequent statements are to be cast. See FINANCIAL STATEMENT.

program. 1. As applied to an AUTOMATIC DATA PROCESSING SYSTEM, a plan consisting of a sequence of operations for receiving, manipulating, and recording data. It is usually expressed first in the form of a FLOW CHART, which shows the major steps in the program, and then as a BLOCK DIAGRAM which shows how each step is performed. 2. As applied to OPERATIONS RESEARCH, a mathematical method of arriving at optimum decisions within the limiting conditions imposed by a problem. 3. As applied to TEACHING MACHINES, a sequence of small units or increments of a course of study, together with questions or problems intended to test the student's comprehension of each unit.

progression. As applied to numbers, a sequence in which each number bears a constant relation to the one immediately preceding it. In *arithmetic progression*, a constant is added to form the sequence. Thus, in the progression 1, 2, 4, 6, 8, 10, 12, etc., the constant added is 2. In *geometric progression,* each number is multiplied by a constant to form the sequence. Thus, in the progression 2, 4, 8, 16, 32, 64, etc., 2 is also the constant, but in this case a multiplier. In *harmonic progression,* the reciprocals of the numbers form an arithmetic progression. Thus, in the progression 1/2, 1/4, 1/6, etc., the reciprocals, 2/1, 4/1, 6/1, are in arithmetic progression.

progressive taxation. A tax system, the rates of which increase as the base amount taxed increases—for example, a rate of 2 per cent applied to a base of $1,000, 4 per cent applied to a base of $10,000, and 6 per cent applied to a base of $100,000.

proletariat. The wage-earning class. As defined by Marxian Socialist ideologues, the whole class of wage-earners who are exploited by those owning the instruments of production, and who, at the appropriate time, will revolt and assume social and economic control.

promissory note. A written promise to pay a specific amount of money to some person at a given place and time with interest at a specific rate, or without interest, as the case may be. See NOTE.

promoter. One who undertakes to launch a new business project, especially one who assumes responsibility for selling a new project's stock or securities in order to obtain necessary capital for the enterprise.

propensity to consume. A Keynesian statistical phrase denoting the relation, expressed as a percentage, between total income and total consumer expenditures. For total income some authorities use NATIONAL INCOME, others GROSS NATIONAL PRODUCT, and still others DISPOSABLE PERSONAL INCOME. The relation is expressed in the equation:

$$P = \frac{C}{Y}$$

when

P = propensity to consume,
C = consumer expenditures,
Y = income.

351

Thus, if the national income is 282.9 billion dollars, and consumption expenditures are 193.6 billion dollars, the propensity to consume is $\frac{193.6}{282.9}$ or 68.4 per cent.

The term "consumption FUNCTION" is frequently used for this percentage because the percentage expresses a relationship between two variables. When the percentage is calculated on the basis of a specific increase or decrease in income and in consumption expenditures compared with some previous period, it is called the *marginal propensity to consume.* The marginal propensity to consume is thus a ratio of change in consumption expenditures to a change in income. The ratio is expressed in the equation

$$M = \frac{\Delta C}{\Delta Y}$$

when

M = marginal propensity to consume
ΔC = change in consumption expenditures
ΔY = change in income

Thus, if the national income increases 12.9 billion dollars, and consumer expenditures increase 8 billion dollars, the marginal propensity to consume is

$$\frac{8.0}{12.9} = 62 \text{ per cent}$$

Occasionally, the terms "propensity to consume" and "marginal propensity to consume" are used to denote the spending disposition of a single consumer or other individual spending unit.

propensity to hoard. A Keynesian term indicating a disposition on the part of the investing public to sell securities and accumulate cash. (See LIQUIDITY PREFERENCE.) The securities thus offered compete in the market for cash, the quantity of which is limited by the monetary policies of the banking system. As a result, security prices decline and interest rates advance. (See LIQUIDITY-PREFERENCE THEORY OF INTEREST.) This condition inhibits CAPITAL FORMATION and has the effect of reducing NA-

TIONAL INCOME and threatening increased unemployment. See also INCOME AND EXPENDITURE EQUATION.

propensity to invest. A statistical phrase, used especially by Keynesian economists, denoting the relation, expressed as a percentage, between total NATIONAL INCOME and that part of income expended on new CAPITAL FORMATION. Under conditions of equilibrium, propensity to invest is identical with PROPENSITY TO SAVE (*q.v.*), as demonstrated in the INCOME AND EXPENDITURE EQUATION (*q.v.*). But under conditions of disequilibrium the propensity to invest may be greater or less than the propensity to save. Under such conditions, however, income tends to bring savings and investment into balance because if savings exceed investments, income is reduced, and if investments exceed savings, income is increased. See also KEYNESIAN ECONOMICS.

propensity to save. A Keynesian statistical phrase denoting the relation, expressed as a percentage, between total income and that part of the income not devoted to consumer expenditures. For total income some authorities use NATIONAL INCOME, others GROSS NATIONAL PRODUCT, and still others DISPOSABLE PERSONAL INCOME. The relation may be expressed by the equation:

$$S = \frac{Y - C}{Y}$$

when

S = propensity to save,
Y = income,
C = consumer expenditures.

Thus, if the gross national product in the United States is 282.6 billion dollars, and consumer expenses are 193.6 billion dollars, propensity to save is:

$$\frac{282.6 - 193.6}{282.6} = 31.49 \text{ per cent}$$

When the percentage is calculated on the basis of a specific increase or decrease in the total income and in that part of the income not devoted to consumption expenditures between two chosen periods, it is called the *marginal propensity to save.* The marginal propensity to save is thus a ratio of change in savings to change in income. The ratio is expressed in the equation:

$$\Delta M = \frac{\Delta Y - \Delta C}{\Delta Y}$$

when

M = marginal propensity to save
ΔY = change in income
ΔC = change in consumer expenditures

Thus, if the national income increases 12.9 billion dollars, and consumer expenditures increase 8.0 billion dollars, the marginal propensity to save is

$$\frac{12.9 - 8.0}{12.9} = 37.98 \text{ per cent}$$

Occasionally the terms "propensity to save" and "marginal propensity to save" are used to denote the saving disposition of a single consumer or other individual saving unit.

property. The right to the present and future benefits of economic goods—material and nonmaterial—as determined by law. Although, technically, the term means a right or interest in things rather than the things themselves, common usage makes it applicable to the things rather than to the right or interest. See (30).

property account. See REAL ACCOUNT.

property capital. See CAPITAL.

property tax. Generally, a tax levied on any kind of property. The property may be real, as in the case of lands or buildings, or it may be personal, as in the case of stocks and bonds or home furnishings. Sometimes property is classified for tax purposes. In such cases a *personal property tax* may be applied at a rate different from the rate applied to real property. A distinction may also be made in the case of real property, a *land tax* being applied to such lands as are unimproved, as distinct from a *real-estate tax* which may apply to both improved and unimproved land. Often called *general property tax. See* TAX.

proportionality, law of. A term sometimes applied to the relationship between production and the FACTORS OF PRODUCTION.

It implies that in any enterprise there is some ideal relationship among the factors of production that will produce optimum returns. Also called *law of variable proportions*. See also DIMINISHING RETURNS.

proportional taxation. A tax using the same rate regardless of the base amount taxed. A rate of 2 per cent, for example, applied to a base of $1,000, $10,000, or $100,000 would be a proportional rate.

proprietorship. See INDIVIDUAL PROPRIETORSHIP.

prospectus. A document or communication offering securities of a corporation for sale that must meet the standards and specifications of the Securities and Exchange Commission concerning full disclosure of the financial standing, operations, and prospects of the corporation making the offer.

protectionism. Advocacy of protective tariffs as a means of developing national wealth and power, a policy supported by such American economists as Henry C. Carey (1793-1879) and S. N. Patten (1852-1922). The chief arguments in support of the policy were: *(a)* encouragement of infant industries; *(b)* opportunity for the employment of a variety of individual talents through industrial diversification; *(c)* savings in the cost of transportation; *(d)* conservation of natural resources for home use; and *(e)* national power in the form of a self-reliant economy. The infant-industry and national-power arguments received support particularly from the German economist Friedrich List (1789-1846). The other arguments, in English-speaking countries at least, have been rejected with practical unanimity, although in recent years protection has occasionally been defended because contemporary specialization has made capital and labor less mobile and therefore a liberal trade policy might induce at least short-term unemployment.

protective tariff. A tariff high enough to assure domestic producers against any effective competition from foreign producers. See TARIFF.

protest. A formal written declaration by a notary public certifying to a demand for payment of some instrument and to the refusal to honor that demand. Checks, for example, drawn on insufficient funds may thus have a protest attached to them when they are returned to the maker unhonored. See also AC-CEPTANCE SUPRA PROTEST.

prudent-investment-cost standard. In determining the value of an enterprise the original cost of the assets less such of the cost as represents dishonest, wasteful, or imprudent investments. See VALUATION.

psychic income. Satisfactions, other than material ones, derived from economic activity. The nature, place, or conditions of a person's work, for example, may offer such satisfactions in a high degree; they may transcend the material satisfaction of a higher money income which could be derived from work under less favorable circumstances. See INCOME.

Psychological school. A school of economic thought developed particularly in the writings of three economists—a German, Karl Menger; a Briton, W. Stanley Jevons; and a Frenchman, Léon Walras—and their followers who, near the last quarter of the 19th century, explained the relationship between desirability and price by reference to the conception of marginal utility. Earlier economists had pointed out the apparent absence of any logical relationship between the usefulness of certain commodities and their prices. Water, for example, was essential to life but virtually free; diamonds, on the other hand, though of relatively little practical use, were very high in price. The writers of the marginal utility school pointed out that, in the case of any one individual, each successive increment of a commodity lessened the subjective value of every increment possessed by that individual. Any one increment of a common substance like water, therefore, would be sacrificed with little or no return despite the fact that water is essential to life itself. But one increment of a rare commodity, like diamonds, would be sacrificed only for a substantial return even though that commodity has no such essential use as water. Also called the *Austrian school* because it was in Austria that the conception of marginal utility first rose to dominance. See SCHOOLS OF ECONOMIC THOUGHT.

psychological theory of the business cycle. A theory that explains business cycles largely by ascribing causative factors to mental attitudes and human emotions. General optimism, based upon favorable economic conditions, stimulates economic activity.

Overoptimism, it is held, then becomes widespread, and the cycle becomes overdeveloped. When economic disturbances occur, some degree of pessimism is felt, and the turning point of the cycle is reached. This, it is argued, engenders deeper pessimism, and a depression follows. See also BUSINESS CYCLE.

public bond. See BOND.

public consumption monopoly. A government monopoly conducted for the purpose of regulating the consumption of certain commodities believed to be harmful; for example, a government monopoly in alcoholic beverages, established primarily for the purpose of limiting their consumption. Such a monopoly, however, is often established for the dual purposes of regulation and revenue, in which case it is partly a FISCAL MONOPOLY. See MONOPOLY.

public corporation. A corporation created by government for a public purpose. The federal government has created many such corporations to permit the relatively autonomous administration of some activity, such as publicly-owned utilities, or agricultural loan agencies, or various government fiscal institutions. In the states of the United States the charter of such a corporation, unlike the charter of a private corporation, may usually be altered or revoked at any time at the will of the legislature unless that body is estopped by the Constitution, and the corporation's powers are strictly construed by the courts. See CORPORATION.

public debt. The total governmental debt of any country, including that of the central government and of political subdivisions, as distinct from the debts of private persons, corporate or natural. The debt of the central government, as distinct from the debts of the political subdivisions of the nation, is usually referred to as the NATIONAL DEBT. See DEBT.

public domain. 1. Lands over which a government exercises proprietary rights, generally called *public lands*. **2.** The condition which exists when a copyright or patent right expires and the composition or process involved may be exploited by anyone.

public finance. The financial operations of all levels of government. Such operations include budgeting, taxing, appropriating, purchasing, borrowing, lending, disbursing funds, and regulating the currency.

public good. As applied to economic goods, a commodity or a service supplied gratuitously to individuals by the government. Public fountains, recreation parks, museums, public education, and food distributed to ameliorate distress are examples. The distinction between a public good and a FREE GOOD should be noted. See GOOD.

Public Health Service. Established in 1798, the Public Health Service is now part of the U.S. Department of Health, Education, and Welfare. Under the direction of the Surgeon General, the Service cooperates with state and local governments in maintaining public health programs; enforces legislation on atmospheric and water pollution; seeks to control the introduction into the United States of communicable diseases originating abroad; administers grant programs for hospital and health-care centers; collects vital statistics pertaining to health matters; and itself provides health-care services to eligible federal employees and certain other groups. Through its affiliated National Institutes of Health, it carries on research, or finances research by others, in medical, biological, and related fields; gathers and disseminates information on research findings; investigates the effects of environmental hazards on health; and provides fellowships and other grants for the training of personnel in the health-care fields.

public lands. Lands owned by the federal government. See PUBLIC DOMAIN. The individual states also have title to large tracts of land.

public-opinion survey. A method of determining the opinion of the public or of segments of the public on specific issues by consulting, in one way or another, a representative cross section of the population. A survey service based on what is known as the sampling method was established during the 1930's. Since then, numerous such services have been organized, some conducting national surveys, some making regional surveys, and others confining themselves to surveys among special-interest groups. See SAMPLE.

public ownership. Ownership and operation by a government unit of some service or productive enterprise, presumably for the benefit of the citizenry.

public relations. The practice of deliberately creating or seeking to create favorable public opinion through publicity, as distinct from advertising.

public revenue. Government income from taxes and from all other sources.

public-service commission. A regulatory body, found in most of the states of the United States, which is responsible for supervising the operations of public-utility companies and passing upon their rates, services, capital structure, issuance of securities, and accounting practices.

public-service corporation. A private corporation which provides a service of peculiar importance to the public's welfare, such as the production of gas or electric power, the operation of a telephone system, or the distribution of water. Such corporations frequently operate under a FRANCHISE granting them a monopoly or a partial monopoly and for this and other reasons they are subject to government regulations in various matters, including the rates charged. Also known as *quasi-public corporation* or *public utility*. See CORPORATION.

public utility. See PUBLIC-SERVICE CORPORATION.

public-utility bond. See BOND.

Public Utility Holding Company Act. An act of Congress, 1935, which required public-utility HOLDING COMPANIES to register with the SECURITIES AND EXCHANGE COMMISSION and to simplify corporate structures by eliminating regional networks of subsidiary operating companies. See also DEATH SENTENCE.

public welfare. 1. The well-being of the people as a whole in contrast to the well-being of only a few. 2. In a much more restricted sense, the economic relief given to indigent elements of the population or to those near the poverty level of subsistence.

public works. Construction projects designed for public welfare or convenience, executed by the government with public funds. Highways, canals, bridges, parks, and public buildings are examples. The term refers to public improvements in contrast to mere maintenance activities, such as street lighting, disposal of rubbish, grading of roads, and the like.

public works and ways system. The employment of convict labor on public works and highways.

pump priming. Any policy of large-scale public expenditure for public works and other activities, the purpose being to increase employment and purchasing power and raise the level of economic activity during a depression. See also DEFICIT FINANCING.

punched-card data processing. The manipulation of information by automatic and semiautomatic machines actuated by electrical circuits, the manipulation being determined by cards containing perforations to which meanings have been assigned. The processing consists of recording, classifying, computing, and printing information. Recording from primary sources is done on a key punch machine which perforates the cards. A sorter separates the cards into any desired classification. An accounting machine interprets the perforations in the form of numerical or alphabetical characters, performs addition and subtraction, if desired, and prints the results all in accordance with "instructions" given by means of a panel wired for the particular report desired. Various other machines perform such operations as verifying, reproducing, merging, matching, selecting, interpreting, posting, and calculating.

purchase-money mortgage. A mortgage given wholly or in part in lieu of cash for the purchase of tangible property. See MORTGAGE.

purchasing power. The ability to buy—especially, the ability of consumers to make purchases as distinguished from investors, although the latter are not excluded.

purchasing-power parity. 1. In international economics, that rate of exchange between the currencies of two countries, both of which may be on a fiat standard, in which the units of national currency expressed in the exchange rate command equivalent or comparable purchasing power, in terms of specified commodities, in either the domestic or world markets. Assuming relatively unhampered world trade and no arbitrary manipulation of national currency, a purchasing-power parity exchange rate of this sort, once established, is likely to maintain a certain equilibrium. Thus if $1 in the United States has a purchasing power equivalent to the purchasing power of 100 francs in France, the price of franc bills of exchange in New York will be 1 cent per franc and the price of dollar exchange in Paris will be 100 francs to the dollar. If the price of franc bills of exchange should advance, this would tend to discourage French imports into the United States and encourage United States exports to France. This process would, it is said, tend to restore the rate of exchange to its former parity. The same equalizing process would occur, according to the doctrine, but in the reverse direction, if the price of francs in terms of dollars should decline. **2.** The concept of equalizing, or seeking to equalize, the income or purchasing power of one economic group in a society with other groups—for example, raising the income or purchasing power of farmers by guaranteeing farm prices or providing subsidies. See PARITY.

pure competition. See COMPETITION.

Pure Food and Drugs Act. An act of Congress, 1906, which has been supplemented and extended by the FEDERAL FOOD, DRUG, AND COSMETIC ACT of 1938 (*q.v.*). The original legislation prohibited interstate traffic in adulterated or misbranded food and drugs, forbade fraudulent claims on patent medicine labels, and established standards of quality to be identified on the labels of canned foods.

pure interest. A price paid for the use of capital excluding all sums to cover risk and all other costs incurred because of the loan. Sometimes called *net interest,* or *true interest.* Pure interest is a theoretical concept because all payments for the use of capital include items other than pure interest. See INTEREST.

pure profit. See PROFIT.

purposive sample. A limited number of observations selected from an entire aggregate of phenomena on the basis of some known attribute. For example, if there is known to be a high correlation between taxable incomes and property valuations, and an estimate of property valuations in a state is desired, a few counties in which the average of taxable incomes is the same as that of the entire state might be selected as a sample. It would then be assumed that the average property valuations found to obtain in the sample would apply to the state as a whole. See SAMPLE.

put. As applied to security trading, an option purchased for a fee, which permits an investor to sell a specified security at an agreed price within a stipulated period of time. Thus, by purchasing a put at the prevailing market price, instead of selling a security at that price, the investor is entitled to exercise his option and escape a loss if the market declines; but if the market advances, he can still sell at a profit.

quadratic mean. See STANDARD DEVIATION.

qualified indorsement. An indorsement that limits the liability of the indorser to that of a mere assignor, thus relieving him of all responsibility in the event of the nonpayment or nonacceptance of the instrument. A qualified indorsement is often indicated by the words "without recourse." See INDORSEMENT.

quality control. The policies and methods of government agencies, manufacturers, and others, who seek to establish and observe, or require adherence to certain qualitative specifications as to the workmanship, serviceability, and technological sophistication of a product, or certain standards of performance in the rendition of services. See CONTROL.

quantity theory of money. The assertion that the general PRICE LEVEL depends directly upon the amount of money in circulation. Thus, according to the theory, an increase in the quantity of money in circulation will increase prices, assuming the supply of goods remains constant; conversely, a decrease in the amount of money in circulation will lower prices. One of the oldest definitely postulated economic theories, its first explicit formulation is attributed to John Locke (1632-1704). With some qualifications and additions it became one of the basic tenets of the CLASSICAL SCHOOL. Early advocates of the theory recognized the importance of CREDIT, that is, deposit currency or money substitutes, but paid insufficient attention to the effect of velocity, or the rapidity of money circulation. In its modern form the theory is expressed in various versions of the EQUATION OF EXCHANGE (*q.v.*).

quarter stock. See CAPITAL STOCK.

quartile deviation. A statistical measure of the extent of absolute dispersion, variability, or scatter in a FREQUENCY DISTRIBUTION (*q.v.*), obtained by subtracting the value of the first QUARTILE (*q.v.*) from the value of the third quartile and dividing by 2.

quartiles. As applied to a FREQUENCY DISTRIBUTION in economic or other analyses, points on the X axis which separate the total number of items into four groups of an equal number of items each. There are three quartiles. The second quartile is the same as the MEDIAN. A quartile is found by first ascertaining the class interval in which it is located and then finding its value within that class interval by INTERPOLATION.

Example:

Class interval	Frequency	Cumulative frequencies	
		To second-class interval	To third-class interval
−0.5 to 0.4	10	10	10
0.5 to 1.4	30	40	40
1.5 to 2.4	40		80
2.5 to 3.4	50		
3.5 to 4.4	25		
4.5 to 5.4	8		
	163		

First quartile (Q_1):

$$\frac{163}{4} = 40.75.$$

$$40.75 - 40.00 = 0.75.$$

$$Q_1 = 1.5 + \left(\frac{0.75}{40} \times 1\right) = 1.5 + 0.01875$$
$$= 1.51875.$$

Third quartile (Q_3):

$$\frac{163}{4} = 40.75.$$

$$40.75 \times 3 = 122.25.$$

$$122.25 - 80.00 = 42.25.$$

$$Q_3 = 2.5 + \left(\frac{42.25}{50} \times 1\right) = 2.5 + 0.845$$
$$= 3.345.$$

In a similar manner, frequency distributions may be divided into *deciles* or *percentiles*. The former are points on the X axis which divide the total number of items into 10 groups; the latter into 100 groups.

quasi corporation. A term sometimes applied to an unincorporated political subdivision of one of the states of the United States. A New England town, for example, is not incorporated but enjoys practically all the rights and privileges of a municipal corporation. See CORPORATION.

quasi-public corporation. A private corporation engaged in a business of a public nature such that it must under regulatory legislation serve all who apply for its goods or services. Also called PUBLIC-SERVICE CORPORATION. See CORPORATION.

quick asset. Cash, or some other asset which can quickly be converted into cash at approximately its book value. See ASSET.

quickie strike. See ILLEGAL STRIKE.

quick ratio. See ACID-TEST RATIO.

quitrent. In the United States a term used to indicate a nominal perpetual rent sometimes made a condition of a conveyance of land. The term harks back to the feudal usage of having a tenant substitute a perpetual money payment to the lord of the manor for all other feudal obligations. See RENT.

quota. A proportionate share of a particular statistical population or universe, e.g., an immigration quota, or a sample quota, or an import quota.

quota sample. A limited number of observations selected from an entire aggregate of phenomena by separating the entire aggregate into constituent parts on the basis of some known attribute and selecting a certain number of cases from each part. Quota samples are used extensively in PUBLIC-OPINION SURVEYS. For example, the population (entire aggregate) might be separated into groups according to sex, political party, income status, or some other known attribute, and a number chosen from each group corresponding to the proportion which that group bears to the total aggregate. See SAMPLE.

R

racism. Belief in the socio-economic, intellectual, and cultural significance of alleged racial differences, and social and political action based on such belief; justification of a discriminatory policy against any group because of alleged racial difference.

rack rent. Rent in amount equal or nearly equal to the entire value of the products produced on the property rented. Hence, in general, an unreasonably high rent. See RENT.

railroad bond. See BOND.

Railroad Commission of Wisconsin* v. *Chicago, Burlington and Quincy R. R. Co. See WISCONSIN RATE CASE.

Railroad Retirement Act. An act of Congress, 1935, which, as amended by the *Railroad Unemployment Insurance Act* of 1938 and subsequent legislation, provides for monthly pensions to retired or disabled railroad, express, and pullman company employees, and survivors' benefits to their families. It also establishes a placement service for unemployed railroad personnel. The legislation is administered by the RAILROAD RETIREMENT BOARD (*q.v.*) created by the Act.

Railroad Retirement Board. A three-member board, appointed by the President and Senate, which administers the pension, unemployment insurance, and employee placement provisions of the RAILROAD RETIREMENT ACT (*q.v.*) and related legislation.

Railroad Unemployment Insurance Act. See RAILROAD RETIRE-
MENT ACT.

railroad valuation case. A case, *St. Louis and O'Fallon Ry. Co.* v.
United States, 279 U.S. 461 (1929), in which the Supreme Court
invalidated the valuation criteria which the Interstate Commerce Commission sought to use for rate-making purposes and
for determining recapture of railway earnings under the TRANS-
PORTATION (ESCH-CUMMINS) ACT of 1920. The Court was dis-
satisfied with the commission's use of the reproduction-cost
standard in determining a particular road's valuation.

Railway Labor Act. An act of Congress, 1926, which, with
amendments, governs the relations between the management of
railroads and airlines and their employees. It guarantees
employees the right of collective bargaining and authorizes the
NATIONAL MEDIATION BOARD (*q.v.*) to mediate grievances and
disputes arising out of the interpretation of labor agreements.

random sample. A limited number of observations selected by
chance from an entire aggregate of phenomena. In random
sampling, each item in the population (the entire aggregate)
must have the same chance of being selected for the sample as
any other item. This can be accomplished by a blind chance
drawing, by the selection of items at stated intervals, or by
means of a table of random numbers prepared for such purpose. See SAMPLE.

range. As applied to a FREQUENCY DISTRIBUTION (*q.v.*), a statistical measure indicating the approximate extent of absolute dispersion, variability, or scatter, obtained by ascertaining the difference between the lower limit of the lowest class interval and
the upper limit of the highest class interval. Applied to the
original data, the range is the difference between the smallest
and the largest items. It is commonly used as a measure of
stock-market variations, but, because one unusual item at
either extreme can materially affect its value, it is seldom used
in economic analysis. For an example, see FREQUENCY DISTRI-
BUTION, which shows a range of 9.99.

rate. 1. A term expressing a fixed relationship between two magnitudes and used as a means of measurement by economists,
businessmen, and statisticians. It may be a unit price for a
service, e.g., 3 cents per mile; a formula for computing wages,
e.g., $1 per hour; a formula for computing taxation, e.g., $10

per $1,000 of assessed valuation; a formula, called *interest rate,* for expressing interest or a discount, e.g., 4 per cent, meaning $4 per $100. See (1). **2.** In England, especially, the term is popularly synonymous with a tax levied by a nonsovereign governmental body.

rate discrimination. Charging persons who are similarly situated different rates for essentially identical services. The practice is normally outlawed because of its inherent unfairness or, especially in the case of transportation companies, because it lessens competition.

rate regulation. The determination by a public-service commission or similar authority of the maximum and occasionally the minimum charge which public-utility corporations may exact for their services.

rate war. See CUTTHROAT COMPETITION.

ratio. 1. A fixed relationship between two magnitudes expressed as a/b or a:b. **2.** In accounting, any one of numerous relationships—for example, between the market price of a company's stock and its earnings—used as an aid in determining the credit rating or the financial standing of an enterprise. See (1).

ratio chart. A graphic representation of statistical data showing the rate of change in a series of values. It differs from an *arithmetic chart,* which shows the absolute amounts of change. The most common type of ratio chart is the *semilogarithmic* type with logarithmic divisions along the vertical or *Y* axis and

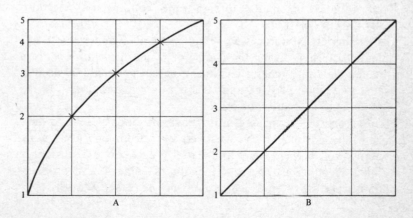

arithmetic divisions along the horizontal or *X* axis. Thus, in the series 1,2,3,4,5, the accompanying semilogarithmic chart A shows a tapering off in the rate of change, while the accompanying arithmetic chart B, showing absolute amounts of change, shows no such tapering off.

rationalization. As applied to industry, improved methods of an administrative nature which increase efficiency.

rationing. Any large-scale plan, either voluntary or enforced by law, for allocating goods and services among consumers. Such plans, resorted to on a national scale in times of scarcity brought on by war or other emergency, usually embrace a system of priorities by which essential commodities, particularly raw materials and certain manufactured articles, are supplied to users in such quantities as will best serve the national or social interest. At the same time the total supplies of the necessities of life are distributed among consumers on an equal basis, some form of stamp usually being issued, which the consumer surrenders when he makes a purchase. Also called *priority system.* See also RATIONING OF FOREIGN EXCHANGE.

rationing of foreign exchange. The policy of requiring holders of BILLS OF EXCHANGE to relinquish them to the government in return for domestic currency at a stipulated legal rate, and of obliging importers to apply to the government for such exchange to finance their operations. The purpose of the policy is to allocate available "earned" exchange to importers whom the government wishes to encourage and to deny it to those whose imports are considered less essential or perhaps harmful to the government's plan for foreign-trade equilibrium. See also EXCHANGE CONTROL.

raw material. Nonprocessed or nonfabricated material used in manufacturing, during the course of which the nature or form of the material is changed. Thus, iron is a raw material used in the production of steel, and steel is a raw material used in the manufacture of automobiles.

real account. A term used in double-entry bookkeeping to indicate an account which is carried over from one accounting period to another. Asset and liability accounts are examples. Such accounts usually bear the title of some sort of property and hence are often called *property accounts.* See ACCOUNT.

real-estate tax. See PROPERTY TAX.

real investment. Expenditure that creates a new and additional CAPITAL ASSET. Real investments thus result in new CAPITAL FORMATION. The term is used in contradistinction to FINANCIAL INVESTMENT. See INVESTMENT.

realistic method. See INDUCTIVE METHOD.

real property. A right or interest in land or whatever is attached to that land in such a way that it cannot be readily moved. The term is used in contradistinction to PERSONAL PROPERTY. See PROPERTY.

real wage. What the money received as wages will buy. As the general price level advances, a MONEY WAGE will buy less, and as the PRICE LEVEL declines, a money wage will buy more. Real wages may change, therefore, while money wages remain the same. Money wages may be converted into real wages by the use of INDEX NUMBERS (*q.v.*). See WAGE.

rebate. An amount returned out of a sum already paid, or the equivalent in the form of a deduction or discount.

recapitalization. Changing the capital structure of a company by increasing or decreasing its capital stock.

recapture of earnings. 1. A term descriptive of a clause in the TRANSPORTATION ACT of 1920 which permitted the railroads to apply to their reserves one-half of all earnings in excess of those which the act identified as constituting a fair return on the valuation of the capital assets. The other half of such earnings was made subject to "recapture"; that is, such earnings were to be paid into a government revolving fund to aid the weaker railroads. **2.** Generally, any policy requiring a public utility to transfer to the government earnings in excess of a return on investment which may be fixed in a statute or a franchise.

receipt. A written acknowledgment that money, goods, or some other property has been received. See (17).

receiver. A person usually appointed by a court to exercise control over a property or business when, in the interests of all parties concerned, it appears necessary to the court that some impartial, qualified person assume such authority. A receiver is appointed, for example, when a company cannot pay its creditors and faces bankruptcy.

receiver's certificate. A short-term note sold by a RECEIVER with the approval of the court which appointed him. The purpose is to realize immediate funds with which to carry on the business for which the receiver was appointed. A receiver of a railroad or other public utility will sometimes issue this form of security in order to keep the business, essential to the public welfare, in operation. A receiver's certificate is usually secured by a first lien upon the property and net earnings of the business in receivership. See CERTIFICATE.

recession. As applied to business conditions, a mild tapering off of economic activity, not sufficient to mark a major phase of a BUSINESS CYCLE and hence not identified as a depression.

reciprocal trade agreement. 1. An international trade treaty or agreement in which two or more nations agree to make trade concessions to one another which are considered to be of equal value. **2.** An international agreement consummated by the U.S. Department of State under the authority of the TRADE AGREEMENTS ACT of 1934, and amendments, and, more recently, of the TRADE EXPANSION ACT of 1962. The Act of 1934 authorized the increase or decrease of existing American duties up to 50 per cent for the purpose of negotiating with foreign countries on a reciprocal basis in the interest of promoting mutually profitable international trade. The Act of 1962 authorized negotiations to achieve reciprocal free trade for certain industrial products. In the case of the United States at least, all concessions received must be extended to countries with which it has most-favored-nation agreements.

reciprocity principle. In international relations, the granting of trade, tariff, or other concessions by one nation in return for equivalent concessions from the grantee.

reclamation. 1. Any method for making useful and economically valuable something which, in its existing state, is useless or nearly so. Thus, desert land may be reclaimed through irrigation, forest lands may be restored by artificial seeding and planting, and fields, if not too badly eroded, may be restored through proper methods of cultivation. **2.** In banking, the correction of a clearinghouse entry for a check or other commercial paper, the face value of which has been incorrectly listed.

Reconstruction Finance Corporation. A corporation of the United States Government organized in 1932 to combat the existing economic depression. It extended financial assistance to agriculture, industry, and commerce by granting loans or purchasing the obligations of banks, trust companies, railways, building and loan associations, insurance companies, mortgage-loan companies, local government bodies, other federal corporations, and various agricultural credit and cooperative agencies. The capital stock of the corporation was originally fixed at $500,000,000, all of which was subscribed by the government through the Secretary of the Treasury. The corporation was abolished in 1957.

reconversion. An over-all change in the direction and operation of a nation's economy when, having been modified to meet the exigencies of a major war, it is readjusted to satisfy peacetime needs and objectives. In a more limited sense, the retooling and administrative changes required in a particular industry or other establishment because of a return to normal peacetime market conditions following a period in which a national military emergency had dictated the type and volume of goods and services produced.

recourse. As applied to loans, the right to collect from an indorser or other guarantor in the event the person obtaining the loan fails to pay it.

redeemable bond. See BOND.

redeemable preferred stock. See CAPITAL STOCK.

redemption agent. See CLEARINGHOUSE AGENT.

rediscount. 1. To discount a second time. 2. The practice of a federal reserve bank discounting a second time eligible promissory notes which have already been discounted by a member bank for its customers. The proceeds of the discounted paper are credited to the member bank's account normally to increase its reserve balance. The more customary procedure, however, is for a member bank to present its own promissory note to the federal reserve bank, secured by United States bonds or other acceptable collateral. A loan made in this way is often called an *advance*.

rediscount rate. The rate of interest at which, in the United States, the federal reserve banks rediscount eligible commercial paper offered by their member banks. The rediscount rate is determined by each federal reserve bank for the member banks in its district, subject to the approval of the Board of Governors of the Federal Reserve System, or the board itself may specify the rate. If rediscounting occurs among the federal reserve banks, the Board of Governors determines the rate. See RATE.

re-export. The exportation of imported commodities in substantially the same form in which they were originally imported, the interval between importation and exportation being relatively brief—essentially, goods in transit to a third country. To avoid payment of duties, goods destined for re-export are stored in bond in FOREIGN-TRADE ZONES, usually provided by the importing countries for re-export transactions.

referee. 1. A person appointed by a court to investigate and to report to the court regarding some controversy involved in a legal action. 2. A person who arbitrates a dispute.

refined birth rate. See BIRTH RATE.

refined death rate. See DEATH RATE.

reforestation. The renewal of forests by either artificial or natural seeding. The term should not be confused with AFFORESTATION.

refunding. 1. The substitution of a new issue of bonds for an older issue, or part of an older issue, the purpose of the operation often being to prolong an existing debt or to change, usually to reduce, the interest rate on such a debt. 2. The act of returning a sum of money from an amount already paid.

refunding bond. See BOND.

regional division of labor. See LOCALIZATION OF LABOR.

regional economic commissions of the United Nations. Four separate bodies, the *Economic Commission for Asia and the Far East, for Europe, for Africa,* and *for Latin America,* established at different times since 1945 under the aegis of the United Nation's Economic and Social Council to facilitate economic collaboration among member governments of each region and to provide a means of coordinating economic policies and practices on a regional basis. The Commissions have also served as instruments for expanding the technical, administrative, and credit resources of countries undergoing development or planning for development.

regional pension system. See PENSION POOL.

registered bond. See BOND.

registered coupon bond. See BOND.

registry. A public recording of information or documents. In commercial law, a listing by a nation of ships which fly its flag on the high seas and are governed by its maritime laws.

regressive supply curve. A graphic representation of the condition that exists when a commodity or service is offered in increasing quantities as the MARKET PRICE declines. With the X axis representing quantity, and the Y axis price, the supply curve slopes downward from left to right and is hence called *regressive*. The condition is frequently found in the agricultural economy. Because they are themselves proprietors, farmers can often increase production by working longer hours without additional monetary outlay. Relatively high fixed monetary expenses may make this increased production necessary in the face of declining market prices. See also SUPPLY.

regressive taxation. A tax system, the rates of which decrease as the base amount taxed increases. A rate of 6 per cent applied to a base of $1,000, 4 per cent applied to a base of $10,000, and 2 per cent applied to a base of $100,000 is an example. A tax may be regressive in effect, however, even when the rates are uniform. A sales tax, for example, although applied at a uniform rate, takes a larger percentage of the total income of low-income groups than it takes from the total income of higher income groups.

regulation. As applied to economic life, some measure of governmental control over private enterprise.

reinsurance. A risk insured by one company which is, in turn, partially insured by a second company. The first company thereby reduces its CONTINGENT LIABILITY. See INSURANCE.

relative-value index number. An INDEX NUMBER (*q.v.*) computed by assigning the index number 100 to each item in a list of figures representing a period of time designated as the base period, finding for each item in each of the other periods under consideration an individual index number or a figure which bears the same relation to 100 that the item in question bears to its corresponding item in the base period, and calculating a GEOMETRIC MEAN of the individual index numbers for each period.

Example:

	Base period 1940		1941		
Item	Value	Individual index number	Value	Calculation	Individual index number
A	9.00	100	10.00	x:100::10.00:9.00	111.11
B	5.00	100	4.00	x:100:: 4.00:5.00	80.00
C	7.00	100	9.00	x:100:: 9.00:7.00	128.57
Index number for 1941, geometric mean					104.55

This method provides no logical means for assigning relative importance to the various items constituting the lists of figures. The resulting index numbers, therefore, even though mathematically valid, may fail to disclose the full significance of changes that may have occurred from one period to another. For example, in calculating variations in the cost of living, changes in consumer buying habits will alter the relative quantities of various commodities purchased, and may affect the cost of living quite as much as do price changes. For this reason a WEIGHTED AVERAGE is often incorporated in this method of constructing an index number. In the case of a cost of living index, the weights might logically be the quantities purchased. For tests to determine the mathematical validity of an index number, see FACTOR REVERSAL TEST, TIME REVERSAL TEST. See INDEX NUMBER.

release. The cancellation or settlement of a claim against another.

Also, the document which validates and provides proof of settlement of a claim.

remainderman. The person designated to receive the principal amount in a TRUST, or of any temporary estate, upon its termination.

remonetization. The reestablishment of a coin as standard money after it has been demonetized. See also DEMONETIZATION.

renegotiation. Reviewing and restating the terms of a contract, usually with the aim of providing more favorable terms for one of the parties—a privilege sometimes reserved by governments in contracts with suppliers during an emergency when the suppliers' profits, under the contract as first negotiated, are deemed to be excessive.

rent. Theoretically, an amount paid for the use of land. In popular usage, however, the term commonly refers to a payment for the use of land as well as the improvements thereon. Such a payment is often designated as *ordinary rent*. Or, in popular usage, the term "rent" may refer to a payment for the use of a CAPITAL GOOD, such as a machine, quite apart from any land. See (12).

rent control. The fixing of ordinary rents by legislation or administrative action regulating the terms of a lease. Rent control was part of market and price-control legislation enacted by Congress in 1942, following precedents established during World War I. Modified federal rent control was continued for some time after the close of World War II. Rent-control legislation has been maintained by state legislation in certain instances or by municipal regulation authorized by the state legislature. See CONTROL.

rent-control case. A case, *Block* v. *Hirsh*, 256 U.S. 135 (1921), in which the Supreme Court upheld state and federal legislation fixing rents and extending leases at the close of World War I. The wartime housing emergency, said the Court, had temporarily clothed the landlord-tenant relationship with a preponderant public interest and, as a consequence, had brought that relationship within the scope of the same sort of regulatory power that government normally exerted over public utilities.

377

rentier. A person who receives a fixed income from land, stocks, or bonds.

reorganization bond. See BOND.

reparations. Cash or materials collected from or charged to defeated nations by the victor nations as a war indemnity. The term was used by the Allied and Associated Powers in the Treaty of Versailles following World War I, and was used after World War II particularly with reference to the collection of war indemnity from current production in occupied Germany.

repatriation. 1. Restoration of prisoners of war or others to full citizenship in their country of origin. **2.** Liquidation of foreign investments and reinvestment of the proceeds in the investor's own country.

replacement-cost standard. In determining the value of an enterprise, the cost of replacing equipment with new models and designs capable of performing operations identical to those performed by the old equipment. See VALUATION.

replacement demand. Demand for capital goods or durable consumer goods created because of depreciation or obsolescence. See DEMAND.

representative good. A document which is evidence of ownership, or an interest in the ownership, of wealth; for example, a stock certificate, a bond, or a mortgage. Thus, theoretically, a representative good is one kind of ECONOMIC GOOD. See GOOD.

representative money. Paper money issued in lieu of its face value in gold or silver, the metal being kept from circulation. In the United States, a sizable amount of silver certificates, a form of representative money, is still outstanding, but the certificates are no longer issued. See MONEY.

repressive tax. A tax which discourages production and thus reduces potential tax income.

reproduction-cost standard. In determining the value of an enterprise the cost, as of a specific date, of reproducing its assets less an allowance for depreciation for the period during which the existing assets have been in use. See VALUATION.

repudiation. As applied to finance, refusal to honor a debt, especially the refusal of the government of a state to pay its public debt in whole or in part.

resale price agreements. See FAIR-TRADE PRACTICES ACTS.

resale price-maintenance cases. See BEECH-NUT PACKING CASE and *OLD DEARBORN DISTRIBUTING CO. V. SEAGRAM DISTILLERS CORP.*

reservation price. The highest offered price at which a seller still refuses to sell. He will sell at any figure above the reservation price. Sometimes the term is used to indicate the minimum price at which a seller will sell. See PRICE.

reserve bank credit. Bank credit created by the federal reserve banks which may take the form of (*a*) loans to member banks through REDISCOUNT operations, (*b*) loans to member banks with appropriate security, and (*c*) OPEN-MARKET OPERATIONS. See CREDIT.

reserve city banks. 1. National banks in some 45 cities in the United States which, under the NATIONAL BANK ACT (*q.v.*), were required to maintain reserves at 25 per cent of deposits but, unlike CENTRAL RESERVE CITY BANKS (*q.v.*), were not required to maintain more than one-half of that total in their own vaults, the other half usually being on deposit with a central reserve city bank. **2.** A similar classification of federal reserve member banks which are required to maintain a greater minimum reserve than COUNTRY BANKS (*q.v.*). See BANK.

reserve currency. A national currency, such as the dollar or pound sterling, or an international currency, such as drawing rights at the International Monetary Fund used by many countries to settle debit balances in their international accounts or as a reserve for their own currencies. See CURRENCY.

reserve ratio. In the United States, the percentage of a bank's total deposits which the bank keeps in liquid assets either in its vaults or with the district federal reserve bank, as a reserve against deposits. Normally the law establishes a minimum reserve ratio for various classes of banks. The higher the reserve ratio, the less opportunity there is for the creation of bank loans through DEPOSIT CURRENCY (*q.v.*). Hence, regulation of the reserve ratio is often suggested as a means of controlling inflation or deflation. See RATIO.

reserves. Funds segregated for specific purposes. See (20).

residuary estate. That portion of an estate which remains after the testator has made specific legacies and bequests.

restraint of trade. Price fixing, the creation of a monopoly, or practices of a related nature which are designed to hamper the free exchange of goods and services or have the effect of reducing competition especially when undertaken by private business although public measures may have a similar effect.

restrictive indorsement. An indorsement which limits the further negotiability of the instrument indorsed. See INDORSEMENT.

Resumption Act. An act of Congress, 1875, which provided for the redemption of GREENBACKS in specie after 1878 and for the gradual reduction of greenbacks in circulation.

retaliatory duty. A DIFFERENTIAL DUTY (*q.v.*), intended to penalize foreign countries for alleged discriminatory trade practices or to coerce them into making trade concessions. See CUSTOMS DUTY.

returns to scale of plant. The relation between quantity of output of a business enterprise and the various FACTORS OF PRODUCTION used in attaining that output, a relation which indicates variation in the degree of productivity as the enterprise develops. As the enterprise first begins to expand its activities, assuming that the factors of production are acquired in optimum proportions as needed, output normally increases at an accelerated rate relative to the increments of the factors added. As economies consequent upon DIVISION OF LABOR and other cost-saving methods are exhausted, there follows a period when output increases more or less in proportion to new increments of the factors. As expansion continues, additional increments of the factors may produce a disproportionately low rate of increased output because of lack of intimate firsthand knowledge of operations on the part of management, delegation of responsibilities, inevitable delays in rendering decisions, and, in general, the complicated routine associated with very large organizations.

revaluation. Restoration of the value of a depreciated currency within a country. The principal methods are to reduce the demand for, or to increase the supply of, foreign BILLS OF EXCHANGE by restricting imports and encouraging exports; to lower the domestic price level through increased productivity; to decrease the credit supply; or to employ other deflationary policies.

revenue. 1. Government income from taxation, duties, etc. According to some authorities, the term may also be applied to government receipts from the sales of stock, land, and other such property, and from fees; hence all PUBLIC REVENUE. **2.** Less commonly, the income of corporations and private individuals.

revenue bond. See BOND.

revenue expenditure. An expense of a business enterprise, to be distinguished from a CAPITAL EXPENDITURE which adds to the value of the enterprise.

revocable letter of credit. See LETTER OF CREDIT.

revolving credit fund. An arrangement whereby a consumer may purchase goods up to a stipulated amount and is given 6 months or more to pay for them, new purchases being permitted as payments for previous ones are made. A revolving credit fund is thus a form of INSTALLMENT BUYING. In recent years such funds have replaced, to a substantial extent, the conventional 30-day retail-store charge accounts in the purchase of soft goods. See FUND.

revolving fund. A sum of money which is constantly renewed as it is used, either by further appropriations or by income from the activities it finances, thus maintaining a balance at all times. See FUND.

revolving letter of credit. See LETTER OF CREDIT.

Ricardian theory of rent. See ECONOMIC RENT.

rigged market. The condition which exists when purchases and sales are manipulated to such an extent as to distort a normal supply-and-demand price. See MARKET.

right-to-work laws. Legislation in more than one-third of the states of the United States, supported by Section 14b of the LABOR-MANAGEMENT (*Taft-Hartley*) ACT (*q.v.*), which makes illegal labor contracts providing for the establishment of a UNION SHOP (*q.v.*).

risk. The possibility of loss. The term is commonly used to describe the possibility of loss from some particular hazard, as fire risk, war risk, credit risk, etc. It also describes the possibility of loss by an investor who, in popular speech, is often referred to as a risk bearer.

risk capital. See VENTURE CAPITAL.

risk-capital pooling. Augmenting the available volume of venture capital in a particular area, or for any particular constituency of potential borrowers, through the establishment of a fund to which various individuals or institutions, particularly banks, contribute assets or credit. Plans of this sort are occasionally broached especially to help small business.

rival demand. See COMPOSITE DEMAND.

rival supply. See COMPOSITE SUPPLY.

Robinson-Patman Act. An act of Congress, 1936. It prohibits those engaged in interstate commerce from either receiving or granting special price or service concessions in the sale of commodities when such concessions substantially lessen competition. Different prices to different customers are permitted when those price variations are caused by genuine differences in production and selling costs, or by efforts to meet some new form of competition. The act authorizes the Federal Trade Commission to determine limits for discounts on quantity sales, a provision designed particularly to prevent abuses by CHAIN STORES.

Rochdale principles. Criteria for conducting a consumer co-operative, generally attributed to Charles Howarth and a group of fellow workers in Rochdale, England, who, in 1844, organized there one of the earliest successful cooperative enterprises. The principles include: *(a)* granting of one vote only to each member regardless of the number of shares owned; *(b)* sale of goods for cash and at current market prices; *(c)* apportioning any income, beyond expenses and RESERVES, pro rata according to the total amount of purchases made; *(d)* permitting no restrictions on membership; *(e)* allowing only nominal interest payments on capital invested; and *(f)* requiring a reserve for educational purposes. See also COOPERATIVE.

roll-back. A popular expression denoting a governmental policy of establishing, as the legal price, an earlier and lower price than the existing market price. Normally this is accomplished by a public subsidy to producers or distributors to compensate them for the difference between the higher existing market price and the lower legally fixed price.

rolling stock. The physical property of a railroad that operates on its own wheels on rails. Locomotives, passenger and freight cars, wrecking derricks, etc., are a part of the rolling stock of a railroad.

rotating shifts. In an enterprise where a 24-hour interval is divided into two or three shifts or working periods, the practice of interchanging employees in such a way that over a period of time they will have taken a turn on each of the two or three shifts instead of being confined to a particular shift. See SHIFT.

roundabout production. See INDIRECT PRODUCTION.

round-of-wage increases. A popular term to identify an occasion, occurring each year or two, when labor agreements between major unions and basic industries, such as steel, other metals, automobiles, electrical goods, etc., are renewed and the resulting settlements, which since World War II have invariably been upward, roughly set the standard for the economy as a whole—hence, a round of increases.

royalty. Compensation resulting from the use of a patent, copyright, or other property. The royalty is usually a percentage of the sales value of an article or service in the production of which the patent, copyright, or other property has been exploited.

rule of reason. A criterion for judging alleged infringements of the antitrust laws, first adopted by the Supreme Court in 1911 in the cases of *Standard Oil Company* v. *United States* and *United States* v. *American Tobacco Company.* Mere size was not to be considered evidence of monopoly; the intent to restrain trade or to monopolize was set forth as the crucial factor. See also STANDARD OIL CASE.

runaway inflation. Serious and unusually severe INFLATION (*q.v.*).

runaway shop. A business organization that moves from one location to another primarily to escape unionization of its employees or the application of labor laws. See SHOP.

running cost. See VARIABLE COST.

run on a bank. A sudden demand by a large number of depositors for the withdrawal of their funds on deposit in a bank, usually caused by fear that the bank in question is financially unsound.

Rural Electrification Administration. A unit of the U.S. Department of Agriculture which makes loans, preferably to public bodies, cooperatives, and nonprofit and limited-dividend corporations, to be used to provide electric power and telephone service to families living in rural areas.

S

sabotage. In industrial disputes, the deliberate slowing down of production, or other action to make production unprofitable, by employees who believe they have a grievance against their employer. Sabotage may take the form of merely wasting time, or it may take the form of actual destruction of machinery or of the manipulation of machinery to make it temporarily unworkable or less efficient.

safe-deposit company. Generally, a corporation which has a vault containing safes and similar receptacles which are rented to users for the custody of securities, important papers, jewelry, and other valuable personal property. Access to the vault is provided during certain hours of the day. Commercial banks frequently provide such safe-deposit facilities. See COMPANY.

safety-fund bank system. A plan put into effect in 1829 by the state of New York whereby all the banks within the state were required to contribute to an insurance fund designed to protect BANK DEPOSITS and to guarantee the redemption of bank notes at par. The plan required of each bank annual contributions equal to ½ of 1 per cent of its capital until such a time as the fund reached an amount equal to 3 per cent of the total banking capital employed in the state. Thereafter, pro rata contributions were required to maintain the fund at this level. The

384

fund was the predecessor of various state and federal schemes to insure bank deposits. See BANKING SYSTEM.

St. Louis and O'Fallon Ry. Co.* v. *United States. See RAILROAD VALUATION CASE.

Saint-Simonians. The followers of Claude Henri de Rouvroy, Comte de Saint-Simon (1760-1825), who is credited with founding French socialism. The movement early took the form of a religious cult, the disciples of which believed that private property was the cause of human exploitation and wished to abolish it. They maintained that, through the laws of inheritance, private property fell into the hands of those incompetent to use it for the benefit of society; hence, the state, they argued, should become the sole inheritor of all forms of wealth.

salary. Compensation for services rendered, paid at fixed intervals. The term implies work of an executive or clerical nature in contrast to manual labor. Occasionally called *stipend.*

sales finance company. See COMMERCIAL CREDIT COMPANY.

sales finance company. A financial institution which buys installment contracts from dealers and finances dealers' inventories. See COMPANY.

sales tax. A tax levied on the sale of goods and services at one or more stages in the process of distribution. The tax may, for example, be levied on the sale of a commodity every time it changes hands. Such a tax is commonly called a *turnover* or a *transactions tax.* Or the tax may be levied on the sale of a commodity only upon its transfer of ownership at one particular time. Thus, only the sales of manufacturers may be taxed when those sales represent completed products; only the sales of wholesalers may be taxed when goods pass into the hands of retailers; or only retail sales may be taxed as the goods pass into the hands of consumers. See TAX.

sample. A limited number of observations from which, by a process of inductive mathematical reasoning, qualified quantitative generalizations are made with respect to an entire aggregate of phenomena. There are various methods of sampling and various mathematical techniques for arriving at generalizations. A simple illustration may be cited in the case of a large aggregate such as the price per dozen of grade-A eggs in New York City. Suppose a RANDOM SAMPLE of 1,600 *(N)* representative prices is gathered, the results are arranged in a FREQUENCY DISTRIBUTION, and the ARITHMETIC MEAN and STANDARD DEVIATION (σ) are calculated at 80 cents and 5 cents, respectively. From this one sample it can be estimated what the standard deviation, called the *standard error of the mean,* would be in a frequency distribution constructed from the means of an indefinite number of samples, such as the above, all containing the same number of items. The generalized equation of the standard error of the mean ($\sigma_{\bar{x}}$) is:

$$\sigma_{\bar{x}} = \frac{\sigma}{\sqrt{N}}$$

and, in the above example,

$$\sigma_{\bar{x}} = \frac{0.05}{\sqrt{1,600}} = 0.00125.$$

In a NORMAL CURVE OF DISTRIBUTION, 99.7 per cent of the items fall within three standard deviations of the mean. It may be assumed, then, in this example, that there are 99.7 chances out of 100 that the obtained mean of 80 cents is not more than $0.00375 ($3 \times 0.00125$) away, plus or minus, from the assumed mean of the total aggregate. See (10).

satiety, law of. See MARGINAL UTILITY.

saving. 1. Accumulation of wealth through the postponement of consumption. **2.** The economical use of want-satisfying goods. See (12).

savings and loan association. A privately owned financial corporation chartered by the federal or a state government. All associations operating under a federal charter, and many operating under a state charter, are MUTUAL COMPANIES; the other state-chartered associations are stock companies. Some state-chartered associations are known by other names such as BUILDING AND LOAN ASSOCIATIONS *(q.v.).* Savings are recorded in passbooks similar to those used in mutual savings banks and are insured up to $15,000 in all *federal savings and loan associations,* in most mutual state associations, and in some stock companies by the FEDERAL SAVINGS AND LOAN INSURANCE CORPORATION.

Mortgages on homes are the chief form of investment by savings and loan associations.

savings bank. A bank, the principal function of which is to accept time deposits and to invest its funds in such securities as the law permits for such banks. A savings bank may be a MUTUAL SAVINGS BANK, a STOCK SAVINGS BANK, or a GUARANTY SAVINGS BANK. See BANK.

savings bond. See BOND.

savings notes. See FREEDOM SHARES.

Say's law. The assertion that the total supply of economic goods must necessarily always equal the total demand for them. The assertion is supported by the argument that goods really exchange for goods, money being merely a medium of exchange. All goods produced, therefore, represent a demand as well as a supply. Hence, any increase in production is an increase in demand, and any general overproduction is impossible. The law is derived from Jean Baptiste Say (1767-1832). Also identified as *Say's theory of markets.*

Say's theory of markets. See SAY'S LAW.

scab. A person who works under conditions contrary to those prescribed by a labor union, or who accepts employment in an establishment where the regular employees are on strike.

Scandinavian Monetary Union. An agreement by Denmark, Norway, and Sweden (1873 and 1875) which provided that the gold and silver coins of any one of these states would be lawful money in all three, and later that bank notes issued by any one state would be accepted in the others at par. Difficulties arose during the period of World War I and in 1924 Sweden withdrew. The Union has not been revived.

scarcity value. Value caused by a demand for a good, the supply of which cannot be increased. Antique furniture is an example. See VALUE.

scatter chart. A graphic device which displays actual relationships between two variables by spot markings, and usually the average relationship between them by a mathematically constructed curve. In the diagram black dots indicate actual relationships between two variables A and B over a period of time.

Time interval	Variables	
	A	B
1	77.1	17.2
2	86.2	18.5
3	70.3	9.2
4	72.5	10.3
5	84.3	15.6
6	83.4	13.3
7	90.0	15.3
8	95.3	16.8
9	93.5	15.2
10	95.6	14.9
Number of cases 10 (N)		

The solid line, called the *line of regression*, indicates the average relationship between these two variables during the same period. Its mathematical equation is:

$$y = -2.58 + 0.2029x.$$

The equation is computed according to the LEAST-SQUARES METHOD. The *standard error of estimate* (S_y) measures the significance of this line, that is, the extent to which the spot markings are in close proximity to it. The standard error of estimate is the STANDARD DEVIATION (σ) measured from the line of regression. Its value in the present example is 2.17. It may be computed by means of the following equation:

$$S_y^2 = \frac{(\Sigma y^2) - a\Sigma(y) - b\Sigma(xy)}{N}.$$

In the same diagram the dotted lines show the limits of the standard error of estimate. Within these limits are about 68 per cent of the cases, this being the approximate constant proportion of cases within one standard variation plus and one standard variation minus the ARITHMETIC MEAN. The *coefficient of correlation (r)* is an abstract measure indicating the degree of relationship between the two variables. It is used extensively in economic calculations to compare the degree of relationship between one pair of variables with that between another. The coefficient of correlation in the present example is 0.6311. It may be computed from the following equation:

$$r = \sqrt{1 - \frac{S_y^2}{\sigma_y^2}}.$$

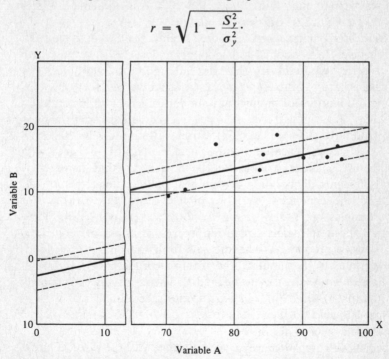

Unity indicates perfect correlation; zero indicates the absence of any correlation. A correlation of 0.6311 is considered medium.

Schechter case. A case, *Schechter Poultry Corp.* v. *United States,* 295 U. S. 495 (1935), in which the Supreme Court invalidated the National Industrial Recovery Act and the fair-practice codes which that statute authorized. Also known as NRA case. The Court held the statute unconstitutional on two principal grounds. These were: *(a)* that Congress did not establish adequate standards for the code-making authority confided to the President under the law, and thus delegated the substance of legislative power to the President; and *(b)* that production and trade, which the statute attempted to regulate, are primarily matters of state concern, and their attempted regulation had only an indirect relation to interstate commerce; consequently the regulation could not be justified under Congress' commerce power and constituted, in fact, an attempt to regulate matters reserved to the states under the 10th Amendment. See also UNITED STATES V. DARBY LUMBER CO.

Schechter Poultry Corp. v. **United States.** See SCHECHTER CASE.

schedule. 1. As applied to economic analysis, a list setting forth a series of quantities that depend upon two variables. For example, a LIQUIDITY PREFERENCE schedule sets forth the various quantities of money that are demanded at various interest rates, a PROPENSITY TO CONSUME schedule lists consumer expenditures that are made at varying income levels, etc. Such schedules are customarily shown in the form of a graph with the independent variable, that is, the quantity that increases by increments deliberately determined, plotted along the X axis, and the dependent variable plotted along the Y axis. For examples, see DEMAND, SUPPLY. **2.** As generally used in industry, the term means a plan for future operations or procedure. Thus, a production schedule sets forth the quantity of goods expected to be manufactured within a certain time, and a sales schedule the quantity to be sold. **3.** The term may refer merely to a list of some kind, such as a price schedule.

schedule demand. See DEMAND.

schedule supply. See SUPPLY.

school desegregation cases. See *BROWN* V. *BOARD OF EDUCATION OF TOPEKA.*

school lunch program. A program funded by federal and state governments, largely an outgrowth of the National School Lunch Act of 1946, to provide midday meals to children in elementary and secondary schools. The aim is to improve the children's nutrition and, in part, provide an additional outlet for surplus commodities held by the Department of Agriculture.

schools of economic thought. More or less systematic bodies of doctrine concerning fundamental aspects of economic behavior developed by certain leading economic theorists and further expounded by their disciples. See (9).

Schuman Treaty. See EUROPEAN COMMUNITY FOR COAL AND STEEL.

scrip. Various kinds of documents indicating that the bearer is entitled to receive something; for example, fractional paper money issued in the past by banks and the government in the United States, or certificates issued by employers and exchangeable for goods at a COMPANY STORE. The term is sometimes applied to CERTIFICATES OF INDEBTEDNESS and to certificates issued provisionally to identify partial payment on a subscription for stocks, bonds, or like instruments. During the depression years following 1929, the term was used to indicate temporary currency used within the boundaries of some communities.

scrip dividend. A corporation dividend paid in the form of a promise to pay at a specified time in the future, or when a specified event transpires, or at the will of the corporation. See DIVIDEND.

S.D.R.'s. SPECIAL DRAWING RIGHTS *(q.v.).*

seasonal fluctuations. A characteristic often discernible in a time series wherein, over a period of years, each of the 12 months shows more or less regular variations in the SECULAR TREND. There are various statistical methods of calculating seasonal fluctuations in a time series. The appended diagram shows the general seasonal pattern for hypothetical data over a 5-year period. The curve may be computed by ascertaining the secular trend according to the LEAST-SQUARES METHOD, finding for each month the percentage that the original data bear to the trend value, calculating the ARITHMETIC MEAN of these percentages by months, and finally adjusting these average percentages to a mean of 100 per cent. For the original data, see TIME SERIES.

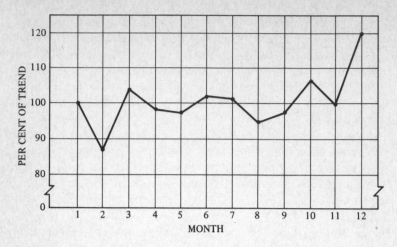

seasonal industry. An industry, such as food processing or toy manufacturing, which is subject to substantial increase or decrease in production or sales volume at different seasons of the year. See INDUSTRY.

seasonal unemployment. Unemployment caused by seasonal variations in the volume of production of certain industries. The building-construction, clothing, and coal-mining industries, for example, normally maintain full production only during certain seasons of the year. As a rule, therefore, few workers in these industries enjoy full employment the entire year. See UNEMPLOYMENT.

seasoned security. A security which has a good record of interest or dividend payments, which has been on the market for a period of time, and which has attained a reasonably stable price. See SECURITY.

seat on the exchange. Membership in a stock exchange organization.

secondary boycott. See BOYCOTT.

secondary offering. The sale of a large block of securities by a large stockholder, as by a pension fund or charity or by the executors of a will. The sale is handled specially on an exchange in order to soften its impact on the market.

secondary picketing. Picketing of an establishment not directly engaged in a labor dispute but associated in some way with an establishment that is so engaged. See PICKETING.

secondary strike. See SYMPATHETIC STRIKE.

Second Industrial Revolution. Greatly increased productivity, and more sophisticated products and services, brought about by automation, jet airplane transport, SYSTEMS RESEARCH, improvements in electronic communication, advances in organic chemistry and in nuclear and other fields of physics, and other advances in science, technology and management—manifested especially after 1960.

secular stagnation. A low level of economic activity over a considerable period of time.

secular trend. Any general tendency of values in a time series to increase or decrease over a period of years. The heavy line in the appended diagram shows the secular trend of hypothetical data over a 5-year period. There are various methods of estimating secular trend in a time series. The linear curve in the diagram may be computed by the LEAST-SQUARES METHOD, the equation being:

$$y = 16.7386 + 0.3682x.$$

For the original data, see TIME SERIES.

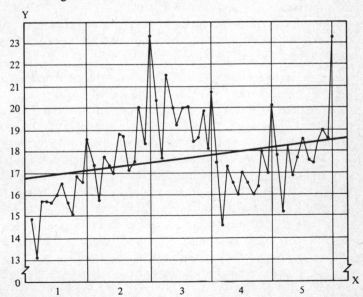

secured debt. A debt for which collateral has been pledged. See DEBT.

Securities Act. An act of Congress, 1933, designed to protect investors in new issues of securities. The act requires that specific information covering some 32 points on most new security issues be filed with a federal supervising agency before the securities in question are offered to the public, and those issuing the securities are made responsible for the accuracy and completeness of the information thus disclosed. The act's provisions are intended to secure full and accurate information regarding new security issues for the public, but they do not prohibit speculative issues. Originally the FEDERAL TRADE COMMISSION was named the supervising agency, but with the enactment of the SECURITIES EXCHANGE ACT of 1934 administrative authority was vested in the newly created SECURITIES AND EXCHANGE COMMISSION.

Securities and Exchange Commission. An independent, quasi-judicial federal agency, created under the authority of the SECURITIES EXCHANGE ACT of 1934 to administer the provisions of that act, the SECURITIES ACT of 1933, and other comparable legislation. Its primary purpose is to protect investors against malpractices in the securities markets. To this end, it restricts trading on margin, limits speculative credit, enforces disclosure rules on new security issues, and supervises activities of investment companies and investment counselors.

Securities Exchange Act. An act of Congress, 1934, supplementing the Securities Act of 1933. It is designed to protect investors purchasing seasoned securities through brokers. The act provides for the registration of all but a few exempted STOCK EXCHANGES with the SECURITIES AND EXCHANGE COMMISSION and their disclosure of the holdings and transactions of directors and officers of companies. The Board of Governors of the FEDERAL RESERVE SYSTEM is made responsible for the control of credit used in the purchase and carrying of securities and the Commission is given power to regulate short sales, floor trading, odd-lot sales, and margin requirements. The manipulation of security prices is prohibited. Companies having securities listed on the registered exchanges are required to file information pertaining to their affairs with exchanges and with the Commission.

security. 1. A document establishing a right to some form of property; for example, a corporate stock certificate, a bond, or a mortgage. See (21). **2.** Property pledged as collateral. **3.** Insurance against risk.

security capital. Capital which is subject to minimum risk. The term is used in contradistinction to VENTURE CAPITAL or RISK CAPITAL. A loan in which valuable property is pledged as surety for the principal is an example. Security capital is usually represented by bonds or mortgages with a stipulated amount of interest guaranteed. See CAPITAL.

Security Council. One of the major organs of the UNITED NATIONS, composed of 5 permanent members (France, Republic of China, Russia, United Kingdom, United States) and 10 members chosen by the General Assembly for 2-year terms, whose primary function is to preserve the peace of the world. To that end, the Charter of the United Nations authorizes it to take direct action in the form of diplomatic, economic, and military sanctions if such action is supported by 9 of the council's 15 members, but the 9 affirmative votes must include those of all 5 permanent members. On procedural or "nonsubstantive" actions, any 9 of the 15 members can authorize action.

security exchange. See STOCK EXCHANGE.

segregated appropriation. See ITEMIZED APPROPRIATION.

segregation. 1. The physical separation of people of different races in educational institutions, transportation facilities, housing, places of accommodation or entertainment, etc., now legally outlawed in the United States but still existing, de facto, especially in ghetto areas of large urban centers. **2.** Authorization of appropriated funds for specific purposes. **3.** Limitation of the proceeds of tax revenues to particular purposes such as highway contruction or local government grants.

seigniorage. 1. A charge, high enough to yield a profit, made by a government for converting bullion into coins. **2.** The profit made by a government in marking subsidiary coins at a face value higher than the cost of their metal content. **3.** Occasionally a synonym for BRASSAGE.

self-interest. A greater regard for personal welfare than for the welfare of others. Self-interest as an actuating force in human affairs, gave rise to the concept of the ECONOMIC MAN used extensively by the CLASSICAL SCHOOL.

self-interest, law of. See HEDONISTIC PRINCIPLE.

self-liquidating. A characteristic of an investment which enables its original cost to be paid from its earnings.

self-sufficient nation. A nation which produces all that it consumes. The attempt to attain such an end is called *economic nationalism.* Modern wants are so numerous and so sophisticated that no nation can be absolutely self-sufficient and maintain high levels of living. Self-sufficiency is contrary to the principle of COMPARATIVE ADVANTAGE *(q.v.)* and hence requires the uneconomic production of some things.

sellers' market. A market situation, subject to competitive conditions, under which the schedules of supply and demand establish market prices at a relatively high level, giving the sellers an advantage. Sellers are disposed to retain their goods and services rather than to sell them at a low price, and buyers are disposed to acquire the goods and services even if they have to pay a high price. The term is used in contradistinction to BUYERS' MARKET. See MARKET.

sellers seven sale. A stock sold on the floor of an exchange with the understanding that delivery will be delayed possibly as much as 7 days, possibly longer, according to whatever time is agreed upon.

seller's surplus. The hypothetical difference between what a seller actually receives for a product and what he would have been willing to sell for if necessary. See SURPLUS.

selling short. The practice of selling a temporarily borrowed security to effect delivery. Short selling is done in anticipation of a decline in the market price. If a decline occurs, the trader can buy the security at a price lower than that for which he sold it, pay the cost of borrowing the security, and make a profit. If the market advances, however, the trader may be forced to buy the security at a higher price than that for which he sold it, and he will have to pay the cost of borrowing the security besides. To avoid too great a loss on an advancing market, the trader may give a STOP-LOSS ORDER to his broker.

semilogarithmic chart. See RATIO CHART.

seniority. As applied to labor relations, an employee's length of service in a given establishment, often used as a basis for wage rates and promotion.

Senn v. Tile Layers Protective Union. A case, 301 U. S. 468 (1937), in which the Supreme Court, in upholding a Wisconsin statute which prohibited the issuance of injunctions against peaceful PICKETING, substantially altered its view in an earlier case [*Truax* v. *Corrigan,* 257 U. S. 312 (1921)] that statutory prohibition of the weapon of injunction in certain labor disputes constituted violation of the equal-protection clause of the 14th Amendment. The court attempted to reconcile the two cases by suggesting that the earlier anti-injunction statute tended to legalize militant actions of labor unions which were illegal before the statute was passed, whereas the subsequent Wisconsin anti-injunction statute had no such effect, the picketing in question being peaceful.

sensitive market. The condition which exists when market prices fluctuate widely in response to good or bad news. See MARKET.

serial bond. See BOND.

series bond. See BOND.

service. 1. Any work or activity of immediate economic value to another, such as medical or other professional assistance, or the provision of some facility, such as power, heat, or transportation, usually distinguished from a tangible good or commodity and also from any work involved in the production of a tangible good or commodity. **2.** The delivery of a writ or other official document.

Servicemen's Readjustment Act. See G. I. BILL OF RIGHTS.

service utility. Utility created by the rendering of a personal service, such as the service of a lawyer, physician, or teacher. See UTILITY.

servitude. 1. Any form of coerced labor. **2.** A restriction on ownership, often sanctioned by prescription or usage, usually relating to the ownership of land, which qualifies the right of ownership of the land in favor of others.

settlor. A person who makes a property settlement; specifically, the creator of a TRUST.

severance tax. A tax levied upon the value of natural resources removed from land or water. See TAX.

severance wage. See DISMISSAL WAGE.

sharecropper. A tenant farmer who works the land, receiving seed, stock, and implements from the landlord in addition to cultivable land and living quarters, and who shares the crops with the landlord. Credits advanced by the landlord are deducted from the tenant's share as are occasionally, also, certain charges for maintenance and improvements.

shares. See CAPITAL STOCK.

share the wealth. A slogan suggesting the desirability of greater equality in income and wider distribution of ownership of capital goods.

share-the-work plan. See WORK-SHARING.

Sheppard-Towner Act. An act of Congress, 1921, which provided federal funds to supplement state appropriations for maternity care and infant welfare.

Sherman Antitrust Act. An act of Congress, 1890, which prohibited combinations or conspiracies—especially trusts—in restraint of interstate or foreign trade, and forbade monopoly or the attempt to monopolize. It allowed any person injured by another's violation of the act to sue the offending party and, if the fact of his injury was established judicially, to recover three times the amount of the ascertained damage. The act authorized the use of the injunction, and various penalties, including confiscation of property, could follow successful prosecutions under the act.

Sherman notes. See TREASURY NOTES.

Sherman Silver Purchase Act. An act of Congress, 1890, inspired by the western silver lobby, which provided that the Secretary of the Treasury purchase 4,500,000 oz. of silver each month at the market price, but at a maximum of $1 for 371.25 grains of silver or $1.29 an ounce, with payment to be made in treasury notes issued as currency of full legal tender. The value of the silver purchased under the act was about $50 million per year and such purchases were continued until the act was repealed in 1893.

shift. As applied to labor, a period of working time, usually an interval between stipulated hours of a 24-hour day. For example, a day shift may begin at 8 A.M. and stop at 5 P.M. and a night shift may begin at 9 P.M. and stop at 6 A.M., or a 24-hour day may be divided into three eight-hour shifts. See (29).

shifting of taxation. See INCIDENCE OF TAXATION.

shinplaster. A derisive term applied at various times in United States history to depreciated paper currency. After the American Revolution it was applied to Continental paper currency; later, about 1837, to various notes issued by private bankers; and again, during the Civil War, to Confederate currency.

ship broker. An individual who, for a fee or commission, obtains cargoes for vessels and secures freight space on ships for shippers.

shoe machinery case. A case, *United States* v. *United Shoe Machinery Corp.*, 258 U. S. 451 (1922), in which the Supreme Court held that tying clauses in contracts, which provided for the leasing and selling of patented or unpatented articles on condition that purchaser or lessee did not deal with competitors of lessor or seller, lessened competition and violated Sec. 3 of the CLAYTON ACT. See also TIE-IN SALE.

shop. 1. A commercial emporium. 2. An establishment where a particular kind of work is carried on, as a paint shop, machine shop, or a carpenter shop. 3. In labor relations, an individual factory or an entire enterprise. See (29).

shopping center. See SHOPPING MALL.

shopping mall. A community of retail stores and related establishments, frequently found on the outskirts of cities, where spacious automobile parking space is provided adjacent to the mall. In an attempt to meet this suburban competition city merchants have developed similar shopping malls in downtown districts by prohibiting vehicular traffic on certain city blocks, by providing more sidewalk area, often attractively landscaped, and by eliminating the hazards of street crossing, thus adding to the comfort and safety of shoppers. Merchants in a shopping mall often engage in joint promotional activities such as advertising the mall, as a convenient and desirable place to shop. Also called *shopping center.*

short interest. At any given time, the difference between the number of shares of stock which short sellers have borrowed and sold and the number they must purchase to replace shares borrowed and sold.

Shreveport case. A case, *Houston East and West Texas Ry. Co.* v. *United States,* 234 U. S. 342 (1914), in which the Supreme Court decided that in order to overcome injurious discrimination to interstate commerce resulting, in certain special situations, from the relation of interstate and intrastate railway rates, Congress, acting through an appropriate authority like the Interstate Commerce Commission, could order the discrimination removed. Such an order could issue even if it should result in the federal government fixing rates on commerce between points which are wholly intrastate.

sight bill. See BILL.

sight draft. See DRAFT.

silent partner. A person participating in a PARTNERSHIP business enterprise who supplies capital but assumes no active responsibility in the management.

silver certificate. A form of United States paper money redeemable in silver. Silver certificates were first issued in 1878, but have been recalled from circulation and replaced by FEDERAL RESERVE NOTES. See CERTIFICATE.

Silver Purchase Act. An act of Congress, 1934, which authorized the Treasury to purchase silver bullion under certain conditions and up to specified amounts, and to issue SILVER CERTIFICATES for the silver thus purchased. The silver bullion was to be added to the monetary reserves until the value of the silver reserve was at least one-third that of gold. The price paid for the silver was above market price.

simple interest. Interest calculated on a principal sum but not on any interest that has been earned by that principal sum. See INTEREST.

sinecure. A position, with perquisites or/and income, which involves limited or no responsibility and requires little, if any, labor or active service.

single entry. A general term for all methods of keeping accounts other than double-entry BOOKKEEPING. The term is usually used to indicate a method of bookkeeping containing only cash and personal accounts. See DOUBLE ENTRY.

single-schedule tariff. A tariff that specifies only one rate of duty for any given article regardless of the country of origin of that article. There may be exceptions as, for example, when special rates are established in a reciprocity agreement, but such special rates do not constitute a second or supplementary schedule. Also called *general tariff* and *unilinear tariff.* See TARIFF.

single standard. See MONOMETALLISM.

single tax. Any tax which constitutes a government's sole source of tax revenue. There have been various proposals for supporting a government on a single tax, such as a tax levied on expenses, on houses, on income, or on capital. The term has come to be applied particularly to Henry George's ideas of a LAND VALUE TAX *(q.v.)* as the sole source of public revenue. See TAX.

sinking fund. A fund to which contributions are made periodically for the purpose of ultimately paying a debt or replacing assets of some kind. See FUND.

sinking-fund bond. See BOND.

sit-down strike. A strike in which the employees cease work but do not leave the establishment in which they are employed. See STRIKE.

situs picketing. Picketing a sub-contractor at a construction site. The courts have held the practice illegal as a secondary boycott under the Taft-Hartley Act. See PICKETING.

sixteen to one. The ratio of the weight of pure metal in the United States silver dollar to the pure metal in the United States gold dollar as fixed by Congress in 1834, this action modifying an earlier ratio of fifteen to one. In 1834 the pure-metal content of the silver dollar was established at 371.25 grains, and that of the gold dollar at 23.2 grains. In the presidential campaign of 1896 this phrase became the slogan of the Democratic party and its candidate, William Jennings Bryan, in their effort to remonetize silver at the 1834 ratio to gold and re-establish BIMETALLISM. See REMONETIZATION.

skewness. The extent to which a FREQUENCY DISTRIBUTION *(q.v.)* is asymmetric. It may be measured by subtracting the MODE *(q.v.)* from the ARITHMETIC MEAN *(q.v.)* and dividing the result by the STANDARD DEVIATION *(q.v.)* or by the following formula:

$$sk = \frac{q_2 - q_1}{q_2 + q_1}$$

when

q_2 = the difference between the third QUARTILE *(q.v.)* and the MEDIAN *(q.v.)*,

q_1 = the difference between the median and the first quartile.

sliding-scale tariff. A system of tariff duties in which the duties vary with the current prices of the articles imported. The duties may be AD VALOREM or SPECIFIC. The usual practice is to reduce the duties as prices rise, and advance the duties as prices decline. See TARIFF.

slow asset. An asset which can be converted into cash at approximately its book value only after a considerable length of time. See ASSET.

slowdown strike. 1. A deliberate and purposeful reduction of production by employees. **2.** A literal interpretation of work rules having the effect of greatly reducing production output. See STRIKE.

slum clearance. The razing of old buildings, usually tenements, in congested slum areas, and the construction in their stead of modern low-priced housing for low- and middle-income families and of various commercial structures and public works, thereby rehabilitating the entire area. Such operations by private corporations or by specially organized authorities are frequently encouraged by a promise of tax exemption, tax reduction, or other incentives.

small business. As defined by the U. S. SMALL BUSINESS ADMINISTRATION: wholesalers with annual sales of not more than $10 to $15 million; retailers with annual sales of not more than $5 million; manufacturers with from 250 to 1,000 employees. These limits often depend upon the nature of the business.

Small Business Administration. An independent federal agency, created by the Small Business Act of 1953, to aid small business concerns, especially proprietorships and small corporations, by providing financial, technical, and managerial assistance; by assuring small business enterprises a proportionate share of government purchases and contracts; and by making loans to small businesses seriously damaged by natural disasters.

small business investment company. A closed-end, non-diversified investment company, licensed under the Small Business Investment Act of 1958, which provides long-term loans to small businesses, purchases the equity securities of such concerns, and makes available to them consulting and managerial services. See COMPANY.

small-loan law. Laws enacted in many of the states of the United States limiting the interest rate usually to 3 or 3½ per cent per month on loans of less than $300 made by finance companies and banks.

Smith-Hughes Act. An act of Congress, 1917, which authorized the first sizable federal appropriations for grants to the states in support of vocational education. Vocational programs have been expanded and appropriations increased through the *George Reed Act,* the *George-Ellzey Act,* the *George-Deen Act,* the *Vocational Education Act of 1946,* and subsequent legislation.

Smith-Lever Act. An act of Congress, 1914, which granted federal funds to the states for agricultural extension work carried on jointly by the U. S. Department of Agriculture and the state agricultural colleges and land grant universities.

smuggling. Clandestine importation into a country of dutiable articles without passing them through the customhouse or submitting them to the revenue officers for examination and the payment of duties.

Smyth v. Ames. One of the first cases, 169 U. S. 466 (1898), in which the question of the power of a state legislature (Nebraska) to fix the maximum rates of transportation companies came before the Supreme Court under the due process clause of the 14th Amendment, and in which that tribunal annulled such maximum rates because they were deemed to be unreasonably low and therefore to constitute a deprivation of property. The Court, however, implied that a state legislature, and public-service bodies operating under its authority, might fix rates and that the courts would interpose no objection if they found the rates to be reasonable. The Court also laid down certain standards for the evaluation of the property of a public utility which public rate-making bodies might consider in seeking to establish reasonable rates and insure a fair return. The degree of judicial control over the fact-finding activity and over the general discretion of public rate-making bodies, evinced in this decision, has since been considerably modified.

Social and Rehabilitation Service. A unit of the Department of Health, Education, and Welfare which finances in whole or in part and otherwise assists local governments and community agencies with medical, social welfare, and rehabilitation programs in aid especially of needy families, children, and the aged.

social costs. Costs of production or distribution in an economy, such as the impairment of health of workers, the pollution of the environment, and the depletion or nonrenewal of natural resources, for which private entrepreneurs normally bear no responsibility, the costs being borne by society as a whole. See COST.

social credit. An economic doctrine which claims that there exists a constant deficiency of purchasing power in the prevailing capitalistic type of economic system, compensation for which must be provided by credit created by the government. The doctrine was advanced by Major C. H. Douglas, (1879–1952), an English engineer and social economist. Shortly after World War II the system was investigated by a committee of eminent economists representing the British Labor party and was rejected as fallacious.

social insurance. A term embracing various kinds of insurance, usually offered by the government and designed to protect wage earners and those in lower income brackets against various hazards. Unemployment, accident, health, and maternity insurance and old-age pensions are examples. Also called *national insurance.* See INSURANCE.

socialism. A collective system of ownership and operation of the means of production, usually by the government. By "means of production" is meant CAPITAL GOODS *(q.v.).* During the course of the 19th century the terms "socialism" and "COMMUNISM" *(q.v.)* reversed their meanings. Socialism at one time referred to the ideas of certain social reformers who were called Christian Socialists and utopian socialists, some of whom established colonies in America based on the principles they taught. On the other hand, Karl Marx, generally regarded as the architect of modern socialism, at first referred to his program as communism. As the experiments of the above-mentioned social reformers gradually fell into disrepute, Marx and his followers began referring to their program as socialism, and it is by that term that their own program is known today, although regimes such as Soviet Russia regard Marx, as supplemented and interpreted by V. I. Lenin, as their principal theoretician and they profess to be moving from what they identify as a transitory period of socialism to full communism. In popular speech, socialism and communism are frequently confused and each has various meanings. See (11).

Social Security Act. An act of Congress, 1935, which, with subsequent amendments, provides insurance to certain wage earners for loss of income due to unemployment or old age, and protection for their families in the event of death. OLD-AGE AND SURVIVORS' DISABILITY INSURANCE is administered by the federal government. UNEMPLOYMENT INSURANCE is administered under a joint federal and state plan. In addition, the original act provided joint federal and state aid to needy old people, dependent children, and blind persons, a program which has since been expanded. Federal grants to the states, supplementing state and local funds, are also provided for maternal and child-health aid, and for crippled children and child-welfare services.

Social Security Administration. A division of the U. S. Department of Health, Education, and Welfare whose various bureaus administer the federal retirement (old-age), disability, and survivors' insurance legislation, medicare or medical insurance, and legislation chartering and stipulating management standards and objectives for federal credit unions.

social security cases. Two cases, *Helvering* v. *Davis,* 301 U.S. 619 (1937) and *Steward Machine Co.* v. *Davis,* 301 U. S. 548 (1937), in which the Supreme Court held constitutional the taxes levied under the SOCIAL SECURITY ACT of 1935 *(q.v.).* The taxes were levied for the maintenance of an extensive system of social insurance for wage earners in the administration of which both the federal and state governments participated. The Court declared that such taxes were levied for the general welfare and that the program they financed did not result in coercing the states in violation of the 10th Amendment to the Constitution.

social security tax. A tax levied usually upon employers and/or employees, directly or indirectly, to finance public insurance plans, such as the OLD-AGE (RETIREMENT) AND DISABILITY INSURANCE system, MEDICARE, and the UNEMPLOYMENT INSURANCE system in the United States. See TAX.

social wealth. All useful things, material and immaterial, free and scarce, enjoyed by a people. The term is broad enough to include such things as the inventive genius of a people, knowledge acquired from the past, climate, and beautiful scenery. Some authorities, however, give this phrase the same narrow economic significance as they give the word wealth, and use these two terms interchangeably. Others make social wealth synonymous with NATIONAL WEALTH. See WEALTH.

social workshop. Historically, an association of workers in the same trade who cooperatively pool their tools and skills and share their earnings in common. Each such workshop was envisaged as a unit. The various units would, it was believed, center about some main establishment, and these main establishments, scattered throughout a nation, would reinforce one another by giving mutual aid and assistance. It was anticipated that an economy, devoid of the evils of COMPETITION would thus develop. The idea was espoused by Louis Blanc (1811-82), a French economist and historian, especially during the revolutionary period, 1848-50. Although not so comprehensive a scheme as others, notably the PHALANSTERY or some aspects of OWENISM, the idea gave impetus to the later establishment of numerous cooperative productive societies. See also UTOPIAN SOCIALISM.

soft loan. A loan providing liberal terms for repayment and sometimes a low interest rate. See LOAN.

soft money. 1. Paper money in contrast to metallic currency. **2.** Any national money which is subject to unusual fluctuations in value, both internally and in international exchange. See MONEY.

soil bank program. A program whereby farmers in the United States contracted with the government to divert certain lands from the production of unneeded crops to conservation uses for a period of years. Participating farmers receive advice in the particular conservation practices to be pursued and an annual rent for the unused croplands. The program is administered by the Agricultural Stabilization and Conservation Service of the Department of Agriculture.

soil conservation. Any one or all of various methods of preventing soil depletion and of restoring soil productivity. Soil conservationists attempt to replace chemical elements in the soil, lost through cropping or leaching, by the application of chemical or organic fertilizers. They try to correct the breakdown of soil structure by proper methods of tillage and crop rotation, and to lessen erosion of topsoil by terracing, contour cultivation, and other methods.

soil-conservation district. A local public agency established under state law in the United States when a majority of the land users in a given area so decide by vote. It is governed by a board of supervisors usually composed of farmers locally elected. The United States government, through its SOIL CONSERVATION SERVICE and appropriate state agencies, cooperates with the soil-conservation districts to provide technical help in surveying soil-conservation problems and in devising methods for the better use of the land.

Soil Conservation Service. A unit of the U. S. Department of Agriculture, primarily concerned with the department's soil-conservation program. It seeks to secure such physical adjustments in the use of land as will promote a better balanced agriculture, to conserve natural resources, and to reduce the hazards of flood.

soil erosion. The carrying away of the topsoil through the action of either water or wind.

sole corporation. A corporation which is composed of only one member. See CORPORATION.

solidarism. A doctrine of mutual dependence. Those who have prospered owe a debt to others who have contributed toward making their prosperity possible, according to the doctrine; and those who have been less fortunate consequently have a moral and even economically justifiable claim upon the more fortunate. Hence, gratuitous insurance against the risks of life, a minimum level of living, free education, minimum-wage-and-hour legislation, public housing, etc., are supported as measures expressing this sense of social solidarity and social equity. To finance these activities, progressive taxation applied to unearned wealth and larger incomes is advocated. The doctrine is a French version of socioethical economics popular at the end of the 19th century. Its chief proponent was Léon Bourgeois (1851-1925), a French statesman and social philosopher.

solvency. The condition which exists when liabilities, other than those representing ownership, amount to less than the total assets. In the statement given below, for example, the liabilities representing ownership amount to $1,200,000. Other liabilities amount to $800,000, while the total assets amount to $2,000,000. A solvent condition therefore exists.

Assets		Liabilities	
Plant	$1,500,000	Bonds	$ 800,000
Cash	500,000	Capital stock	1,200,000
	$2,000,000		$2,000,000

South Carolina v. United States. A case, 199 U. S. 437 (1905), in which the Supreme Court declared that state-owned liquor stores might be taxed by the federal government since the rule exempting state instrumentalities from federal taxation involved only such instrumentalities as were strictly governmental in character and did not embrace proprietary activities.

Southeastern Power Administration. A unit of the U. S. Department of the Interior which disposes of surplus electric power generated at reservoir projects and other sites under federal control in ten Southeastern states, by sales to private companies, public bodies, and cooperatives.

South Pacific Commission. An organization created after World War II by Australia, France, New Zealand, the United Kingdom, and the United States to extend economic aid to and advance the social welfare of the peoples of the Pacific Islands area. Newly independent Western Samoa has recently joined. Its headquarters are in Noumea, New Caledonia.

South Sea Bubble. A highly speculative joint-stock venture undertaken in England at the beginning of the 18th century, the chief concern involved having been the South Sea Company. In return for an annual subsidy and a monopoly of the British South Sea trade, this company assumed responsibility for a larger part of the national debt. The venture collapsed with substantial losses.

Southwestern Power Administration. A unit of the U. S. Department of the Interior which disposes of the surplus electric energy generated at federal sites in Oklahoma, Arkansas, and adjacent states by selling it to private companies, cooperatives, and public bodies at prices favorable to the consumer. The Administration is authorized to provide transmission facilities for electric power when necessary, and to plan for effective integration of the region's public and private power resources.

space. The unlimited area beyond the earth's atmosphere which is not subject to any national jurisdiction. It has become politically and economically important because of military and communications vehicles which have been launched into it in recent years and because of the landing on the moon by United States' astronauts which presaged the possibility of planetary exploration. In 1967 a treaty was signed by representatives of most of the states of the world which is intended to govern the peaceful exploration of space and which prohibits the launching of vehicles carrying weapons of mass destruction.

span of control. In organization theory, the number of subordinates who receive direction or supervision from a common leader or superior. The subordinates may in turn be leaders of subgroups with their respective spans of control.

spearhead money. See OCCUPATION MONEY.

special assessment. As applied to public finance, a charge made by a government against a landowner for a public improvement adjacent to his property which, while generally beneficial to the community, is especially beneficial to the landowner assessed. It differs from a tax in that there is a direct relationship between the value of the benefit received and the amount of the ASSESSMENT.

special-assessment bond. See BOND.

Special Drawing Rights. A new reserve asset to be used in international exchange transactions as a supplement or substitute for gold or reserve currencies (dollar and pound), hence, sometimes called *paper gold.* Creation of the S.D.R.'s was recommended by a group of nine leading financial countries, the GROUP OF TEN *(q.v.)* without France, at the Stockholm Monetary Conference, March 30, 1968. Member countries of the International Monetary Fund agreed to accept the new reserve asset during the IMF meeting in Washington on October 3, 1969, and authorized distribution of $9.5 billion of the new S.D.R.'s as reserves among member IMF countries. Each participating country has agreed to regard the new asset as exchangeable for gold or reserve currencies in settling its international account.

special indorsement. An indorsement that specifies to whose order a check, note, or similar paper is payable or to whom the paper is assigned, and which requires the additional indorsement of the indorsee before payment can be made or the paper can be assigned to another. The term is used in contradistinction to BLANK INDORSEMENT. See INDORSEMENT.

specialist. As applied to stock trading, a broker or trader on the floor of an exchange who confines his operations to certain securities and maintains a degree of price equilibrium in the market for them through orderly buying and selling for others and purchase and sale on his own account.

specialization of labor. The condition which exists when certain craftsmen confine their work to the production of a specific commodity. Thus, certain craftsmen may make shoes, others may make hats, etc.

specialized agency. As applied to the UNITED NATIONS, an international organization operating within a particular social and economic field, either newly created by the ECONOMIC AND SOCIAL COUNCIL, or already established and brought under the council's jurisdiction and cooperating with it for the accomplishment of its general objectives.

specialized capital good. A capital good which can be used for only one purpose or for a very limited number of purposes. The term is used in contradistinction to FREE CAPITAL GOOD. See GOOD.

special-privilege monopoly. 1. A monopoly resulting from legislative enactments or special favors granted by private companies. Thus, a tariff sufficiently high to prohibit the importation of a commodity might conceivably give a domestic producer complete control of the domestic supply of the commodity in question. The practice, once common among railroads, of granting rebates to certain shippers often enabled those so favored to drive competitors out of business. See MONOPOLY. **2.** Historically, a special grant of the sovereign to a company or group of private individuals giving them an exclusive trading or other valuable franchise.

special stock. See CAPITAL STOCK.

specie. **1.** Metallic money. **2.** Bullion.

Specie Circular. An order by President Jackson in 1836 directing that payments for public lands be made in SPECIE, that is, in gold or silver coins.

specific duty. A customs duty based on weight, quantity, or other physical characteristics of imported goods. The term is used in contradistinction to AD VALOREM DUTY. See CUSTOMS DUTY.

specific performance. Originally, an equity writ which required the performance of a contractual obligation in exact accord with the contract's terms.

speculation. The practice of buying at one time and selling at another time to take advantage of price changes that have occurred during the interval.

speed-up. Any means used to secure more work from employees per hour or day. This may be attempted by raising the minimum standards of work performance, or, if the operations are controlled wholly by machinery, by increasing the speed of the machines.

spending unit. A statistical term normally used to identify a family or other collective group that pools resources and income and spends as a single unit. The term may, however, also embrace individuals.

spill-over. See SPIN-OFF.

spin-off. **1.** Technology developed in the defense and space programs that is usable in the civilian economy, also called *spillover*. **2.** Distribution of the capital stock of a subsidiary corporation to the stockholders of the parent company. **3.** A BY-PRODUCT.

split investment company. A CLOSED-END INVESTMENT COMPANY *(q.v.)* that issues two classes of capital stock: the first, called income shares, receives dividends derived from income generated by its investments; the second, called capital shares, receives dividends resulting from the appreciation of investments.

411

Also called *dual purpose (*or *leverage) fund.* See INVESTMENT COMPANY.

split-up. The issuance of two or more shares of stock for each share outstanding. This increase in the number of shares outstanding decreases the value per share but does not change the total liability of the issuing corporation for the outstanding capital stock.

spot delivery. Immediate delivery.

spread. As applied to security trading, two separate options, a PUT *(q.v.)* specifying a price below the prevailing market, and a CALL *(q.v.)* specifying a price above the prevailing market, both options applying to the same security and expiring on the same date. The investor is thus assured of a sale at a price not less than the put price if the market declines, and a purchase at a price not more than the call price if the market advances—hence, the spread.

stabilization. The prevention of fluctuations in some phase of economic life. Thus, price stabilization means an attempt either by legislation or by voluntary action of producers to keep prices at a constant level. Business stabilization suggests any policy designed to maintain a steady volume of economic activity.

stabilization fund. A profit of about $2 billion which accrued to the Treasury when the United States abandoned the gold standard in 1933. The proceeds were applied toward keeping the international currency exchange rates stable, hence, the name. See FUND.

stable money. Money that maintains a reasonably constant value in terms of the commodities and services which it will purchase. See MONEY.

stamped bond. See BOND.

stamp tax. A tax, payment of which is secured through the purchase by the taxpayers of revenue stamps of various denominations issued by the taxing authorities, the latter requiring that such stamps be affixed to articles or documents before they may be lawfully sold, purchased, or used. See TAX.

standard deviation. A statistical measure of the extent of absolute dispersion, variability, or scatter in a FREQUENCY DISTRIBUTION *(q.v.),* obtained by extracting the square root of the ARITH-

METIC MEAN of the squares of the deviations from the arithmetic mean of the frequency distribution.

The standard deviation, although the most commonly used measure of dispersion, emphasizes extreme values because the deviations are squared.

This computation is known also as the *quadratic mean*, the generalized formula being:

$$M_q = \sqrt{\frac{\Sigma(X)^2}{N}}$$

when

M_q = quadratic mean,
X = the numbers to be averaged,
N = the total number of items to be averaged.

Example:

Class interval	Mid-point	Frequency	Deviation from mean (2.454)	Deviation from mean squared	Multiplied by frequency
−0.5 to 0.4	0	10	−2.454	6.022	60.220
0.5 to 1.4	1	30	−1.454	2.114	63.420
1.5 to 2.4	2	40	−0.454	0.206	8.240
2.5 to 3.4	3	50	0.546	0.298	14.900
3.5 to 4.4	4	25	1.546	2.390	59.750
4.5 to 5.4	5	8	2.546	6.482	51.856
		163			258.386

$$\text{Standard deviation} = \sqrt{\frac{258.386}{163}} = \sqrt{1.585} = 1.26.$$

standard error of estimate. See SCATTER CHART.

standard error of the mean. See SAMPLE.

standardization. As applied to marketing, the identification of a definite grade, quality, or size of a product by a known term or symbol. Certain standards are first determined, then the product thus standardized is inspected and graded according to those standards and is assigned the appropriate term or symbol.

standard metropolitan area. A U. S. Census Bureau concept of a central city with at least 50,000 people and with economically integrated suburban areas, usually the rest of the county in which the city is located and, possibly, contiguous territories.

standard money. Money consisting of a commodity of specified weight and purity, the value of which, as a commodity, equals its value as money. It should be noted, however, that in legal nomenclature the United States silver dollar is referred to as standard money although its value may be more or less than its face value. As defined elsewhere in this dictionary, the silver dollar is FIDUCIARY MONEY. There has been no standard money, as here defined, in circulation in the United States since 1933. Prior to that time, standard money was in circulation in the form of gold coins. The government accepted gold bullion in unlimited quantities at the rate determined by law which was then $20.67 per ounce of fine gold. Gold could not be bought for less than that price and could always be secured as bullion from the mint at that amount. Hence, it could not be sold for more and its price was stable. The face value of gold coins, therefore, always equaled their value as a commodity. Also called *primary money.* See MONEY.

standard of living. The minimum of the necessities or luxuries of life to which a person or a group may be accustomed or to which they aspire—essentially a relative concept which is measured by a country's gross national product and per capita income.

Standard Oil case. The first of two cases (decided simultaneously,) *Standard Oil Co.* v. *United States,* 221 U. S. 1 (1911) and *United States* v. *American Tobacco Co,* 221 U. S. 106 (1911), in which the Supreme Court formulated the famous RULE OF REASON *(q.v.)* in interpreting the provisions of the SHERMAN ANTITRUST ACT. The Court declared that the act did not intend that every combination in interstate commerce should be considered ipso facto invalid; on the contrary, rational criteria should be used in identifying the combinations which the act intended to prohibit. Unless such an interpretation were used, said the Court, the act would be so absolute as to be unworkable. The actual combinations involved in the American Tobacco and Standard Oil cases were mergers of competing companies effected through stock purchase. These the Court ordered dissolved.

Standard Oil Co. v. United States. See STANDARD OIL CASE.

standby controls. Government credit, commodity, or other economic controls that are legally authorized but are held in abeyance by administrative authorities pending conditions that may require their invocation. See CONTROL.

state bank. A banking institution chartered, or carrying on business, under the laws of one of the states of the United States. A state bank may be a COMMERCIAL BANK, a PRIVATE BANK, or a SAVINGS BANK. See BANK.

state bond. See BOND.

state capitalism. A somewhat ambiguous term usually indicating some degree of state ownership and control of CAPITAL. As thus used, it is often made synonymous with SOCIALISM or STATE SOCIALISM. See ECONOMIC SYSTEM.

state socialism. A term loosely used to denote the nationalization of key industries or government regulation of industry to curb monopolistic tendencies and to stabilize economic life. Sometimes it is used to describe social-welfare legislation or other paternalistic measures, and it may even be used to describe a policy of PROGRESSIVE TAXATION to reduce high incomes. See SOCIALISM.

state tax immunity case. A case, *Graves* v. *New York* ex rel. *O'Keefe,* 306 U. S. 466 (1939), in which the Supreme Court reversed the old rule that salaries of federal employees were immune from state taxation and sustained the application of the New York income tax law, and hence of any state income tax, to the salary of an employee of an administrative instrumentality of the United States government—in this instance, of the Home Owners Loan Corporation.

state use system. The use of convict labor for the production of commodities not for public sale but exclusively for the use of the institutions of the state and its subdivisions. See also CONTRACT SYSTEM, CONVICT LEASE SYSTEM, PUBLIC WORKS AND WAYS SYSTEM.

static economics. See GENERAL EQUILIBRIUM.

statism. Any trend toward government control of economic life, especially any situation where government, through public economic planning and the nationalization of key industries, acquires a predominant influence in shaping and directing the economic life of a nation. See ECONOMIC SYSTEMS.

statute of limitations. A law which bars action to recover a debt or enforce a judgment after the expiration of a specific interval of time.

stay law. A legislative act prescribing a delay in the execution of legal remedies; in case of nonfulfillment of contractual obligations, for example, a mortgage moratorium or a postponement of the execution of judgments.

sterilized gold. Gold placed by the United States government in an inactive fund where it is not used for credit expansion. When buying new gold, instead of paying for it from its deposit account in a federal reserve bank and crediting that bank's gold certificate account, thus increasing reserves for possible credit expansion, the Treasury may make payment by issuing a check on a commercial federal depositary bank. No additional gold reserves are then created and the gold is said to be sterilized.

sterling. A popular term for British currency or for documents, such as bills of exchange, which are drawn in terms of British currency.

sterling area. An aggregation of countries, most of them having had a former political connection with the United Kingdom or still having membership in the Commonwealth, who carry on a sizable volume of trade with the United Kingdom, are heavily dependent on the British capital market, and maintain reserves in London in sterling to settle their international balances and sometimes as backing for their respective domestic currencies. This aggregation of countries came into being in 1931 when the United Kingdom abandoned the gold standard, and until World War II it was usually identified as the *sterling bloc.* Membership has varied, and though the group has somewhat less coherence at present than when first formed, that the sterling area is still of consequence became apparent at the end of 1967 when, following the United Kingdom devaluation of the pound sterling to $2.40, some twenty-two other countries immediately followed suit with a proportionate devaluation of their currencies. Still other countries devalued their currencies later in sympathy with the direction taken by the pound sterling.

sterling bloc. See STERLING AREA.

steward. As applied to labor relations, an employee elected by his fellow employees within an establishment or department to represent them in negotiations with the employer.

Steward Machine Co. v. Davis. See SOCIAL SECURITY CASES.

stipend. See SALARY.

stock certificate. See CAPITAL STOCK.

stock clearing agency. An organization, such as the Stock Clearing Corporation of the New York Stock Exchange, which periodically balances and clears accounts among trading members of the exchange, settles their debit cash balances, and assists them in distributing stocks and other securities which have been bought and sold.

stock dividend. A dividend paid in shares of capital stock. A stock dividend does not change the financial condition of the corporation. The ASSETS remain the same and the LIABILITIES are changed only in that the undivided profits are decreased and capital stock is increased. See DIVIDEND.

stock option. A privilege frequently given to an executive of a corporation to purchase the corporation's stock at a guaranteed price during some future period. Should the market price advance, the possessor of this privilege may buy the stock on which he has such an option at the guaranteed price and sell it at the higher market price, thus realizing capital gains; or alternatively, he may purchase the stock and hold it for possible further appreciation.

stock exchange. 1. A place where buyers and sellers meet to trade in securities. **2.** An organization, usually unincorporated, which provides a place where members trade in securities both on their own account and for the account of others. Also called *security exchange.* See EXCHANGE.

stockholder. A person who holds a share or shares of the capital stock of a corporation.

stockpiles. See STRATEGIC MATERIALS.

stock rights. The privilege accorded stockholders to purchase shares of a new issue of a corporation's stock at a stipulated price, in quantities limited to some proportion of their existing holdings. Such rights are customarily evidenced by a document called a *stock warrant.* If the relation between the market price of the existing stock and the purchase price of the new issue is favorable, the stock rights may have cash value. See also CUM RIGHTS, EX RIGHTS.

stock savings bank. A bank organized under state laws as a profit-making institution, with the customary capital stock and stockholders, and which accepts time deposits for the purpose of saving. Stock savings banks in the United States are located in the Middle West and are relatively small institutions. Many now accept DEMAND DEPOSITS as well as TIME DEPOSITS, and make short-term loans; hence they are hardly distinguishable from COMMERCIAL BANKS. See BANK.

stock transfer tax. A tax levied by some states of the United States upon the transfer of shares of stock from one owner to another by purchase or gift—essentially a tax on the operations of stock exchanges. See TAX.

stock warrant. See STOCK RIGHTS.

Stone* v. *Farmers' Loan and Trust Co. A case, 116 U. S. 307 (1886), in which the Supreme Court suggested that rates charged by a public utility, fixed in a legislative enactment, might not necessarily be final, despite an apparently contrary doctrine developed in the Granger cases and *MUNN* v. *ILLINOIS (q.v.)* since the courts would necessarily be the tribunals of last resort in determining whether or not rates thus fixed, were reasonable. Four years later, in a Minnesota rate case, *Chicago, Milwaukee, and St. Paul Railroad Co.* v. *Minnesota,* 134 U. S. 418 the Supreme Court definitely established the finality of judicial review of legislative rates by declaring that the reasonableness of a rate was a judicial question, and any rate found by the court to be unreasonable would be set aside.

stop-loss order. An order to a stockbroker to sell at a stipulated price on a falling market, or to buy at a stipulated price on a rising market. Stop-loss orders are usually given in cases where a trader has been BUYING ON MARGIN or SELLING SHORT *(qq.v.).*

store credit. Credit extended by means of a charge account covering merchandise bought. Also called *book credit.* Store credit was used extensively to finance the colonial planters along the North Atlantic seaboard during the 17th and 18th centuries. With the development of more formal methods of extending long- and intermediate-term credit, store credit has ceased to occupy its former position of importance, being confined today largely to use in emergencies and in extending short-term consumer credit in retail establishments. See CREDIT.

straddle. As applied to security trading, an option, purchased for a fee, permitting an investor to buy or to sell a specific security at an agreed upon price within a stipulated period of time. A straddle is thus a combination PUT *(q.v.)* and CALL *(q.v.),* but differs from a SPREAD *(q.v.)* in that the put price and the call price are identical. Hence, the investor is assured of a purchase or sale at the agreed upon put and call price whether the market advances or declines.

straight bill of lading. A nonnegotiable bill of lading stating that the goods are consigned to a person specified. See BILL OF LADING.

straight letter of credit. See LETTER OF CREDIT.

straight-life plan of life insurance. A plan according to which a life insurance company agrees to pay a stipulated sum of money upon the death of an insured person in return for an annual premium of a fixed amount during that person's lifetime. See LIFE INSURANCE.

strategic materials. Raw materials or other commodities essential to national defense, of which a particular nation's actual or potential supply falls below needs anticipated for a period of national emergency and which are therefore accumulated or stockpiled before an emergency develops. Under the Strategic and Critical Materials Stockpiling Act of 1946, agencies of the United States government were authorized to determine from time to time which materials are strategic and which are critical, the only difference between these two categories being the magnitude of the supply which it is thought desirable to accumulate. Recommendations were also to be made as to the quantities of such commodities to be accumulated in national *stockpiles.* In recent years these responsibilities have been delegated to appropriate agencies in the General Services Administration.

stratified sample. A limited number of observations selected from an entire aggregate of phenomena by separating the entire aggregate into homogeneous groups and drawing samples from each group at random. For example, suppose that an estimate is desired of the price of grade-A eggs in New York City, and there is known to be a price differential between the chain stores and the independents. The proportion of chain stores to independents in the sample, then, might be made to conform to the proportion obtaining in the whole area. See SAMPLE.

street certificate. A stock certificate evidencing ownership of a specified number of shares of the capital stock of a corporation and containing a BLANK INDORSEMENT by a registered owner whose signature is guaranteed by a broker. A street certificate may be sold and resold in the financial market without formal transfer on the books of the corporation. See CERTIFICATE.

stretch-out. An increase of work without a commensurate increase in wages.

strike. A planned and concerted work stoppage by employees in a plant or industry, in an effort to enforce certain demands having to do with their continued employment. Also called *walkout.* See (29).

strikebreaker. One employed during a labor dispute to replace an employee on strike. The term refers particularly to a person employed only for the duration of the strike. See also SCAB.

structural unemployment. The condition which exists when workers are unemployed because their skills must be combined with some other factor in short supply, or they are unable to move out of a depressed area, or their productivity is too low to justify the lowest legal or acceptable wage, or they cannot find remunerative employment because of age, sex, race, or some other personal characteristic. See UNEMPLOYMENT.

Sturges* v. *Crowninshield. A case, 4 Wheaton 122 (1819), in which the Supreme Court established the rule that, although the Constitution delegates powers over bankruptcy to Congress, the states of the United States may make their own bankruptcy laws and such laws are valid as long as they do not conflict with federal legislation or are not superseded, by federal legislation. Also known as the *bankruptcy case.*

subordinated debenture. A debenture BOND *(q.v.).* When the debenture is issued with the privilege of conversion into stock at a fixed price, this privilege may become profitable to the owner if the market rises above the fixed conversion price.

subscription price. As applied to stock purchases, the fixed price at which new or additional shares issued by a corporation may be purchased. The subscription price may, and usually does, differ from the MARKET PRICE that is ultimately established for the stock in question. See PRICE.

subsidiary coin. In the United States, a coin of a value less than $1. In the Coinage Act of 1965, the government abandoned its traditional alloy of 90 per cent silver and 10 per cent copper for its major subsidiary coins, substituting 10- and 25-cent pieces with an outer layer of 75 per cent copper and 25 per cent nickel, bonded to a copper core, and a 50-cent piece with an outer layer of 80 per cent silver and 20 per cent copper bonded to an inner core of approximately 20 per cent silver and 80 per cent copper. Bronze and copper coins, being made of base metal, are usually called MINOR COINS. See COIN.

subsidiary company. A business enterprise, the operations of which are subject to the control of another corporation. The control is usually established through the ownership of a sufficient quantity of capital stock. See COMPANY.

subsidy. 1. Financial assistance, or its equivalent, given for a service which, though uneconomic from a profit-making standpoint, is considered essential to the public welfare. 2. A grant made by a central government to its political subdivisions for the support of certain public services.

subsistence. A sufficient quantity of the necessities of life to maintain a bare livelihood.

subsistence law of wages. See IRON LAW OF WAGES.

substitution, law of. The principle that when one commodity can be substituted for another, the price of the latter commodity, if it is to continue in use, cannot be much higher than that of the substitute.

subtreasury system. See INDEPENDENT TREASURY SYSTEM.

subvention. Financial support or assistance, particularly a grant or subsidy from a government or a foundation.

Suffolk Bank system. A plan put into effect after the economic crisis of 1837 whereby the Suffolk and seven other banks in Boston, Mass., agreed to accept and pay only the notes of those out-of-town banks that maintained a redemption deposit account with the Suffolk and its sister Boston banks. The plan had the effect of maintaining at par value the entire bank note circulation of the state. See BANKING SYSTEM.

sumptuary law. 1. A law which seeks to prevent consumption of goods believed to be injurious to the health of individuals or to the welfare of society. **2.** A law which limits the purchase of certain goods, particularly of wearing apparel, food, etc., in order to curb extravagance and ostentatious living.

sunk cost. An initial, nonrecurring item in production costs. In manufacturing metal stampings, for example, the cost of the die is a sunk cost. Once it is made, an indefinite number of units can be produced from it. See COST.

Sunshine Anthracite Coal Co. v. Adkins. See BITUMINOUS COAL CASES.

sunspot theory of the business cycle. See ASTRONOMICAL THEORY OF THE BUSINESS CYCLE.

supermarket. A spacious retail store, usually located in one story on the street level, where goods are conspicuously displayed and so arranged that customers may select what they want without clerical service. Purchases are customarily collected in a small pushcart and conveyed to a check-out counter where the cost is computed. Sales are generally for cash, with an extra charge for delivery if such service is provided. Food products and household supplies are commonly sold in supermarkets, although a wide variety of other consumer goods are often offered. Most supermarkets are units of large corporations operating over a wide area.

superseniority. A preferred rank given special groups in the interpretation of seniority privileges. The term is frequently applied to the seniority accorded to veterans.

supplementary cost. See FIXED COST.

supply. The quantity of an economic good available for sale in the market. In its most limited sense the term may mean the quantity of an economic good that will be offered at a given price at a particular time. Thus, if 200 units will be offered for sale at $5 and 100 units at $4, we may say that the supply is 200 at $5 and 100 at $4.

The term also has the broader meaning of the quantity of an economic good that will be offered at all possible prices at a particular time. This is called *schedule supply*.

Price	First-period Supply	Second-period Supply
$5	500	600
4	400	500
3	300	400
2	200	300
1	100	200

In the table below the schedule supply of a good is indicated at various prices, at two different periods.

Note that during the interval between the first and second periods, the schedule supply increased; that is, there was an increased offering of the good at all prices. These two schedule supplies are represented by lines *a-a'* and *b-b'* in the following diagram.

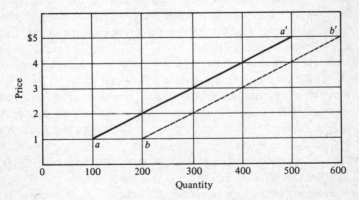

supply and demand, law of. The assertion that price varies directly, but not necessarily proportionately, with demand, and inversely, but not necessarily proportionately, with supply. See also DEMAND, DEMAND AND SUPPLY CURVES, SUPPLY.

surety bond. A contract in which one party guarantees a second that the first party will fulfill an obligation originally assumed by a third party, if the latter fails to fulfill it.

surplus. 1. That which remains after immediate needs have been fulfilled. **2.** In business corporations, surplus is the amount of stockholders' equity in excess of the stated value of the capital stock, usually designated as EARNED, PAID-IN, or CAPITAL SURPLUS, depending upon its source. See (1).

surplus labor and value theory. A theory, developed by Karl Marx and other socialist writers, which assumes that the value of a commodity is determined solely by the amount of human labor necessary to produce it, no consideration being given to the capital cost of the equipment the worker uses. From this premise it is argued that although the worker is entitled to all the value he produces, he receives only that portion necessary for his upkeep, the remainder passing to the capitalist as profit or surplus value. In addition to ignoring capital and managerial cost, the theory assumes that the labor expended on the commodities necessary for the worker's upkeep is less than the labor expended on the commodities he creates. Also called *theory of surplus value.* See also LABOR, VALUE.

surplus value, theory of. See SURPLUS LABOR AND VALUE THEORY.

surtax. An additional tax on the same tax base after one tax has been applied or, as in the case of the 1968 United States federal income surtax, an additional tax calculated as a percentage of a tax already levied.

survivorship annuity. 1. An annuity paid to a beneficiary after the death of the person providing for such annuity. **2.** An annuity which continues in whole or in part to a surviving beneficiary after the death of the annuitant in the case of the federal OLD-AGE (RETIREMENT), SURVIVORS', AND DISABILITY INSURANCE system. See ANNUITY.

survivors' insurance. See OLD-AGE (RETIREMENT), SURVIVORS', AND DISABILITY INSURANCE.

suspense account. 1. A bookkeeping account containing a balance which is of doubtful value and hence is placed in suspense before finally being charged to the profit-and-loss account. **2.** An account containing items which temporarily have not been allocated to a regular account. See ACCOUNT.

swap credits. Standby credits set up on a reciprocal basis from time to time among major CENTRAL BANKS and the BANK FOR INTERNATIONAL SETTLEMENTS which enable the central bank of a country which is party to this arrangement to settle a debit balance in its international account with another participating country by using the latter country's currency instead of having to resort to gold or foreign exchange. Such swap credits are used especially in periods of emergency when a particular country's currency, for example the U.S. dollar, comes under heavy pressure because speculators are selling it on the world markets. See CREDIT.

sweating. Employing labor, usually on a piecework basis, at low wages and long hours, and perhaps under unhealthful conditions.

sweetheart contract. A labor agreement, the terms of which are likely to be influenced by criminal elements, which benefits management and the leaders of a union but confers little, if any, benefit upon employees and, indeed, is often detrimental to their welfare. See CONTRACT.

symmetallism. **1.** An amalgam of precious metals in coins. **2.** A monetary system in which paper money is backed by gold and silver bullion and is redeemable in specified proportions of each. See MONETARY SYSTEM.

sympathetic strike. A strike by workers who have no grievance against their own employer, but who stop work in order to aid other workers, presumably members of some allied union. Also called *secondary strike.* See STRIKE.

syndicalism. An economic system that would place the ownership and control of the means of production in the hands of the workers. Each industry would be organized as an autonomous unit managed by the workers, and these autonomous units would be combined in a federation for the promulgation of measures in the common interest of the workers and of the public. Coercive government would hold no important place in a syndicalist regime and, theoretically, might disappear altogether. Ideas of this nature were given a vogue in France during the late nineteenth century by Georges Sorel and Hubert Lagardelle, and in the United States during the early twentieth century by the Industrial Workers of the World (IWW), a labor organization. See ECONOMIC SYSTEM.

syndicate. 1. A group of individuals, business organizations, or banks associated together for the purpose of carrying out an undertaking requiring a large amount of capital. See COMBINATION. **2.** A labor union, especially in Southern European countries.

systems research. An analysis of the routine operations of an enterprise which seeks to improve procedures, increase efficiency, and hence reduce costs—often a prelude to the installation of an automatic data processing system.

T

Tableau économique. A graphic representation of what was believed to be the flow of wealth in an economy, published in 1758 by François Quesnay (1694-1774), a French physician. The *Tableau économique* envisaged three classes in the economy: (*a*) a productive class consisting principally of agriculturalists; (*b*) a proprietary class made up of property owners and government officials; and (*c*) a sterile class consisting of merchants, manufacturers, and servants. All wealth was thought to be created by the productive class; some was retained for its maintenance, and the rest circulated in the economy, only to return to that class eventually. In his presentation Quesnay used the figure of 5 milliard (billion) francs as the value of wealth created by the productive class within a specified period of time. Of this, 2 milliard francs were retained for maintenance, 1 milliard francs were paid to the sterile class for manufactured goods required in agriculture, and 2 milliard were paid to the proprietary class for taxes and rents. Of the 2 milliard paid to the proprietary class, 1 milliard were spent for food and hence returned to the original source, and 1 milliard were paid to the sterile class for various purchases. This 1 milliard francs received by the sterile class together with the 1 milliard francs originally received from the productive class were both repaid to the productive class for food and raw materials. Thus, of the

427

3 milliard francs originally emanating from the productive class, all were eventually returned to that source.

Although an ingenious conception, and the first attempt at MACROECONOMICS in the field of DISTRIBUTION, the explanation has little relation to the operation of economic life as now interpreted.

tabular standard of value. A plan to introduce greater equity in contractual obligations, according to which such obligations, in terms of money, may be altered according to the purchasing power or real value of money at the time the payment is due. A number of specific commodities are selected, and the sum or average of the prices of these commodities is accepted as a standard. If, at the time the payment is due, this sum or average has advanced or declined, a proportionate additional or lesser amount of money is paid in settlement of the contractual obligation. See VALUE.

Taft-Hartley Act. See LABOR-MANAGEMENT RELATIONS (TAFT-HARTLEY) ACT.

Taft-Hartley injunction case. A case, *United Steelworkers of America* v. *United States,* 361 U.S. 39 (1959), in which the Supreme Court upheld the action of a federal district court in enjoining the nationwide steel strike of 1959. The strike had lasted 116 days and was the longest on record. The Court held that the injunction was an appropriate exercise of judicial power in overcoming a threat to the "national health," authority for its exercise having been conferred upon the courts by Congress in Sections 208-210 of the LABOR-MANAGEMENT RELATIONS (TAFT-HARTLEY) ACT. The injunction was issued following the expiration of the Act's so-called cooling-off period of 80 days and had the effect of compelling some one half million steelworkers to return to their jobs.

take-home-pay. The net amount received by an employee as a periodic wage or salary after various deductions by the employer for taxes, union dues, and benefits.

tangible property. A right or interest in things that have substance, as distinct from property rights in relatively immaterial concepts such as a patent, a claim against a debtor, or the good will of a business. The term may also refer to any property that can be accurately appraised. See PROPERTY.

tare. A deduction from a gross weight for the weight of a container.

tariff. 1. A schedule of fixed rates or charges of a common carrier; for example, a passenger tariff published by a railroad. **2.** A schedule or system of duties authorized by a government and imposed upon commodities exported or imported. See (27).

Tariff Commission. See UNITED STATES TARIFF COMMISSION.

tariff for revenue only. A system of tariff duties which, theoretically, is not intended to protect home industry but only to produce revenue for the government. See TARIFF.

Tariff Information Catalogue. An encyclopedia compiled by the United States Tariff Commission giving information concerning commodities subject to import duties, the volume of commodities imported and exported, costs of production, and the extent of foreign competition.

Tariff of Abominations. The United States Tariff Act of 1828. It represented the most extreme protectionist legislation up to that date, was rather generally criticized, and, because it favored New England trade and manufacturing over Southern agriculture, led to the nullification movement in South Carolina.

tariff union. See CUSTOMS UNION.

tariff war. Competition between two or more countries, carried on by means of tariff discriminations, commercial concessions and demands, and the like.

task. As applied to wage systems, the amount of work that must be done within a given length of time in order to secure the minimum wage assigned to any particular job. The term is usually applied to cases where a bonus of some kind is paid for production beyond a certain prescribed minimum within a given length of time.

tax. A contribution exacted of persons, corporations, and other organizations by the government, according to law, for the government's general support and for the maintenance of public services. Besides its compulsory character another distinguishing characteristic of a tax is the fact that there is no exact correlation between the amount paid and the value of the public services from which the taxpayer benefits. See (35).

tax and loan accounts. See GOVERNMENT DEPOSITARY.

tax-anticipation bond. See BOND.

tax assessment. See ASSESSMENT.

tax avoidance. Exploitation by a taxpayer of legally permissible alternative tax rates or methods of assessing taxable property or income, or of reporting taxable property or income, in order to reduce tax liability. The term may be extended to include situations where a person refrains from engaging in some activity or enjoying some privilege in order to avoid the incidental taxation; for example, failure to import goods because of unwillingness to pay the duty. Sometimes described as *tax dodging.* See also TAX EVASION.

tax base. The unit of value or some privilege or object upon which a tax is actually levied and the tax return is calculated. It may be property owned by the taxpayer, annual net income, the value of the estate of a deceased person, a corporate franchise, an occupation, or the volume, number, quality, or other characteristic of certain specified articles. In the case of the poll tax, the tax base would be the individual taxed.

tax collector. 1. A local government official charged with the responsibility of collecting taxes, particularly those levied on property. **2.** Generally, any official who collects taxes as, in the United States, the Director of Internal Revenue.

tax commission. An administrative agency of a state of the United States whose members are either elected or appointed to supervise local taxation, administer taxes not collected locally, and attend to the EQUALIZATION OF ASSESSMENTS throughout the state.

Tax Court of the United States. A 16-member tribunal, created by the Revenue Act of 1924 and given its present title in 1942, whose most important prerogative is to decide cases or controversies arising under most of the federal tax laws which involve alleged overpayment of taxes or tax deficiencies certified by the Commissioner of Internal Revenue. It may also review denials by the Commissioner of excess-profits-tax refund claims. A few of its decisions are final but many may, under certain circumstances, be reviewed by a federal appellate court and in some cases an appeal may be taken to the Supreme Court.

tax dodging. See TAX AVOIDANCE.

tax evasion. Illegal efforts to avoid payment of a tax: for

example, failure to report taxable income or property. See also
TAX AVOIDANCE.

tax exemption. Freedom from the charge of taxes, a privilege
accorded to properties used by educational or eleemosynary
organizations, to the income of certain nonprofit corporations,
and to certain securities such as federal, state, and municipal
bonds.

tax farming. A practice, common in the ancient Greek cities and
in the early period of the Roman Republic, of delegating to
private individuals or institutions the right to collect public
revenue in return for specified lump-sum payments to the public treasury. As a rule, a profit or commission was derived by
collecting from taxpayers more than was paid to the treasury.

tax lien. A lien held against real property by a government,
usually a political subdivision, for nonpayment of taxes.

tax limit. A constitutional or statutory limitation upon the kind
of tax or the maximum rate of taxation which a tax authority,
usually a political subdivision, may impose. Normally, this is
coupled with provisions for securing additional funds to meet
emergencies.

taxpayer. **1.** Any individual who pays taxes or is liable for taxes.
2. A building the income from which is sufficient to cover real
estate taxes, operating expenses, and amortization charges.

tax rate. The proportion of the appraised monetary value of a
TAX BASE which a government actually collects as a tax. See
RATE.

tax sharing. The practice of having one political jurisdiction levy
and collect a tax and share the proceeds with other political
jurisdictions. In certain states of the United States a general
property tax is sometimes levied and collected by the county or
other local governmental body, part of the proceeds then being
allocated to the central state government and to lesser political
subdivisions according to a formula previously established. Sometimes, as in the case of a sales or other excise tax the central
administration of the state may levy and collect the tax and
then apportion a part of the proceeds to the state's subdivisions. The procedure of having the federal government assess
and collect a tax (normally the income tax), and then share its
proceeds with the states, has been recommended.

Taylorism. A term used to designate scientific management and work efficiency, so called because of the pioneer research in the field done by Frederick W. Taylor early in the twentieth century.

Taylor Law. A New York State law enacted in 1967, also known as the *Civil Service anti-strike law,* which prohibits strikes by unions of public employees and subjects violating unions to maximum fines of $10,000 per day for every day of a strike, or one week's dues from members, whichever is less. The law guarantees the right of collective bargaining and establishes a board to resolve threats of strikes through mediation and other procedures.

teaching machine. A manual, mechanical, or electrical device designed for self-instruction. It presents the student with a sequence of small units or increments of a course of study, one unit at a time; tests the student's comprehension of each unit; and informs him immediately whether or not his response is correct. See also PROGRAM.

technical assistance. As applied to economically underdeveloped regions, technical knowledge and resources provided by gift or loan, usually under a special program of the United Nations or directly by technologically more advanced states, to help those regions equip themselves with the economic infrastructure of a more developed society, including transportation and power facilities, communications, hospitals, scientific and technological centers, educational institutions, and managerial and scientific manpower.

technocracy. A body of doctrine prominent in the depression years of 1932 and 1933. The technocrats—economists, architects, and industrial engineers—claimed that industrial efficiency was being maintained at a high cost by premature obsolescence of machines. They argued that the savings resulting from laborsaving machinery never reached consumers but were absorbed by creditors and investors. This, they said, deprived the mass of people of purchasing power and created a surplus of goods. The goods were wanted and needed, but could not be bought at the prices asked.

technological unemployment. The unemployment that results when machines replace men. If the machines reduce production costs, competition reduces selling prices, reduced selling prices increase demand, and new products and markets are created, re-employment may occur in due course providing new skills to meet the new conditions can be acquired by the workers. To the extent that prices are not reduced and new products and markets are not realized, technological unemployment tends to be prolonged. See UNEMPLOYMENT.

technology. **1.** Industrial science, particularly its application to the replacement of skilled labor by modern machinery. **2.** The application of scientific discovery to production and distribution resulting in the creation of new products, new processes of manufacture, and radical changes in methods of distribution.

teller. A bank employee who receives deposits, issues withdrawals, or collects amounts due on promissory notes and other commercial paper payable to the bank.

temporal distribution. See TIME SERIES.

temporary admission. The practice of admitting goods to a country for eventual export. Under specified conditions no CUSTOMS DUTY is paid on such goods, and hence no DRAWBACK is claimed.

Temporary National Economic Committee. A committee authorized by congressional resolution in 1938 to conduct a comprehensive study of monopoly and the concentration of economic power in the United States. The committee consisted of three senators, three representatives, and appointees from the Departments of Justice, Treasury, Commerce, and Labor, the FEDERAL TRADE COMMISSION, and the SECURITIES AND EXCHANGE COMMISSION. Among the important monographs published by the committee were *Competition and Monopoly in American Industry, The Structure of Industry,* and *Distribution of Ownership in the 200 Largest Nonfinancial Corporations.*

ten-forty bond. A popular name for certain United States bonds issued in 1864. The bonds were redeemable any time after 10 years, were payable at the end of 40 years, and yielded 5 per cent interest. See BOND.

Tennessee Valley Authority. A public corporation chartered by Congress in 1933 to build dams, power structures, and flood-control works along the Tennessee River and tributary streams, to produce hydroelectric power, and to manufacture fertilizer.

The TVA's power output is sold to consumers through cooperatives, local governments, and private power companies. Its activities have greatly aided in promoting rehabilitation throughout the Tennessee Valley, an area of some 41,000 square miles. The work of the authority is financed through the sale of bonds to the investing public, by public appropriations, and by the income from the sale of products and services. Three directors, appointed by the President and Senate, and a general manager, control its operations.

tenure. 1. The term of a position or office which may be guaranteed by law, by contract, or by custom. **2.** The legal or contractual condition determining the way in which property is held.

terminal bond. See BOND.

terminal wage. See DISMISSAL WAGE.

term plan of life insurance. A policy under which a life insurance company agrees to pay a stipulated sum of money upon the death of the insured if his death occurs within the term fixed by the policy—usually 5 or 10 years. In return for the protection, the insured pays an annual premium of a fixed amount during the period for which the insurance is in force. See LIFE INSURANCE.

terms of trade. The conditions under which a nation carries on foreign trade, with reference particularly to the question whether such conditions are favorable or unfavorable. Among the factors which determine the terms of a nation's trade are the nature of its economy and the degree of its dependence on foreign trade; the presence or absence of certain advantages in production, particularly production for export; and the world price level. In an inflationary period, for example, a nation that imports most of its foodstuffs and raw materials for industry is likely to find that the value differential between imported raw commodities and finished goods is less than in a period when prices are declining on world markets. Hence, the terms of trade for such a nation are likely to be more favorable when the world price level is declining than when it is rising.

territorial bond. See BOND.

Texas and New Orleans R.R. Co. v. Brotherhood of Railway and Steamship Clerks. A case, 281 U.S. 548 (1930), in which the Supreme Court sustained an act of Congress, passed in 1926, protecting the rights of railway employees to organize and select collective-bargaining representatives without employer interference. The Court virtually overruled earlier decisions like that in *COPPAGE* v. *KANSAS* and *ADAIR* v. *UNITED STATES* (*qq.v.*) by declaring the employees' rights of collective bargaining to be beyond question, and by further stating that such rights would become a "mockery" if employers were permitted to interfere with employees' freedom in choosing their bargaining representatives.

theory. A statement setting forth an apparent relationship among observed facts, the relationship having been repeatedly verified by independent investigators. See also INDUCTIVE METHOD.

thin market. See NARROW MARKET.

through bill of lading. A bill of lading used for shipments which are handled by more than one carrier before they reach their destination. It relieves the shipper of the necessity of accepting and reshipping the goods at connecting points. See BILL OF LADING.

tidelands oil cases. See OFFSHORE OIL CASES.

tied loan. A term sometimes applied to a foreign loan which has been made on the condition that the borrower will purchase in the lending country such materials as are required to carry out the purpose of the loan. In practice, such a condition is more likely to be stipulated in a governmental than in a private loan. See LOAN.

tie-in sale. A sale made with the stipulation that some article other than the one purchased must also be purchased. See also TYING CONTRACT.

till money. A relatively small reserve of money kept in the vaults of banks for the purpose of paying out such cash as is demanded. See MONEY.

time and motion study. In industrial relations, a measurement of the amount of time an employee requires to perform some task or part of a task and an analysis of his attendant physical movements, to determine ways in which the employee can make his actions more efficient and productive or to rate his performance.

time bill. See BILL.

time deposit. A bank deposit subject to withdrawal only after a certain number of days' notice. See BANK DEPOSIT.

time draft. See DRAFT.

time loan. A loan made for a definite period of time. The term is used in contradistinction to CALL LOAN. See LOAN.

time reversal test. A method of determining the mathematical validity of an INDEX NUMBER (*q.v.*). The calculated index numbers of two periods (period A and period B) are considered. Period A is first considered the base period (index 100) and an index number for period B is calculated accordingly. Period B is then considered the base period and an index number is calculated for period A. If the product of the ratio of the index number for period B to the index number for period A and the ratio of the index number for period A to the index number for period B is unity, there is no inherent bias in the method used for computing the prices on which the index numbers are based.

Period	Price	Index Number	Period		Price	Index Number
A	$21.00	100	B	1941	$23.00	100
B	$23.00	109.5238	A	1940	$21.00	91.3044

$$\frac{109.5238}{100} \times \frac{91.3044}{100} \pm .9999$$

See also FACTOR REVERSAL TEST.

time series. Statistical data arranged according to periods of time, usually months or years, sometimes called *temporal distribution*. When displayed in graphic form, the time periods are plotted along the horizontal axis, and whatever other data is considered is plotted along the vertical axis. On page 437 the chart is a time series of hypothetical data, the time intervals being represented by 1 to 5, and 1 to 12. For general tendencies in a time series, see SEASONAL FLUCTUATIONS, SECULAR TREND, CYCLICAL FLUCTUATIONS.

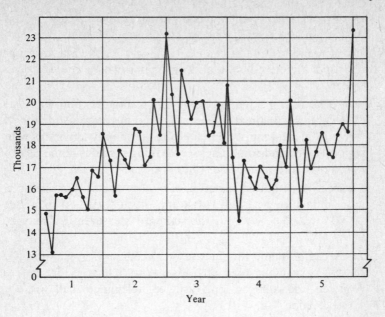

	Year				
	1	2	3	4	5
1	14,983	17,499	20,383	17,597	17,860
2	13,111	15,766	17,620	14,623	15,201
3	15,754	17,866	21,605	17,363	18,211
4	15,745	17,497	20,151	16,597	16,832
5	15,655	16,998	19,292	16,013	17,763
6	15,914	18,880	20,019	17,160	18,676
7	16,657	18,617	20,152	16,677	17,683
8	15,644	17,106	18,409	16,023	17,496
9	15,016	17,586	18,642	16,440	18,526
10	16,962	20,142	19,923	18,096	19,029
11	16,696	18,475	18,160	17,039	18,636
12	18,689	23,238	20,825	21,087	23,385

(Month — left axis label for rows 1–12)

time utility. The accessibility of goods at a time when they are wanted to satisfy human desires. When goods are stored, a time utility may be created. Ice harvested in the winter and distributed in summer is an example. See UTILITY.

timework. A wage system under which an employee is paid a certain amount per hour or per day for a given job.

title. Evidence of conditions establishing a legal claim to property and the instrument or instruments which provide such evidence.

token coin. A coin, the face value of which is less than its value as metal. Thus defined, the term is used in contradistinction to standard-money coins. Sometimes the term is synonymous with MINOR COINS, and sometimes its meaning includes both SUBSIDIARY COINS and minor coins. See COIN.

tolerance. A permitted variation of quality or size. For example, in manufacturing certain INTERCHANGEABLE PARTS a tolerance of .003 in., plus or minus the standard measurement, may be permitted.

toll. A charge made for the use of something, for example, for the use of a public road or bridge. Also, a charge for services rendered, as for a long-distance telephone call or for transportation.

tonnage. 1. As applied to ships, the cubical contents expressed usually in units of 100 cu. ft. Each such unit is called a registered ton, the word "ton" as thus used having no relation to the unit of weight. **2.** A tax on ships, based on their capacity.

total utility. The sum of the utility of all units constituting a supply of goods, such supply being affected by the principle of diminishing utility. Thus, if the diminishing utility of a supply of five units of a good is represented by the figures 5, 4, 3, 2, 1, then the total utility of the supply is 15. The term is sometimes defined, however, as the marginal utility times the number of items constituting the supply. Considered thus, the total utility in the above example would be 5 X 1 (marginal utility) or 5. See UTILITY.

Townsend plan. A proposal known as Old Age Revolving Pensions, originated by Dr. Francis E. Townsend during an economic depression in 1934, which advocated that the United States government grant a pension of $200 a month to every person 60 years of age or over, the entire amount to be spent within a month to insure that the money would "revolve." According to the sponsors of the plan, the money spent by the recipients of the pensions would stimulate a demand for goods and services and thus assure prosperity.

trade acceptance. A time draft drawn by a seller on a buyer and accepted by the buyer, who promises to pay at a specific time and place the amount of an invoice covering a current sale of goods. See ACCEPTANCE.

trade agreement. 1. A contract between a labor union and an employer or employers, setting forth the terms of employment for a stipulated length of time. Also known as a *labor agreement* or labor contract. **2.** A trade or commercial treaty. See also RECIPROCAL TRADE AGREEMENT.

Trade Agreements Act. An act of Congress, 1934, which amended the Hawley-Smoot Tariff Act of 1930 and permitted the President to negotiate trade agreements on a reciprocal basis with foreign countries, with power to reduce duties as much as 50 per cent. The act was amended several times and was extended by the TRADE EXPANSION ACT of 1962 (*q.v.*). See also RECIPROCAL TRADE AGREEMENT.

trade association. An organization of business establishments in one trade or field of work which aims to further the common interests of that particular activity. According to the U.S. Department of Commerce, a trade association is concerned with statistics, cost accounting, research, public relations, trade relations, credit, insurance, employer-employee relations, and traffic and transportation, insofar as these relate to the area of interest of the particular association and of its constituent business establishments.

trade barrier. Any interference with the free exchange of goods and services among different political jurisdictions. CUSTOMS DUTIES and IMPORT QUOTAS are common trade barriers, but international EXCHANGE CONTROL and sanitary and health regulations may be used for the same purpose.

trade bloc. Two or more countries which have adopted a common policy regarding customs duties and trade regulations applicable to other countries, and which apply preferential policies to trade among themselves on a reciprocal basis, such preferential policies not being extended to other countries.

trade deficit. See UNFAVORABLE BALANCE OF TRADE.

trade discount. A deduction from a basic or list price expressed as a percentage. By using a trade discount, manufacturers and jobbers need not constantly reissue catalogues or price lists as market prices change. The published prices thus remain fixed, but the actual selling prices are advanced or reduced by adjusting the amount of trade discount.

trade dollar. A special United States silver coin minted from 1873 to 1885. It contained more silver than the standard silver dollar and was intended to facilitate trade with China and Japan. See MONEY.

Trade Expansion Act. An act of Congress, 1962, expanding the principle of the flexible tariff and authorizing the President to arrange reductions of existing tariffs, and even to establish free trade for certain manufactured commodities, by appropriate international negotiation. During the following five years such negotiation, conducted through GATT, resulted in two major agreements to reduce tariffs and ease restrictions on international trade. See DILLON ROUND, KENNEDY ROUND.

trademark. A mark or symbol used to identify a specific seller or manufacturer. A trademark is usually stamped on, or attached to, a commodity and frequently appears in the advertising and on the letterhead of the individual or concern making or marketing the product. A trademark may be registered with the Patent Office of the United States.

trade monopoly. A special-privilege monopoly created by the government of a country, permitting a private trading company to monopolize commerce between that country and some other area, usually a colony. Such companies were especially active during the 17th and 18th centuries. Probably the most famous was the British East India Company which monopolized trade between England and India and enjoyed governmental powers in India. Similar companies existed in France, Holland, and elsewhere. See MONOPOLY.

trading stamp. A stamp given to customers by retail merchants, usually with each 10 cents' worth of goods purchased, which the customer may redeem for various articles when he has accumulated a sufficient quantity of stamps. The trading stamp is thus a promotional device to attract and hold customers. The retail merchant customarily buys the stamps in bulk from a stamp company which advertises the premiums available and redeems the stamps from collectors.

transactions tax. See SALES TAX.

transfer agent. A person who records changes in the ownership of a corporation's stock as the stock of the corporation is bought and sold. If a corporation does not maintain its own transfer office, it appoints an agent, frequently a bank or a trust company, for the purpose.

transfer payment. As used by the U.S. Department of Commerce in determining national income, a term indicating a payment made by business or government which does not result from current production and for which no services were currently rendered. Examples are a pension, social security payments, relief payments, and veterans' aid payments.

Trans-Missouri Freight Association case. An early antitrust case, *United States* v. *Trans-Missouri Freight Assn.,* 166 U.S. 290 (1897), in which the Supreme Court ruled that a contract between railroads to maintain rates violated the Sherman Antitrust Act. The court interpreted the Sherman Act rather broadly and implied that it proscribed any contract in restraint of interstate trade whether or not the contract might be construed as reasonable.

Transportation Act. 1. An act of Congress, 1920, known also as the ESCH-CUMMINS ACT (*q.v.*). **2.** An act of Congress, 1940. It authorized the Interstate Commerce Commission to assume jurisdiction over coastal and inland waterways in order to achieve a more unified national system of water, rail, and motor transportation.

traveler's check. A check or draft payable at sight, issued principally by banks in various denominations and sold to a traveler who signs the document once when purchasing it, and again, for purposes of identification, in the presence of the person who is asked to cash it. See CHECK.

traveler's letter of credit. See LETTER OF CREDIT.

Treasurer of the United States. See OFFICE OF THE TREASURER OF THE UNITED STATES.

treasury bill. See BILL.

Treasury currency. Paper money, especially United States notes (GREENBACKS), $300 million of which are still technically in circulation, and coins, including silver dollars and subsidiary coins, which are issued by the U.S. Treasury. The nation's principal money, federal reserve notes, is not considered to be treasury currency. See CURRENCY.

treasury note. A short-term obligation of the United States government, usually maturing in from 1 to 5 years. The term also applies to two kinds of United States paper money—GREEN-BACKS and *United States notes* of 1890, (*Sherman notes*). The latter have been called for redemption. See NOTE.

treasury stock. See CAPITAL STOCK.

Trenton Potteries case. A case, *United States* v. *Trenton Potteries Co.*, 273 U.S. 392 (1927), in which the Supreme Court ruled that a specific agreement among producers in a trade association to fix and maintain prices for their commodities however reasonable the prices may be, is a violation of the federal antitrust statutes and therefore void.

trial balance. The sum of all the debit balances in a general ledger compared with the sum of all the credit balances. When the two sums are equal, the ledger is said to be in balance; that is, for every amount debited there is a corresponding amount credited.

triangular trade. A situation in foreign trade in which equilibrium—that is, a balance of exports and imports—is maintained over a period of time by an exchange pattern involving 3 rather than only 2 countries. Where such a pattern exists, Country A may export to Country B which, in turn, may export to Country C. Country C then completes the 3-way pattern, or triangle, by exporting goods to Country A, thereby offsetting, or balancing, the flow of goods from Country A to Country B. A classic example of such a situation is afforded by part of the trade of the American colonies in the 18th century. The colonies exported rum to the West Coast of Africa in exchange for slaves; the slaves were transported to the West Indies in exchange for sugar; in turn, the sugar was taken back to the colonies to be manufactured into more rum for the African trade.

Tripartite Currency Agreement. A declaration issued by France, Great Britain, and the United States in 1936, joined later by Switzerland, the Netherlands, and Belgium, in which cooperation in the stabilization of their respective currencies was pledged. The understanding became inoperative after the occupation of France and other countries by Germany in 1940.

Truax v. Corrigan. A case, 257 U.S. 312 (1921), which involved a statute of the state of Arizona barring the use of injunctions in labor disputes. By a bare majority, the Supreme Court invalidated the Arizona statute on the ground, among others, that the denial of injunctive relief in labor disputes, access to such relief being continued in practically all other situations where principles of equity were applicable, constituted an arbitrary and unreasonable legislative classification and violated the equal protection clause of the 14th Amendment to the United States Constitution.

true interest. See PURE INTEREST.

Truman Plan. See POINT FOUR PROGRAM.

trust. 1. An arrangement, developed under equity jurisprudence whereby property is held by one person for the benefit of another. A trust may be created by a will or by an agreement. There are innumerable kinds of trusts, depending upon their purpose, duration, and terms. **2.** A corollary to the above definition, applied to business organization, is a plan whereby the voting rights of the majority of the voting stock of two or more corporations are assigned to a designated number of trustees who then direct the affairs of the corporations to the mutual advantage of all the stockholders. See also MASSACHUSETTS TRUST. **3.** More recently, the term has been used to designate any large corporation or combination of corporations exercising a monopolistic or semimonopolistic control over the production or distribution of some commodity or service. See COMBINATION.

trust company. A financial organization, usually performing the customary commercial banking functions of accepting deposits and making loans, and in addition having the authority to act as a trustee under the rules of equitable jurisprudence. To exercise that role, it serves as an agent or fiduciary and also as executor or administrator of estates. See BANK, COMPANY.

trustee. 1. The administrator of a public or private TRUST *(q.v.)*. **2.** A member of the governing board of an ELEEMOSYNARY CORPORATION or some similar body who, by law, has the responsibility of an administrator of a trust. **3.** An administrator of an insolvent or bankrupt concern and conservator of its assets, appointed, usually, by a court.

Trusteeship Council. A major organ of the UNITED NATIONS which has responsibility for protecting the peoples of dependent areas, particularly those areas administered as trusteeships or *trust territories* by member states of the United Nations. Membership of the Council includes those states administering such trust territories, the five permanent members of the SECURITY COUNCIL, and a sufficient number of other countries chosen by the General Assembly for three-year terms, to insure that half of the membership at all times consists of states not administering trust territories.

trust fund. A fund administered by a trustee, frequently a bank, which assumes trustee functions. The investment policies pursued by the trustee may be specified by the maker of the trust fund. Where they are not so specified, the investment policies pursued by the trustee are governed by law. See FUND.

Trust Indenture Act. An act of Congress, 1939, which supplements earlier securities legislation. It requires that the investment agency or corporation serving as trustee of the indenture under which debt securities, such as certain bonds and debentures are sold to the investing public must meet various standards to protect that public, among them maintenance of minimum capital resources, avoidance of conflict of interest with the corporation issuing the securities and borrowing the funds, and adequate reports to the investors.

trust receipt. A document acknowledging responsibility for property enumerated therein and held in trust for some designated party. A trust receipt is sometimes executed when a DRAFT attached to an ORDER BILL OF LADING cannot be met by the buyer. The bank through which the draft has been drawn may then issue a trust receipt which is signed by the buyer. The bank retains title to the property; the buyer sells the property and remits the proceeds to the bank. See RECEIPT.

trust territory. See TRUSTEESHIP COUNCIL.

Truth-in-Lending Act. An act of Congress, 1968, requiring that a consumer borrower be informed of the true cost of a loan. Among specific regulations in the act are: (*a*) the interest rate on revolving charge accounts must be disclosed; (*b*) the true annual interest rate on home mortgages must be revealed; (*c*) the actual interest rate must be given in a credit advertisement if the advertisement is in figures; (*d*) the cost of credit life insurance on a loan must be stated; and (*e*) a specific limitation, effective in 1970, is placed on the power to garnishee wages. See also INSTALLMENT INTEREST.

Truth-in-Packaging Act. An act of Congress, 1966, which requires that goods sold in containers in grocery, drug, and other stores be honestly labeled as to quality, content, net weight, and manufacturer; that names in common use be applied to ingredients in non-food items; and that manufacturers avoid "slack-filling" practices.

turnover. A statistical measure of the extent of the diminution and replacement of some entity, such as a labor force, a sum of money, or a stock of goods, over a given period of time. For example, if the average number of employees in a given year is 5,000, and 1,000 of them leave and are replaced during the 12-month period, the labor turnover for that year is 20 per cent.

turnover tax. See SALES TAX.

two-dollar broker. A stockbroker who transacts business only with other brokers. The term originated from the commission once charged, which was $2 for every 100 shares of stock bought or sold. The commissions now depend upon the price of the stock. Two-dollar brokers absorb overflow business from other brokers during busy periods.

two-name paper. One of various types of short-term negotiable instruments in which two persons guarantee payment.

two-tier gold price. An agreement made early in 1968 among central bank members of the GOLD POOL *(q.v.)*, the INTERNATIONAL MONETARY FUND, and the BANK FOR INTERNATIONAL SETTLEMENTS, to suspend the pool's sale of gold on the free market at the United States price of $35 per troy ounce; to confine gold sales at that price to the central banks and international financial institutions; and to restrict non-fiduciary buying and selling of gold to the supply of the precious metal that might become available from mines and other sellers on the free market where prices would seek their own level. The principal purpose of the plan was to insulate the dollar, and other currencies based on the dollar, from the speculative gyrations of the free gold market, and to keep stable the value of the dollar which has become a principal international reserve currency since World War II. After the agreement was adopted, the free market price of gold sometimes exceeded the official price of $35 per ounce by five dollars or more.

tycoon. A popular designation for a very wealthy and influential businessman. Taken from the Japanese *taikun,* meaning "great prince," the term is used sometimes in derision and sometimes in approbation.

tying contract. A contract to sell goods or lease property which contains clauses compelling the buyer or lessee to abstain from using goods of competing sellers or lessors in connection with the goods or property bought or leased. Various statutes, including the CLAYTON ACT, prohibit tying clauses in contracts. See CONTRACT.

Tyson v. Banton. A case, 273 U.S. 418 (1927), in which the Supreme Court invalidated a New York statute attempting to regulate the resale price of theater tickets. The court based its adverse decision on the ground that selling tickets for theatrical exhibitions was not "business affected with a public interest" and hence not subject to regulation under the state's police power.

unconfirmed letter of credit. See LETTER OF CREDIT.

underdeveloped area. A term popularly used to indicate a region which, compared with Western standards, suffers from low levels of living. Ineffective use of natural resources and lack of industrialization are often associated with the concept of underdevelopment, although an area may be underdeveloped in other respects.

underemployment equilibrium. A condition in which the sum of the investment items and consumer expenditures in the GROSS NATIONAL PRODUCT balances with a NATIONAL INCOME insufficient in volume to absorb the entire working force of the nation. Some authorities hold that this is the trend in a highly industrialized economy. The reasons cited are: (*a*) decline in the PROPENSITY TO CONSUME; (*b*) decline in the MARGINAL EFFICIENCY OF CAPITAL; and (*c*) strengthening of LIQUIDITY PREFERENCE because of low interest rates, which, in turn, results in a low PROPENSITY TO INVEST and national income insufficient to absorb the entire working force. See also KEYNESIAN ECONOMICS, KEYNES'S LAW OF CONSUMPTION.

underlying bond. See BOND.

Underwood Tariff. The United States Tariff Act of 1913. It enlarged the FREE LIST, increasing only a few items to correct previous errors. Certain COMPENSATORY duties were abolished, and in many cases SPECIFIC DUTIES were replaced by AD VALO-REM DUTIES. In general, this tariff attempted to reduce duties, such a policy being advocated as a means of bringing foreign competition to bear upon domestic monopolies.

underwriting. As applied to INVESTMENT BANKING (*q.v.*), the purchase for resale of a large block of a new security issue by one or more investment bankers. Also the written agreement pertaining to such a transaction.

undistributed-profits tax. A progressive tax on corporation profits not distributed as dividends. Such a tax, for example, was levied by the United States government in 1936. See TAX.

unearned income. 1. Income received as rent, interest, dividend payments, or in any form other than gain or compensation resulting directly from the recipient's personal efforts. 2. As applied to accounting, payments received that have not been earned. Such items as rent and interest are frequently received in advance of the time when they are earned. The sums thus received are treated as liabilities until such time as they are actually earned. The items are then credited to an income account. Sometimes called *deferred income*. See INCOME.

unearned increment. Generally, appreciation in the value of property, not anticipated by the owner and not in any way due to his personal efforts, intelligence, or skill. More particularly, the value added to land because of increased population, the growth of cities, and the building of transportation facilities and other such improvements; hence, value added to land apart from any effort or expense applied on the land in question by the owners thereof.

uneconomic. 1. A term applicable to any action or process which does not add to the total sum of useful goods and services. 2. Descriptive of any action or process which produces goods or services less effectively or at a greater cost than is warranted by existing technical knowledge.

unemployment. The condition of being unable to find gainful employment when able and willing to work. See (12).

unemployment insurance. A system of insurance for protection of workers against financial loss due to unemployment. In the United States, nation-wide compulsory unemployment insurance for most categories of employed workers is authorized principally by the SOCIAL SECURITY ACT of 1935 and the Federal Unemployment Tax Act. Actual planning and administration of such insurance, which provides that unemployed workers receive a weekly income for a limited period, is left to each state. A federal tax on payrolls finances the system as a whole, but an employer's federal payroll tax may be offset, within limits, by his contributions to a particular state's plan provided the state plan is approved by the Bureau of Employment Security of the U.S. Department of Labor. The bureau imposes acceptable standards for each state's employment security or insurance plan, keeps the plans under review, and coordinates their programs with the objectives of other federal manpower and employment security legislation. See INSURANCE.

unfair labor practice. Any action by management which is prohibited by labor legislation such as the NATIONAL LABOR RELATIONS (WAGNER-CONNERY) ACT or the LABOR-MANAGEMENT RELATIONS (TAFT-HARTLEY) ACT (*qq.v.*), for example, discrimination by management against workers because of their union activities or management's refusal to bargain collectively. Under the LABOR REFORM (LANDRUM-GRIFFIN) ACT of 1959 (*q.v.*), labor as well as management is enjoined from committing acts that may be labeled unfair.

unfavorable balance of trade. A condition in the international trade of a given country when the money value of its merchandise imports exceeds the money value of its merchandise exports for a particular period of time. The term originated in the theory of the MERCANTILIST SCHOOL (*q.v.*) and should not today be considered synonymous with "undesirable balance of trade." Also called *passive trade balance* and *trade deficit.* See also BALANCE OF TRADE.

unified bond. See BOND.

unified budget. A form of budget first used by the United States Government in 1968 which includes all types of disbursements whether from general funds or from so-called trust funds. As a result of the consolidation under the new practice, total budget outlays rose in one year from approximately $100 billion to approximately $186 billion. See BUDGET.

uniform laws. Codes of laws on various matters of business and commerce, such as the Uniform Commercial Code governing stock transfers, bills of lading, and other business transactions, which have been drawn up by the Commissioners on Uniform State Laws and various legal and professional bodies in the expectation that state legislatures will adopt the codes and thus make the regulations on these matters uniform throughout the United States.

unilinear tariff. See SINGLE-SCHEDULE TARIFF.

union. See LABOR UNION.

union certification. Certification by an appropriate government agency, in the United States by the National Labor Relations Board, to the effect that a particular labor union has fulfilled the legal requirements to qualify as the bargaining agent for the employees of an establishment and is to be recognized as such. See CERTIFICATE.

union label. A label or stamp placed on commodities to indicate that they have been made in a union shop or that the labor expended upon them has been that of workers belonging to a labor union.

union security clause. Any provision in a labor agreement that protects a labor union against loss of dues-paying members during the life of the agreement, the provision usually being enforced by a compulsory CHECKOFF (*q.v.*).

union shop. A plant or enterprise in which all the workers must belong to the union; nonunion workers may be employed, however, on condition that they join the union. See SHOP.

unissued stock. See CAPITAL STOCK.

unit banking. A banking system under which chartered or unchartered banks operate as independent entities, in contrast to CHAIN BANKING or BRANCH BANKING (*qq.v.*). See BANKING SYSTEM and CHARTER.

unit cost. The total cost of a single article or unit of service. It includes the VARIABLE COST, plus a proportionate share of the FIXED COST. See COST.

United Mine Workers v. Coronado Coal Co. See CORONADO CASE.

United Nations. An association of most of the nations of the world organized to maintain international peace and security and to encourage such economic and social conditions throughout the world as promise to further this objective. A conference at Washington, D.C. (Dumbarton Oaks), laid the foundations of the United Nations and led to the calling of the United Nations Conference on International Organization at San Francisco in 1945, at which place and time the charter of the United Nations was drafted and signed by 50 participating nations. The two principal organs are the GENERAL ASSEMBLY and the SECURITY COUNCIL *(qq.v.).*

United Nations Conference on Trade and Development (UNCTAD). A conference of United Nations members which meets periodically—a session was held in New Delhi, India, in 1968—to recommend ways of improving the international trading position of the less developed nations of the world. Policy recommendations of the conference, such as tariff and other concessions for the developing countries, sometimes run counter to the efforts of GATT industrial nations to liberalize trade. See UNITED NATIONS.

United Nations Educational, Scientific and Cultural Organization (UNESCO). A specialized agency of the UNITED NATIONS organized in 1945, which promotes collaboration among nations by advancing knowledge, particularly through instruments of mass communication; by establishing educational standards and opportunities; and by maintaining, increasing, and diffusing mankind's cultural heritage.

United Nations Relief and Rehabilitation Administration. An international agency of some 52 states which was established in 1943 and terminated in 1946. It was organized to provide direct relief, and funds for economic reconstruction and rehabilitation, to victor and vanquished European belligerent countries of World War II, and later extended its relief operations worldwide. See UNITED NATIONS.

United States Chamber of Commerce. A federation of local boards of trade, chambers of commerce, and similar organizations, including some trade associations. It represents the commercial interests of the United States as a whole, its chief functions being to give voice to the views of its member bodies in matters relating to public commercial policies and to furnish information having to do with industrial and commercial interests.

United States Civil Service Commission. An independent federal agency created by Congress on January 16, 1883, and authorized to establish a merit system based on demonstrated fitness for public employment—as opposed to a spoils system—in the recruiting, appointing, and promoting of federal civilian officials and employees. The commission is composed of 3 members, not more than 2 of whom may belong to one political party. Since its inception, the commission has become far more than an examining and recruiting agency; its broad objective is to promote a career service in the federal government, and to that end it has instituted the essentials necessary to attract career personnel: adequate compensation, incentives for professional competence, systematic promotion opportunities, protection against unwarranted dismissal, and adequate retirement provisions.

United States Court of Claims. A special court created in 1855 which, since 1866, has been empowered to adjudicate contractual claims against the federal government and, more recently, has been given similar power over certain types of damage suits arising out of acts of public employees. The court consists of a chief judge and 6 associate justices.

United States Court of Customs and Patent Appeals. A specialized federal appellate court of 5 justices which reviews controversies arising from customs and patent matters. It was established in 1909 under a clause in the Payne-Aldrich Tariff Act. In 1929 its jurisdiction was extended to include appeals from decisions of the United States Patent Office in matters relating to patents and trademarks.

United States Customs Court. A court composed of 9 judges, located in New York City, which reviews and interprets tariff laws and customs regulations and adjudicates disputes arising under such laws. The court was created in 1890 and was given its present name in 1926.

United States Employment Service. A part of the U.S. Labor Department's Bureau of Employment Security which supervises a system of nationwide, free, public employment offices, administered by the states and paid for with federal funds when minimum federal standards are maintained.

United States Fish and Wildlife Service. A unit of the U.S. Department of the Interior, created in 1940 and reorganized under this title in 1956, which through its Bureau of Commercial Fisheries and Bureau of Sport Fisheries and Wildlife supervises the commercial fishing industry, enforces international agreements on fishing, and develops programs to conserve and to promote the efficient economic and recreational use of the country's wildlife resources.

United States note. See TREASURY NOTE.

United States Steel case. A case, *United States* v. *United States Steel Corp.,* 251 U.S. 417 (1920), in which the Supreme Court refused to order the dissolution of the United States Steel Corporation which counsel for the government had indicated controlled more than one-half of the business of the industry and which counsel had sought to partition on the ground that it violated the antitrust statutes. The Court held that the antitrust statutes did "not make mere size an offense," and pointed out, in support of its decision, that competition existed in the industry and that price-fixing agreements had been terminated.

United States Tariff Commission. An independent federal agency, generally known as the Tariff Commission, created by Congress in 1916 and consisting of 6 members, not more than 3 of whom may be members of the same political party, appointed for 6 year terms by the President and Senate. The commission studies the effects of tariff and related legislation on the economic life of the nation and conducts research on matters relating to international commercial policy. Its investigations cover such matters as foreign export bounties, the effect of tariffs upon competition among domestic producers, competition of foreign products with those produced domestically, and preferential provisions in trade treaties. It also advises the President on the negotiation of RECIPROCAL TRADE AGREEMENTS with foreign countries and on the administration of the FLEXIBLE TARIFF.

United States Travel Service. A unit of the U.S. Department of Commerce established in 1961 to stimulate travel to the United States by residents of foreign countries, partly in order to help overcome the then existing adverse balance of payments. It seeks to insure adequate accommodations and transportation for foreign tourists at reasonable rates, to overcome legal and cultural obstacles which foreign tourists may encounter in visiting this country, and to develop appropriate advertising campaigns to encourage tourism in the United States.

United States v. Addyston Pipe and Steel Co. See ADDYSTON PIPE AND STEEL CO. CASE.

United States v. American Linseed Oil Co. See LINSEED OIL INDUSTRY CASE.

United States v. American Tobacco Co. See STANDARD OIL CASE.

United States v. Brown. A case, 381 U.S. 437 (1965), in which the Supreme Court invalidated, as being equivalent to an attainder, the provision in the Labor Reform (Landrum-Griffin) Act of 1959 which denied the right of an enrolled Communist party member to hold office in a labor union and designated such action as a crime.

United States v. Butler. See HOOSAC MILLS CASE.

United States v. Darby Lumber Co. A case, 312 U.S. 100 (1941), in which the Supreme Court upheld the constitutionality of the minimum-wage and maximum-hour provisions and, by implication, other provisions (including the proscription of child labor) contained in the FAIR LABOR STANDARDS ACT of 1938. Hence, often called the *fair labor standards case.* In coming to this decision, the Court developed the doctrine that the power of Congress over interstate commerce includes authority to prevent the transportation of proscribed goods—in this instance goods made under substandard working conditions. This authority, moreover, is not vitiated even if it results in congressional regulation of manufacture. By implication, therefore, an implication expressly confirmed in the court's opinion, this case overrules the CHILD-LABOR CASE (*q.v.*) of *Hammer* v. *Dagenhart.* It also opens the way for national regulation of almost every phase of production and changes materially the historic distinction between the powers of Congress and those of the states.

United States v. E. C. Knight Co. See KNIGHT CASE.

United States v. Florida. See OFFSHORE OIL CASES.

United States v. International Harvester Co. See INTERNATIONAL HARVESTER CASE.

United States v. Louisiana. See OFFSHORE OIL CASES.

United States v. South-Eastern Underwriters Assn. See INSURANCE CASE.

United States v. *Trans-Missouri Freight Assn.* See TRANS-MIS-SOURI FREIGHT ASSOCIATION CASE.

United States v. *Trenton Potteries Co.* See TRENTON POTTERIES CASE.

United States v. *United Shoe Machinery Corp.* See SHOE MACHINERY CASE.

United States v. *United States Steel Corp.* See UNITED STATES STEEL CASE.

United Steelworkers of America v. *United States.* See TAFT-HARTLEY INJUNCTION CASE.

Universal Postal Union. An organization with headquarters in Bern, Switzerland, established in 1874 for the purpose of fostering international cooperation in the improvement of postal services. The union is now a specialized agency of the United Nations and its membership comprises most of the countries and territories of the world. Under the terms of various conventions, developed by quinquennial congresses of the Union, member states have agreed to the reciprocal free exchange of mailable matter; and, for reasonable compensation, each member has agreed to forward external mail to its destination in its own territory by the most expeditious means. Information on changing mail costs and services is distributed by the Union's Swiss bureau.

unlisted stock. See CAPITAL STOCK.

unparted bullion. Bullion from which baser metals have not been extracted.

unproductive consumption. A term sometimes applied to the utilization of services which do not produce goods for the market; for example, the services of household servants. Some early economists argued that increased unproductive consumption of this nature was the way out of a depression, for wages paid for these services created more spending but did not add to the accumulation of goods. Most contemporary economists consider any services that have economic value as a part of production, and such services are included in the GROSS NATIONAL PRODUCT (*q.v.*). See CONSUMPTION.

unsecured debt. A debt for which no specific collateral has been pledged. See DEBT.

455

Urban Mass Transportation Act. An act of Congress, 1964, which offers assistance for the development of mass-transit facilities in major urban and suburban areas. The act provides for financing of research and demonstration projects, and encourages the establishment of long-range programs to set up and maintain mass-transit facilities on an area-wide coordinated basis.

urban renewal. Efforts by private enterprise, public corporations, and government at all levels to rehabilitate housing and to construct new dwellings in slum areas of cities, and to redesign and rehabilitate existing public buildings, streets, parks, and transportation facilities, with the aim of checking the physical and cultural decay of the central or core areas of large cities or metropolitan communities. Government often encourages such a program by appropriate use of its regulatory power and its power of condemnation under eminent domain, and by providing tax rebates, subsidies, loans on favorable terms, and insurance for private loans to those enterprises aiding in the renewal.

usance. A period of time, established by law or custom, for the payment of certain BILLS OF EXCHANGE.

use-and-occupancy insurance. Insurance to cover the loss of net profits, or to cover specific charges, such as taxes, royalties, or salaries, when a fire or other catastrophe makes it impossible to carry on a business for a certain length of time. Also called *business interruption insurance.* See INSURANCE.

user cost. A Keynesian term which identifies DEPRECIATION in UNIT COST on the basis of the amount that the discounted expected future earnings of the capital equipment has been reduced because of producing that unit. Instead of being calculated on the basis of a percentage which absorbs the cost of the capital equipment over a span of years, presumably its period of usefulness, depreciation is thus made dependent upon future costs and selling prices as reflected in the estimated future earnings of the capital equipment. See COST.

use tax. A tax levied on the use of particular articles. During World War II the United States imposed a use tax on automobiles and boats. A use tax is frequently resorted to in order to reach persons who attempt to escape a local sales tax by pur-

chasing in localities where the sales tax is not applicable. See
TAX.

usury. Interest in excess of a maximum established by laws applicable to various types of loan transactions. In popular
speech the term is frequently applied to any rate of interest
considered to be unfair and unjust.

utility. The ability to satisfy a human want or desire. There is no
unit of measure for utility. It is a subjective appraisal depending upon the individual concerned and the object considered.
See (12).

utility theory of value. The theory that explains value according
to the degree to which the thing valued contributes to man's
most urgent necessities. The obvious objection that some commodities like diamonds, which contribute nothing to the actual
physical needs of existence, may stand high in value, and other
commodities like water, which do contribute to basic physical
needs, may stand low in the scale of values, led to the modification of the utility theory of value and the development of the
FINAL UTILITY THEORY OF VALUE (*q.v.*).

utopia. An imaginative account of an ideal society. Examples
are Francis Bacon's *New Atlantis,* Edward Bellamy's *Looking
Backward,* Tommaso Campanella's *City of the Sun,* Laurence
Gronlund's *Cooperative Commonwealth,* Sir Thomas More's
Utopia, William Morris's *News from Nowhere,* Plato's *Republic.*

utopian socialism. A name applied to the ideas of a number of
social reformers of the latter part of the 18th and early part of
the 19th centuries who believed that the ills of society could all
be resolved by some preconceived plan of voluntary association.
Among the prominent utopian socialists were Robert
Owen, a wealthy English manufacturer; Charles Fourier, the
son of a wealthy French merchant; and Louis Blanc, a French
historian. Their ideas as to the specific organization of an ideal
society differed, but all were essentially communistic. Numerous colonies, both in Europe and in the United States, were
established by the utopian socialists. Robert Owen established
such a colony in New Harmony, Indiana, in 1825; and in Massachusetts, the Brook Farm experiment was begun in 1841. See
also SOCIALISM.

V

Vaca v. Spies. A case, 386 U.S. 171 (1967), in which the Supreme Court held that union members may sue their union for damages if the officials of such union acted in proven bad faith in their supposed efforts to secure redress of members' grievances and did not, in fact, protect the interests of the members.

validation certificate. An instrument which confirms or attests the authenticity or formal legality of some action; especially, a document required by the Treasury since 1967, to legalize sale of foreign securities by Americans to other Americans under the *Interest Equalization Tax* (*q.v.*) and to prevent evasion of that tax. See CERTIFICATE.

valorization. The establishment of an arbitrary price or value for a commodity, usually through government action such as, for example, price fixing or making public loans to agricultural producers on commodities the value of which may be established by government order above or below prevailing market prices.

valuation. 1. The process of appraising the worth of property according to some recognized criteria, a process necessarily preliminary to the fixing of fair and reasonable rates for a public utility by a public-service commission. See (1). **2.** The determination of value for tax purposes by an assessor.

value. The quantity of one thing that will be given in exchange for another thing. Thus, if 2 bu. of corn will exchange for 1 bu. of wheat, the value of corn in terms of wheat is ½, whereas the value of wheat in terms of corn is 2. The value of goods and services is usually expressed in terms of the standard medium of exchange; that is, the amount of money for which they can be exchanged at any given time. See (1).

value added. For a given enterprise, the market price of a good, less the cost of materials purchased from others and used to fabricate that good. Value added may be gross or net. Gross value added includes payments for taxes, interest, rent, profits, reserves for depreciation, and compensation to management and other employees, including social security. Net value added excludes depreciation. The GROSS NATIONAL PRODUCT is the total gross value added by all the productive enterprises in the economy. See VALUE.

value-added tax. See ADDED VALUE TAX.

variable annuity. An annuity, based on a capital sum usually invested in common stocks, that pays the annuitant at regular intervals (usually monthly or quarterly) amounts which may vary from year to year. The market value of the investments at a specified annual date, together with the earnings from the investments less expenses, determine the amounts of the periodic payments during the following year. See ANNUITY.

variable cost. A cost which increases or decreases as the total volume of production increases or decreases. Material and direct labor costs are usually variable. Also called *direct, prime, running,* and *operating cost.* See COST.

variable proportions, law of. See PROPORTIONALITY, LAW OF.

***Veazie Bank* v. *Fenno*.** A case, 8 Wallace 533 (1869), in which the Supreme Court upheld a federal tax of 10 per cent on all state bank notes circulating as money on the ground, among others, that such a tax was an exercise of Congress's constitutional power to provide a sound and uniform currency for the entire country, and that the exercise of such a right included the power under its taxing authority to restrain the circulation of bank notes issued under state rather than under federal law. The practical effect of the tax, thus sustained, was to drive all state bank notes out of circulation and to ensure that the circulation privilege for bank notes would, at the time the decision was rendered, belong to the then recently created national banks.

velocity of circulation. The rapidity with which MONEY or money substitutes (especially DEPOSIT CURRENCY), or both combined, changes hands during a given period of time. The velocity of circulation of money alone has been estimated at from 20 to 25 times a year. Inasmuch as payments by check account for approximately 90 per cent of the goods and services purchased in the United States, velocity of circulation is often calculated on the basis of BANK DEPOSITS alone. Income velocity, that is, payments for final goods and services, is usually measured by dividing the NET NATIONAL PRODUCT for a given year by the sum of the total MONEY IN CIRCULATION and the total DEMAND DEPOSITS standing to the credit of bank customers during that year. Exchange or transactions velocity, which includes not only transactions involving final goods and services but also all intermediate transactions, is measured by dividing BANK DEBITS during a specific period of time by demand deposits existing during that same period.

venture capital. Capital subject to a considerable risk; hence, also called *risk capital.* The term is used in contradistinction to SECURITY CAPITAL. Capital invested in a new business, where the chances of success are uncertain, is an example. Venture capital is usually represented by common stock in the case of incorporated organizations. See CAPITAL.

vertical expansion. Expansion of a business establishment by gaining control of all the operations involved in the production and sale of its output, from obtaining the original raw materials through fabrication and final marketing.

vertical labor union. See INDUSTRIAL UNION.

vested interests. 1. Established claims to real or personal property. **2.** The moneyed or property-owning classes in society.

Veterans Administration. An independent federal agency, established in 1930, which administers the laws providing benefits for war veterans and their dependents. The benefits include special compensation and allowances for service-connected disability or death, pensions, vocational rehabilitation, provision for support of surviving dependents and education for dependents, insurance loans or guaranty of loans for the purchase of homes or business, and hospitalization and medical care.

veterans' preference. The practice of waiving various standards usually required of prospective employees, such as physical fitness, proper age, or minimum intelligence and experience ratings, or of reducing such standards, in order to provide employment for veterans and their immediate relatives. Veterans' preference is frequently authorized by state and federal legislation for employment by public agencies, and sometimes is accorded by private industry.

vice-consul. See CONSUL.

visible items of trade. Exports and imports of merchandise and specie. The term is used in contradistinction to INVISIBLE ITEMS OF TRADE. Both the visible and invisible items are considered in the BALANCE OF PAYMENTS.

VISTA. An acronym for "Volunteers in Service to America." For little more than maintenance expenses, members of this organization serve in hospitals, health and welfare institutions, and employment camps, their broad objective being to combat poverty and juvenile delinquency and otherwise to carry out the national policy, expressed in such legislation as the Economic Opportunity Act, to help Black, Indian, and other minorities to surmount economic and cultural barriers erected against them by poverty and discrimination.

vital statistics. Statistics having to do with births, deaths, marriages, health, disease, and related matters.

Vocational Education Act. See SMITH-HUGHES ACT.

voluntary bankruptcy. See BANKRUPTCY.

voluntary checkoff. See CHECKOFF.

voting-trust certificate. A document issued to stockholders of a corporation when they assign the voting rights of their stock to a trustee or trustees. The voting-trust certificates are evidence of an interest in the corporation identical with the interest evidenced by the stock certificates, except for the voting rights. Unlike voting rights transferred by means of a proxy, a voting-trust certificate indicates that such rights have been assigned for a relatively extended period of time. See CERTIFICATE.

voucher. A document that establishes the accuracy of the entries in books of account or other alleged facts. The term often refers specifically to a receipt for a sum of money.

W

wage. A payment for labor or services. The term is usually applied to payment for manual labor, as distinguished from the term SALARY which is used to identify compensation for clerical and managerial personnel. See (29).

Wage and Hour and Public Contracts Divisions. A unit of the U.S. Department of Labor that administers and enforces the provisions of the FAIR LABOR STANDARDS ACT and other legislation governing minimum wages, overtime compensation, child labor, and safety and health standards, and the provisions of the WALSH-HEALEY PUBLIC CONTRACTS ACT governing standards required of government supply contractors. Within the department it operates under the Wage and Standards Administration.

Wage and Hour Law. See FAIR LABOR STANDARDS ACT.

wage-and-price guidelines. Recommendations to labor and management, such as those made by the Council of Economic Advisers in 1962, which are intended to discourage inflationary wage and price trends by suggesting (*a*) that except under certain special circumstances, increases in wages, including fringe benefits, should not exceed the annual overall productivity increase per man-hour, averaged over a period of years; and (*b*) that price decreases or increases in particular industries should be geared to the average overall rate of productivity increase.

wage and salary control. Any effort to fix the level of wages or salaries by law or administrative decree. See CONTROL.

wage dividend. A bonus which is paid to employees of a corporation in addition to their regular salaries and, which bears a definite relation to dividends paid on the capital stock of the corporation. See DIVIDEND.

wage-fund theory. A doctrine developed by John Stuart Mill, to the effect that wages depend upon the relationship that exists at any particular time between the number of workers and the quantity of capital employed for the payment of wages. The only way wages can be increased, he held, is to reduce the number of workers or to increase the amount of capital used for the payment of wages.

wage leadership. The influence exerted over the wage level of an entire industry or labor market by a wage settlement arrived at in one large industrial establishment or group of establishments.

Wagner-Connery Act. See NATIONAL LABOR RELATIONS ACT.

Walker Tariff. The United States Tariff Act of 1846. It embodied the principle of TARIFF FOR REVENUE ONLY. Maximum duties were placed on luxuries.

walkout. See STRIKE.

Walsh-Healey Public Contracts Act. An act of Congress, 1936, which, with subsequent amendments, requires the inclusion, in government supply contracts involving sums in excess of $10,000, of stipulations calling for the payment of prevailing minimum wages as certified by the Secretary of Labor, overtime pay at the rate of time-and-one-half, a basic 8-hour day or a 40-hour week, safety and health standards, and restrictions on child and convict labor.

want. A need or desire for an economic good or service, not necessarily accompanied by the power to satisfy it.

war economy. The condition obtaining in economic life when, through governmental CONTROLS, allocations of scarce materials, rationing, and the imposition of similar restrictions, production for civilian use is curbed and the production of war materials is greatly expanded.

war-profits tax. A tax designed to divert to the public treasury excessive private profits resulting from abnormal war demands, especially excess profits due to the demand for goods by the government in wartime. See TAX.

warrant. As applied to the purchase of stock, a right granted a stockholder to buy additional shares at a specified price within a certain period of time.

wash sale. A fictitious sale in which the seller becomes the buyer of what he sells. The term is usually applied to a fictitious stock transaction in which the purpose is, as a rule, to induce others to buy and thus to stimulate demand.

wasting asset. An asset which cannot be replaced, and the life of which cannot be prolonged by repairs. A coal mine is an example of a wasting asset. See ASSET.

watered stock. See CAPITAL STOCK.

waybill. A receipt listing the goods accepted for shipment, issued to a shipper by a common land carrier.

wealth. **1.** Material objects that are external to man, inherently useful, appropriable, and relatively scarce. Some economists exclude from the meaning of the term "wealth" all property rights such as stocks, bonds, and mortgages, these being regarded as evidences of ownership of wealth, but not wealth itself. Others argue that such property rights must be included in the concept because the manner or degree in which ownership of wealth is divided may affect the usefulness of that wealth, and the division, therefore, cannot be considered apart from the thing divided. Likewise there is a difference of opinion regarding the inclusion of money within the meaning of wealth. Money as such—that is, exclusive of its possible usefulness as a commodity—is not generally regarded as wealth in the technical sense of that term. However, some authorities argue that, aside from any intrinsic usefulness which certain forms of money may have, money is a particular kind of wealth because it is external to man, appropriable, relatively scarce, and useful indirectly as a medium of exchange. Wealth as defined above is often referred to as *economic wealth.* **2.** In general business practice the term "wealth" includes money, evidences of ownership, and, in general, anything that has money value. **3.** Popularly "wealth" is sometimes given a still broader meaning by the inclusion of attributes of man such as health and skills and, in fact, even man himself when he is not a legal chattel. Likewise, in popular speech, the term may include inappropriable items such as climate or a beautiful landscape. Such items are sometimes designated as SOCIAL WEALTH but it should be noted that the term "social wealth" is given other meanings as well. See (12).

Webb-Pomerene Act. An act of Congress, 1918, which authorizes American exporters to organize approved *export associations* for the carrying on of export trade, such associations being exempted from the operation of the antitrust laws.

weighted average. An average in which the numbers to be averaged are multiplied by certain values called "weights" according to the relative importance of the numbers being averaged. Following are examples of a weighted ARITHMETIC MEAN, GEOMETRIC MEAN, and HARMONIC MEAN.

Weights (*w*)	Numbers to be averaged *(m)*
1	10
2	8
3	5

Weighted arithmetic mean $= \dfrac{\Sigma wm}{\Sigma w} = \dfrac{41}{6} = 6.833.$

Weighted geometric mean $= \sqrt[\Sigma w]{m_1^{w1} \times m_2^{w2} \times m_3^{w3}}$
$$= \sqrt[6]{80,000} = 6.564.$$

Weighted harmonic mean $= \dfrac{\Sigma w}{\dfrac{w_1}{m_1} + \dfrac{w_2}{m_2} + \dfrac{w_3}{m_3}} = \dfrac{6}{0.95} = 6.316.$

In economic computation, weighted averages are frequently used in the construction of INDEX NUMBERS. In computing central tendency in a FREQUENCY DISTRIBUTION, the frequencies are weights. See AVERAGE.

welfare economics. Consideration of the extent to which an economic system attains predetermined goals assumed to maximize human welfare, and the evaluation of public policies designed to effect economic changes directed to those ends. The term is associated with the work of Arthur Cecil Pigou, a British economist, who conceived costs of production as including certain social costs such as the impairment of the health of employees or air pollution due to fumes from a factory chimney, and who recognized social gains that may result from production quite apart from private profit. The phrase is also applied to current economic policies of government which seek to improve social conditions. See ECONOMICS.

welfare state. A term used to characterize a government sponsoring social welfare programs such as public housing, farm subsidies, health insurance, and the like. The term is sometimes used in a derogatory sense.

West Coast Hotel Co. v. Parrish. See MINIMUM-WAGE CASES.

Western Hemisphere trade corporation. A United States trade or business corporation which conducts all of its business in North, Central, or South America, or the West Indies, and derives at least 95 per cent of its gross income from sources outside of the United States. Certain tax advantages are granted to Western Hemisphere trade corporations for the purpose of encouraging trade with, and promoting the economic development of, countries within the Western Hemisphere. See CORPORATION.

wetback. See MIGRANT WORKER.

Wheeler-Lea Act. An act of Congress, 1938, which amended the FEDERAL TRADE COMMISSION ACT (*q.v.*) in several important respects. As thus amended, that Act prohibits not only "unfair methods of competition" but also "unfair or deceptive acts or practices in commerce," and authorizes the commission temporarily to enjoin dissemination of false advertising of foods, drugs, and other products, pending a final order of the commission regarding such dissemination or the institution of appropriate suits through the Justice Department. It also provides for civil penalties in suits instituted by the Department of Justice when any final order of the Federal Trade Commission under this legislation is defied or ignored.

wildcat banking era. The period following the dissolution of the second Bank of the United States in 1836. Because state banking laws of the time lacked conservative standards and varied greatly from state to state, banks inspired little confidence in prospective depositors, and the nation's money and credit structure was most unstable.

wildcat strike. See ILLEGAL STRIKE.

Willcox v. *Consolidated Gas Co.* A case, 212 U.S. 19 (1909), in which the Supreme Court, in attempting to provide a definition for "fair return" to a utility, declared that there was no particular rate of return which was to be deemed "fair" for invested capital. Degree of risk, location, prevailing interest rates on investment, and other factors must all be considered in determining the fairness of a rate for any particular enterprise.

Wilson-Gorman Tariff. The United States Tariff Act of 1894. It changed the tariff rates only slightly, and such changes as were made were in the direction of lower duties.

Wilson v. *New.* A case, 243 U.S. 332 (1917), in which the Supreme Court upheld the provisions of the ADAMSON ACT (*q.v.*) establishing a maximum 8-hour day and an appropriate wage structure for interstate railway employees. The Court ruled that failure of employers and employees to secure a collective wage-and-hour agreement on railways justified such legislation even if it involved the fixing of wages. The Court also suggested that Congress could compel adjustments by arbitration of labor disputes on interstate railways.

windfall profit. A profit in excess of that which can be considered normal. See PROFIT.

Wisconsin rate case. A case, *Railroad Commission of Wisconsin* v. *Chicago, Burlington and Quincy R.R. Co.,* 257 U.S. 563 (1922), in which the Supreme Court extended the doctrine of the SHREVEPORT CASE that the federal government, operating through appropriate administrative authority, may remove discrimination between interstate and intrastate railway rates by ordering the latter to be raised to a level with interstate rates. The power was held to belong to the federal government because it is necessary to any effective policy of national control of interstate commerce.

withholding tax. See CURRENT TAX PAYMENT ACT.

Wolff Packing Co. v. *Industrial Court of Kansas.* A case, 262 U.S. 522 (1923), in which the Supreme Court invalidated provisions of a Kansas statute setting up an industrial-relations court and empowering it to hear and determine labor controversies in certain businesses declared to be "affected with a public interest." The Court held that some of the businesses subjected to this statutory regulation, notably those having to do with food, fuel, and clothing, did not come within the judicially accepted category of businesses "affected with a public interest"; hence, the statute's requirement that labor controversies in which such businesses might be involved must in certain instances be submitted to compulsory adjudication constituted an unreasonable interference with the contractual freedom of employer and employee and violated the due process clause of the 14th Amendment. Subsequent cases, notably the MILK-CONTROL CASE, have greatly modified at least the judicial premises upon which the decision turned in this case.

Women's Bureau. A unit of the U.S. Department of Labor, established in 1918, which is concerned with the welfare of gainfully employed women. It formulates standards for improving their working conditions and suggests ways for advancing their employment opportunities and increasing their efficiency. Research is carried on to provide the necessary data for carrying out the Bureau's program.

working capital. Current assets of an enterprise less the amount of the current liabilities. That part of the current assets which is equal to the current liabilities must be reserved to meet the enterprise's short-term debts. What remains of current assets is available for other uses in the business and hence is working capital. See CAPITAL.

workmen's compensation laws. In the United States, laws enacted by the states and by the federal government which set forth the liability of employers in cases of industrial accidents or employment-connected illness. Such laws replace or supplement the common-law rules of liability of employers to employees. The Bureau of Employees' Compensation administers federal workmen's compensation laws and most states establish special boards or commissions to administer their laws. Also called *employers' liability laws.*

work relief. Employment provided by the government or by private social agencies primarily to ameliorate distress and to stimulate recovery from a depression stage in the BUSINESS CYCLE by increasing PURCHASING POWER.

work-sharing. As applied to labor relations, an attempt to prevent dismissal of some employees by placing all employees on a part-time basis. Also known as *share-the-work plan.*

world bank. See INTERNATIONAL BANK FOR RECONSTRUCTION AND DEVELOPMENT.

World Bank Group. Collectively, the INTERNATIONAL BANK FOR RECONSTRUCTION AND DEVELOPMENT (*World Bank*) and its affiliates, the INTERNATIONAL FINANCE CORPORATION and the INTERNATIONAL DEVELOPMENT ASSOCIATION.

World Federation of Trade Unions. An international organization founded in Paris in 1945 to further trade union interests throughout the world. Sixty countries were represented at the first organizational meetings, and by the end of 1945 the Federation claimed a membership representing some 71 million workers. During 1949, dissension arose within the Federation, in part because many of the member national unions were from Communist countries and were creatures of their governments. Many national groups subsequently withdrew and under the leadership of American, British, and other Western trade-union organizations, these seceding national groups, together with other national groups which had never joined the Federation, formed the INTERNATIONAL CONFEDERATION OF FREE TRADE UNIONS (*q.v.*).

World Health Organization. A specialized agency of the United Nations, with headquarters in Geneva, Switzerland, which is devoted to improving health conditions throughout the world. To that end, it collects and disseminates epidemiological information, recommends uniform standards for therapeutic drugs, establishes uniform systems of health statistics, and seeks to prevent the spread of disease or epidemics on an international scale.

write-up. An increase in the book value of an asset which does not result from additional costs, or the adjustment of an asset account to correspond to an appraisal value.

Y

Yakus v. United States. A case, 321 U.S. 414 (1944), in which the Supreme Court ruled there had been no unconstitutional delegation of legislative power to an administrative agency when Congress authorized such an agency, in this instance the wartime Office of Price Administration, to establish and enforce ceiling-price and rationing regulations under the Emergency Price Control Act of 1942.

yardstick. 1. A criterion for forming judgments or comparisons. **2.** As applied by the TENNESSEE VALLEY AUTHORITY in 1933, a schedule of rates for light and power kept deliberately low in order to find out whether a low rate would increase demand and income, and how profits would be affected. It was anticipated that such data might influence the rates of privately owned establishments.

yellow-dog contract. An agreement entered into by an applicant for employment stating that he will not become a member of a labor union if employed. Yellow-dog contracts are generally illegal in the United States. See CONTRACTS. See also ANTI-INJUNCTION (NORRIS-LAGUARDIA) ACT, and *ADAIR* v. *UNITED STATES.*

yellow seal dollar. See OCCUPATION MONEY.

yield. 1. As used in finance, the annual net return on an investment. **2.** The net return to a public authority of a tax. See (21).

yield to maturity. The annual return on a bond from the date of acquisition to the date of maturity. If the bond is bought at PAR VALUE, the yield to maturity is the same as the NOMINAL YIELD; if bought at a PREMIUM, the yield to maturity is less than the nominal yield; if bought at a DISCOUNT, the yield to maturity is more than the nominal yield. Yield to maturity may be approximated by the following equations:
When bought at a premium:

$$X = \frac{\dfrac{B - D'}{A} + \dfrac{B - D'}{A - D'\,(C-1)}}{2}$$

When bought at a discount:

$$X = \frac{\dfrac{B + D}{A} + \dfrac{B + D}{A + D\,(C-1)}}{2}$$

X = yield to maturity
A = purchase price
B = nominal yield in dollars
C = years to maturity
D = annual ACCUMULATION
D' = annual AMORTIZATION
See YIELD.

Young plan. A plan for the payment of reparations owed by Germany under the Treaty of Versailles and put into effect in 1929. The Young plan superseded the DAWES PLAN. It reduced the total amount of reparations to be paid, specified a definite schedule of sums to be paid during a stipulated length of time (59 years), and did away with most of the supervisory controls on German economy then in existence. The plan was named for Owen D. Young, chairman of the committee that devised the plan. A meeting of the creditor powers at Lausanne in 1932 sought to reduce Germany's reparations to a token payment because of the prevailing economic depression; but the United States refused to accept the stipulated condition that, as net creditor, it cancel all war debts. Even so, Germany paid no more reparations thereafter and she defaulted on her obligations under the Young plan.

Youngstown Sheet & Tube Co. v. Sawyer. A case, 343 U.S. 579 (1952), in which the Supreme Court passed upon the so-called emergency powers of the President. The case arose out of an executive order by President Truman for governmental seizure and operation of the nation's steel mills because of a threatened strike in 1952. Although the Court left open the question of executive discretion in the absence of pertinent Congressional legislation, and although it suggested that there might be occasions when the President could rely upon inherent constitutional authority to counter threats to the nation's safety, the majority of the Court took the position that the President had failed to follow the procedure for settling labor disputes which Congress had provided in the LABOR-MANAGEMENT RELATIONS (TAFT-HARTLEY) ACT (*q.v.*), and that, hence, his order invaded the legislative province of Congress.

youth employment service. Any organized effort to provide young people with vocational training or apprenticeship experience in order to equip them with marketable skills. The efforts of the federal government in this direction are largely centered in the Manpower Administration and its Bureau of Apprenticeship and Training of the U.S. Department of Labor.

Z

Zollverein. The German word for a CUSTOMS UNION. Such unions were formed in 1833 between Prussia and various independent German states wherein it was agreed to impose no tariff duties among themselves, and to adopt uniform duties applicable to the rest of the world.

zoning. The practice of planning a municipality or metropolitan area in such a way that, as population increases, maximum convenience, utility, and beauty are assured the residents. To that end districts are zoned or designated primarily for manufacturing enterprises, or for retail establishments, or for various classes of residences, or for a combination of these uses. See also *EUCLID* V. *AMBLER REALTY CO.*

zoning case. See *EUCLID* V. *AMBLER REALTY CO.*

APPENDICES

DESCRIPTIVE CLASSIFICATION OF DEFINED TERMS

(1) Accounting

accelerated appreciation
account
  accounts payable
  accounts receivable
  controlling
  custodian
  expense
  impersonal
  nominal
  open
  personal
  property
  real
  suspense
  tax and loan
accrual basis
amortization
appraisal
appreciation
asset
  asset enter mains
  capital
  contingent
  current
  fixed
  floating
  frozen
  intangible
  legal
  liquid
  ordinary
  quick
  slow
  wasting
audit
bills payable
bills receivable
bookkeeping
budget
  administrative
  capital
  double
  national income accounts
  unified
capital gain
certified public accountant
cost
  bulk line
  comparative
  constant

  decreasing
  direct
  factor
  fixed
  imputed
  increasing
  indirect
  joint
  marginal
  operating
  opportunity
  overhead
  prime
  running
  social
  sunk
  supplementary
  unit
  user
  variable
cost accounting
debit
deficit
depreciation
double entry
earnings
fifo
financial statement
  asset and liability
  balance sheet
  cash flow
  income
  profit-and-loss
  pro forma
fiscal year
good will
income
  adjusted gross
  deferred
  disposable personal
  earned
  gross
  guaranteed annual
  national
  net
  personal
  psychic
  unearned
inventory
liability
  capital
  contingent

477

current
double
fixed
limited
long term
lifo
net worth
nonrecurring expense
notes payable
notes receivable
overextended
per contra item
petty cash
prepaid expense
profit
  gross
  net
  operating
  pure
  windfall
rate
  anticipation
  bank
  base
  birth
  combination
  cross
  crude birth
  crude death
  death
  discount
  economic growth
  exchange
    floating
    official
    par
  interest
  joint
  legal
  local
  measured day
  minimum
  prime
  rediscount
  refined birth
  refined death
  tax
ratio
  acid test
  current
  dividend payment
  man land
  mint

operating
prime earnings
quick
reserve
revenue expenditure
segregated appropriation
single entry
solvent
surplus
  buyer's
  capital
  earned
  paid-in
  sellers
trial balance
valuation
  capitalized-value standard
  earning-capacity standard
  foreign
  original-cost standard
  prudent-investment-cost standard
  replacement-cost standard
  reproduction-cost standard
value
  book
  capitalized
  denominational
  face
  going
  intrinsic
  market
  par
  scarcity
  tabular standard of
  value added
write up

(2) Agriculture—Farm Organizations

American Farm Bureau Federation
farm bloc
Farm Bureau
Farmers Union
4-H Club
Grange
National Farmers' Union
National Grange Order of Patrons of
    Husbandry
Patrons of Husbandry

(3) Agriculture—General Terms

agricultural ladder
agricultural price support
basic crops

Brannan plan
chemurgy
conservation
county agricultural agent
crop insurance
dry farming
ever-normal granary
extensive cultivation
farm subsidies
farm surpluses
Federal Extension Service
home demonstration agent
industrial type farming
intensive cultivation
irrigation
marketing agreement
parity
    agricultural
    purchasing-power
share cropper
soil conservation
soil erosion

**(4) Business and Professional
      Non-financial Organizations and
      Quasi-organizations**

advertising agency
American Arbitration Association
American Economic Association
American Management Association
American Statistical Association
American Stock Exchange
board of trade
bonded warehouse
bucket shop
captive mine
chamber of commerce
Chicago Board of Trade
combination
    amalgamation
    cartel
    conglomerate
    consolidation
    holding company
    merger
    pool
    syndicate
    trust
Committee for Economic
      Development
commodity exchange
common law trust
company (non-financial)

    controlling
    holding
    joint-stock
    management
    mutual
    safe deposit
    subsidiary
condominium
consumer cooperative
corporation
    aggregate
    civil
    close
    ecclesiastical
    eleemosynary
    foreign
    lay
    limited-dividend
    municipal
    private
    public
    public-service
    quasi
    quasi-public
    sole
    Western Hemisphere trade
depository
discount house
duopoly
employers' association
employment agency
enterprise
Executive Peace Corps
export association
factor
forms of business organizations
    cooperative
    corporation
    individual proprietorship
    limited partnership
    partnership
    proprietorship
guild
incorporation
International Executive Service Corps
Massachusetts trust
mercantile agency
monopoly
    bilateral
    buyer's
    fiscal
    monopsony
    natural

partial
public consumption
special privilege
trade
National Academy of Sciences
National Association of
    Manufacturers
national security exchange
New York Stock Exchange
Paunch Corps
public utility
shop
stock exchange
trade association
United States Chamber of Commerce

(5) Business and Professional Non-financial General Terms

arbitration
arms length
assembly-line technique
assurance
backing
big business
big steel
board of directors
bonanza
boom
breakthrough
business
by-product
coaxial cable
commodity
company town
composites
contract research
cumulative voting
decentralization
development
diagonal expansion
director
    dummy
    inside
    outside
diversification
division of labor
downtown
dummy incorporators
employment
entrepreneurship
expendable
gentlemen's agreement

going business
hallmark
heat pipe
hoarding
holography
horizontal expansion
incentive
industrial relations
industrial research
industry
    extractive
    genetic
    infant
    key
    seasonal
integration
interchangeable parts
interlocking directorate
invention
inventory control
jetsam
junket
laborsaving machinery
large-scale production
laser technology
lead time
liquidation
little steel
maintenance
management
management science
mediation
modular housing
moonlighting
obsolescence
operations research
order
panic
payola
permit
policy
prefabricate
production
public opinion survey
public relations
quality control
rationalization
raw material
reconversion
referee
Second Industrial Revolution
silent partner

sinecure
small business
span of control
spill-over
spin-off
subsidy
subvention
systems research
take-home pay
Taylorism
technology
time and motion study
tolerance
turnover
tycoon
vertical expansion

(6) Commerce, Transportation, and Securities Trading Terms
(*See also* International Trade and Exchange)

advice
arbitrage
at the market
auction sale
back spread
bantam store
barter
basing-point system
bazaar
bear
bid
bill
bill of lading
   order
   straight
   through
boot
bourse
buying on margin
brand
bull
buyers' strike
call
capsule cargo
caveat emptor
caveat venditor
chain store
commerce
combination rate
commerce

commodity
company store
competition
   cutthroat
   destructive
   free
   imperfect
   monopolistic
   open
   perfect
   pure
concentration
conditional sale
consignment
containerized freight
convenience stores
conversion
corner
cross purchase
cum rights
customers' net debit balance
demurrage
descriptive labeling
discount store
diversification
drayage
dumping
Dutch auction
embargo
emporium
equity trading
exchange
   blocked
   domestic
   foreign
   forward
   national security
   pecuniary
   stock
ex dividend
ex interest
ex rights
forced sale
grade labeling
hard sell
hedging
higgling
highway
hire purchase
inherent vice
in kind
installment buying

481

international transit
interstate commerce
interstate trade barriers
intrastate commerce
invoice
long and short haul
loss leader
marginal trading
market
  black
  broad
  buyers'
  capital
  continuous
  discount
  federal funds
  free
  gray
  money
  narrow
  open
  over-the-counter
  rigged
  sellers'
  sensitive
  thin
markon
markup
merchantman
merchant marine
middleman
open commitments
open contracts
open interest
open price system
pegging
piggyback
pit
polypoly
preclusive buying
premium
price
  administered
  American selling
  class
  conversion
  fair
  gold
  list
  market
  net
  nominal

  normal
  price loco
  reservation
  subscription
price leadership
pricing out of the market
procurement
put
rate discrimination
rebate
registry
resale price agreements
seat on the exchange
sellers seven sale
selling short
shopping center
shopping mall
short interest
space
speculation
spot delivery
spread
standardization
stock option
stock rights
stop-loss order
straddle
supermarket
tare
tariff
tie-in sale
tonnage
trade discount
trade-mark
trading stamp
unfair trade practice
warrant
waybill
yardstick

(7) Data Processing

analog computer
automatic data processing system
automation
binary notation
block diagram
computer
computer-assisted instruction
cybernetics
datamation
digital computer
electronic data processing

flow chart
program
punched-card data processing
teaching machine

(8) Economics—Principles and Theories

abstinence theory of interest
acceleration principle
agio theory of interest
antagonistic co-operation
appropriation, law of
astronomical theory of business cycle
brazen law of wages
capillarity, law of
commodity theory of money
compensatory principle of money
cost-of-production theory of value
credit theory of the business cycle
declining-marginal-efficiency-of-
	capital theory
diffusion theory of taxation
diminishing utility, law of
Dow theory
Engel's law
equimarginal principle
falling-rate-of-profit theory
final utility theory of value
general equilibrium
general equilibrium theory of
	international trade
Gresham's law
harmonies
hedonistic principle
increasing misery, theory of
iron law of wages
Keynes' law of consumption
labor theory of value
law of supply and demand
liquidity-preference theory of interest
loanable-funds theory of interest
make-work fallacy
Malthusian theory of population
marginal-productivity theory of wages
marginal utility theory of interest
markets, law of
Marxian law of capitalist
	accumulation
multiplier principle
neoclassical theory of value
overinvestment theory of the business
	cycle

oversaving theory of the business cycle
Pareto's law
Parkinson's laws
price specie-flow theory
proportionality, law of
psychological theory of the business
	cycle
quantity theory of money
reciprocity principle
Ricardian theory of rent
Rochdale principles
satiety, law of
Say's law
Say's Theory of Markets
self-interest, law of
social credit
subsistence law of wages
substitution, law of
sunspot theory of the business cycle
surplus labor and value theory
surplus value, theory of
technocracy
underemployment equilibrium
utility theory of value
variable proportions, law of
wage-fund theory

(9) Economics—Schools of Thought

schools of economic thought
	Austrian
	Cambridge
	Cameralism
	Classical
	historical
	individualist
	Kameralism
	liberal
	Manchester
	Marxian
	mercantilist
	neoclassical
	optimist
	Organic
	Orthodox
	Physiocrats
	psychological

(10) Economics—Statistics and Statistical Measurements

arithmetic chart
autonomous variable

483

average
  arithmetic mean
  geometric mean
  harmonic mean
  median
  mode
  moving
  quadratic mean
  weighted
bank credit proxy
bank debits
base period
birth rate
block diagram
break-even chart
business barometer
capital consumption allowance
capitalization of land taxes
capitalized value
car loadings
cobweb chart
coefficient of acceleration
coefficient of correlation
coefficient of cross-elasticity
coefficient of elasticity
coefficient of variation
column diagram
common stock index
consumer price index
crude birth rate
crude death rate
cyclical fluctuations
death rate
decile
decreasing returns
deflationary gap
demand-and-supply curves
diminishing productivity
diminishing returns
disposable personal income
dollar deficit
dollar gap
Dow Jones averages
econometrics
economic growth rate
equation of exchange
extrapolation
factor cost
factor reversal test
flow chart
frequency curve
frequency distribution
frequency polygon

frequency table
Gantt chart
gross national product
gross national products deflator
histogram
income and expenditure equation
increasing returns
index number
  aggregative
  Fisher's ideal
  relative-value
indifference curve
indifference map
indifference schedule
inflationary gap
input and output analysis
international unit
interpolation
inventory valuation adjustment
kurtosis
least-squares method
line of regression
logistics
Lorenz curve
man-land ratio
mean
mean deviation
national income
national income and product account
national product
net national product
normal curve of distribution
normal curve of error
ogive
optimum population
per capita
percentile
per diem
Phillips curve
point of ideal proportions
point of indifference
population pyramid
price consumption curve
probability curve
probable error
process effects
production factors
productivity
progression
  arithmetic
  geometric
  harmonic
propensity to consume

propensity to hoard
propensity to invest
propensity to save
quartile
quartile deviation
quota
range
ratio chart
refined birth rate
refined death rate
regressive supply curve
sample
  area
  purposive
  quota
  random
  stratified
scatter chart
seasonal fluctuations
secular trend
semilogarithmic chart
skewness
spending unit
standard deviation
standard error of estimate
standard error of the mean
time reversal test
time series chart
transfer payment
vital statistics

(11)   Economics—Systems

economic systems
  capitalism
  communism
  controlled economy
  cooperative commonwealth
  directed economy
  domestic industry
  domestic system
  factory system
  family industry
  fascism
  handicraft economy
  home industry
  household system
  middle way
  mixed economy
  plantation system
  socialism
    Christian
    democratic
    Fabian

    guild
    municipal
    state
    utopian
  state capitalism
  statism
  syndicalism

(12)   Economics—General Terms

agents of production
atomistic society
automatic balance
automatic stabilizer
autonomous investment
boom
built-in
bourgeoisie
buffer stock plan
business cycle
buyer's surplus
capital
  artificial
  consumers'
  equity
  frozen
  instrumental
  liquid
  lucrative
  money
  natural
  producer's
  property
  risk
  security
  venture
  working
capital formation
compensatory spending
constant dollar
consumer sovereignty
consumption
  conspicuous
  induced
  unproductive
cross-elasticity
debt monetization
deductive method
deflation
demand
  composite
  deferred
  derived
  effective

Appendix A

elastic
inelastic
joint
market
potential
replacement
rival
schedule
depression
dishoarding
disinflation
distribution
functional
personal
physical
temporal
disutility
division of labor
duopsony
economic
economic abundance
economic democracy
economic determinism
economic equality
economic friction
economic good
economic growth rate
economic harmonies
economic history
economic imperialism
economic independence
economic interpretation of history
economic law
economic liberalism
economic man
economic mobilization
economic nationalism
economic planning
economic rent
economic royalist
economic sanctions
economic scarcity
economic self-sufficiency
economic union
economic warfare
economic wealth
economics
agricultural
applied
consumer
descriptive
dynamic

econometrics
home
institutional
international
Keynesian
macroeconomics
mathematical
microeconomics
static
welfare
endogenous change
end product
entrepreneur
exchange
exogenous change
factors of production
flight of capital
flight of the dollar
frame of reference
full employment
function
good
capital
circulating capital
consumer
economic
final
fixed capital
free
free capital
improved
intermediate
public
representative
specialized capital
hypothesis
illth
impair investment
imputed
induced investment
inductive method
inflation
hidden
runaway
labor
land
leakage
level of living
liquidity preference
management
marginal
marginal borrower

486

marginal buyer
marginal cost
marginal desirability
marginal disutility of labor
marginal efficiency of capital
marginal land
marginal lender
marginal producer
marginal product
marginal productivity
marginal propensity to consume
marginal propensity to save
marginal rate of substitution
marginal revenue
marginal seller
marginal trading
marginal utility
margin of cultivation
mature economy
medium of exchange
national economy
nature
oligopoly
overheating
partial or particular equilibrium
plane of living
political economy
price level
price rigidity
production
  capitalistic
  direct
  indirect
  large scale
  mass
  overproduction
  roundabout
public finance
purchasing power
realistic method
real wage
recession
reconversion
rent
  capital
  contract
  dead
  economic
  ground
  imputed
  ordinary
  peppercorn

quitrent
rack
returns to scale of plant
saving
  fluid
  offsets to
  oversaving
schedule
secular stagnation
seller's surplus
service
stabilization
standard of living
subsistence
supply
  composite
  elastic
  inelastic
  joint
  rival
  schedule
  theory
unearned increment
uneconomic
unemployment
  cyclical
  disguised
  frictional
  seasonal
  structural
  technological
utility
  form
  marginal
  ownership
  place
  possession
  service
  time
  total
velocity of circulation
want
war economy
wealth
  national
  social
work-sharing

(13) Environment and Resources

afforestation
Appalachia
blighted area

conservation
development
dry farming
ghetto
impacted area
irrigation
national forests
natural resources
pollution control
reclamation
reforestation
soil conservation
soil erosion
standard metropolitan area
technical assistance
underdeveloped area
urban renewal

(14) Financial Documents—Bills

bill
  acceptance
  advance
  bankable
  banker's
  blank
  clean
  continental
  credit
  demand
  documentary
  domestic
  finance
  foreign
  inland
  investment
  payment
  prime
  sight
  time
  treasury
bill of credit
bill of sale

(15) Financial Documents—Bonds

bond
  adjustment
  annuity
  assented
  assumed
  blanket
  bottomry
  callable

collateral trust
colonial
consol
consolidated
continued
convertible
coupon
currency
debenture
deferred
divisional
equipment trust
extended
extension
fidelity
first-lien
gold
guaranteed
income
indorsed
industrial
industrial revenue
installment
insular
interchangeable
interest
interim
irredeemable
joint and several
junior-lien
land-grant
legal-tender
liberty
mortgage
municipal
nonassented
noninterest-bearing discount
optional
overlying
participating
passive
perpetual
plain
prior-lien
profit-sharing
public
public-utility
railroad
redeemable
refunding
registered
registered coupon

reorganization
revenue
savings
serial
series
sinking-fund
special-assessment
stamped
state
surety
tax-anticipation
terminal
territorial
underlying
unified

(16) Financial Documents—Stocks

capital stock
  active
  assented
  assessable
  barometer
  bonus
  callable preferred
  classified
  clearinghouse
  common
  convertible
  corporate
  cumulative
  curb
  debenture
  donated
  equity
  full-paid
  full
  guaranteed
  half
  inactive
  international
  listed
  management
  nonassented
  nonassessable
  nonclearinghouse
  noncumulative
  no-par-value
  ordinary
  original-issue
  paid-up
  participating preferred
  part-paid

par-value
potential
preference
preferred
premium
prior
quarter
redeemable preferred
rolling
special
treasury
trustee
unissued
unlisted
watered

(17) Financial Documents—Other

acceptance
  acceptance supra protest
  bank
  trade
accommodation paper
allonge
binder
certificate
  debenture
  gold
  participating
  receiver's
  silver
  stock
  street
  union
  validation
  voting trust
certificate of beneficial interest
certificate of deposit
certificate of incorporation
certificate of indebtedness
certificate of origin
certificate of public convenience and
    necessity
check
  cashier's
  certified
  counter
  traveler's
commercial paper
commodity paper
credit card
deed
definitive

draft
  sight
  time
eligible paper
Freedom Shares
instrument
invoice
letter of credit
  circular
  confirmed
  irrevocable
  open
  revocable
  revolving
  straight
  traveler's
  unconfirmed
letter of lien
letter of trust
money order
mortgage
  chattel
  closed
  direct reduction
  open
  purchase money
note
  balloon
  bank
  federal reserve bank
  federal reserve
  promissory
  saving
  Sherman
  treasury
  United States
open-market paper
receipt
  American depository
  European depository
  trust
script
stock warrant
subordinated debenture
two-name paper
voucher

(18)   Financial Institutions—Banks

bank
  Asian Development Bank
  bank for cooperatives
  Bank for International Settlements

bank of issue
Bank of North Dakota
Bank of the United States
central
central reserve city
commercial
correspondent
country
deposit
Edge banks
Export-Import Bank of Washington
Federal
federal intermediate credit bank
federal land bank
federal reserve bank
guaranty savings
industrial
Inter-American Development Bank
International Bank for
      Reconstruction and
      Development
joint-stock land
labor exchange
land
member
Morris plan
mutual savings
national
par-list
private
reserve city
savings
state
stock savings
trust company
World

(19)   Financial Institutions—Other

American Stock Exchange
benefit society
building and loan association
building society
clearing house
company
  commercial credit
  investment
    closed end
    open end
    split
  personal finance
  sales finance
  small business

trust
credit union
depositary
Federal Land Bank Association
federal savings and loan association
government depositary
homestead-aid benefit association
investment trust
mutual funds
mutual loan association
national security exchange
New York Stock Exchange
savings and loan association
security exchange
stock clearing agency
stock exchange

(20) Financial Terms—Banking

bank call
bank clearings
bank credit
bank deposit
  demand
  derivative
  primary
  time
bank holiday
banking system
  branch
  chain
  federal home loan
  federal reserve
  group
  safety-fund
  Suffolk
  unit
bank rate
Board of Governors of the Federal
    Reserve System
check credit
check currency
clearinghouse agent
clearings
common trust
custodian account
deposit currency
deposit slip
discount market
discount rate
eligible paper
federal funds market
Federal Open Market Committee

federal reserve bank float
federal reserve city
idle money
interdistrict settlement fund
investment banking
kiting
multiple expansion of credit
Open Market Committee
open-market operations
order
overcertification
overdraft
overdraw
passbook
prime rate
protest
reclamation
redemption agent
rediscount
rediscount rate
reserve bank credit
reserve ratio
reserves
  bank
  excess
  legal
  monetary
  net borrowed
  net free
  run on a bank
  swap credits

(21) Financial Terms—Other
(*See also* Accounting)

accumulation
advance
amortization
annuity
  deferred
  life
  suvivorship
  variable
appropriation
  itemized
  lump-sum
  segregated
assessment
assimilation
at the market
avail
bear
bearer

big board
bill
blue chip
boiler room
bonus
borrow
brokerage
bubble
budgetary control
bull
buying on margin
call
capitalist
Central Certificate Service
collateral
commission
credit
  bank
  book
  check
  commercial
  consumer
  reserve bank
  social
  store
  swap
creditor
credit rating
cum rights
customers' net debit balance
days of grace
debt
  floating
  funded
  gross national
  interallied
  national
  private
  public
    external
    internal
  secured
  unsecured
debt service
debtor
direct financing
discount
discounting the news
disintermediation
disinvestment
dissaving
diversification

dividend
  accumulated
  accumulative
  cumulative
  optional
  scrip
  stock
  wage
emolument
end money
endorsement
equalization fee
equity capital
equity trading
ex dividend
ex interest
ex rights
extended
factorage
fee
fine
fiscal
fund
  carryover
  contingent
  counterpart
  dual purpose or leverage
  endowment
  exchange stabilization
  federal trust
  general
  hedge
  imprest
  interdistrict settlement
  International Monetary
  revolving credit
  revolving
  sinking
  stabilization
  trust
gift
give up
grace period
grant
gratuity
growth stock
hypothecate
increment
indorsement
  blank
  conditional
  qualified

restrictive
special
institutional investor
interest
  accrued
  compound
  gross
  imputed
  installment
  legal
  loan
  net
  pure
  simple
  true
investment
  autonomous
  financial
  impair
  induced
  negative
  real
investment portfolio
irredeemable
issue
loan
  add-on
  bank term
  call
  day
  discount
  forced
  nonrecourse
  soft
  tied
  time
loan shark
marginal trading
maturity
mortgagee
mortgagor
near money
negotiability
net yield
perquisite
point
poundage
premium
  premium for risk
  premium pay
  premium stock
proceeds

profit
prospectus
put
rate war
recapitalization
refunding
rentier
reparations
repatriation
repudiation
revenue
risk
risk-capital pooling
royalty
salary
secondary offering
security
  eligible
  gilt-edge
  legal
  listed
  seasoned
self-liquidating
selling short
shares
spin-off
split-up
spread
stipend
stockholder
stock option
stock rights
straddle
toll
transfer agent
trustee
underwriting
warrant
wash sale
yield
  basic
  current
  nominal
  yield to maturity

(22) Government—Agencies and Officials

Agency for International
    Development
Agricultural Stabilization and
    Conservation Service
Antitrust Division

Appendix A

Area Redevelopment Administration
assay office
assessor
Atomic Energy Commission
Bonneville Power Administration
Bureau of Employees' Compensation
Bureau of Employment Security
Bureau of Engraving and Printing
Bureau of Family Services
Bureau of Federal Credit Unions
Bureau of International Commerce
Bureau of Labor Standards
Bureau of Labor Statistics
Bureau of Land Management
Bureau of Mines
Bureau of Public Roads
Bureau of Reclamation
Bureau of the Budget
Bureau of the Census
Bureau of the Customs
Bureau of the Mint
Bureau of the Public Debt
Civil Aeronautics Board
collector of the customs
Commissioner of Customs
commissioner of deeds
Commissioner of Internal Revenue
Commodity Credit Corporation
Commodity Exchange Authority
conservator
consul
consular agent
consul general
Consumer and Marketing Service
Consumers Advisory Council
Council of Economic Advisers
county agricultural agent
Department of Agriculture
Department of Commerce
Department of Defense
Department of Health, Education,
    and Welfare
Department of Housing and Urban
    Development
Department of Justice
Department of Labor
Department of State
Department of the Interior
Department of the Treasury
Department of Transportation
director of internal revenue

Economic and Social Council
Economic Cooperation
    Administration
Environmental Science Service
    Administration
Executive Office of the President
Extension Service
Fannie Mae
Farm Credit Administration
Farmers Home Administration
Federal Advisory Council
Federal Aviation Agency
Federal Communications Commission
Federal Crop Insurance Corporation
Federal Deposit Insurance
    Corporation
Federal Extension Service
Federal Home Loan Bank Board
Federal Housing Administration
Federal Maritime Commission
Federal Mediation and Conciliation
    Service
Federal National Mortgage
    Association
Federal Power Commission
Federal Prison Industries, Inc.
federal reserve agent
Federal Savings and Loan Insurance
    Corporation
Federal Trade Commission
Federal Water Pollution Control
    Administration
Food and Drug Administration
foreign service officer
Forest Service
Fort Knox
General Accounting Office
General Service Administration
Government Printing Office
home demonstration agent
industrial relations court
Internal Revenue Service
Interstate Commerce Commission
Joint Economic Committee
Kansas Industrial Court
Maritime Administration
National Advisory Council on
    International and Financial
    Problems
National Aeronautics and Space
    Administration

494

National Bureau of Standards
National Institutes of Health
National Labor Relations Board
National Mediation Board
National Railroad Adjustment Board
National Science Foundation
National Security Council
National Transportation Safety Board
notary public
Office of Business Economics
Office of Comptroller of the Currency
Office of Economic Opportunity
Office of Education
Office of Emergency Planning
Office of Science and Technology
Office of Special Representative for
    Trade Negotiations
Office of Tax Legislative Counsel
Office of Treasurer of the United
    States
Patent Office
Peace Corps
port authority
Port of New York Authority
Post Office Department
President's Committee of Equal
    Employment Opportunity
Public Health Service
public service commission
Railroad Retirement Board
Reconstruction Finance Corporation
Rural Electrification Administration
Securities and Exchange Commission
Small Business Administration
Social Security Administration
soil conservation district
Soil Conservation Service
Southeastern Power Administration
Southwestern Power Administration
Tariff Commission
tax collector
tax commission
Tax Court of the United States
Tennessee Valley Authority
Treasurer of the United States
trust territory
United States Civil Service
    Commission
United States Court of Claims
United States Court of Customs and
    Patent Appeals

United States Customs Court
United States Employment Service
United States Fish and Wildlife
    Service
United States Tariff Commission
United States Travel Service
Veterans Administration
vice-consul
Vocational Rehabilitation
    Administration
Wage and Hour and Public Contracts
    Divisions
Welfare Administration
Women's Bureau

(23) Government—Policies

agricultural parity
agricultural price support
antitrust
austerity program
bounty
ceiling prices
child labor
codetermination
collective ownership
commercial policy
community-property principle
compensatory fiscal policy
contract system
control
    budgetary
    credit
    exchange
    inventory
    manpower
    pollution
    price
    quality
    rent
    standby
    wage and salary
convict labor
convict lease system
critical material
debt ceiling
deficit financing
development
disability benefits
disaster relief program
dole
economic planning

equalization fee
ever normal granary
export bounty
farm subsidies
fiscal policy
food stamp plan
franking
functional finance
guaranteed annual income
holding the line
immigration
internal improvement
land-grant college
marketing agreement
means test
medicaid
medicare
minimum wage
monetary policy
monetary sovereignty
national minimum
nonrecourse loans
open-door policy
original-package doctrine
paternalism
pay-as-you-go
planning
policy
price fixing
price support
priority system
production allocation program
protectionism
public domain
public lands
public ownership
public works
public works and ways system
pump priming
rate regulation
rationing of foreign exchange
rationing system
recapture of earnings
regulation
roll-back
school lunch program
slum clearance
soil bank program
special assessment
state use system
stockpiling
strategic materials

valorization
veterans' preference
VISTA
wage and price guidelines
work relief
youth employment service
zoning

(24)   Historic Terms, Events, Institutions, and Movements

agricultural revolution
American Federation of Labor
American system
antibank movement
Anti-Corn Law League
assignat
atomistic society
bank holiday
Bank of the United States
Beveridge plan
black Friday
blue eagle
bubble
bulk-line costs
central reserve cities
central reserve city banks
Chartism
chrematistic
codes of fair competition
Colombo Plan
commercial revolution
Compromise Tariff
Congress of Industrial Organizations
corn laws
Crédit Mobilier
Crime of 1873
cross of gold
curb exchange
Dawes Plan
death sentence
deposit bank
dismal science
eagle
enclosures
essential industry
European Recovery Program
fair deal
feudal system
five-twenty bond
Fourierism
free banking system of New York

guild
  craft
  merchant
headright
Hoover moratorium
indentured servant
independent treasury system
Industrial Revolution
Industrial Workers of the World
Interallied debts
invisible hand
joint stock land bank
Knights of Labor
labor exchange bank
laissez faire
land bank
land grant
Latin Monetary Union
London Economic Conference
Luddite
manorial system
Marshall plan
Mississippi bubble
monetary union
mutualism
National Monetary Commission
natural order
net product
New Deal
nonimportation agreement
Owenism
patroon
pet banks
phalanstery
Plumb plan
point 4 program
political arithmetic
postal savings
privateering
safety-fund bank system
Saint-Simonians
Scandinavian Monetary Union
shinplaster
sixteen to one
social workshop
South Sea Bubble
Specie Circular
sterling bloc
subtreasury system
Suffolk Bank system
Tableau économique
Tariff of Abominations

Temporary National Economic
  Committee
ten-forty bond
trade dollar
trade monopoly
Tripartite Currency Agreement
Truman Plan
wildcat banking era
Young plan
Zollverein

(25) Insurance

insurance
  business interruption
  casualty
  coinsurance
  crop
  deposit
  employers' liability
  fidelity
  group
  health
  life
    credit
    endowment
    industrial
    leased
    limited-payment plan
    straight-life plan of
    term plan of
  national
  old-age (retirement), survivors, and
    disability
  reinsurance
  social
  survivors
  unemployment
  use-and-occupancy

(26) International—Organizations,
**   Conferences, and Agreements**

Alliance for Progress
Asian Development Bank
Bank for International Settlements
Benelux
Caribbean Organization
COMECON
commercial treaty
commodity agreement
Common Market
Comsat

Council for Mutual Economic
    Assistance
counterpart fund
customs union
Dillon Round
Economic Commission for Africa
Economic Commission for Asia and
    the Far East
Economic Commission for Europe
Economic Commission for Latin
    America
economic union
Empire preference
Euromarket
Euromart
European Atomic Energy Community
European Commission
European Community for Coal and
    Steel
European Economic Community
European Free Trade Association
European Monetary Agreement
European Payments Union
Food and Agriculture Organizations
    of the United Nations
General Agreement on Tariffs and
    Trade
General Assembly of the United
    Nations
Gold Pool
Group of Ten
Intelsat
Inter-American Development Bank
Intergovernmental Maritime
    Consultative Organization
International Atomic Energy Agency
International Bank for Reconstruction
    and Development
International Chamber of Commerce
International Civil Aviation
    Organization
international commodity agreement
International Confederation of Free
    Trade Unions
International Cotton Advisory
    Committee
International Court of Justice
International Development
    Association
International Finance Corporation
International Labor Organization
International Monetary Fund

International Patents Bureau
International Rubber Study Group
International Statistical Institute
International Telecommunication
    Union
International Wheat Agreement
Kennedy Round
monetary union
Organization of American States
Organization for Economic
    Cooperation and Development
Organization for European Economic
    Cooperation
Ottawa agreements
Outer 7
Pan-American Union
reciprocal trade agreements
Regional Economic Commissions of
    the United States
Schuman Plan
Security Council
South Pacific Commission
specialized agency
sterling area
swap credits
trade bloc
Trusteeship Council
two-tier gold price
United Nations
United Nations Conference on Trade
    and Development
United Nations Educational,
    Scientific and Cultural
    Organization
United Nations Relief and
    Rehabilitation Administration
Universal Postal Union
World Bank
World Bank Group
World Federation of Trade Unions
World Health Organization

**(27)   International—Trade and
       Exchange**

absolute advantage
active trade balance
admission temporaire
agio
American selling price
arbitration of exchange
balance of payments
balance of trade

bank post remittance
bill of exchange
blocked exchange
bonded goods
cable transfer
cambist
capital movement
certificate of origin
clearing agreement
comparative advantage
comparative costs
consular invoice
creditor nation
cross-rate
customhouse
customs
customs duty
   ad valorem
   antidumping
   compensatory
   contingent
   countervailing
   countervailing excise
   differential
   discriminating
   preferential
   retaliatory
   specific
debenture certificate
debtor nation
del credere agreement
disagio
dollar deficit
dollar exchange
dollar gap
drawback
dumping
duty
earmarked gold
entrepot
Eurobonds
Eurodollars
exchange control
exchange rate
export
fair, international trade
favorable balance of trade
floating exchange rate
foreign exchange
foreign-trade zone
foreign valuation
forward exchange

free list
free port
free trade
fundamental disequilibrium
futures
immigrant remittances
import
import duty
import license
import quota
impost
indent
indirect exporting
infant industry
invisible items of trade
most-favored-nation clause
multiple currency system
navicert
nostro overdraft
official exchange rate
paper gold
par exchange rate
parity
passive trade balance
peril point
port of entry
purchasing-power parity
rationing of foreign exchange
reciprocity principle
re-export
S.D.R's
smuggling
Special Drawing Rights
tariff
   autonomous
   convention
   educational
   flexible
   general
   maximum and minimum
   multilinear
   multiple
   protective
   single schedule
   sliding-scale
   tariff for revenue only
   unilinear
Tariff Information Catalogue
tariff union
tariff war
temporary admission
terms of trade

499

tied loan
tourist expenditures
trade barrier
trade deficit
trade monopoly
triangular trade
unfavorable balance of trade
usance
visible items of trade

(28) Judicial Decisions

Adair v. *United States*
Addyston Pipe and Steel Co. case
Adkins v. *Children's Hospital*
Adler v. *Board of Education*
Agricultural Adjustment Act case
(second)
American Column and Lumber Co.
v. *United States*
American Communications Association
v. *Douds*
American Tobacco Co. v. *United States*
Apex Hosiery case
Bailey v. *Drexel Furniture Co.*
bankruptcy case
Bedford Cut Stone Co. v. *Journeymen*
Stone Cutters' Assn.
Beech-Nut Packing case
bituminous coal cases
Block v. *Hirsh*
Bolling v. *Sharpe*
Brown v. *Board of Education of Topeka*
Brown v. *Maryland*
Bunting v. *Oregon*
Carter v. *Carter Coal Co.*
cement case
Cement Mfrs'. Protective Assn.
v. *United States*
Chicago, Milwaukee and St. Paul
Railroad Co. v. *Minnesota*
child-labor cases
Collector v. *Day*
Commonwealth (Mass.) v. *Hunt*
Commonwealth (Pa.) v. *Cordwainers*
Cooley v. *Board of Wardens*
Coppage v. *Kansas*
Coronado case
Danbury Hatters' case
Daniel Ball case, The
Dayton-Goose Creek Ry. Co. v. *United*
States
Debs case

Duplex Printing Co. v. *Deering*
Eastern States Retail Lumber Assn.
v. *United States*
Euclid v. *Ambler Realty Co.*
fair labor standards case
Fansteel case
federal tax immunity case
Frothingham v. *Mellon*
German Alliance Insurance Co.
v. *Lewis*
Gibbons v. *Ogden*
Gold-clause cases
Gompers v. *Bucks Stove and Range Co.*
Granger cases
Graves v. *New York ex rel. O'Keefe*
Green v. *Frazier*
Hammer v. *Dagenhart*
Helvering v. *Davis*
Helvering v. *Gerhardt*
Hepburn v. *Griswold*
Home Building and Loan Association
v. *Blaisdell*
Hoosac Mills case
hot-oil case
income-tax case
insurance case
International Harvester case
Juilliard v. *Greenman*
Knight case
Knox v. *Lee*
legal-tender cases
Leisy v. *Hardin*
linseed oil industry case
Lochner v. *New York*
Loewe v. *Lawlor*
lumber industry case
McCray v. *United States*
McCulloch v. *Maryland*
milk-control case
minimum-wage cases
mortgage-moratorium case
Mulford v. *Smith*
Muller v. *Oregon*
Munn v. *Illinois*
National Labor Relations Act case
National Labor Relations Board
v. *Fansteel Metallurgical Corp.*
National Labor Relations Board v.
Jones and Laughlin Steel Corp.
National Woodwork Manufacturers
Association v. *N.L.R.B.*
Nebbia v. *New York*

New York, et al., v. *United States, et al.*
Noble State Bank v. *Haskell*
Norman v. *Baltimore and Ohio
    R.R. Co.*
Northern Securities Co. v. *United
    States*
NRA case
offshore oil cases
Old Dearborn Distributing Co.
    v. *Seagram Distillers Corp.*
oleomargarine case
original-package cases
Panama Refining Co. v. *Ryan*
Parker v. *Davis*
Paul v. *Virginia*
Perry v. *United States*
Plessy v. *Ferguson*
Pollock v. *Farmers' Loan and Trust Co.*
Railroad Commission of Wisconsin v.
    *Chicago, Burlington and Quincy
    R.R. Co.*
Railroad valuation case
rent-control case
resale price-maintenance cases
St. Louis and O'Fallon Ry. Co.
    v. *United States*
Schechter case
Schechter Poultry Corp. v. *United
    States*
school desegregation cases
Senn v. *Tile Layers Protective Union*
shoe machinery case
Shreveport case
Smyth v. *Ames*
social-security cases
South Carolina v. *United States*
Standard Oil case
state tax immunity case
Steward Machine Co. v. *Davis*
Stone v. *Farmers' Loan and Trust Co.*
Sturges v. *Crowninshield*
Sunshine Anthracite Coal Co. v. *Adkins*
Taft-Hartley Injunction case
Texas and New Orleans R.R. Co.
    v. *Brotherhood of Railway and
    Steamship Clerks*
tidelands oil
Trans-Missouri Freight Association
    case
Trenton Potteries case
Truax v. *Corrigan*
Tyson v. *Banton*

United Mine Workers v. *Coronado
    Coal Co.*
United States Steel case
United States v. *Addyston Pipe and
    Steel Co.*
United States v. *American Linseed
    Oil Co.*
United States v. *American Tobacco Co.*
United States v. *Brown*
United States v. *Butler*
United States v. *Darby Lumber Co.*
United States v. *E.C. Knight Co.*
United States v. *International
    Harvester Co.*
United States v. *South-Eastern
    Underwriters Assn.*
United States v. *Trans-Missouri Freight
    Assn.*
United States v. *Trenton Potteries Co.*
United States v. *United Shoe
    Machinery Corp.*
United States v. *United States Steel
    Corp.*
Veazie Bank v. *Fenno*
Yace v. *Spies*
West Coast Hotel Co. v. *Parrish*
Willcox v. *Consolidated Gas Co.*
Wilson v. *New*
Wisconsin rate case
Wolff Packing Co. v. *Industrial Court
    of Kansas*
Yakus v. *United States*
Youngstown Sheet and Tube Co.
    v. *Sawyer*
Zoning Case

**(29) Labor—Terms and
    Organizations**

accelerated premium
across the board
allowed time
American Federation of Labor and
    Congress of Industrial
    Organizations
apprentice
arbitration
area agreement
association agreement
automatic checkoff
automatic wage adjustment
backtracking
bargaining unit

501

base pay
base rate
bidding
black list
bonus
boondoggling
boycott
  primary
  secondary
bumping
business agent
call-back pay
call pay
casual workers
chapel
checkoff
coalition bargaining
collective bargaining
compulsory arbitration
compulsory checkoff
conciliation
contract labor
contributory pension
cooling-off period
cost-of-living adjustment
cutback
dead time
down period
dual pay system
early vesting
escape clause
featherbedding
fink
flexible schedule
fringe benefit
gain sharing
garnishment
grievance
guaranteed-wage plan
guild
hold-back pay
homework
impartial chairman
industrial democracy
industrial relations
industry-wide bargaining
instant vesting
involuntary servitude
job action
job classification
job evaluation
joint agreement

joint council
kickback
labor
  child
  contract
  division of
  labor agreement
  labor dispute
  labor force
  labor grade
  labor piracy
  labor relations
  localization of
labor union
  closed
  company
  craft
  horizontal
  independent
  industrial
  international
  multicraft
  national
  open
  vertical
lockout
maintenance of membership
man-hour
measured day rate
mediation
merit rating
migrant worker
more-favorable-terms clause
noncontributory pension
occupational level
pace setter
peg point
pension
pension pool
picketing
  cross
  mass
  secondary
  situs
piecework
portable pension
portal-to-portal pay
premium pay
profit sharing
proletariat
regional division of labor
regional pension system

round-of-wage increases
sabotage
scab
seniority
share-the-work plan
shift
  fixed
  graveyard
  rotating
shop
  agency
  closed
  modified union
  open
  preferential
  runaway
  union
specialization of labor
speed-up
steward
stretch-out
strike
  buyers'
  direct
  general
  illegal
  jurisdictional
  outlaw
  quickie
  secondary
  sit-down
  slowdown
  sympathetic
  wildcat
strikebreaker
superseniority
sweating
sweetheart contract
task
timework
trade agreement
union
union certification
union label
union security clause
voluntary checkoff
wage
  annual
  dismissal
  going wage
  guaranteed annual
  incentive

  minimum
  money
  real
  severance
  terminal
wage dividend
wage leadership
walkout
wetback
yellow-dog contract

(30) Legal and Quasi-legal Terms

acknowledgment
affidavit
article of incorporation
asset enter mains
assignee
assignment
assumption of risk
bad faith
bailment
bankruptcy
beneficiary
bequest
bilateral agreement
bootlegging
borrowing power
business affected with a public interest
cadastre
charter
chattel
combination in restraint of trade
common carrier
composition
concession
condemnation
confiscation
conflict of interest
consent decree
contract
  cost-plus
  open
  open-end
  sweetheart
  tying
  yellow dog
contract clause
contributory negligence
copyright
covenant
days of grace
debt limit

dedication
deductible clause
defalcation
devise
easement
embezzlement
eminent domain
entail
equity
escalator clause
escheat
escrow
estate
excess condemnation
executor
ex officio
export license
expropriation
fair return
fellow-servant doctrine
fiduciary
fine
flotsam
foreclosure
franchise
free and clear
freedom of contract
gold clause
gold cover
good faith
grace period
grant
head of family
holography
homestead
indemnity
indenture
injunction
insolvent
involuntary bankruptcy
just compensation
land patent
lease
lease-back
legacy
legal asset
legal person
legal reserve
legal security
legal tender
lending authority
letter of marque

letters patent
license
lien
life estate
malfeasance
malpractice
manifest
misfeasance
moratorium
multilateral agreement
net lease
nonfeasance
obligational authority
one-thousand-hour clause
option
patent
pauper
peonage
permissive wage-adjustment clause
power of attorney
prescription
primogeniture
property
   intangible
   personal
   private
   real
   tangible
protest
quasi corporation
quitrent
receiver
recourse
referee
release
remainderman
renegotiation
residuary estate
restraint of trade
rule of reason
servitude
settler
specific performance
statute of limitations
stay law
sumptuary laws
tax lien
tenure
title
uniform laws
usury
voluntary bankruptcy

(31) Legislation—General Terms and Specific Statutes

Adamson Act
Agricultural Adjustment Act (first)
Agricultural Adjustment Act (second)
Agricultural Credit Act
Air Quality Act
Aldrich-Vreeland Act
Anti-injunction (Norris-LaGuardia) Act
Antiracketeering Act
Antistrikebreaking (Byrnes) Act
antitrust acts
Atomic Energy Act
Bankhead-Jones Farm Tenant Act
Banking (Glass-Steagall) Act
bankruptcy acts
Bland-Allison Act
blue-sky laws
Budget and Accounting Act
Byrnes Act
Civil Service anti-strike law
Clayton Act
Clean Waters Act
Coinage Act of 1965
Co-operative Marketing (Capper-Volstead) Act
Current Tax Payment Act
Defense Production Act
deficiency supply bill
Economic Opportunity Act
Edge Act
employers' liability laws
Employment Act of 1946
Erdman Act
Esch-Cummins Act
fair-employment practices legislation
Fair Labor Standards Act (Wage and Hour Law)
fair-trade practices acts
Federal-Aid Highway Acts
Federal Farm Loan Act
Federal Food, Drug, and Cosmetic Act
Federal Home Loan Bank Act
Federal Power Act
Federal Reserve Act
Federal Trade Commission Act
Foreign Investors Tax Act
Foreign Securities Act
Frazier-Lemke Act

George-Deen Act
George-Ellzey Act
George-Reed Act
G.I. Bill of Rights (Servicemen's Readjustment) Act
Glass-Steagall Act
Gold-cover Repeal Act
Gold Reserve Act
Gold Standard Act
Grain Futures Act
Grain Standards Act
granger legislation
Guffey Coal Act
Hatch Act
Hawes-Cooper Act
Hepburn Act
Homestead Act
Interstate Commerce Act
Investment Advisers Act
Investment Companies Act
Johnson Act
Keating-Owen Act
Labor-Management Relations (Taft-Hartley) Act
Labor Reform (Landrum-Griffin) Act (1959)
La Follette Seamen's Act
Landrum-Griffin Act
Lend-Lease Act
Manns-Elkins Act
McFadden Act
McNary-Haugen Bill
maximum-hour legislation
Miller-Tydings Act
Morrill (Land-Grant College) Act
Motor Carrier Act
National Bank Act
National Currency Act
National Defense Education Act
National Industrial Recovery Act
National Labor Relations (Wagner-Connery) Act
Natural Gas Act
Newlands Act
Nonimportation Act
Nonintercourse Act
Norris-LaGuardia Act
Packers and Stockyards Act
Portal-to-Portal Act
price-control legislation
Public Utility Holding Company Act
Pure Food and Drugs Act

505

Railroad Retirement Act
Railroad Unemployment Insurance
    Act
Railway Labor Act
Resumption Act
right-to-work laws
Robinson-Patman Act
Securities Act
Securities Exchange Act
Servicemen's Readjustment Act
Sheppard-Towner Act
Sherman Antitrust Act
Sherman Silver Purchase Act
Silver Purchase Act
small-loan law
Smith-Hughes Act
Smith-Lever Act
Social Security Act
Taft-Hartley Act
Taylor Law
Trade Agreements Act
Trade Expansion Act of 1962
Transportation Act
Trust Indenture Act
Truth-in-lending Act
Truth-in-packaging Act
uniform laws
Urban Home Transportation Act
Vocational Education Act
Wage and Hour Law
Wagner-Connery Act
Walsh-Healey Public Contracts Act
Webb-Pomerene Act
Wheeler-Lea Act
workmen's compensation laws

(32)   Legislation—Tariff Acts

Compromise
Dingley
Fordney-McCumber
Grundy
Hawley-Smoot
McKinley
Morrill
Payne-Aldrich
Tariff Act of 1922
Tariff of Abominations
Underwood
Walker
Wilson-Gorman

(33)   Money and Monetary Terms

abrasion
agio
assaying
bank note
bill
bill of credit
brassage
bullion
cash
circulating medium
coin
    minor
    subsidiary
    token
coinage
    free
    gratuitous
commodity dollar
compensated dollar
currency
    blocked
    check
    deposit
    fractional
    reserve
    Treasury
debasement
demonetization
denominational value
devaluation
earmarked gold
federal reserve bank note
federal reserve note
free silver
functions of money
gold certificate
gold cover
gold points
gold price
greenbacks
inconvertible money
legal tender
mint
mint par of exchange
mint price of gold
mint ratio
monetary system
    bimetallism
    commodity standard

composite commodity standard
double standard
fiat standard
fiduciary standard
gold-bullion standard
gold-exchange standard
gold standard
indirect foreign exchange standard
international gold bullion standard
irredeemable foreign exchange
    standard
limping standard
managed money
monometallism
multiple-commodity reserve dollar
parallel standard
polymetallism
single standard
symmetallism
monetary unit
money
  cheap
  convertible
  counterfeit
  credit
  dear
  elastic
  fiat
  fiduciary
  hard
  hot
  idle
  irredeemable
  lawful
  near
  occupation
  paper
  primary
  representative
  soft
  spearhead
  stable
  standard
  till
money in circulation
multiple currency system
remonetization
revaluation
seigniorage
Sherman notes
silver certificate

specie
sterilized gold
sterling
trade dollar
Treasury note
United States note
unparted bullion
yellow seal dollar

**(34) Politico-Economic and Social
      Terms, Theories, Customs, and
      Movements**

anarchism
autarchy
bondage
caste system
class
class struggle
collectivism
colonial system
culture lag
discrimination
economic democracy
economic determinism
economic equality
economic interpretation of history
economic nationalism
establishment
Fourierism
free enterprise
group medicine
individualism
industrial democracy
institutionalism
nationalization
natural rights
organic school
peasant movement
plutocracy
poverty
price system
private enterprise
public welfare
racism
segregation
self-interest
self-sufficient nation
share the wealth
solidarism
Townsend plan
utopia

507

vested interests
welfare state

(35)   Taxes and Taxation

ability-to-pay principle of taxation
assessment
benefits-received principle of taxation
cadastre
canons of taxation
capitalization of land taxes
capital levy
carry back
compensatory principle of taxation
cost-of-service principle of taxation
degressive taxation
depletion allowance
discriminatory taxation
double taxation
equalization of assessments
faculty principle of taxation
incentive taxation
incidence of taxation
income maintenance
internal revenue
international double taxation
joint return
proceeds
progressive taxation
proportional taxation
public revenue
regressive taxation
repressive taxation
shifting of taxation
surtax
tax
   accumulated profits
   added value
   apportioned
   betterment
   capital-gains
   capital-stock
   capitation
   chain-store
   classified
   consumption
   corporation income
   delinquent
   direct
   estate
   excess profits
   excise

   export
   franchise
   general property
   gift
   graded
   graduated
   head
   hidden
   income
   indirect
   inheritance
   interest equalization
   land
   land-value
   luxury
   negative income
   nuisance
   occupation
   payroll
   personal property
   poll
   privilege
   processing
   property
   real-estate
   sales
   severance
   single
   social security
   stamp
   stock transfer
   tonnage
   transactions
   turnover
   undistributed-profits
   use
   value added
   war profits
   withholding
tax assessment
tax avoidance
tax base
Tax Court of the United States
tax dodging
tax evasion
tax exemption
tax farming
tax limit
taxpayer
tax rate
tax selling
tax sharing

(36) Vocations and Occupations
(*See also* Government—Agencies and
  Officials)

accountant
actuary
adjuster
administrator
advertising
agent
artisan
assessor
auditor
bank examiner
broker
cambist
checkweighman
compliance director
comptroller
customs broker
drummer

economist
efficiency engineer
executive
expediter
five percenter
floor trader
forwarding agent
investment counselor
jobber
journeyman
mediator
odd-lot broker
pawnbroker
plunger
promoter
share cropper
ship broker
specialist
teller
two-dollar broker

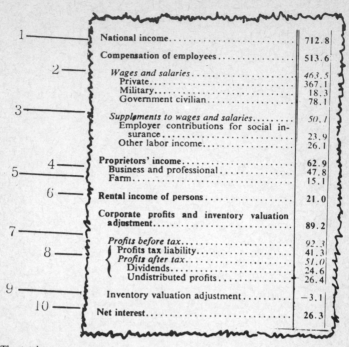

National income		712.8
Compensation of employees		513.6
Wages and salaries		*463.5*
Private		367.1
Military		18.3
Government civilian		78.1
Supplements to wages and salaries		*50.1*
Employer contributions for social insurance		23.9
Other labor income		26.1
Proprietors' income		62.9
Business and professional		47.8
Farm		15.1
Rental income of persons		21.0
Corporate profits and inventory valuation adjustment		89.2
Profits before tax		*92.3*
Profits tax liability		41.3
Profits after tax		*51.0*
Dividends		24.6
Undistributed profits		26.4
Inventory valuation adjustment		−3.1
Net interest		26.3

1. The total FACTOR COSTS of all goods and services produced by the nation's economy during a specific period of time.

2. BONUSES, COMMISSIONS, GRATUITIES, payments in kind, SALARIES, WAGES, etc.

3. Employee contributions to SOCIAL INSURANCE, compensation for injuries, payments to welfare and private pension funds by employers, compensation to part-time military reservists, and such items as fees paid to juries, DIRECTORS, witnesses, etc.

4. Income of non-corporate enterprises such as PROPRIETORSHIPS and PARTNERSHIPS as well as non-corporate INVENTORY VALUATION ADJUSTMENTS.

5. Net return to farmers, and other agricultural services such as forestries, fisheries, etc.

6. Net rental returns from REAL PROPERTY, net IMPUTED rent from nonfarm dwellings received by owner-occupants, and personal income received from PATENTS, COPYRIGHTS, and similar sources.

7. Corporation earnings whether paid as dividends or retained as undistributed profits before deduction of federal, state, and local taxes.

8. Profit before taxes, less dividends and undistributed profits equals profits tax liability.

9. Corporate INVENTORY, VALUATION ADJUSTMENTS.

10. Net monetary and IMPUTED interest such as the value of bank clearings and collection services and investment returns to life insurance companies and mutual financial institutions accruing to but unpaid to individuals.

11. The market value of goods and services produced in the national economy during a given period of time.

12. Monetary payments for goods and services or payments in kind for services purchased by individuals and nonprofit organizations.

13. Gross private domestic investments such as equipment, new residential, nonresidential, and farm buildings; also farm and nonfarm INVENTORY VALUATION ADJUSTMENTS.

---

*As published periodically in the *Federal Reserve Bulletin,* Board of Governors of the Federal Reserve System, Washington, D.C.—Billions of Dollars.

11	Gross national product...................	860.7
	Final purchases...........................	*853.1*
12	Personal consumption expenditures.........	533.7
	Durable goods.......................	82.5
	Nondurable goods.....................	230.2
	Services............................	221.0
13	Gross private domestic investment..........	127.5
	Fixed investment....................	*120.0*
	Nonresidential....................	*90.0*
	Structures.....................	29.2
	Producers' durable equipment.......	60.8
	Residential structures.................	30.0
	Nonfarm......................	29.4
	Change in business inventories..........	7.6
	Nonfarm......................	7.2
14	Net exports of goods and services..........	2.4
	Exports.............................	50.6
	Imports.............................	48.2
15	Government purchases of goods and services..	197.1
	Federal...........................	*100.0*
	National defense....................	78.9
	Other............................	21.1
	State and local......................	97.1
	Gross national product in constant (1958) dollars................................	706.9

14. The difference between: (1) the value of domestic output exported; (2) materials produced abroad by United States-owned resources; (3) cash gifts and contributions received from abroad, and: (1) imports from foreign producers; (2) materials produced in the United States by foreign-owned resources; and (3) cash gifts and contributions to foreigners.
15. Purchases of goods and services by federal, state, and local government bodies including both outlays for operating expenses and investments in CAPITAL GOODS.
16. CAPITAL CONSUMPTION allowance.
17. INDIRECT TAXES such as SALES and EXCISE TAXES, and nontax liabilities such as fines and penalties.
18. Business TRANSFER PAYMENTS.
19. Statistical discrepancy.
20. Subsidies less surplus of government enterprises.

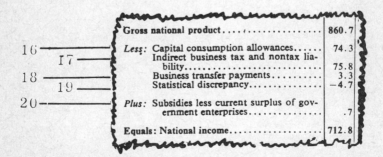

16	Gross national product.................	860.7
17	*Less:* Capital consumption allowances......	74.3
	Indirect business tax and nontax liability.................	75.8
18	Business transfer payments..........	3.3
19	Statistical discrepancy..............	−4.7
20	*Plus:* Subsidies less current surplus of government enterprises..............	.7
	Equals: National income..................	712.8

COMBINED STATEMENT OF CONDITION OF

Assets	
Gold certificate account............................	10,025
Cash...	228
Discounts and advances:	
Member bank borrowings.........................	926
Other..	....
Acceptances:	
Bought outright.................................	50
Held under repurchase agreements...............	....
Federal agency obligations—Held under repurchase agreements.......................................	....
U.S. Govt. securities:	
Bought outright:	
Bills..	18,144
Certificates—Special........................	....
Other'.......................	....
Notes.......................................	28,706
Bonds.......................................	5,475
Total bought outright...........................	52,325
Held under repurchase agreements...............	....
Total U.S. Govt. securities.......................	52,325
Total loans and securities........................	53,301
Cash items in process of collection...............	8,637
Bank premises....................................	114
Other assets:	
Denominated in foreign currencies..............	1,984
IMF gold deposited[2]...........................	231
All other..	631
Total assets.....................................	75,151

1. Credits to Federal Reserve Banks by the U.S. Treasury in return for funds withdrawn from its deposit account in payment for newly acquired gold.

2. Coins and paper money (other than Federal Reserve notes) in the vaults of the Federal Reserve Banks.

3. Discounts are rediscounted short-term eligible commercial, agricultural, and other business paper. Advances are promissory notes secured by satisfactory COLLATERAL.

4. Prime bankers' ACCEPTANCES purchased in the open market sometimes with the understanding that sellers may buy them back within a stipulated period of time.

5. Obligations (both guaranteed and nonguaranteed) issued by agencies of the Federal government.

6. TREASURY BILLS, CERTIFICATES OF INDEBTEDNESS, TREASURY NOTES and Treasury bonds sometimes purchased from nonbank dealers with the understanding that they may be bought back within a stipulated period of time.

7. Cash items deposited in the Federal Reserve Banks and in process of collection on the date of a financial statement.

8. REAL PROPERTY occupied by the Federal Reserve Banks.

*As published in the *Federal Reserve Bulletin,* Board of Governors of the Federal Reserve System, Washington, D.C.—Millions of dollars.

ALL FEDERAL RESERVE BANKS*

Liabilities	
F.R. notes...................................	42,991
Deposits:	
Member bank reserves........................	22,902
U.S. Treasurer—General account...............	498
Foreign....................................	124
Other:	
IMF gold deposit[2]..........................	231
All other..................................	242
Total deposits................................	23,997
Deferred availability cash items..................	6,326
Other liabilities and accrued dividends.............	358
Total liabilities..............................	73,672
Capital accounts	
Capital paid in...............................	633
Surplus.....................................	630
Other capital accounts.........................	216
Total liabilities and capital accounts.............	75,151

9. Value of foreign currencies.

10. Gold deposited with INTERNATIONAL MONETARY FUND.

11. Accrued interest, accounts receivable, premiums on securities owned, balances due from foreign CENTRAL BANKS, and various other items of lesser significance.

12. Federal Reserve notes. The principal type of currency in circulation may be secured by the Gold Certificate Account, U.S. Government securities and eligible short-term paper discounted or purchased by the Reserve Banks.

13. Legal BANK RESERVES of member banks deposited in the Federal Reserve Bank of the district where the member bank is located.

14. Checking account of the U.S. Treasury used to make payments for government purchases.

15. Deposits of foreign CENTRAL BANKS and governments.

16. Gold deposits of the INTERNATIONAL MONETARY FUND.

17. Deposits of nonmember banks used as clearing accounts with the Federal Reserve Bank of their districts as a matter of convenience, also deposits of certain government agencies and international organizations.

18. Counterpart of cash items in process of collection.

19. Principally unearned discount on notes and securities, miscellaneous accounts payable and dividends accrued between semiannual dividend payment dates.

20. Capital stock of Federal Reserve Bank purchased by member banks.

21. Retained net earnings.

22. Unallocated net earnings for the current year to the date of the statement.

NATIONAL MONETARY UNITS

Courtesy of Manufacturers Hanover Trust Co.
International Division, New York

Country	Currency	Consisting of
Abu Dhabi	Dinar	1000 Fils
Aden	Dinar	1000 Fils
Afghanistan	Afghani	100 Puls
Albania	Lek	100 Qintar
Algeria	Dinar	100 Centimes
Andorra	Peseta	100 Centimos
Angola	Escudo	100 Centavos
Antigua	Dollar	100 Cents
Argentina	Peso	100 Centavos
Australia	Dollar	100 Cents
Austria	Schilling	100 Groschen
Azores	Escudo	100 Cents
Bahamas	Dollar	100 Cents
Bahrain	Dinar	1000 Fils
Balearic Island	Peseta	100 Centimos
Barbados	Dollar	100 Cents
Belgium	Franc	100 Centimes
Bermuda	Pound	20 Shillings = 240 Pence
Bolivia	Peso	100 Centavos
Botswana	Rand	100 Cents
Brazil	New Cruzeiro	100 Centavos
British Honduras	Dollar	100 Cents
Brunei	Dollar	100 Cents
Bulgaria	Lev	100 Stotinki
Burma	Kyat	100 Pyas
Cambodia	Riel	100 Sen
Cameroons	Franc	100 Centimes
Canada	Dollar	100 Cents
Canary Islands	Peseta	100 Centimos
Cape Verde Islands	Escudo	100 Centavos
Central African Republic	Franc	100 Centimes
Ceylon	Rupee	100 Cents
Chad	Franc	100 Centimes
Chile	Escudo	100 Centesimos
China	NT Dollar	100 Cents
Colombia	Peso	100 Centavos
Congo (Kinshasa)	Zaire	100 Makutu
Congo (Brazzaville)	Franc	100 Centimes
Costa Rica	Colon	100 Centimos
Cuba	Peso	100 Centavos
Cyprus	Pound	1000 Mils
Czechoslovakia	Crown	100 Hellers
Dahomey	Franc	100 Centimes
Denmark	Krone	100 Ore

Country	Currency	Consisting of
Dominica	Dollar	100 Cents
Dominican Republic	Peso	100 Centavos
Dubai	Gulf Royal	100 Dirhams
Ecuador	Sucre	100 Centavos
Egypt	Pound	100 Piasters = 1000 Mill.
El Salvador	Colon	100 Centavos
Ethiopia	Dollar	100 Cents
Fiji Islands	Pound	20 Shillings = 240 Pence
Finland	Markka	100 Pennis
France	Franc	100 Centimes
French Somaliland	Franc	100 Centimes
Gabon	Franc	100 Centimes
Gambia	Pound	20 Shillings = 240 Pence
Germany (Western)	Deutsche Mark	100 Pfennig
Ghana	New Cedi	100 Pesewas
Gibraltar	Pound	20 Shillings = 240 Pence
Grand Cayman Island	Pound	20 Shillings = 240 Pence
Greece	Drachma	100 Lepta
Grenada	Dollar	100 Cents
Guadeloupe	Franc	100 Centimes
Guam	U.S. Dollar	100 Cents
Guatemala	Quetzal	100 Centavos
Guiana, French	Franc	100 Centimes
Guinea	Franc	100 Centimes
Guyana	Dollar	100 Cents
Haiti	Gourde	100 Centimes
Honduras (Republic)	Lempira	100 Centavos
Hong Kong	Dollar	100 Cents
Hungary	Forint	100 Fillers
Iceland	Krona	100 Aurar
India	Rupee	100 Paise
Indonesia	New Rupiah	100 Sen
Iran	Rial	100 Dinars
Iraq	Dinar	1000 Fils
Ireland (Republic)	Pound	20 Shillings = 240 Pence
Israel	Pound	100 Agorot
Italy	Lira	100 Centesimi
Ivory Coast	Franc	100 Centimes
Jamaica	Pound	20 Shillings = 240 Pence
Japan	Yen	100 Sen
Jordan	Dinar	1000 Fils
Kenya	Shilling	100 Cents
Korea (South)	Won	100 Chon
Kuwait	Dinar	1000 Fils
Laos	Kip	100 At
Lebanon	Pound	100 Piasters
Lesotho	Rand	100 Cents
Liberia	U.S. Dollar	100 Cents
Libya	Pound	1000 Milliemes
Liechtenstein	Franc	100 Centimes

515

Country	Currency	Consisting of
Luxembourg	Franc	100 Centimes
Macao	Pataca	100 Avos
Madeira	Escudo	100 Centavos
Malagasy	Franc	100 Centimes
Malawi	Pound	20 Shillings = 240 Pence
Malaysia	Dollar	100 Cents
Mali	Franc	100 Centimes
Malta	Pound	20 Shillings = 240 Pence
Marshall Islands	U.S. Dollar	100 Cents
Martinique	Franc	100 Centimes
Mauritania	Franc	100 Centimes
Mauritius	Rupee	100 Cents
Mexico	Peso	100 Centavos
Monaco	Franc	100 Centimes
Montserrat	Dollar	100 Cents
Morocco	Dirham	100 Moroccan Francs
Nepal	Rupee	100 Pice
Netherlands	Guilder	100 Cents
Netherlands Antilles	Guilder	100 Cents
Nevis	Dollar	100 Cents
New Caledonia	Franc	100 Centimes
New Guinea	Dollar	100 Cents
New Hebrides Islands	Franc	100 Centimes
New Zealand	Dollar	100 Cents
Nicaragua	Cordoba	100 Centavos
Niger	Franc	100 Centimes
Nigeria	Pound	20 Shillings = 240 Pence
Norway	Krone	100 Ore
Oceania (French)	Franc	100 Centimes
Pakistan	Rupee	100 Paisa
Panama	Balboa	100 Centesimos
Papua	Dollar	100 Cents
Paraguay	Guarani	100 Centimos
Peru	Sol	100 Centavos
Philippines	Peso	100 Centavos
Poland	Zloty	100 Grosze
Portugal	Escudo	100 Centavos
Portuguese East Africa	Escudo	100 Centavos
Portuguese Guinea	Escudo	100 Centavos
Puerto Rico	U.S. Dollar	100 Cents
Qatar	Gulf Riyal	100 Dirhams
Reunion Island	Franc	100 Centimes
Rhodesia	Pound	20 Shillings = 240 Pence
Romania	Leu	100 Bani
Ryukyu Islands	U.S. Dollar	100 Cents
St. Kitts	Dollar	100 Cents
St. Lucia	Dollar	100 Cents
St. Vincent	Dollar	100 Cents
Samoa (British)	Dollar	100 Cents
Saudi Arabia	Riyal	20 Gurshes = 100 Halalah

Country	Currency	Consisting of
Senegal	Franc	100 Centimes
Seychelles	Rupee	100 Cents
Sierra Leone	Leone	100 Cents
Singapore	Dollar	100 Cents
Solomon Islands	Dollar	100 Cents
Somalia	So. Shilling	100 Centesimi
South Africa (Republic)	Rand	100 Cents
South West Africa	Rand	100 Cents
Spain	Peseta	100 Centimos
Sudan	Pound	100 Piasters = 1000 Mill.
Surinam	Guilder	100 Cents
Swaziland	Rand	100 Cents
Sweden	Krona	100 Ore
Switzerland	Franc	100 Centimes
Syria	Pound	100 Piasters
Tahiti	Franc	100 Centimes
Tanzania	Shilling	100 Cents
Thailand	Baht	100 Satang
Timor	Escudo	100 Centavos
Togo	Franc	100 Centimes
Tonga Islands	Dollar	100 Cents
Trinidad and Tobago	Dollar	100 Cents
Tunisia	Dinar	1000 Mill.
Turkey	Pound	100 Piasters
Uganda	Shilling	100 Cents
U.S.S.R.	Rouble	100 Kopecks
United Kingdom	Pound	20 Shillings = 240 Pence
Upper Volta	Franc	100 Centimes
Uruguay	Peso	100 Centesimos
Vatican City	Lira	100 Centesimi
Venezuela	Bolivar	100 Centimos
Viet-Nam	Piaster	100 Cents
Virgin Islands (U.S.)	U.S. Dollar	100 Cents
Yugoslavia	Dinar	100 Paras
Zambia	Kwacha	100 Newee

KEY TO ABBREVIATIONS

Commonly used for certain public agencies and other organizations
described in this dictionary

ADB	Asian Development Bank
ADP	Automatic Data Processing
AEC	Atomic Energy Commission
AFL	American Federation of Labor
AID	Agency for International Development
ARS	Agricultural Research Service
BEC	Bureau of Employees' Compensation
BIS	Bank for International Settlements
BLS	Bureau of Labor Statistics
CAB	Civil Aeronautics Board
CCC	Commodity Credit Corporation
CEA	Council for Economic Advisors
CEA	Commodity Exchange Authority
CED	Committee for Economic Development
CEMA	Council for Economic Mutual Assistance
CIO	Congress of Industrial Organizations
CMN	Common Market Nations
CMS	Consumer and Marketing Service
ECSC	European Community for Coal and Steel
EEC	European Economic Community
EFTA	European Free Trade Association
EIB	Export-Import Bank of Washington
ESSA	Environmental Science Services Administration
EURATOM	European Atomic Energy Community
FAA	Federal Aviation Agency
FAC	Federal Advisory Council
FAO	Food and Agriculture Organization of the United Nations
FCA	Farm Credit Administration
FCC	Federal Communications Commission
FCIC	Federal Crop Insurance Corporation
FDA	Food and Drug Administration
FDIC	Federal Deposit Insurance Corporation
FHA	Federal Housing Administration
FHA	Farmers Home Administration
FHLBB	Federal Home Loan Bank Board
FMC	Federal Maritime Commission
FMCS	Federal Mediation and Conciliation Service
FNMA	Federal National Mortgage Association
FPC	Federal Power Commission
FRS	Federal Reserve System
FTC	Federal Trade Commission

GAO	General Accounting Office
GATT	General Agreement on Tariffs and Trade
GPO	Government Printing Office
GSA	General Services Administration
HEW	Department of Health, Education, and Welfare
HUD	Department of Housing and Urban Development
IAEA	International Atomic Energy Agency
IBRD	International Bank for Reconstruction and Development
ICAO	International Civil Aviation Organization
ICC	Interstate Commerce Commission
ICFTU	International Confederation of Free Trade Unions
ICJ	International Court of Justice
IDA	International Development Association
IDB	Inter-American Development Bank
IFC	International Finance Corporation
ILO	International Labor Organization
IMF	International Monetary Fund
IRS	Internal Revenue Service
ITU	International Telecommunications Union
IWW	Industrial Workers of the World
MA	Maritime Administration
NAM	National Association of Manufacturers
NASA	National Aeronautics and Space Administration
NBS	National Bureau of Standards
NIH	National Institute of Health
NLRB	National Labor Relations Board
NMB	National Mediation Board
NSC	National Security Council
NSF	National Science Foundation
OAS	Organization of American States
OECD	Organization for Economic Cooperation and Development
OEEC	Organization for European Economic Cooperation
OEO	Office of Economic Opportunity
OEP	Office of Emergency Planning
PHS	Public Health Service
REA	Rural Electrification Administration
RFC	Reconstruction Finance Corporation
RRB	Railroad Retirement Board
SBA	Small Business Administration
SCS	Soil Conservation Service
SEC	Securities and Exchange Commission
SSA	Social Security Administration
TVA	Tennessee Valley Authority
UN	United Nations
UNCTAD	United Nations Conference on Trade and Development
UNESCO	United Nations Educational, Scientific and Cultural Organization

519

UNRRA	United Nations Relief and Rehabilitation Administration
UPU	Universal Postal Union
USES	United States Employment Service
USTC	United States Tariff Commission
VA	Veterans Administration
WFTU	World Federation of Trade Unions
WHO	World Health Organization